MASTERS OF RUSSIAN MUSIC

GLINKA
by Repin

Masters of Russian Music

GERALD ABRAHAM
and
M. D. CALVOCORESSI

faber and faber

This edition first published in 2013
by Faber and Faber Ltd
Bloomsbury House, 74–77 Great Russell Street
London WC1B 3DA

Printed by Books on Demand GmbH, Norderstedt

All rights reserved
© Gerald Abraham and M. D. Calvocoressi, 1936

The right of Gerald Abraham and M. D. Calvocoressi to be identified
as author of this work has been asserted in accordance
with Section 77 of the Copyright, Designs and Patents Act 1988

This book is sold subject to the condition that it shall not, by way of
trade or otherwise, be lent, resold, hired out or otherwise circulated
without the publisher's prior consent in any form of binding or cover other than
that in which it is published and without a similar condition including this
condition being imposed on the subsequent purchaser

A CIP record for this book is available from the British Library

ISBN 978–0–571–29652–1

Our authorised representative in the EU for product safety is
Easy Access System Europe, Mustamäe tee 50, 10621 Tallinn, Estonia
gpsr.requests@easproject.com

CONTENTS

	PAGE
PREFACE	9–11
GLINKA	13–64
DARGOMYJSKY	65–75
SEROF	76–96
BALAKIREF	97–146
CUI	147–154
BORODIN	155–177
MUSSORGSKY	178–248
TCHAÏKOVSKY	249–334
RIMSKY-KORSAKOF	335–423
LIADOF	424–430
GLAZUNOF	431–435
LIAPUNOF	436–438
TANEIEF	439–449
SCRIABIN	450–498
CHRONOLOGICAL TABLE	499–500
BIBLIOGRAPHY	501–502
INDEX	503–511

LIST OF ILLUSTRATIONS

GLINKA	*Frontispiece*
BALAKIREF	*facing page* 97
CUI	,, ,, 147
BORODIN	,, ,, 155
MUSSORGSKY	,, ,, 178
TCHAÏKOVSKY	,, ,, 249
RIMSKY-KORSAKOF	,, ,, 335
LIADOF	,, ,, 424
GLAZUNOF	,, ,, 431
LIAPUNOF	,, ,, 436
TANEIEF	,, ,, 439
SCRIABIN	,, ,, 450

PREFACE

THE main reason for bringing out this book is that of late years an enormous quantity of new materials has cropped up and completely changed the state of our information on Russian music—which, not long ago, was scanty, and often inaccurate even in matters of plain facts and dates. Now we have an abundance of trustworthy documents, many accessible only to people who can read Russian, and not a few inaccessible outside Russian libraries and archives. Letters and other materials which had previously been published in censored form are now available in full, with comments by first-rate scholars, such as Andrei Rimsky-Korsakof, Serge Dianin, " Vladimir Karenin " (pseudonym of Varvara Komarova, Vladimir Stassof's daughter), Keldysh, and others. Naturally, all this has altered our perspective of both composers and music. On Mussorgsky, for instance, such a spate of valuable, hitherto unsuspected information has come forth, that all biographies of him written outside Russia, or in Russia before 1931 or so, are put out of court. On Balakiref, too, previous information was inadequate; and no full biography of him has been published in any country. New light has been cast on many aspects of Rimsky-Korsakof's life and thought by the recent editions (from the third onwards) of his " Memoirs ", with a preface and notes by his son Andrei; a big biography of him by the same author is being published. On Tchaïkovsky and Scriabin, too, much important information has come forth of late. And very little has been written in Western Europe on Dargomyjsky and Liadof. Therefore it is hoped that, brief as they are, these " lives " will do away with certain misconceptions and fill certain gaps. Of course, many new critical materials have cropped up too—not only criticism proper, but documents on the composers' outlook, aims, methods, artistic descent, and influence. And all this, naturally, is even more important than purely biographical information could be, since, after all, it is mainly by reason of their musical achievements that the lives of composers interest us, though the curious personalities of several of the Russian masters are of deep interest to all students of human nature, musicians and non-musicians alike. However, no attempt has been made here to combine a study of the music with the story of the lives, beyond defining the main idiosyncrasies of the composers' output and indicating from which angle this output should, in the authors' opinion, be studied.

Both authors are convinced that no purpose can be served by a few vague generalities—substitutes for, and not epitomes of, considered critical judgments; and that Russian music should be submitted to the same careful, minute, and thorough criticism as all other music of importance. This, of course, implies (especially considering how very little has been done in the matter) far more circumstantial treatment than is possible except in extensive monographs. So they have attempted to create no illusion that this book covers more ground than it actually does. It is hoped that this policy will help to stimulate interest in Russian music, and render the book useful both to music-lovers who, having enjoyed this music, may wish to know more about the lives and personalities of the composers, and to students who may find in it a guide to fuller knowledge and a useful reference book, more accurate than any hitherto available in any non-Russian language.

* * * * *

Each chapter bears the initials of its author; and although, of course, much, here and there, is the outcome of work in common, he alone is responsible for its contents.

For the method of transliteration of Russian names (which differs from the " official " English one) responsibility rests with the senior collaborator only. His view is that a reasonably close equivalent of Russian pronunciation is preferable to one of Russian spelling: for instance, final F sounds, here, are represented by F and not by V. Readers who wish for further particulars will find them in a note in the Oxford University Press edition of Mussorgsky's opera " Boris Godunof ", page xxi. It may be added that the transliteration stops short of reproducing minute peculiarities of vowel sounds: " Yeromushka " is used instead of the nearer transliteration " Eremushka ", but not " Byelyayef " for " Belaief ". This, no doubt, is inconsistent, but even the " official " method draws a line somewhere: nobody has insisted, so far, on the correct transliteration " nitchego " replacing " nitchevo ", the correct equivalent of the pronunciation.

*   *   *   *   *

No living composer has been included, except the veteran Glazunof, the only survivor of the *Sturm und Drang* period of Russian music.

According to usage dates are given twice: first according to the Eastern calendar, then according to the Western, differing by twelve days in the nineteenth century, by thirteen in the twentieth. For the reasons stated at the beginning of this Preface, the bibliography (in compiling which care has been taken to select only the most useful and reliable sources) consists almost exclusively of books in Russian; a second section, however, mentions a few works in other languages, the critical contents of which, if not the biographical, may still prove of value to students.

MICHAEL GLINKA

IT would not be quite true to say there were no Russian composers before Glinka. For, in addition to the foreign musicians attracted to the Russian court during the eighteenth century, native nonentities like Fomin and Paskevitch had written pseudo-Italian operas, while cultured *dilettanti* composed sentimental " romances " with alarming fertility and sang their own compositions in every fashionable drawing-room. And, to do them justice, neither they nor the naturalised foreigners were entirely deaf to the songs of the people. But the earliest Russian music of the slightest value was composed by a man whose sister died as recently as 1906. He too was a dilettante who composed for drawing-room performance. He too was saturated with Italianism. Glinka differs from the horde of Verstovskys and Titofs and Alabiefs only in this: that his dabblings reveal something very like genius. He lived very fully; but as a musician he can hardly be said to have had a career.

Michael Ivanovitch Glinka was born on May 20th/June 1st, 1804, in the village of Novospasskoe in the Smolensk Government. His father, a wealthy landowner, though only twenty-seven, had already resigned his commission in the army. He detested activity of any kind and richly endowed his son with the same attitude to life. His wife was a girl of nineteen. Their first-born, Alexei, had died soon after birth, yet the young parents handed over this second child —they were to have eight others—to the care of his grand-mother, who nearly ruined him. The boy may have been naturally delicate, but the old lady, herself an invalid, not only spoiled him by giving him everything he wanted, but insisted on wrapping him in furs and keeping him in her own heated sick-room. Fortunately she died in 1810, but not before she had permanently undermined the child's constitution. He had quickly learned to read; he loved to draw; and he delighted in the solemn festivals of the church. But for a long time he showed no inclination toward music beyond a typically Russian delight in bell-sounds, which he tried to imitate with a couple of copper basins.

Returned to his mother at the age of six, the boy entered a healthier atmosphere. Not that there was any element of Spartanism in his home-life. His parents were far too indolent and easy-going. But he was coddled less and sent into the fresh air. He had drawing-lessons and pored over an old Russian version of Prévost's " Histoire générale des Voyages ", which awakened a lifelong passion for foreign travel and for oriental things in general. But his interest in music lay dormant till he was ten or eleven, when one day he heard a clarinet quartet by the now forgotten Finnish composer Bernhard Crusell," music which produced on me an incomprehensible, new and ravishing impression—I remained all day in a sort of fever ". Being reproached a day or two later by his drawing-master for " thinking about nothing but music, the boy precociously answered: " How can I help it? Music is my soul ". (At least, he thought he did, when he wrote his " Memoirs " forty years later.) This memorable quartet was performed by musicians from the private orchestra maintained by a neighbouring uncle. The boy now succumbed completely to the fascination of this orchestra, which was often lent to Glinka *père* on festive occasions. During supper the musicians would play " Russian songs, arranged for two flutes, two clarinets, two horns and two bassoons ... and it may be that these songs, heard in childhood, were the first cause of my later love of Russian folk-music ". Next to these songs of the people, Glinka liked the overtures to " Lodoiska " by Kreutzer and to Méhul's " Deux aveugles ", which (with Steibelt's " Storm " Rondo) he was soon able to play on the piano. For at about this time he had his first piano lessons, " merely mechanical " instruction given by a governess from Petersburg. Under one of his uncle's violinists he began to learn the fiddle as well, though unfortunately the man taught him his own bad habits of bowing.

In the winter of 1817 the boy was sent to Petersburg, to the Chief Pedagogic Institute, where he stayed till the summer of 1822. His favourite subjects were languages—Latin, French, German, English and Persian—geography and zoology. (His interest in animals remained a prominent trait to the end of his life.) And like so many musicians, he was an excellent mathematician. Music was not included in the curriculum of the Institute, but none the less Glinka was sent to the best available masters in the northern capital. First he had three lessons from John Field. But the latter left Petersburg almost immediately and handed over his young pupil to an older one, a certain Aumann who announced himself on the title-pages of his compositions as " *ci-devant aide de camp du général commandant en chef de l'armée russe en Perse* "! Dissatisfied with the former aide-de-camp and also with his successor, a pedant named Karl Zeuner, Glinka finally turned to another and better-known pianist of the Field school, Charles Mayer. It was to Mayer that Glinka was indebted for most of his musical education. By 1822 he was able to play Hummel's A minor Concerto in public, accompanied by Mayer on a second piano. Not only that, but he played part of the Concerto to the composer himself. As a violinist he was less successful and his master, Böhm, told him despairingly, " Messieu Klinka, fous ne chouerez chamais du fiolon." Still, he learned enough to play in his uncle's orchestra when he went home for the holidays. In Petersburg he was able to go frequently to the opera, hearing Cherubini's " Wasserträger ", Méhul's " Joseph ", Boïeldieu's " Chaperon rouge " and other works of the same calibre. Rossini's overtures particularly delighted him. But "at that time", he says, "I had no real understanding of serious singing and was chiefly attracted by instrumental soloists and by the orchestra".

So the years of adolescence passed pleasantly and uneventfully. Among other acquaintances he met the Lvofs, the father who was soon to succeed Bortniansky as Director of the Imperial Chapel, and the son who ten years later composed the national anthem, "God preserve the Tsar"; young V. P. Engelhardt, to whom we owe the preservation of so many of Glinka's manuscripts; and a certain "beautiful young lady, who played the harp well and possessed a charming soprano voice". This girl, whose name has not been recorded, not only touched Glinka's susceptible heart but mildly jogged his musical imagination, inspiring his first timid attempts at composition, a set of variations on a theme from Weigl's "Schweizerfamilie", of which she was fond, and another set for harp and piano on a theme by Mozart. These first essays must have been amateurish in the extreme; for, as he says, "I as yet knew nothing of thoroughbass and had only just made the acquaintance of the harp". Fully realising his ignorance of musical theory, Glinka partially made good the deficiency by taking lessons from J. L. Fuchs.

When Glinka left the Institute in 1822 there was some talk of his embarking on an official career, but he was quite without ambition. Business of any kind was utterly distasteful to him, and he showed something akin to genius in shuffling even his private affairs into the hands of others—his mother or one of his sisters—and in evading the normal responsibilities of life. Finally, in the spring of 1823, his father recalled him from Petersburg and sent him to the Caucasus for the mineral water cure at Piatigorsk, which was just becoming fashionable. The treatment disagreed with him. (Treatment of any kind nearly always did disagree with him, and in his "Memoirs" of many years later he always recalls both the treatment and the nature of the disagreement with loving care.) But he returned to Novospasskoe with many pleasant memories of the Ukrainian steppes and the mountains of the Caucasus, to say nothing of the Circassian dancing he had seen at Piatigorsk. But the winter at home was more profitable, for he spent it almost entirely in dabbling with his uncle's orchestra, going carefully through each part with the indifferent players, and conducting the rehearsals. The repertoire consisted of the overtures of Cherubini, Méhul and Mozart, with one or two symphonies by Haydn, Mozart (the G minor) and Beethoven (No. 2); and thus, through intimate study of a handful of masterpieces, Glinka almost unconsciously acquired that " understanding of the most secret resources of the instruments "— the phrase is Berlioz's—and that mastery of orchestration, to which both the French composer and Rimsky-Korsakof have paid generous tribute.

Glinka returned to the capital in the spring, still toying with the idea of an official career but very bored at the prospect. Indeed, rather bored by everything but his musical pastimes. Mayer refused to give him any more lessons. " You have too much talent for me to teach you," he said. But he invited the young man to come daily to " make music together." In this informal way Mayer was able to guide his study of Mozart, Cherubini and Beethoven. Glinka might have studied counterpoint thoroughly, of course. But that would have been rather too much like real work. " Perhaps it was all for the best ", he reflected complacently in after years. " Severe German counterpoint doesn't always accord very well with warmth of imagination." In any case, what need was there to bother? There could be no question of his devoting himself seriously to music. His father disapproved even of this persistent dabbling. And in May, 1824, under paternal pressure, Glinka entered the Ministry of Communications. Fortunately his duties were not arduous, occupying only a few hours a day, and his official chief invited him to musical evenings where the young man met some of the most accomplished amateurs in the capital.

Glinka now quickly developed into the perfect social butterfly. " I didn't care for male society, preferring that of ladies and young girls ", he says. He began to take dancing lessons and to study singing under an Italian, Belloli. " My voice was hoarse, rather nasal, and indeterminate, i.e. neither tenor nor baritone." (It developed into a tenor, " of not particularly beautiful timbre, but a pure chest voice, sonorous —with some metallic high notes—unusually well adapted to passionate dramatic expression throughout its register ", according to Serof.) For some months he even sang out of tune " through being unaccustomed to hearing myself ". But Belloli and his later singing masters must have taught him to some purpose, for all who heard him in later years acknowledged the artistry of his singing. Serof, a by no means over-friendly critic, says in his reminiscences that Glinka was equally great as singer and composer, and compares him with the famous Czech tenor, Tichatschek.

Singing naturally led to the composition of songs, and several admittedly " unsuccessful " songs (besides a String Quartet in D and the first movement of a Sonata for viola and piano) date from 1825. Glinka soon became a prolific song-composer. That is, prolific by comparison with his output as a whole; for he wrote only about eighty songs as compared with Schubert's six hundred. But only a tiny handful have permanent value. The vast majority are merely good or average specimens of the dilettante type of romance produced by Turgenef's Panshin and his kind. Most of them circulated only in manuscript, and it was not till 1855 that Glinka took it into his head to make a complete collection of them. Serof comments on the fact that songs which appeared to be masterpieces when the composer himself sang them seemed flat and commonplace when one coldly examined the printed notes.

Most of Glinka's songs must be regarded as improvisations, so unsatisfactorily and incompletely recorded that their vital essence has evaporated.

Toward the end of 1825 Glinka moved to a new flat which he shared with an old school friend, a certain Alexander Rimsky-Korsakof, a very minor poet and a member of the same family as the yet unborn composer. Soon afterwards, for the first and only time in his life, Glinka became involved in political trouble. The succession of Nicholas I was immediately followed by the so-called " Decembrist " rising of December 14th/26th, which the young Tsar crushed with savage severity. Owing to their acquaintance with the poet Küchelbecker, one of the ringleaders, both Glinka and Pushkin came under suspicion, though neither was at all politically minded. Glinka, thoroughly frightened, was interrogated but had no difficulty in clearing himself. But the accession of Nicholas I was not unimportant to the development of Russian art in general and, in the sequel, to Glinka personally. The early part of his thirty years of severe " paternal " government was actually the golden age of Russian romanticism. Though a tyrant, the new Tsar was no fool. Gifted with both subtle intelligence and great personal charm, he was able first to captivate Pushkin and then to muzzle him by undertaking the personal censorship of everything he wrote, the most effective device for bringing the poet to heel being thus disguised as a unique favour. Nicholas considered freedom of thought dangerous, but he saw no reason why art should not be used to support paternal government as well as to undermine it. In 1833 he commissioned the younger Lvof to compose a national anthem. And a year or two later still we shall find Glinka himself helping to create an aureole round the occupant of the throne. Already in this winter of 1825-6 he composed a little cantata to commemorate the accession of the new Emperor.

But music was still only one of the numerous diversions

of this charming little ornament of fashionable drawing-rooms, though it is true some variations of his on an Italian air found their way into print at about this time. Glinka was also collecting birds—he had fifteen or sixteen in his aviary—and weeping over the sentimental poetry of Zhukovsky, whose personal acquaintance he made soon after. For as a youth he was, on his own confession, " of a romantic turn of mind and loved to weep sweet tears of emotion ". One love-affair succeeded another, though none was important enough to be chronicled as he chronicled his dealings with the Parisian grisettes in maturer years. In May, 1828, he added an *adagio* to the Viola Sonata begun three years before.

During the summer of the same year Glinka's official superior having found fault with his punctuation—a piece of pedantry which he ascribed to the machinations of the chief's disappointed daughter—he took the opportunity to resign from the service. But, except that he had more free time, his life changed very little. It would have been a not unenviable life, but for his health. By his own account he was suffering with eye-trouble, nerve-trouble and in half-a-dozen other ways; and though it is true that those who knew him, even his adoring sister Liudmila Shestakova[1], unkindly but unanimously hint that his sufferings were largely imaginary, they were certainly real enough to him. And, as usual, he was quite sure that his doctor was making him worse. But, in spite of his hypochondria, people (as he naïvely boasts) found him a delightful companion—good-tempered, naturally affectionate and gifted with laconic wit.

Always interested in foreign tongues, he now began to learn Italian and, as a pendant to this study, took lessons in

---

[1] According to Liudmila, " he was so afraid of death that he protected himself ludicrously from every trifle which, in his opinion, might affect his health. He was occasionally unwell—as we all are—but he considered himself always ill ". On one occasion (in 1855) he came into her room, pale and frightened, and in a scarcely audible voice groaned : " I'm ill. Look, my blood is already beginning to ooze out of my body ". It appeared that he had cut himself in shaving !

composition from an Italian named Zamboni. He acquired a little knowledge of counterpoint, but now composed principally in the Italian style and to Italian words. In August, 1828, this mania for the Italian took the flamboyant form of public serenades on the Neva. The serenaders—Glinka, Theophil Tolstoy, the Princes Golitsyn, the Counts Vielgorsky, and other young men of their set—sat in one boat, trumpeters from the Regiment of Horse Guards in another; they sang barcarolles and opera choruses, while the trumpeters played, among other things, a march specially written by Glinka, which he afterwards used in the finale of " A Life for the Tsar ". The serenades were so successful that the *entrepreneurs* went a step further and gave operatic performances at various private houses, Glinka playing Donna Anna in " Don Giovanni " and Figaro in " The Barber of Seville ". It was at this period that Glinka made the acquaintance of Pushkin, whom he closely resembled in so many respects, and of other prominent literary men, Delvig, Griboedof, and the Polish poet Mickiewicz, as well as the afterwards celebrated tenor, Ivanof, then a youth of eighteen. On one occasion Glinka made an expedition to the Imatra Falls in Finland with A. Y. Rimsky-Korsakof, the Delvigs, and the celebrated Mme. Kern, who inspired some of Pushkin's most perfect love-poems (though he referred to her in one letter as " our whore of Babylon " and in others in terms still less respectful) and whom we shall meet again in these pages. During the excursion Glinka noted down the song of a postillion, which he used ten years afterwards for the ballad of Finn in " Ruslan and Liudmila ". And a little later he heard from one of the secretaries of the Foreign Ministry the Persian air on which is based the famous " Persian chorus " in the same opera. But continuous neuralgia, for which he took quantities of opium, terminated this pleasant, idle life. By October, 1829, Glinka's health had become so bad that he was obliged to spend the winter in the quietness of his home at Novospasskoe, improving his piano technique and composing a little. (His String Quartet in F was written during the spring of 1830.)

Glinka had long been anxious to go abroad, preferably to Spain, but his father had steadfastly refused his permission. But at last Ivan Glinka had to give way before the doctor's pronouncement that " not less than three years in a warm climate " were absolutely necessary for the restoration of his son's health. Michael was delighted. The singer Ivanof was persuaded to accompany him, and the two left Novospasskoe on April 25th/May 7th, 1830.[1] They travelled by way of Brest-Litovsk and Warsaw to Dresden, where a fashionable doctor advised Glinka to try the treatment at Ems and Aix-la-Chapelle. But the Ems water disagreed with him and after three weeks they moved on to Aix. Here the waters suited him better but he overdid the treatment, just as he had done in the Caucasus, " drinking too much and bathing too often ", as he confessed, and bringing on inflammation of the glands of the neck. At the theatre he and Ivanof heard " Der Freischütz ", which they enjoyed, and " Fidelio ", which they " failed to understand the first time ", though the second performance reduced them both to tears. In August they travelled south with some Petersburg friends, crossed the Alps, and early in September reached Milan, where everything—the Cathedral, the pellucid sky, the black-eyed women—filled Glinka with " indescribable rapture ".

After a month or two, both began to take lessons, Ivanof from the tenor Eliodoro Bianchi, Glinka from Francesco Basili, then head of the Milan Conservatoire. But Glinka was quickly bored by the " dry and unpoetic labour " of Basili's exercises in strict counterpoint and broke off his

---

[1] Glinka's passport description was as follows : " 25 years of age, short (5 ft. 0⅜ in.); medium forehead, dark hair; black eyebrows, chestnut-brown eyes, medium nose " (" longish " is scratched out); " medium mouth; medium chin; pale complexion; special marks: small wart on the left temple and forelock on the right side of the head ".

studies.[1] Besides, Milan was so full of distractions. Through the Russian Ambassador to the Sardinian Court, Glinka soon made friends among the Italian nobility. He had already found a congenial friend of the other sex in a certain Adelaide ("Didina"). And at the end of December both the Milan theatres opened. That season La Scala was thrown into the shade by the smaller Teatro Carcano, where Glinka was allowed to use the Ambassador's stage-box. Pasta and Rubini sang; Bellini and Donizetti directed their own operas. The season opened with the first performance of the latter's "Anna Bolena", and in March came a still more eagerly anticipated *première*, that of "La Sonnambula", at which the emotional little Russian was not behind the Latin audience in "shedding copious tears". At about the same time Glinka made the acquaintance of a remarkable but now forgotten composer, Francesco Pollini, pupil of Mozart, precursor of Liszt and Thalberg in the nineteenth century technique of piano-writing, and inventor of a certain *rob antisyphilitique* ("*Eau de Mr. Pollin*"), the sale of which provided him with a comfortable income. Pollini was honoured by Liszt; "Sonnambula" was dedicated to him; and under his influence and that of the fashionable operas of the day, Glinka began to concoct "Variations on a Theme from 'Anna Bolena'", a "Rondo on a Theme from 'Montecchi e Capuletti'", and similar regrettable productions. He also sampled the *Eau de Mr. Pollin*—which, needless to say, disagreed with him.

In spite of innumerable aches and pains, real or imaginary, and the inevitable wrong treatment, the spring and summer passed pleasantly enough, but uneventfully except for a brief, transitory acquaintanceship with Mendelssohn. In the autumn the two Russians moved on to Naples, where Ivanof began to study with Nozzari and, more informally, with

---
[1] Basili's fame, however, is not chiefly due to his failure to interest Glinka in strict counterpoint, but to his refusal at this very time to accept such an unpromising pupil as Giuseppe Verdi.

Mme. Fodor-Mainvielle, to both of whom Glinka also was indebted for much of his knowledge of vocal technique. In Naples they were introduced to both Bellini and Donizetti, and Ivanof made his stage debut in " Anna Bolena ". Here Glinka took leave of his none too congenial travelling companion and, wandering alone by way of Rome and Bologna, returned in March to Milan and " Didina ".

But " Didina's " reign was not undisputed. Glinka boasts of his more or less serious flirtations with the married daughter of one of his doctors and the niece of another. Each of these ladies being a performer on the piano or harp, he was inspired to more " serenades " on operatic themes (for instance, one on " Anna Bolena " for piano, harp, viola, 'cello, bassoon and horn) as well as to a more serious Sextet for piano and strings, completed in October, 1832. At this period Glinka was drawing in the atmosphere of Italian opera at every breath, renewing and extending his acquaintanceship with Bellini (who had come north for the *première* of " Norma " at La Scala), both in Milan and Venice, and mixing with artists and amateurs of every type. But soon the spell began to lose its potency. As a composer, Glinka had tried to imitate the Italian *sentimento brillante*—and signally failed, as he was the first to recognise. It expressed a delightful view of life, easygoing and warmed through with southern sunshine. But " we northerners feel otherwise; impressions either leave us quite cold or move us to our depths ", he felt. " With us, love is inseparable from sorrow." The very pieces he had written for his Milanese friends and which Ricordi had published, " convinced me that I had not found the right road and that I could not *sincerely* become an Italian. Homesickness gradually led me to the idea of writing in Russian ". This nostalgia, the culmination of a harrowing sequence of pains in head and stomach, nervous disorders (even hallucinations) and insomnia, decided Glinka. He left Italy for ever in July, 1833.

Accompanied by one of his Italian doctors, he made first for Vienna and took the waters at Baden—the Lower Austrian Baden, of course—with the usual result that the " cure " was worse than the illness, or at any rate worsened the illness. His hallucinations returned in the most distressing forms and he had so little control over his feet and hands that he had to be led about by a servant. Then, most dramatically, he found salvation—in homœopathy. On the recommendation of a Catholic priest in Baden, he consulted a Viennese homœopathist whose treatment proved almost miraculously effective. The patient promptly revived, read Schiller, went to hear the Strauss and Lanner bands and composed a melody afterwards used in the *krakoviak* of " A Life for the Tsar ". In October he joined his sister Natalie and her husband in Berlin.

The next few months in Berlin were vitally important to Glinka, the prelude to an entirely new phase of his life. For one thing, he now—at twenty-nine—for the first time grappled seriously, if only briefly, with the technical problems of composition. On the recommendation of an old Milan acquaintance, the vocal teacher Teschner, he went to Siegfried Dehn (later the Librarian of the Music Section of the Royal Library in Berlin, and teacher of Peter Cornelius, Kullak and Anton Rubinstein), and studied with him for four or five months. Dehn, though one of the most distinguished theorists of his day, was no pedant. He knew how to interest his dilettante-pupil, and not only clarified Glinka's rather hazy ideas of harmony and counterpoint but grounded him in the elements of fugal writing. More or less under Dehn's guidance Glinka wrote a " Capriccio on Russian Themes " for piano duet (all things considered, a very remarkable piece of work), two movements of a Symphony in D minor, also on Russian themes though " worked out in the German manner ", and one of the best of all his songs, a setting of Zhukovsky's " The oak-trees murmur ".

Not content with " treating " Russian themes, Glinka also

began deliberately to write " in the Russian style " himself, producing two melodies which he was able to use later in " A Life for the Tsar "—Vania's song and the first subject of the *allegro* of the overture. He was already aflame with the ambition to write an opera of some kind, though of what kind he hardly knew, except that it must be *Russian*. " I have a scheme in my head ", he wrote to a Petersburg friend. " Perhaps this is not the moment to make a complete confession; perhaps if I did, I should be afraid of detecting signs of incredulity in your face. And yet, I ought to warn you that you will find me somewhat changed; I'm sure you'll be astonished to find much more in me than you could ever have believed at the time when I was living in Petersburg.... Must I tell you? I fancy I have the ability to enrich our stage with a big work. It won't be a masterpiece.... but—it won't be so bad! ... The most important point is a well-chosen subject. In every way it will be absolutely national. And not only the subject but the music." But for the time being, he sought this through-and-through " national " subject among the fashionable sentimental-romantic tales of the day, nearly deciding on Zhukovsky's " Marina Grove " and even composing some of the music for it later in the summer.

The months in Berlin were sweetened by an idyllic love-affair with one of Teschner's pupils, a girl of seventeen or eighteen " with the face almost of a Madonna ". Glinka gave her singing-lessons, writing for her little studies, one of which he afterwards developed into the " Hebrew Song " in the incidental music to " Prince Kholmsky ". But idyll and study were both interrupted by bad news from Novospasskoe. Glinka's father had died and the little family party in Berlin were obliged to hasten home. And thus Glinka returned to the great prison-house of Nicholas I's Russia.

His captivity was to be pleasant enough, however. Indeed, like some of the other cage-birds, he was perfectly delighted to sing for his master's pleasure. Yet at first he had had no intention of settling in Russia. After a short stay in Moscow where, with a naïvely acknowledged desire to show off, he played and sang some of his latest compositions in society circles, he intended to return to Berlin and the Madonna-faced Maria. He actually set out in August, 1834, escorting his sister's German maid who wished to return home, and got as far as Smolensk. There he was held up by the fact that the girl's passport was not in order. In order to put the matter right, he was obliged, much to his annoyance, to go to Petersburg—still intending to settle in Berlin before winter set in. But in Petersburg, staying at the house of a relation by marriage, Alexei Stuneef, he met and was attracted by another Maria, the latter's sister-in-law—Maria Petrovna Ivanova. Petersburg suddenly seemed more pleasant. Early in October the snow came and finally settled Glinka's fate. He decided not to go to Berlin after all.

It must be admitted that he was held in Petersburg by other chains than Maria Petrovna's, though his infatuation persisted and he became engaged to her in the following March. But at the house of his friend the poet-critic, Zhukovsky, tutor to the Tsarevitch Alexander and hence a link and mediator between the Court and the literary-artistic world, Glinka renewed his acquaintanceship with Pushkin and was introduced to the new star that had appeared in the firmament of Russian literature during his absence in Italy, Nikolai Gogol. In their circle Glinka constantly met the leaders of intellectual life in the northern capital—the Princes Viazemsky and Odoievsky, Count Michael Vielgorsky and his brother—and through Michael Vielgorsky he was brought into contact with a fifth-rate poet and dramatist, Nestor Kukolnik, vain and self-conscious, who was destined later to play an active part in Glinka's life—according to some, an evil part. During the same winter Glinka also met the twenty-one-year-old Dargomyjsky, whose place in the early history of Russian music is second only to his own. They remained on friendly terms to the end of Glinka's life, but their friendship never ripened to intimacy. Their lives flowed always in different channels.

To Zhukovsky Glinka revealed his ambition to write a Russian opera. As we have seen, he was contemplating a subject by the poet himself. But Zhukovsky, perhaps inspired by a hint from the Tsar, and certainly remembering the new national anthem, now just a year old, for which he had supplied the words, suggested a more obviously patriotic subject, one directly glorifying the monarchy: the heroism of the peasant Ivan Susanin, who in 1613, by misleading a body of Polish troops, saved the life of the founder of the Romanof dynasty at the cost of his own. Zhukovsky promised to write the libretto and did actually make a beginning, but, having little time, handed over the task to his colleague, Baron Rosen, secretary to the Tsarevitch and a German. Poor Rosen had no easy task, for no sooner had Glinka accepted the idea of " Ivan Susanin " than his imagination caught fire[1] and he plunged headlong into the composition, without waiting for his librettist. " As if by magic ", he says, " both the plan of the whole opera and the idea of the antithesis of Russian and Polish music, as well as many of the themes and even details of the working-out— all this flashed into my head at one stroke. I began to work— and from the wrong end; for I started with the part that others write last—the overture, which I wrote out for piano duet, with indications of the scoring." (When the overture was published, only the slow introduction differed from this first draft.) " Themes for the different parts of the opera, often with indications of contrapuntal treatment, I wrote down in notebooks as I invented them!" And all this before the libretto existed; so that the unfortunate Rosen had to fit his verses not only into the fairly detailed scenario prepared

[1] Though, according to Odoievsky, Glinka's original idea was to treat "Ivan" as a sort of "scenic oratorio" in three tableaux.

by the composer but, in many places, to music already written. But he steadily went on manufacturing lines. " Rosen was a clever fellow; you asked for so many verses in such-and-such a metre—it was all the same to him; you came back next day and there they were. Zhukovsky and the others used to say laughingly that Rosen's pockets were filled with ready-made verses, and that I only had to say what kind I wanted, i.e. the metre, and how many lines, and he would produce the right number of each variety, each sort from a special pocket." But in one respect Rosen was less compliant. Although his Russian was not irreproachable, he stubbornly defended every one of his unlucky phrases. " You don'd undersdand; id is de besd boetry ", he told the composer on one occasion, his cheeks flaming with indignation. Was ever an opera so written, and by an apprentice composer?

On April 26th/May 8th, 1835, Glinka married. (When he came to write his " Memoirs " he was not quite sure of the date, though he had reason enough to remember it.) Like Pushkin's, four years before, it was a marriage foredoomed to disaster. And for the same reasons. In both cases the husbands were more or less accomplished Don Juans and in each the wife, a frivolous, empty-headed society woman, was quite unable (even had she wished) to make herself indispensable to her husband and to command a lasting respect and affection which would have held as sheet-anchor through all temporary infidelities. Maria was seventeen and very beautiful, but she was a coquette and a fool. Though her fiancé had taught her to sing a little, she knew nothing whatever of music. Seeing him deeply moved on one occasion after a performance of Beethoven's Seventh Symphony, she had asked him what was the matter. " Beethoven ", he told her. " And what has he done to you, then? " she wanted to know.

But for a little while they lived quite blissfully, Glinka took his bride, his " angel ", and her mother—with the libretto of two acts of his opera—to Novospasskoe. He actually began the lovely bridal chorus in 5/4 time in Act III in the carriage during the journey; and in the familiar surroundings of his old home in the heart of the country, work went easily. " Every morning I sat at the table of the big, cheerful drawing-room in our house at Novospasskoe. It was our favourite room; sisters, mother, wife—in short, the whole family—swarmed there, and the more noisily they laughed and chattered, the quicker went my work. The weather was lovely, and I often worked with the door open into the garden, drinking in the pure, fragrant air." One might conclude from the date on the title-page of the manuscript that the full score was finished on August 27th/September 8th, immediately after their return to Petersburg. But in his " Memoirs " the composer says he wrote the scene of Susanin in the forest " during the winter . . . so vividly imagining myself in my hero's place that my hair stood on end and I felt frozen with fear ". And various additions and alterations were made during the next few months in accordance with the advice of numerous friendly critics—Michael Vielgorsky, Odoievsky and Glinka's old teacher, Charles Mayer, whom he consulted on points of orchestration.

In the beginning of February, 1836, private rehearsals of the First Act began at Prince Yusupof's house, with the Prince's incomplete and not very efficient private orchestra, while at about the same time Glinka succeeded in winning the interest of some of the principal artists of the Imperial Opera. Chief among these were the famous bass Petrof and his wife-to-be, the almost equally celebrated contralto Ann Petrova-Vorobieva, who learned the leading rôles in the work and sang them privately, to the annoyance of the Director of the Theatres, A. M. Gedeonof. Gedeonof complained that Glinka was ruining their voices by inducing them to sing in smoke-laden rooms, but he himself was persuaded to attend a run-through of the First Act at the Vielgorskys', and on April 8th/20th Glinka was able to send him the necessary formal request for the production of the opera. Cavos, the naturalised Italian conductor of the Imperial Opera, who twenty years before had written a highly successful " Ivan Susanin " himself, warmly pressed for acceptance, and Gedeonof agreed—on one condition. The composer was not to claim any fee. Being in no particular need of money at the time, Glinka willingly signed away his rights.

The rehearsals began almost at once, at first in the Alexandrinsky Theatre. Cavos and the musicians were enthusiastic, even spontaneously applauding certain numbers. But an interesting light on the standard of musical performance in Russia at that time is shed by Glinka's information that Cavos, who had a very high reputation for efficiency, paid little attention to dynamic markings ("*pp* usually became a sort of *mf* ") and hardly ever hit on the right *tempi*. The orchestra itself was very unequal; some of the first violins and 'cellos were very good, the first flute, first oboe and first clarinet excellent, the rest decidedly mediocre. And when in the autumn the rehearsals were transferred to the Grand Theatre, singers and orchestra had to compete with the hammers of renovating workmen. Zhukovsky busied himself throughout with the production, and shortly before the first performance the Tsar himself graciously appeared at a rehearsal. A few months previously he had attended the first performance of Gogol's " Revizor " and laughed heartily at its lashing of his corrupt officials, so that his interest in a work centring about an act of devotion to the throne was only to be expected. As an immediate consequence of this visit, Nicholas accepted the dedication of the work, the title of which was now changed from " Ivan Susanin " to " A Life for the Tsar ".[1]

Glinka was not well enough to attend the *répétition générale*, when the theatre was filled by the curious public, but on the following night (November 27th/December 9th)

[1] It is given in Soviet Russia under its original title.

he was present with his wife and enjoyed his triumph to the full. Petrof took the part of the hero, Petrova-Vorobieva that of Ivan's son, Vania. There was one curious, typically Russian incident: the Polish Rebellion had been crushed only five years before and the audience, in the presence of the Tsar, dared not applaud actors representing Poles. Consequently the Second Act, entirely Polish and mostly ballet, ended in deadly silence. Otherwise the reception was enthusiastic. There was every reason why it should be. " A Life for the Tsar " contains nothing that could have shocked the most conservative audience. It is an amateur Italian opera, with a strongly Russian flavour, on a flamboyantly patriotic subject —a very remarkable achievement for a half-trained Russian gentleman in the 1830's but not, in spite of beautiful pages, a work of any great importance to the world in general. It should be regarded as the finest flower of the old dilettantism rather than as the first blossoming of " serious " Russian music which it is usually considered. The happy little composer was summoned to the Imperial Box where, as he wrote to his mother next day, " His Majesty the Emperor took me by the hand, thanked me and had a long conversation with me; the Crown Prince, the Empress and the Grand Duchess Maria Nikolaevna also honoured me with flattering remarks about my music ". A few days later the Tsar acknowledged the dedication of the opera by the gift of a handsome ring (valued at 4,000 rubles, the sum Glinka would normally have received for the production rights), which the composer gave to his wife. In addition he derived a little money from the sale of piano arrangements of separate numbers, made by Mayer and himself, and printed on very bad paper by the music-seller Snegiref, which for years constituted the only printed edition of the opera. More important than financial reward, however, was the satisfaction, as he tells his mother, of being " recognised as the first composer in Russia ". The theatre was filled for ten more performances before the end of the year; and the majority of the audiences must have gone voluntarily, though it is true the Cadet Corps attended in obedience to an Imperial command. Only some of the would-be-Western aristocrats, despisers of everything Russian, including their own language, ventured to sneer at " la musique des cochers ".

The Imperial favour brought Glinka yet one other reward. He had for some time been anxious to obtain some sort of post in connection with the direction of the Imperial Theatres. Even now this was not granted, though he did not give up hope. But on January 1st/13th, 1837, he was appointed Kapellmeister of the Imperial Chapel, with a salary of 2,500 rubles, an additional thousand for the table expenses, and an official residence.[1] Formerly there had only been a Director of the Chapel. But the death of the elder Lvof, who had held this appointment since 1825, gave Nicholas an opportunity to reward both his musical protégés. The younger Lvof, he of the national anthem, was appointed Director in succession to his father, and a new post was created for Glinka's benefit. The two new brooms took their official positions very seriously and subjected the Imperial choristers to an examination which a number of them failed to pass. Lvof was for turning them out. But Glinka, always amusingly proud of his knowledge of vocal technique, undertook to teach them at least to read and to sing in tune, neither of which accomplishments had apparently been usual in the Chapel of His Imperial Majesty.

From this period dates the most famous of all Glinka's songs, his setting of Zhukovsky's " Midnight Review ". He tells us that he composed it directly he saw the words and sang it to Zhukovsky and Pushkin the same evening at his own house, adding that his mother was present and was delighted that her son should entertain such distinguished

[1] In those days, before the Crimean War, the exchange value of the ruble was just over three shillings and its purchasing value a great deal more still.

guests. That last detail is interesting, if correct, for it places the evening in the latter part of January and must have been almost the last occasion on which Glinka saw Pushkin, though he does not say so, as one would naturally expect. For the poet was shot in a duel on January 27th/February 8th and died two days later, a tragedy which deprived Glinka of a possible collaborator of the first rank. Both his operas suffer from very bad libretti, and the successor to " A Life for the Tsar " was to be a Pushkin subject, " Ruslan and Liudmila ". But it is doubtful whether, as has sometimes been asserted, Glinka had actually discussed an operatic version of " Ruslan " with the poet. This assertion rests only on two statements in different parts of Glinka's " Memoirs ": that he had once heard Pushkin say he would have altered a great many things in this youthful work if he had been writing it now in maturity, and that he (Glinka) had intended to ask *what* changes—but was prevented by the poet's death: and that " I had hoped to draw up the plan " (i.e. the scenario) " under Pushkin's guidance, but was prevented by his untimely end ". Intentions, but nothing more. Glinka's project cannot at any rate have been generally known, for after an excerpt from " A Life for the Tsar " sung at a Patriotic Concert during Lent, 1837, the Tsar remarked significantly to the composer's brother-in-law: " Glinka is a great master. It will be a pity if he does nothing more than this one opera ". And we hear nothing of the music for " Ruslan " till December of that year, when the composer speaks, in a letter to his mother, of " all my thoughts being directed towards a new opera ". Are we to conclude that Glinka was thinking of " Ruslan " in the weeks immediately after the production of his first opera and then was so stunned by the poet's death, which he mentions so casually, that he laid the project aside for nearly a year? He gives no hint of all this in his " Memoirs "; but if it, or something like it, is not the truth, the composer's memory or fancy must have played him false as to his " hope of drawing up the plan under Pushkin's guidance ". Unfortunately, we have no means of checking the accuracy of his " Memoirs " at every point.

Perhaps the explanation of the muddled chronology of his account of this period is to be found in his domestic troubles. So far his marriage had appeared superficially to be a success, though even in the earliest days Maria had been so little sympathetic with her husband's work that she had complained of his squandering money on music-paper. But in the spring of 1837 a rather serious illness of hers " shook my faith in conjugal happiness " (her affectionate husband says) " and her caprices after the illness completely destroyed that belief ". Storms were continually provoked by mere trifles, and it is evident that not all the blame was on one side. Instead of humouring the girl, Glinka was determined, he says, to assert his authority. Maria would sob bitterly, while her German mother, who lived with them, would storm at the unhappy little man, getting so excited that her broken Russian was barely understandable and " making a noise like the hissing of a *samovar* ". Glinka gives an amusing wordpicture of himself, marching to and fro across the room, silently and with measured steps, during one of these storms, " at each turn pivoting on my right foot and carefully describing a semicircle with my left leg, which enraged my mother-in-law beyond everything, and thus quickly reduced her to silence. Then I would turn to her and enquire whether she had said all she had to say. Naturally she would start afresh at this; but not for long. Exhaustion would close her lips, and I would slowly put on my gloves, take my hat and, politely bowing to the ladies, betake myself to friends with whom I sometimes stayed for several days ", until the storm had blown over. Chief among these friends with whom he was accustomed to take refuge were the already mentioned Nestor Kukolnik and his younger brother Platon. Kukolnik was a vain, self-conscious *poseur* who had had the impertinence to consider himself a rival of Pushkin. Even before Glinka's marriage he had taken a dislike to Maria; according to an entry in his diary[1] he was "jealous" of her; and there can be no doubt that his influence now widened the breach.

At the end of the summer Glinka found yet another source of consolation. In addition to his pupils of the Imperial Chapel he was teaching various amateur singers (for instance Lodi, a friend of the Kukolniks, who afterwards became a professional and went on the stage). And now Gedeonof asked him to train the voices of four girls specially selected from the Theatrical School. "The time I spent with these charming creatures, half-children, half-coquettes, was perhaps among the best in my life." And one of the quartet, a certain Caroline K., "little by little awakened a poetic emotion in my soul", a feeling which she evidently reciprocated. "When I played and sang, her face expressed genuine delight. The other pupils listened to me eagerly; even quite little girls crowded round the door and listened breathlessly to my singing." But the pleasant hours in the Theatrical School were terminated early in 1838, through a quarrel with Gedeonof.

The compositions dating from this period are of no interest: a few songs, a polonaise for chorus and orchestra written for a reception in honour of the Tsarevitch, and a supplementary scene for "A Life for the Tsar" written in a single day to words by Kukolnik, at the request of Petrof for the latter's wife. From the painter Aïvazovsky, an amateur fiddler who visited the Kukolniks, Glinka acquired three Tatar melodies, two of which he afterwards used in the *lezginka* of "Ruslan" and the third in Ratmir's aria in Act III. But we have no definite information as to the

[1] A document full of interesting information about the composer, though its trustworthiness is not beyond suspicion. If its dates are correct, Kukolnik must occasionally have received letters two or three weeks before they were written.

beginning of work on this opera till the end of April, 1838, when Glinka was despatched to the Ukraine for three months at the head of a small commission charged with the recruiting of singers for the Imperial Chapel. He wrote to Kukolnik (May 26th/June 7th): " As regards music in general and ' Ruslan ' in particular, you must know that my head is like a garden allowed to run wild and overgrown with weeds ". And three weeks later: " You ask about the opera! .... I tell you frankly that as long as Gedeonof is Director, I'm not going to have any dealings with the theatre. My muse is not importunate; she remains silent—thank God ". These letters are unusually full of melancholy, though the expedition was not without amusing incidents. (In one town Glinka, like Gogol's hero, Khlestakof, was taken for a visiting *Revizor*.) As his centre of operations, Glinka stayed at Katchenovka, the house of a very wealthy landowner who maintained a private orchestra good enough to tackle Beethoven's " Egmont " music. Glinka got this orchestra to play for the first time his Persian Chorus and Tchernomor's March, which must therefore have been the first two numbers written for " Ruslan ". Finn's Ballad was actually composed during this visit, Pushkin's verses being adapted for the purpose by a fellow-guest named Markevitch; and the composer sang it with the orchestra.

But the work made little progress after Glinka's return to Petersburg. His wife's extravagance strained even his ample financial resources. (" An income of 10,000 rubles a year— and he can't live as he wants to ", Kukolnik comments in his diary.) And to make his home life more tolerable he had begun to entertain more lavishly, giving a musical evening and conversazione regularly once a week. In the hope of raising a little money, Glinka published early in 1839 an " Album of Musical Pieces " by himself and other composers, which brought him in a thousand rubles. But even this work —to say nothing of his social life and his official duties—

"hindered me", as he complains, "from working at 'Ruslan'". Still, the work made some progress. "I wrote the opera in snatches and fragments." Gorislava's cavatina must have been composed at about this time, for Kukolnik says he heard Petrova sing "the new aria" at one of Glinka's conversazioni in November, and Liudmila's cavatina in Act I was performed, with chorus and orchestra, at a Patriotic Concert in the spring of 1839. "Besides these five pieces" (i.e. the three performed at Katchenovka and these two cavatinas) "I had by this time noted down themes, with bits of counterpoint, in a notebook given me for that purpose by N. Kukolnik". Which is not quite true, for the notebook in question has been published and consists mainly, not of sketches for the music, but of an outline plan of the opera.

Glinka's account of the origin of the scenario and libretto of "Ruslan" is picturesque but misleading. "In the winter of either 1837 or 1838", he says, "I was once playing some excerpts from the opera. N. Kukolnik, always interested in my productions, egged me on more and more. Among the others present was Constantine Bakhturin" (a third-rate poet and dramatist). "He undertook to draw up the plan of the opera and, although drunk, did it in a quarter of an hour. And just imagine: the opera was actually carried out according to this plan!" Kukolnik's diary not only supports this story but settles the date as November 6th/18th, 1838.[1] Yet nearly seven weeks before this Glinka had informed a friend in the postscript of a letter that "my poet has finished the First Act and begun the Second successfully". Why write the ground-plan when the libretto was already partly finished? And who was this poet? In his "Memoirs" Glinka says he was introduced at about this time to a Staff-Captain Shirkof as a possibly suitable librettist. He stipulated

[1] The very same day, he says, Gurskalin ("Odeon") the publisher of the already mentioned "Album of Musical Pieces", agreed to pay another thousand rubles (£150 at that period) for the publication rights in Glinka's songs—Kukolnik's brother, Platon, being the intermediary between composer and publisher in both transactions.

that Pushkin's verses were to be preserved wherever possible and asked Shirkof, by way of trial, to write the words of Gorislava's cavatina and *part* of the First Act. " These turned out very satisfactorily, but instead of thinking out the whole plan and action of the piece beforehand, I at once set to work at the cavatinas of Liudmila and Gorislava, not bothering at all about the dramatic action, but supposing that all this could be settled later." It is difficult to reconcile this with the statement that the librettist had *finished* Act I and begun Act II six weeks before, even if we assume that by "the beginning of the Second Act" Glinka meant the words of Gorislava's song (actually in Act III). The real truth of the " drunken Bakhturin " story appears to be that in that quarter of an hour Bakhturin sketched out some sort of plan for the *rest* of the action.

At Easter, 1839, in his sister's drawing-room, Glinka saw for the first time Ekaterina Kern, daughter of his old acquaintance Anna Petrovna Kern, the lady whom Pushkin had celebrated in lovely verse and defamed in unprintable prose. The girl was in ill-health; his own nerves were upset at the time; but, despite the expression of suffering on her pale face, Ekaterina's " peculiar charm " at once attracted him. " Having fortified myself with a bottle of champagne, I found means to talk to this charming girl, and I remember as if it were now the extraordinary skill with which I expressed what I was feeling." Ekaterina soon reciprocated his sudden passion and his relations with his wife worsened proportionately. When Maria left Petersburg during the heat of the summer, according to custom, her husband spent as little time with her as possible, slipping back to town under various pretexts, staying with the Kukolniks and visiting Ekaterina.

Glinka had for some time been gradually drawing into ever closer relationship with the Kukolniks, who have been accused of trying to monopolise him, of being jealous of his other friends. It was at their house that he had first heard Beethoven's last quartets. And they had formed a mutual admiration society of young poets and artists, calling themselves "The Brotherhood of Russia's Two Greatest Geniuses", the "geniuses" in question being Glinka and—Nestor Kukolnik. Among the "brothers" were the singer Petrof, the caricaturist N. A. Stepanof, to whom we are indebted for a most amusing series of sketches of the composer, the already mentioned tenor Lodi, K. P. Villebois, an artillery colonel who dabbled in composition and published a collection of folk-songs, and others of the same stamp, intelligent men but a very different circle from that of Zhukovsky and Pushkin. Indeed, Glinka's old friends, the Vielgorskys and others, were temporarily estranged from him during the three or four years of his greatest intimacy with the "brothers". The "brotherhood" met to hear music and poetry. But the music was always Glinka's and the poetry Kukolnik's; the two were often mated in songs. Their gatherings are reputed to have generally ended in "orgies", and the "brothers" have been accused by responsible people who knew the circumstances (for instance, Yury Arnold) of having finally ruined Glinka's never very robust health. He frequently spent the night at the Kukolniks' and his connection with the "brotherhood" certainly did not help to improve his relations with his wife. It may be, as he says, that the "brotherhood" was a refuge from domestic unhappiness, but there is plenty of evidence that it was partly the cause of that unhappiness. Considering these nights of absence and her husband's notorious interest in Ekaterina Kern, it is hardly surprising that a woman of Maria's nature and up-bringing turned elsewhere for consolation.

On at least one occasion there was a scene between husband and wife in Ekaterina's presence. Maria having significantly remarked that "all poets and artists come to bad ends" and cited the instance of Pushkin, Glinka retorted that, although he did not consider himself as clever as Pushkin, he had no intention of getting a bullet in his head on account of his wife. " She turned away, making a grimace at me." They found cause for bitter dissension in the fact that whereas Glinka wanted to keep only a pair of horses, his wife felt socially degraded with less than four. And to crown everything, Glinka was embittered by the reflection that, lovely as she appeared in public, he was obliged to see her in untidy *négligé*, a cigar-holder between her lips, her complexion ruined by " the immoderate use of cosmetics ", walking about the room and hurling abuse at her maid. In September he learned beyond doubt that she was as unfaithful to him as he to her. Finally, in November, having overheard his mother-in-law arranging an appointment with Maria's lover, he sent his wife a note explaining that as mutual confidence had long ceased to exist between them, he would live with her no more. " We must separate—but separate as becomes those nobly born, without quarrelling, noise and mutual reproaches." He " prayed heaven to preserve her from new miseries " and, for his part (after due consultation with his mother, to whom the Glinka estate still belonged) he would do what he could to provide for her. (In the sequel he allowed her half his income.) " But let me tell you that tears, explanations, complaints, entreaties, the mediation of relatives and people in high circles—none of these will shake my resolution." Having fired this farewell shot and sent his serfs to fetch away a few specially valued possessions, including the horses which had been so hotly disputed over, he fled to the flat of his friend, Adjutant P. A. Stepanof, the caricaturist's brother. An attempt at reconciliation having completed his fright, he did not venture outside Stepanof's door for a whole month, seeing only a few intimate friends—not even Ekaterina, who was lying ill at the time—but pouring out all his troubles in a series of passionately affectionate letters to his adored mother. " All the old women in

Petersburg" were up in arms against him. There was "no limit to the slanders". At first he was prepared to "care very little for public opinion" but very soon this man of thirty-five was writing that "you alone, dear mamma, can be my guardian angel", whose "experience and sagacity" would get him out of his difficulties, and imploring her to come to Petersburg. On December 18th/30th, under pretext of ill-health, he was permitted to resign his appointment at the Imperial Chapel, in which he had for some time lost interest.

It had been a wretched year, 1839; the unhappiest, he says, of his life. In addition to his domestic troubles he had lost his younger brother Andrei, of whom he had been very fond. He had done nothing at all toward "Ruslan". Except a valse and polonaise for orchestra, dedicated to the Grand Duchess Maria Nikolaevna, and a nocturne for piano, he had composed only the orchestral "Valse-Fantaisie".

His mother having come to the capital, and Ekaterina's health being temporarily better, Glinka pulled himself together a little and the immediate fruit of his recovery was his setting of one of Pushkin's best known poems, "I remember the wonderful moment", one of those addressed to Ekaterina's mother. After some months in the quiet of Novospasskoe, his nerves again in serious disorder, Glinka lived in Petersburg for a time with another sister (Maria) and her husband. He once more began to compose; and it is from this period that we must date Glinka's real, brief maturity as a creative artist. As he confessed, the troubles of the previous year had taught him more about life in a short time than he had learned in all the rest of his existence. The ripening and individualisation of his musical thought at this period are very remarkable.

According to Kukolnik's diary "the Overture and the whole of the First Act of 'Ruslan' were ready" by the middle of May, 1840, which is certainly not true. Nevertheless Glinka had evidently begun to think about the opera again, visiting the librettist Shirkof, trying unsuccessfully to paint water-colours with him, and being introduced to Chopin's music by Shirkof's wife. He also started a piano piece (for three hands!) on the folk-tune, " Kamarinskaya ", but it " turned out such trash " that he did not finish it; it had nothing in common with the well-known orchestral piece based on the same melody. Also from this period dates the album—it is not a connected cycle—of twelve songs to Kukolnik's words, published by Gurskalin under the collective title, " Farewell to Petersburg ", a set which includes some of Glinka's best work in the field of song-writing. One of the songs, " The Lark ", has become widely known through Balakiref's piano transcription. The apparently meaningless title of the collection is a reference to the composer's intention of leaving this city of unpleasant memories.

He wished to go abroad. But Ekaterina's health was worse; she appeared to be consumptive; and her mother would not agree to leave Russia. Finally Glinka handed over his ready money to the Kerns, who were none too well off, so that Ekaterina might take a holiday in the south of Russia. He intended to marry her if he could get a divorce from Maria Petrovna. But the Kerns procrastinated in truly Russian fashion and did not leave Petersburg till the middle of August; and Glinka, after accompanying the ladies part of the way, had to turn sadly aside to Novospasskoe to try to get more money out of his mother.

His time at home was not wasted, however. On the eve of his departure he had written to Shirkof that he had " never composed so much before, never felt such inspiration. I implore you to write Act IV according to the programme sent you ". In three weeks he wrote the introduction to Act I, and on the way back to Petersburg, feverish and ill, sketched out the finale of the last act in a single night. He now made his home first with the Kukolniks, later with the Stepanofs;

he had more or less decided not to go abroad till
" Ruslan " had been completed and produced. But instead
of pressing ahead with the opera, he first, at Kukolnik's
request (though Kukolnik said he had no recollection of
having made it), wrote an overture and incidental music to
the latter's recently completed tragedy " Prince Kholmsky ",
the whole being composed between September 19th and
October 15th (October 1st and 27th, N.S.), the most concentrated piece of sustained work Glinka ever did. But as
the first performance was given on September 30th/
October 12th and the piece survived only three performances,
the entr'actes, " each ", as Tchaïkovsky said, " a little picture
painted by a master-hand ", were not ready in time. Only
the three songs (and possibly the overture) were performed
in the theatre.

Even when the " Kholmsky " music was out of the way,
" Ruslan " progressed very slowly. Glinka's health was
again much worse; at least, he believed it was. In the
intervals of better health, he was pestered to write *piéces
d'occasion*, a curious " Tarantella " for chorus and orchestra,
to accompany a stage-performance compounded of ballet and
declamation, and a chorus for the girls of the Ekaterininsky
Institute. (Both these pieces date from December 1840/
January 1841). And all the time he was tormented by a
fresh personal trouble. His mother had shown her disapproval
of his projected marriage to the daughter of the " whore of
Babylon "; and Glinka, like Gibbon, had " sighed as a
lover " but " obeyed as a son ". Ekaterina's relations also
objected to her connection with a still married man, while
Glinka's own attitude was not too clear. His exquisitely
uncomfortable letters to Mme. Kern, with their references
to " votre petit ange ", give one an unpleasant impression that
he was coldly and clumsily extricating himself from an affair
of which he had wearied. Yet it appears from confidential
letters to other correspondents that the filial devotion was not

a mere pretext. For months both he and Ekaterina were deeply unhappy, and they even continued to correspond. But in any case the scandal-mongers of Petersburg would have made life intolerable for them. The capital had become hateful to him, he told his sister, for it " often led me into a sort of life injurious to both health and morals, since I no longer have *an angel to restrain me* ". His constant desire was to go abroad, " Ruslan " or no " Ruslan ". But as usual he wavered, took no definite step, and was finally held in Petersburg by the fortunate acquisition of documentary proofs of his wife's misconduct with Prince N. N. Vasiltchikof. He began proceedings in May, 1841, but the case dragged on till May, 1846, long after he had left Russia, when the marriage was finally dissolved.

In the autumn Glinka, with his customary resilience, came to life again. He made his home with one of his sisters, Elisabeth Sobolevskaya, happily attached himself to one of her maids, an eighteen-year-old serf, began to study landscape-drawing, and—to work again at " Ruslan ". As usual, domestic happiness quickened his productiveness and he quickly outdistanced his still more dilatory librettist. Moreover, in spite of the famous plan drawn up by the intoxicated Bakhturin—perhaps because of it—the scenario of the opera was in a hopeless muddle. Nestor Kukolnik and Michael Gedeonof, a son of the Director of the Theatres, came to Shirkof's assistance, contributing verses and doing their best to give the whole a little coherence. (In which, it must be confessed, they signally failed; no one who had not read Pushkin's poem or a synopsis of it could possibly make head or tail of the opera.) Even Glinka himself wrote the words for three passages, so that Pushkin's classic was butchered to make a Russian opera by five different poetasters: Shirkof, Kukolnik, M. A. Gedeonof (to whom " Ruslan " is dedicated), Markevitch and Glinka. However, the score was at last completed and sent in April, 1842, to the elder Gedeonof, with whom Glinka had made up his quarrel. Gedeonof at once accepted it, agreeing to Glinka's request for a royalty of ten per cent. of two-thirds of the total takings at each performance, instead of a lump sum of 4,000 rubles,[1] and musical rehearsals began the next month.

When the full stage-rehearsals commenced in November, it was found necessary to make numerous cuts—to the further confusion of the action. Nor was that the only misfortune. Owing to a quarrel with Gedeonof, the scene-painter scamped some of the most important scenes ("Tchernomor's Castle", according to Glinka, "looked like a barrack"); an unlucky, if not malicious, newspaper article caused bad feeling between the composer and the artists, including the orchestra; the conductor, K. F. Albrecht, proved a bad disciplinarian; Petrova, who was to have sung Ratmir, fell ill and had to be replaced by a young understudy who, curiously enough, bore the same name. If not actually in disgrace since his resignation from the Imperial Chapel, Glinka no longer basked in the sunshine of Imperial favour. Nor was the Court likely to interest itself in a mere fairy-tale opera as it had done in a patriotic one. Finally Vielgorsky and other Job's comforters reduced the unfortunate composer to the last stages of nervousness and irritability. Considering also the appalling muddle of the plot, it is hardly surprising that at the first performance (on November 27th/December 9th, the sixth anniversary of the *première* of "A Life for the Tsar") the audience was bored. Indeed the applause was diluted with a little hissing. The twenty-year-old Voin Rimsky-Korsakof, brother of the as yet unborn composer and himself a keen music-lover, wrote home that "in the evening Uncle" (i.e. Admiral N. P. Rimsky-Korsakof) "had to attend His Majesty at the first performance of 'Ruslan and

---

[1] The composer actually received 3,000 rubles from the thirty-two performances given that first winter.

Liudmila' .... Uncle came back at twelve very dissatisfied at the way the opera had gone. The music is beautiful, the *décor* magnificent, but the actors are most unsatisfactory. Petrof as Ruslan is a regular *mujik* and Stepanova sings Liudmila like a cat being strangled. Glinka himself was terribly upset. When he was called out, his face was as long as a fiddle ". But Gedeonof had faith in the work and refused to withdraw it. At the third performance Petrova was able to replace her namesake, and the tide of success turned. Perhaps the astonishing modernity of the music also puzzled the audience. For " Ruslan " is no mere Russianised Italian opera, like its predecessor, but a work almost of genius. Glinka himself said more than once that he " could have made ten operas like ' A Life for the Tsar ' out of ' Ruslan ' ". Some of its pages, notably the *lezginka* in Act IV, are the prototypes of all that is most characteristic in later Russian music. Unlike " A Life for the Tsar " it demands measurement not by local and contemporary, but by universal standards. With it the history of Russian music begins in earnest.

One European musician of the first rank seems to have recognised its worth at once. According to his " Memoirs " Glinka had already made the acquaintance of Liszt during the latter's first visit to Petersburg in March, 1842, when the pianist had played at sight from the manuscript full score of " Ruslan ",[1] and the friendship was renewed and strengthened during his second visit. Liszt's admiration of " Ruslan " puzzled Russian aristocrats like the Grand Duke Michael Pavlovitch, who told the distinguished visitor that he punished his officers " by sending them to Glinka's opera instead of putting them under arrest ", and wanted to know,

---

[1] Youri Arnold in his " Reminiscences " says that the composer's memory is at fault here; that the incident occurred in the course of a festive " Bohemian " evening at Glinka's house during Liszt's return visit the following year. At any rate, Liszt's transcription of Tchernomor's March, with the title " Tscherkessen-Marsch ", dates from 1843.

" Est-ce que c'est une mauvaise plaisanterie à vous de trouver Glinka un génie?"

But after the production of " Ruslan " the " genius " relapsed into indolence, composing only an occasional song or piano piece. Now that there was no reason why he should not go abroad he was no longer eager to do so. Petersburg seemed more tolerable. Ekaterina Kern had returned from the Ukraine, where she had been living since the rupture, and though the old relations were not resumed they were once more on terms of friendship, and her circle of women-friends drew Glinka away from the " brothers ". Ulybyshef's " Nouvelle biographie de Mozart " set him restudying that master's opera scores and " awakened ", he says, " my critical instinct ". (Incidentally, he considered " Don Giovanni " " masterly but not exemplary ".) But at last sheer boredom sent him on his travels again. In June, 1844, with one of his brothers-in-law and a young French girl, the latter's mistress, he set out for Paris, spending a few days in Berlin with Siegfried Dehn, who expressed his warm approval of the famous trio from his pupil's earlier opera.

In Paris the three took a flat and spent the next few months in sight-seeing and theatre-going, but without meeting any French artists of importance. Glinka wished to visit Spain and to that end wrote to his " dear, precious mamma " for money and her permission, which was not too willingly granted. He also took Spanish lessons and was soon able to read " Don Quixote " in the original. In the meantime, having found the ever necessary female companion in a charming young actress (" Adelina ") at the little Théâtre Chantereine in the Rue de la Victoire, Glinka left his brother-in-law and moved to fresh quarters. Through Prince Volkonsky he obtained an introduction to Hector Berlioz, with whom he was quickly on the friendliest terms. Berlioz was giving *concerts monstres* with an orchestra of 160 at the Cirque des Champs Elysées; on March 16th he played the *lezginka* from " Ruslan " (described as a " Grand air de danse sur des thèmes du Caucase et de la Crimée "), and Mme. Solovieva, a leading member of the Petersburg Opera who happened to be in Paris, sang a cavatina from " A Life for the Tsar ". But the *lezginka,* intended for double orchestra, was ineffective when arranged for a normal one, and the cavatina appeared, to at least one of the Parisian critics, to be nearly all on one note. Western Europe had had its first taste of Russian music—and didn't like it.

However, the cavatina was repeated five days later at Berlioz's next concert; and on April 10th, Glinka, with financial backing from the millionaire Prince Golitsyn, gave a concert of his own in the Salle Henri Herz, " on behalf of the local musical society ", the bulk of the programme being devoted to his own works, including the *krakoviak* from " A Life for the Tsar ", Tchernomor's March and the Valse-Fantaisie, played by the orchestra of the Théâtre des Italiens, under Théophile Tilmant. The Russian colony in Paris turned out in force to support their fellow-countryman, the hall was filled, and Glinka enjoyed at least a *succès d'estime.* The " Journal des débats " of April 16th contained a long and flattering article on Glinka by Berlioz, and other papers noticed the concert favourably—all of which Glinka proudly reported to his friends at home, begging Kukolnik to get Berlioz's article translated and published in the Russian press.

At the same time he confided to Kukolnik his intention, suggested by his study of Berlioz's music and the taste of the Parisian public, " to enrich my repertoire with a few—and, if my strength permits, many—concert pieces for orchestra, under the designation *Fantaisies pittoresques.* Up to now, instrumental music has been divided into two opposite categories: quartets and symphonies, valued by a few, but intimidating the mass of listeners by their depth and complexity; and concertos, variations, etc. which tire the ear by their lack of connection and their difficulties. It seems to me that it ought to be possible to reconcile the demands of art with those of the age and ... to write pieces equally accessible to the connoisseurs and to the general public ". He hoped to find in the " original and hitherto unexploited " melodies of Spain, material for such *Fantaisies*, perhaps even for a Spanish opera. " In any case I shall try to transmit my impressions in the form of sounds." Parting with Adelina, not without tears, he set out, accompanied by Don Santiago, the Spanish *major-domo* he had engaged in Paris.

They entered Spain, the Spain of Borrow and Richard Ford,[1] on June 1st, Glinka's birthday. " I was completely enraptured." In Pampeluna Glinka had his first sight of Spanish dancing, and in Valladolid, where they spent the summer with Santiago's sister, he listened with delight to the guitar-playing of a lad, Felix Castilla, one of whose tunes, the Arragonese *jota* and its variations, so took his fancy that, immediately on his arrival in Madrid in September, he wrote on it an orchestral " Capriccio brillant ", afterwards renamed " Spanish Overture, No. I ", the first of the projected *Fantaisies pittoresques*. In the capital he took and furnished a flat overlooking the Puerta del Sol, visited the theatre and continued his not very scientific investigations into the popular music of the country, recording the melodies of singers and guitarists who were brought to his flat in the evenings in a notebook (now preserved in the MSS section of the Leningrad Public Library). His chief source was a muleteer named Zagal, two of whose songs, *seguidillas manchegas*, he afterwards used in " Night in Madrid ". Otherwise he lived precisely as in Paris, making little excursions to Aranjuez and Toledo, and finding the usual " rather charming girl " in a certain Ramona Gonzales, a friend of Santiago's niece.

At the end of November Glinka went to Granada, staying

---

[1] Ford's famous " Handbook " appeared that very year—1845.

there till March, 1846, watching the dances of the gypsies and even learning Spanish dancing himself. " My feet were all right but I couldn't manage the castanets ", he says. A Spanish friend " at my request found me a charming Andalusian girl renowned for her singing of folk-songs ", whose songs and person pleased him so much that he took her back to Madrid. But Dolores proved troublesome and was " sent back to her mother " in June. And soon after this we hear of the " young and pretty " Zefirina. Glinka was certainly successful in healing those " wounds of his heart " from which he had been suffering so long. Our Don Juan also acquired a Leporello in the person of Pedro Fernandez, one of a little group of students and young officials with whom Glinka lived a bachelor life during the summer of 1846. Fernandez became his companion, factotum and piano-pupil, and even accompanied him back to Russia.

Shortly after the wedding of the young Queen Isabella II, the trio from " A Life for the Tsar " was sung at a Court concert (November 27th), but apparently the composer was not present. He spent the winter and spring in Seville, where he was particularly struck by the rhythmic complication of the dance-music, sometimes with three independent rhythms simultaneously; that of the singers, that of the guitar accompaniment, and that of the hand-clapping and feet of the dancers. He also made the acquaintance of the violinist Ole Bull. But in the beginning of May, 1847, Glinka decided to return to Russia. After three weeks in Madrid and three more in Paris, he met P. A. Stepanof at Kissingen and learned from him that Maria Petrovna, whose second husband had died already, was amply provided for. " This news delighted me, for although I did not love Maria Petrovna, it would have been painful for me to see her in want."

From Kissingen, where he was received very graciously by the Tsarevitch Alexander, he and " Don Pedro " travelled home by way of Vienna and Warsaw, reaching Novospasskoe by the end of July. It was in all outward respects the same paternally governed Russia that he had left. But in the literary world new names were beginning to appear. Pushkin was dead; Lermontof was dead; Gogol had been artistically dead since the appearance of " Dead Souls " in 1842, a few months after the first performance of " Ruslan ". But while Glinka was in Spain, a young writer named Dostoevsky had attracted attention with his novel " Poor Folk ", and in 1847 Turgenef had published the first of his " Sportsman's Sketches ", the earliest tokens of that great literary renaissance which accompanied the musical efflorescence and the political reforms of the 'sixties.

At Novospasskoe Glinka's nerves soon became troublesome, as was usually the case when he had nothing to occupy his mind. He set out for Petersburg to consult his doctor, but fell ill on the way, at Smolensk, where his sister Liudmila Shestakova joined him as soon as possible. They spent the winter there, and Glinka wrote one or two piano pieces, including a " Prayer without words " which in January, 1855, he converted into a song—one of his finest—with words by Lermontof, for his pupil Leonova. He superintended Pedro's study of Clementi's " Gradus ad Parnassum "; his friends read to him and played " preference " with him; and the local big-wigs gave an official dinner in his honour.

In March, 1848, he travelled to Warsaw, intending to go abroad. But owing to the disturbed state of Europe the paternal government refused him a passport. Finding Warsaw pleasanter than Petersburg, however, he contentedly settled down with "a rather charming girl named Angélique" whom he had noticed in a café, turned part of his flat into an aviary—he always liked to have birds about him—read Shakespeare and entertained. An evening *chez Glinka* in Warsaw must have been a memorable experience. The guests drank punch and danced. " Angelique danced beautifully, and if other pairs were wanted the cook and chambermaid danced too. Besides the birds flying about in the next room behind a net, there were two tame hares which ran about the drawing-room and sometimes scampered over the feet of the guests." At the request of the Governor, Prince Paskevitch, Glinka also interested himself in the latter's orchestra, writing for that not very efficient body a pot-pourri on four Spanish melodies, first called " Recuerdos de Castilla ", but afterwards revised and styled " Night in Madrid: Spanish Overture No. 2 ". His attempt to construct a similar piece on Andalusian melodies failed, since "the majority of them are based on oriental scales, altogether different from ours ". But another piece, based on two Russian tunes, written for this orchestra (the autograph score is dated September 19th/October 1st, 1848) is perhaps the best known of all Glinka's compositions, the famous " Kamarinskaya " which became the model for all later essays in the symphonic handling of Russian folk-melodies. The piece was at first called simply " Wedding Song and Dance Song ", and like the two Spanish pieces was renamed the following year (after its second theme) on the advice of Prince Odoevsky. Incidentally, Glinka was always very annoyed at any attempt to find a " programme " in " Kamarinskaya ". " I was guided in its composition simply by inward musical feeling, without any thought of what goes on at a wedding ", he said. Like the " Ruslan " Overture, it was written immediately in full score. The unusual instrumentation of " Night in Madrid " and " Kamarinskaya ", with a single bass trombone, is due simply to the deficiencies of Paskevitch's orchestra, which had only one trombonist.

In Warsaw Glinka heard for the first time a composition by Gluck. This was the chorus " Les fureurs d'Oreste " from " Iphigenia in Tauris ", which he considered " exemplary ", as " Don Giovanni ", it will be remembered, was not. He began to study Gluck with ardour. But it was too late. His own career as a composer was practically over—at forty-four and with nearly nine more years to live.

Having quarrelled with Angélique, who had "begun to give herself airs", and wishing to see his mother again, Glinka went to Petersburg in November and did not return to Warsaw till May. During this visit he gathered with the Tsarevitch, Viazemsky, Vielgorsky and other old friends to do honour to the veteran Zhukovsky, in commemoration of the jubilee of the latter's literary activity. Zhukovsky was the most distinguished survivor of a chapter in the history of Russian culture now practically closed. But during the same winter Glinka made the acquaintance of several of the young men who were to play distinguished parts in the next chapter, notably the twenty-four-year-old Vladimir Stassof, whose name was to appear on nearly every page of the later history of Russian music for half a century. Glinka also speaks of other young literary men of the new generation, "some of whom, unfortunately, got themselves into trouble during that very year". The reference is evidently to the very harmless "Petrashevtsy" group of reformers, of which Dostoevsky was a member, which was suppressed by the police with appalling severity about a fortnight after Glinka's return to Warsaw. Twenty-one of them, including the novelist, were sentenced to death, though the sentences were commuted at the last moment. Nicholas's règime was at its worst just before it ended.

Notwithstanding carousals with friends and the Bach playing of the organist August Freyer, which moved him to tears, Glinka now found Warsaw very boring for a time. But his apathy was dispelled by the pretty daughter of a restaurant-keeper, with whom he enjoyed what he styles an "églogue". Under this poetic influence he was inspired to write a few more songs. But other than these, the only product of this second stay in Warsaw was a chorus written for the girls of the Smolny Institute which, being lightly scored, tempted the Autocrat of All the Russias into the field of musical criticism. The composer was informed that " His Majesty the Emperor considered the instrumentation of the chorus *weak* ". Nevertheless sunshine poured on Glinka from other members of the Imperial family. The Empress and one of the Grand Duchesses having visited Warsaw, the Grand Duchess told Prince Paskevitch that she " could not go away without hearing or seeing Glinka ". The happy little loyalist was sent for and the Empress greeted him (as he carefully records) with the remarkable words: " How do you do, Glinka? And what are you doing here?" Being told that he preferred the climate to that of Petersburg, " Her Majesty was pleased to say: ' There is not much difference, but I am glad, very glad to see you ' ".

In June, 1851, Glinka received news of his mother's death. Yet he characteristically lingered on in Warsaw till September, leaving the settlement of the family affairs in the hands of his sister Liudmila and her husband. Liudmila at once set about the task of mothering her helpless brother. She joined him in Petersburg in October, took a flat for him, nursed him through a winter of bad health, and on April 2nd/14th, 1852, arranged a concert by the Petersburg Philharmonic Society at which " Night in Madrid ", " Kamarinskaya " and an aria from " Ruslan " were performed. As Glinka says he heard " Kamarinskaya " for the first time on this occasion, it seems that it was never played by the orchestra for which it was written.

Seven weeks later Glinka and " Don Pedro " again set out on their travels. In Berlin Meyerbeer called in the most friendly way at Glinka's hotel and wanted to know, " How is it, Monsieur Glinka, that we know you so well by reputation, but don't know your works?" To which the Russian replied that it was " not a habit of his to *colporter* his productions ". Dehn regaled his former pupil " with quartets and *Moselwein* ", and from Berlin the travellers went on to

Cologne and Strasbourg, inspecting the cathedrals, and reached Paris on July 1st. But Glinka's intended goal was Andalusia. After three weeks in Paris he set off by way of Lyons, Avignon and Toulouse, but there the state of his health constrained him to change his mind and return to Paris.

Settled in a flat in the Rue Rossini, Glinka was once more troubled by the stirrings of inspiration. He procured "scoring paper of enormous size" and began to write a "Ukrainian Symphony" based on Gogol's story, "Taras Bulba". " I wrote the first part of the first *allegro* (C minor) and began the second part, but being unable to get out of the German rut in the development, I abandoned the work—which Don Pedro afterwards destroyed."[1] So having laid this troublesome ghost, Glinka declined again into idle domesticity, the present incarnation of the eternal " charming young girl" taking the form of a nineteen-year-old Léonie. " She was quiet but not very robust," Glinka remarks reminiscently. He read Homer and Sophocles in French translations and haunted the Jardin des Plantes, fascinated by the animals, but stayed away from the theatres on account of their intolerably stuffy atmosphere, though he twice heard his old favourite Méhul's " Joseph " and took Léonie to the first performance of Auber's " Marco Spada ", which he found " very unsatisfactory ". Hearing Beethoven's Fifth Symphony at one of the Concerts du Conservatoire, he renewed a former impression of the " affectedness " and " exaggeration " of the French conception of Beethoven. Evidently Habeneck's tradition was continued by his successor, Girard: *f* became *fff*, *p* became *ppp*. It was " *not* Beethoven ", in Glinka's opinion. His own predilection was always for the " simple " interpretation of music.

[1] Balakiref and Engelhardt heard him play it after his return to Russia, and Stassof attempted a fragmentary reconstruction of it from their recollections. Glinka told Kukolnik that the general character of his " Cossack Symphony " was Little Russian.

Spring came and the exile began to think of going home. Léonie was dismissed. But Glinka disliked the railway and it was tiresome to find other means of travelling; so, after all, the only result of this upheaval was that he took a fresh flat and replaced Léonie with "a rather charming young *grisette* from Bordeaux ". However, she " often wearied me with her excessive liveliness " and was quickly succeeded by a spirited Andalusian, who in turn was replaced by a " fairly well-bred " milliner. Instead of Homer and Sophocles, Glinka studied the " Arabian Nights " (regretting that he had not known them before he wrote " Ruslan "), Boccaccio and " almost the whole of Paul de Kock ". In the summer of 1853 he again came into contact with Meyerbeer who, for all his affability, seems to have had a knack of provoking unusual flashes of spirit from the amiable little Russian. For on one occasion, when Meyerbeer remarked on the loftiness of his artistic standards, he retorted that he had a perfect right to set a high standard, for " I begin with my own works, with which I am seldom satisfied ". And he stayed away from the *première* of Meyerbeer's " L'Étoile du Nord " in February, 1854, on patriotic grounds, since the person of Peter the Great is treated in it " very disrespectfully ".

Glinka's patriotism was rather on edge that winter, for the Eastern Question had embittered Russia's relations with France and England. She had been at war with Turkey since October. France declared war on March 27th, followed by England a day later, and on April 4th, Glinka and Pedro left for Brussels *en route* for home. In Berlin he heard and delighted in Gluck's " Armida " at the Royal Opera and enjoyed more of Dehn's " quartets and Moselle ". He reached Petersburg on May 16th/28th—the very day on which Richard Wagner in Zürich completed the full score of " Das Rheingold ". Wagner had been in Paris with Liszt for a short time the previous October; and if Glinka, sitting at home in his overheated room with his *grisettes* and his Paul de Kock, had not allowed his artistic friendships to lapse, he might have been one of the privileged company who heard the poem of the " Ring " read by the composer himself. As it was, Glinka never knew of Wagner's existence, except perhaps by hearsay as " the uncle of the celebrated soprano ", whom he did meet later.

Glinka spent the summer quietly at Tsarskoe Selo, with Liudmila Shestakova, who humoured his every whim, and her little daughter Olga, of whom he was passionately fond. At Liudmila's request he began to write those amusing " Memoirs " which give one such a clear impression of his weak, amiable, hypochondriacal character, with its naïve vanity so curiously divorced from ambition. This labour occupied him for a few hours each morning from June, 1854, till the beginning of April, 1855, each instalment being sent to Kukolnik for revision. Later in the day visitors would come from Petersburg—Lvof, Engelhardt, the young critic Serof (not yet a composer), Villebois, or Stassof's younger brother, Dimitri, who was to live to see the Great War and the Bolshevist Revolution. In the autumn Liudmila took a flat in Petersburg, and her brother lived with her, Olga, and his birds till he left Russia for the last time in May, 1856. Shortly after the removal little Olga fell dangerously ill and her adoring uncle devoted all his time to her. When she recovered, he wrote a little polka " for her Christmas tree ", and tried to teach her to sing Ilyinishna's song from " Prince Kholmsky ". Dargomyjsky brought him the numbers of his " Russalka " as he wrote them. But the two men never got on very well. Dargomyjsky's nature was more than a little acid, and Glinka, much as he resented criticism of his own work, had developed a weakness for telling other people how to compose. Glinka visited the theatre only twice the whole winter, once to hear " A Life for the Tsar ", which he had not heard for nearly twenty years. The work was now only given occasionally as a stop-gap and was never rehearsed, while

"Ruslan" had completely disappeared from the repertory. This particular performance was so bad that the composer left the theatre in a rage, ignoring the applause. Nevertheless, he interested himself in the young contralto, Daria Leonova, who had sung the part of Vania, took her as a pupil, and orchestrated several of his songs for a concert she was giving.

In March, 1855, Nicholas I died, bitterly mortified by the Crimean reverses, and was succeeded by his comparatively liberal son. In preparation for the coronation ball of Alexander II, Glinka at once wrote a "Festival Polonaise" for orchestra, taking for the chief theme a Spanish bolero melody, "since", he told Engelhardt, "I can't offer anything Polish to the White Russian Tsar". During the winter he had also orchestrated a Nocturne of Hummel's and Weber's "Invitation to the Waltz".

A performance of the "Crucifixus" from Bach's B minor Mass, which profoundly impressed him, turned Glinka's attention to church music for the first time since his Imperial Chapel days. He began to study the old ecclesiastical modes, then turned aside to work at a new opera, the subject of which, Kukolnik's drama, "The Bigamist", had "long been revolving in my head". He found a librettist, a certain Vasilko-Petrof who taught elocution in the Theatrical School, and sketches for the music began to accumulate. His sister left him in June, well, happy and busy. But he took a dislike to the librettist, found it impossible, he said, to write "Russian music" without lapsing into the vein of "A Life for the Tsar", and very soon sent for Liudmila in a panic. Petersburg had become intolerable again; he must go at once to Warsaw. Yet Liudmila had no sooner hastened to join him, than he immediately changed his mind. He would stay on in Petersburg. But there was an end to "The Bigamist" and to all other composition, though early in 1856 he revised and re-scored his "Valse-Fantaisie" of 1839 for another of

Leonova's concerts. But his one thought now was to go to Berlin and " study the old church modes " with Dehn. Most of his time was spent with his little niece, playing with her and telling her stories. He decided that her future music-master should be a lad named Balakiref, who had been introduced to him that winter by Ulybyshef. " No one else ", he said, " has ideas so like my own. One of these days he will be a second Glinka ".

Glinka left the city he hated so bitterly on April 27th/May 9th, 1856, and never saw it again. His sister and Vladimir Stassof, who accompanied him as far as the city-barrier, have left it on record that at the barrier he spat symbolically. In Berlin he settled down to a quiet routine, working in the morning with Dehn, giving a few singing lessons, going to theatres and concerts—he preferred the Berlin musicians to those of any other city—and getting into rages with the political writers who dared to attack Russia. His work with Dehn consisted of study of the famous " Istitutioni armoniche " of the sixteenth century theorist, Zarlino, and critical analysis of Bach's " Well-Tempered Clavichord ". He even wrote two fugues himself. His last orchestral score, finished on July 10th (N.S.), was an arrangement for small orchestra of Alabief's song, " The Nightingale ", made for the singer Valentina Bianchi.

On January 21st, 1857, Meyerbeer, who was *Generalmusikdirektor* to the King of Prussia, honoured Glinka by including the trio from " A Life for the Tsar " in the programme of the annual Court Concert. It was a brilliant social function; " Petrova's part was sung very, very satisfactorily by Mme. Wagner ";[1] and Glinka was delighted. But going into the cold night air from the over-heated Palace he caught a chill. There appeared to be nothing seriously wrong, and after a few days he began to work again with Dehn.

---

[1] Johanna Wagner, Richard Wagner's niece, though really a soprano, had a remarkable compass which enabled her to sing contralto rôles.

Then one day he appeared to have received worrying news and Dehn, good-naturedly anxious to soothe him, visited him as often as four or five times daily. He wished to tell Dehn something, not now " but later, perhaps in a few days ". In the meantime he drew on Dehn, who was looking after his money, for large sums which he sent away, no one knows whither. He became more and more moody, and complained of his liver. But still the doctor did not consider him in any danger. On Februry 13th, he joked with Dehn, talked about his fugues, and discussed his plan of spending the next winter in Italy with Liudmila. But the next morning his friend found him very exhausted and apathetic, rousing himself only to abuse the doctor. At five o'clock on the morning of the 15th, he died suddenly but peacefully. The postmortem examination showed that death was due to excessive distention of the liver and that in any case he could not have lived much longer.

Glinka was buried in Berlin on the 18th, the funeral being attended only by Meyerbeer, Dehn, an Embassy official and one or two acquaintances. But he rested finally in Russia. Engelhardt went to Berlin in May to superintend the exhumation. The body was brought by sea to Kronstadt and taken to the Alexander Nevsky Monastery in Petersburg.

Glinka was honoured immediately after his death by a concert of his works given by the Petersburg Philharmonic Society, and almost at once he became a sort of legendary hero. And such he has remained in Russia, revered beyond all reason by men as diverse in their artistic ideas as Anton Rubinstein, Tchaïkovsky and Rimsky-Korsakof. As yet very little of his music had even been printed, only the separate numbers of his first opera in piano arrangements, with a few songs and other odds and ends. His masterpiece, " Ruslan ", was still in manuscript and long remained so. It was left for Liudmila Shestakova to give her brother's work to the world in permanent form and, in a sense, to continue it by mothering the younger generation, of which he had caught only one glimpse in the person of the nineteen-year-old Balakiref.

*   *   *   *   *

Leo Tolstoy made a blunder characteristic of the literary man dealing with music when he remarked to the pianist Goldenweiser that " in Glinka's work I feel that he was an unclean, sensual man ". Tolstoy happened to know that Glinka was " an unclean, sensual man ", and he proceeded to read this uncleanliness and sensuality into the music. Tchaïkovsky was very much nearer the mark when, in his diary, he expressed astonishment that the man who has unconsciously drawn his own portrait in the " Memoirs " —" a pleasant, kindly sort of fellow, but empty, insignificant, commonplace "—could have been Glinka the composer, that " such colossal artistic power could exist side by side with such insignificance ". Tchaïkovsky even goes on to talk nonsense about Glinka's having "at one stride placed himself on a level (yes! on a level!) with Mozart, with Beethoven, with whomever you like ". No Russian seems to be able to keep his head where Glinka is concerned. Nationalist and " Westerner ", academic and ultra-modernist —all are alike. Even Anton Rubinstein could speak, in one breath, of " Beethoven and Glinka ". But apart from the exaggeration of this patriotic fervour, Russian admiration of Glinka is fully justified. When Tchaïkovsky wrote (in his diary) that " the present Russian symphonic school is all in ' Kamarinskaya ' just as the whole oak is in the acorn ", and (to Mme. von Meck) that " from ' Kamarinskaya ' all later Russian composers (including myself) draw contrapuntal and harmonic combinations whenever they have to deal with a Russian dance-tune ", he was stating nothing more than the truth.

Apart altogether from elements like the orientalism of

"Ruslan", which has exercised considerable influence on later Russian music, Glinka's purely musical innovations are astonishing. He used the whole-tone scale as the *leitmotif* of Tchernomor in "Ruslan" a quarter of a century before Dargomyjsky and half a century before Debussy; and the *lezginka* from the same opera is amazingly bold and modern. Glinka was the founder of an entirely new school of orchestration, an orchestration (characterised by bright, pure, transparent colouring) which has since been employed by almost every Russian composer of note, modified only in later years by Lisztian and Wagnerian influences. And, like all good orchestration, Glinka's has as its foundation not tone-colour alone but characteristic harmony and part-writing—in his case, part-writing of the most delightful purity and spontaneity. His handling of individual instruments (e.g. the clarinet) is extraordinarily subtle. He understands perfectly what one may call the "personality" of each instrument.

Glinka's melody is always fresh and spontaneous, springing from a genuine lyrical impulse. In "A Life for the Tsar" and in the great majority of the songs, there are far too many lapses into commonplaceness and pseudo-Italian conventionalism. But such lapses are easily understandable, only to be expected, while on the other hand "Ruslan" is full of the loveliest and most original melody. The songs of Finn and Ruslan himself in Act II are the obvious models, both in melody and in the simple, directly effective harmonic background, of the best lyrical pages of "Igor" and the operas of Rimsky-Korsakof, just as the *lezginka* in "Ruslan" and the Prelude to Act V of "Prince Kholmsky" clearly foreshadow Borodin's Polovtsian dances. The choruses in both Glinka's operas are particularly fine—the opening chorus, the nuptial chorus and the "Slavsia" in "A Life for the Tsar", the choruses in the First Act of "Ruslan" (and the famous four-part canon of the terrified princes), the Persian chorus which opens Act III, the choruses of spirits in Act IV—a string of gems.

Everyone knows that polished little masterpiece of concision, the " Ruslan " Overture. Presumably, Glinka took a certain amount of trouble with it. But " Kamarinskaya " and the two so-called " Spanish Overtures " were written in the most casual way, almost by accident; yet in " Kamarinskaya " the composer does wonders with an extraordinarily banal little tune, while the two Spanish pieces, apparently no more than brilliant orchestrations of popular melodies, come to life in his hands and infect one as many far more pretentious things fail to do. The " empty, commonplace " little man must have been something of a magician, and for these feats one can easily forgive him his banalities, his occasional technical flounderings, his architectural incompetence and the rest of his obvious shortcomings. All things considered—his passive character, his training and his surroundings—Glinka the composer remains an inexplicable natural phenomenon of a kind almost unique in the history of music.

G. A.

DARGOMYJSKY

To the average well-informed music-lovers of most European countries, Alexander Dargomyjsky is, so to speak, the mystery man of Russian music. His name is given an important place in history; he is described as the link between Glinka and the moderns, as a great realist in music, and in that capacity the immediate predecessor of Mussorgsky. Praise has been lavished on his sense of musical humour, on the originality and effectiveness of the recitatives in his opera " Russalka " (" the Mermaid "), and especially on his " Stone Guest ", in which he achieved to the full his own ideals of dramatic declamation, or " melodic recitative ". But his music is never heard, remains difficult to procure, and has never been the subject of searching criticism.

Even the circumstances connected with his name are remarkable. He was born on February 2nd/14th, 1813, on a country property in the Government of Tula, whose name no biographer has mentioned. His father was the illegitimate son of a magnate of Catherine the Great, who was given the Christian name Sergei, the patronymic Nikolaievitch, and a family name derived for the occasion from that of his native village, Dargomyjskoe, in the Government of Smolensk. Sergei Dargomyjsky was a postal official in Moscow, had married (after eloping with her) a certain Princess Koslovskaya, and was to be granted, in 1829, letters of nobility. The couple had six children: three sons, of which Alexander was the last-born, and three daughters. But none of the sons was to have issue, so that the name became extinct with the second generation. Alexander spent his childhood partly in the country, partly in Moscow. He was delicate in health, had been born dumb, and became able to speak only at the age of five (his voice always remained highly-pitched and squeaky).

He showed an early disposition for piano-playing, and also for composing little pieces. His father encouraged him —which is the more noteworthy considering that he was a creature of habits and thoroughly unimaginative. He had, it is recorded, a great taste for satire: and when his children achieved a piece of sarcasm which pleased him, he used to reward them with small silver in order to encourage them to further efforts. This taste of his may have contributed to develop in Alexander that sense of characterisation and caricature which is now regarded as his greatest asset. As for the mother, the one positive trait of hers that is recorded is that she disliked music. The eldest son, Victor, was a good amateur violinist; and one of the daughters played the harp.

In 1817, the whole family left Moscow for Petersburg, where the father had been transferred. Alexander was educated, not at a school, but at home, as was usual at the time. His first piano teacher was a young German governess bearing the amazing name Luise Wohlgeboren, " who did nothing but kiss him and taught him nothing ", he ungratefully records in his autobiography. The second was a pianist and composer named Danilevsky, " a really good musician, but unable to rid himself of the idea that musical composition was not a fit occupation for a young Russian nobleman. He used to tear to shreds every scrap of staved paper on which I had written down a piano piece or a song. Only once, after he had read two of my songs at the piano, did I succeed in whisking the manuscripts away before his hands had finally left the keyboard, and so saved them from destruction. I have them still ".

In 1822 he received violin lessons from a professional player named Vorontsof; and after that, piano lessons from Schoberlechner, who was a pupil of Hummel and in great demand as a teacher. Another teacher then in fashion, Zeibich, " taught him the first principles of the art of singing, and also gave him a certain amount of information as to the intervals ".

" By 1830 or so ", the autobiography continues, " I was known in the Petersburg society as a good pianist. I could play everything at sight, and took part in many charity concerts, I often played the second violin or the viola part in quartets, and my playing won unanimous praise from the best artists of the period. But, apparently, I did not always tune my instrument carefully enough; my elder brother, who was an excellent violinist, commemorated the sad fact in a piece of satirical poetry. At that time I composed a quantity of brilliant (although certainly not flawless) pieces for piano and violin, two quartets, cantatas, and a quantity of songs. A few of them were published "—in all likelihood, Findeisen says, at his own expense.

In 1831 (or according to other sources, as early as 1827) he entered the Civil Service, Department of Justice. Although his regularity and efficiency were greatly appreciated and promotion came speedily, he was to resign in 1843—at a time when his first opera " Esmeralda " had already been lying four years unheeded in the files of the Petersburg Opera.

In 1834 he started setting to music a libretto in French, derived from Victor Hugo's drama " Lucréce Borgia ". At that time, he was very much under the influence of French literature and music; and a mere tyro in the matter of musical composition. A few months later, however, a piece of good fortune came to him, he was introduced to Glinka, who not only gave him much encouragement and useful advice, but lent him the five copy-books in which he had noted down all the substance of the lessons in technique he had received from Dehn in Berlin. " I copied down all these instructions and thus assimilated the so-called wisdom of thoroughbass and counterpoint. Glinka and I played all kinds of music in piano duet form, and studied the scores of Beethoven's symphonies and Mendelssohn's overtures. My first attempts at orchestration were carried out in view of charity concerts which we two organised. These attempts were successful." No record of these concerts having taken place has been discovered. The remark about the "so-called wisdom of thoroughbass and counterpoint" is as characteristic of Dargomyjsky as his naïvely-asserted conviction as to the merits of his early compositions. He never acquired much technical efficiency; and it was years later that his realistic ambitions began to develop.

Upon the poet Zhukovsky's advice, he gave up "Lucréce Borgia" and started work upon "Esmeralda", a French libretto which Victor Hugo had prepared for the composer Louise Bertin (her setting of it was produced in Paris in 1836). By 1839, the score was finished, the text translated, and the work submitted to the management of the Imperial Opera. " Despite all my efforts and the fact that all the conductors approved of 'Esmeralda', it was not produced until eight years later, thanks to the ignorance of the high official in charge of the repertory and to the caprice of the manager—eight long years of waiting in vain, during the very keenest and most fervid period of life! This experience weighed heavily upon the whole of my artistic career. And during those eight years, operas by other Russian composers —Bernard, Lvof and Tolstoy—were produced!"

The sense of injury under which he smarted—and which the fate of his later works contributed to heighten—led him gradually to become jealous even of Glinka's fame and success. He suspected Glinka of wishing to monopolise the limelight, of intriguing and cajoling in order to get his works performed. He could not understand why Glinka's music found greater favour than his own. "In which respect am I inferior to Glinka?" he asked in 1862, his friend Youri

Arnold (the critic), only to receive the reply: " My dear Alexander, you are endowed with sufficient sagacity and artistic sense to be able to find the answer for yourself."

Dargomyjsky not only hankered (quite naturally) for success, but had a weakness for adulation—especially when it came from the fair sex, to whose charms he was sensitive in the extreme. He once told Alexander Sokolof (an amateur composer, whose " Recollections " appeared in 1885): " But for the existence of such human beings as lady singers, I should never have become a composer. It is they alone who inspired me throughout my career."

He liked to be surrounded by women. They were welcome guests at his musical parties—the programmes of which consisted mainly of works of his own—and he used to give them singing lessons. " I may boldly say ", he writes in his autobiography " that every single lady singer of repute in Petersburg has had the benefit of my teaching or at least of my advice ". He did not accept male pupils; and he made no charge for his lessons. He found his reward in their appreciation. He once wrote to a friend (a lady, of course): " My opera ' Russalka ' displeases the great majority of male listeners. But at each performance I have the solace of seeing the charming ladies in full sympathy with poor Natasha and her unfortunate father (N.B. the principal characters). This is the only kind of success I wish for." His friend Youri Arnold, in his " Recollections ", gives the following portrait of him at the age of twenty-seven (1840):

> He was of small stature—no taller than Glinka; and his head was remarkably big in proportion to the rest of him, especially on account of its great breadth at the top. He had chestnut hair, high cheek bones, a slightly-flat snub nose, rather thick lips, and small eyes that continually blinked. A tiny scrap of moustache imparted a highly-original character to his pale, sickly-looking face—a mobile

and expressive face, which betokened thoughtfulness and will-power. His carriage and manner bore the stamp of perfect breeding.

The delay in the production of " Esmeralda " was but the beginning of a long series of disappointments. In 1840 Dargomyjsky began " The Triumph of Bacchus ", an opera-ballet in one act. This was not produced until 1867—at Moscow. It fell flat, was never given elsewhere, and remained unpublished. " Esmeralda ", first produced at Moscow on December 5th/17th, 1847, had to be withdrawn after three performances. It was given at Petersburg in 1851, with indifferent success, revived at intervals in both cities, until 1867, and then sank into oblivion. He fared better as a composer of songs. But the first public successes he enjoyed came with a big charity concert given in April, 1853, at which several of his compositions were played or sung; and with the production in 1856 of his " Russalka " of which more hereafter.

In 1844/1845 he went abroad, visiting Brussels, Paris and Vienna. In Paris, the autobiography tells us, he met Auber, Meyerbeer and Halévy; in Brussels, he saw a good deal of Fétis, the historian and critic; and in all three cities " private performances of works of his won praise from a few Press critics ". Shortly after his return (March, 1845) to Petersburg, he wrote to a friend: " There is no better people in the world than the Russian. If, indeed, any element of poetry exist in Europe, it is in Russia only." And maybe this feeling was the germ of the ambition he developed to write a " truly Russian " opera—exactly, Findeisen remarks, as Glinka, after a journey abroad, had decided to write " A Life for the Tsar ". He selected for its subject Pushkin's play the " Russalka " and began working on it in the summer of 1848. While engaged on the task, he wrote to a friend: " I have great difficulties with the libretto. I am writing the additional verse myself. All our poets are men of genius—

not one of them is just a man of talent, like you or me. So there is no coming to terms with them: they just stare at you contemptuously." And in 1853, while hard at work on the music, he wrote to another: " The more I study the elements of our folk-music, the more I realise how many and diverse they are. Glinka, who has been the only one so far to extend the boundaries of Russian music, has, it seems to me, touched but one side of it—the lyrical. He has given us melancholy drama only; there is nothing national in the comic parts of his works. In the 'Russalka' I try to develop our national dramatic elements. And I shall be glad if I succeed half as well as Glinka."

The " Russalka ", finished in 1855, was given on May 4th, 1856, at Petersburg; and although the production was in many respects unsatisfactory, the opera pleased the performers, the public and the Press. The dramatic and comic scenes in it created a great impression; and had the management felt greater confidence in the new work, it might have established itself forthwith as a success. Under the unfavourable circumstances, it had only a short run, despite the splendid readings of the principal parts by Petrof, Bulakhova and Leonova. It was produced at Moscow in 1858, revived at Petersburg in 1866; and it gradually won a permanent place in the Russian repertory. It is the only one of Dargomyjsky's works to be known in other countries to the present day.

The " Russalka "—and especially, let it be repeated, the comic and dramatic scenes in it, with their bold and telling recitatives—aroused the interest of the younger Russian composers who meanwhile had appeared on the horizon: Balakiref, Cui, and also the eighteen-year-old Mussorgsky. They mustered a while around him, but did not find the atmosphere of his circle congenial (the critic Vladimir Stassof [see page 105] had nicknamed this circle " the Russian invalids "), and all except Cui ceased to frequent his house until years later, when he had already begun work on his last opera " The

Stone Guest "—the one which Cui was to describe as " the very keystone of the new Russian opera ".

But even in 1857 Dargomyjsky stood firm in his new artistic creed. It was on December 9th of that year that he wrote to Liubov Karmalina the letter containing the profession of faith which has so often been compared to Mussorgsky's:

> My position as an artist is very unsatisfactory. The great majority of our public and journalists regard me as uninspired. I do not intend to debase music to the level of a mere amusement for their sake. I wish the notes to express exactly what the words express: I want truth.

At that moment he had already begun a second " really Russian " opera " Rogdana ", the subject of which was comic and fantastic. But he soon gave the scheme up, because, the last sentence in his autobiography says, " he had not the faintest hope for support, and so decided to turn his attentions to composing orchestral works which, in the course of time, might be performed abroad ".

These orchestral works, none of them very important, were a " Kosachok " (a Ukrainian Dance) a " Finnish Fantasy ", and a tone picture entitled " Baba Yaga, or from Volga to Riga ". The composer's sense of picturesque effects and of orchestral treatment being hardly greater that his sense of form, the new venture, naturally, did not fulfil his expectations. His desire to find outlets abroad led him to undertake, in 1864, a second tour abroad. At Brussels, his " Kosachok " and orchestral excerpts from the " Russalka " were successfully performed; and the management of the opera considered the question of producing " Esmeralda ". He, however, was no longer interested in this early work; and he vainly tried to persuade them to do " The Triumph of Bacchus " instead. He moved about a good deal in social circles, and scored many successes with his songs, which he had translated into French for the occasion. It was in that city that he composed a " Tarentelle Slave " for piano duet " to be played " the sub-title said " with people who are unable to play the piano ". The bass part consisted only of one repeated note, and had been devised to suit the limited ability, at the piano, of a charming young dancer in whom Dargomyjsky had developed an interest.

He stayed a few weeks in Paris, and paid a short visit to London. The latter city struck him as " a splendid, enchanting village, to which Paris might serve as a gay suburb ". He returned to Petersburg in May, 1865. And although his health, which for years had been poor, was growing steadily worse, he started work the following spring on the opera " The Stone Guest ", a musical setting of Pushkin's play of the same name, " just as it stood, without altering a single word of it. Of course, nobody will care to hear a thing of that kind ". As he proceeded he derived increasing satisfaction, not only from the work itself, but from the interest Balakiref, Cui, Mussorgsky and the other members of their circle took in it. " Sitting at the piano ", he wrote in January, 1868, " ailing and all twisted by rheumatism, I was able to turn out more music for it than I should have done in two months in the ordinary course of things. . . . And what I have written delights not only the Cui-Balakiref circle but the Purgolds and Platonova, and friend G., who is so taken with my new achievement that he goes proclaiming my ' Russalka ' to be no good at all! "

He was aware of the difficulties of the task, and also the fact that the result would appeal only to a limited circle. To Nadejda Purgold (the future Mrs. Rimsky-Korsakof) he explained that " to compose music according to his principles was far more difficult that to use current methods, because for every single phrase he had to devise a new musical idea whereas the usual method consisted in the working out of a few themes ". A note appended to his autobiography says: " I would never expect a sensational success in Russia, because I kept too strictly to the higher ideal of art and wrote with the sole object of achieving my ends to my own satisfaction. I destroyed many quite effective compositions of mine simply because they did not come up to the standards I had set myself."

The tone of the above excerpts is very different from that of the letters in which he rejoiced in the success of his music with " the charming lady listeners ". He was, at that time, moving in a circle very different from the one that had previously surrounded him. Not only were the keenest and most progressive musicians regarding him as their leader, but in 1866 he had been appointed President of the Imperial Music Society—which testified to the fact that he had won recognition, in official circles as well as in the advanced, highly non-official one. Repeatedly, performances of excerpts from " The Stone Guest " took place at his house. He sang the part of Don Juan, Mussorgsky those of Leporello and Don Carlos, Alexandra Purgold those of Dona Anna and Laura, and her sister Nadejda was at the piano. On November 15th, 1868, the whole of what he had composed was given. That same day he had written to a friend:

> My work is drawing to a close. Many people are eager to hear it. But after hearing it, many of them will wonder, I fear, whether it is music or blind stupidity.

He had the satisfaction of seeing his audience delighted; but that of witnessing the public performance of the opera was to be denied to him. A few days later, the Court Minister enquired when it would be ready for production, and what his views as to the casting were. Alas! the first draft was not finished, the scoring not even begun, and his strength was failing fast. On January 5th, 1869, he died. According to his expressed desire, Cui completed the final scene of " The

Stone Guest" and also another scene left not quite finished; and Rimsky-Korsakof took charge of the scoring. Their work was done by September, 1870.

Dargomyjsky's testamentary dispositions delayed its production. He had stipulated—as a mere matter of principle, obviously: for he had always been well-off—a higher fee for the performing rights than the management of the Imperial Opera was empowered by law to pay. A public subscription was opened to make up the difference; and so on February 16th, 1872, the work was produced with a splendid cast comprising Komissarjevsky, Petrof, Melnikof, Platonova and Ilissa—the best singers in the company. It was received coldly; and no attempt to revive it has proved successful.

The truth is that Dargomyjsky was endowed with a real sense of characterisation and dramatic expression, but lacked the lyrical and poetic faculty proper—or, more generally, the supreme gift of flowing and far-reaching musical imagination. Even in the best of his music—the tragic and comic scenes in the " Russalka ", the songs which the Balakiref circle held in highest esteem (" The Paladin ", " The Worm ", the " Titular Counsellor ", for instance) and " The Stone Guest "—there is a dryness and short-windedness which often prevent its winning its point. Yet its qualities were significant enough to render him the acknowledged leader of the new national school with which the next chapters will deal. The question of the actual importance of his part as such is a complex one, and its discussion does not come within the scope of this book. What may be said, however, is that nowadays —two-thirds of a century after his death—marking how none of his works (not excluding the comparatively popular " Russalka ") has really gained a hold upon music lovers in his own or any other country, it is impossible not to come to the conclusion that he will be remembered for his influence rather than for his actual achievements.

M. D. C.

ALEXANDER SEROF

"Ma position? C'est l'opposition", Serof is said to have replied to a foreigner who enquired what official position he held in the musical life of Russia. He did not exaggerate. The first Russian musical critic worthy of the name; the first Russian Wagnerian; a man of wide culture yet narrow mind but, according to his lights, the highest ideals; vain, witty, self-contradictory, malicious, hot-tempered; Serof was for a couple of decades the Ishmael of Russian music, a supreme master of the " gentle art of making enemies ". Add to this that he wore the same hat for twenty years and that he was a composer who wrote his first serious work when he was over forty, winning with it extraordinary success and the admiration of the young Tchaïkovsky and the young Rimsky-Korsakof, and it will be seen that we have to do with a striking personality if not a great creative genius.

Alexander Nikolaevitch Serof was born in St. Petersburg on January 11th/23rd, 1820, the son of a cultured high official of the Ministry of Finance, a Voltaire-worshipper and despiser of music. Through his German mother, the boy inherited a strain of Jewish blood of which he was inordinately proud. He soon showed himself to be gifted, though not specially so as a musician; at eight he could read French and German (English came later) and began to have piano lessons, though he was much more fond of drawing; at eleven we hear of his saving up his pocket money to buy Buffon's " Natural History ". But Serof's musical development really began at fifteen when he entered the recently founded School of Jurisprudence—where, queerly enough, music was studied almost as assiduously as law. The study of an orchestral instrument was compulsory and Nicholas I himself sometimes deigned to attend the concerts of the School orchestra. Under Karl Schubert, Serof took up the 'cello and became a reasonably good player—for an amateur. As a pianist he was already capable of tackling a Hummel concerto, but instead of continuing his studies under Henselt, who was on the school staff, he characteristically preferred to go his own sweet way, sight-reading through the opera scores of Bellini and Donizetti, Spontini, Weber and Meyerbeer. As for theory, he seems to have been frightened by a few peeps into the harmony-books of one of the masters, a keen, ungifted amateur. Yet he already wanted to compose. The trouble was that Serof was a born dilettante and that music was by no means his only love. With his bosom friend, a boy named Vladimir Stassof, four years younger than himself, who was also to make some little noise in the world later, he devoured Goethe and E. T. A. Hoffmann, and pored over reproductions of the world's great paintings with an eagerness equalled only by his " sleepy apathy " toward anything which did *not* particularly interest him, an apathy which infuriated his father and angered even the hero-worshipping Stassof. At that time no one was comparable with Serof in Stassof's eyes. They differed only on one point. Serof passionately admired German music, while Stassof was intolerant of every German composer except Beethoven. " One could live with Serof for a century and not feel a moment's boredom ", he wrote long afterwards, when they had become bitter enemies. " His mind was as plastic as wax." It was a gift which turned out in the long run to be as fatal as it was useful. Serof was naturally an eclectic, in so far as a man of limited sympathies can be an eclectic. (May one put it that he was a highminded, narrow-minded champion of broad-mindedness?) He already announced to Stassof his *credo* that " music as a world art . . . is as many-sided and universal as human thought. And owing to its immateriality, far superior to painting in this respect . . . *En musique on doit être cosmopolite*". (The mixture of French and Russian is characteristic.) Next to Beethoven, Serof's idol at this period was—Meyerbeer! Though, in fairness, it must be admitted that quite early he suspected "*le favori de mon âme*" of a certain falsity, "real Jewish" falsity, unpardonable and yet—on second thoughts—pardonable.

In 1840 Serof left the School of Jurisprudence and meekly entered the civil service, where his duties came into the category of things for which he felt that profound apathy. Not even antipathy. As for the *other* things, his sympathies were still too widely distributed. It annoyed him to feel that his abilities " could be turned to account in all directions, yet would not make him great in any single one ". He was attracted by "*all* beauty in *every* possible form "—the underlinings are characteristic—and felt it " cruel that, in order to win immortality, all the others must be sacrificed for the sake of *one* ". Only *on the whole* it seemed to him that his musical gift, of which his father was so contemptuous, was worth just a little more than any of the others. " To win immortality " in music, of course, one must compose. Stassof, who was to spend the greater part of his life in egging on composers, egged on his first friend. And so Serof devoted his ample leisure to the fabrication of fantasias for 'cello and piano—on themes for " Les Huguenots " and " en forme de valse "—and grand " song scenas ". He anticipated Hugo Wolf in setting Goethe's " Rattenfänger ", while the success of another Goethe piece, the " Mailied " for voice, piano, and 'cello, privately performed at the Prince of Oldenburg's in June, 1840, really worried him. For he had " read the biographies of all sorts of great artists and found that they had all had to overcome obstacles and face defeat ". And his own way was so smooth! Without learning even the most elementary points of musical theory, he was already turning out what appeared to be real compositions, guided only by his innate gifts, his knowledge of musical literature and his teeming theories of æsthetics. And after all, with a flash of real insight, " even if I don't do much in the way of creative work, I shall most certainly achieve something in the sphere of æsthetic analysis, of higher criticism. To be a Winckelmann would not be too bad!".

One of the most important keys to the understanding of Serof's curious nature is his tendency to almost insane hero-worship, particularly to worship of artists with whom he came into personal contact. The year 1842 brought him two such experiences. First, in March, Liszt came to Petersburg and through his playing gave Serof " the highest revelation that has yet been vouchsafed to me ". And a personal meeting, when Liszt played him his " Don Juan " Fantasia, completely finished him off. " In a few moments I lived through years of undreamed of concentration of existence." The impact of Glinka, naïve, amiable little Glinka, was even more curious in its effect, for Serof had not been particularly attracted by " A Life for the Tsar ". Yet—" since I have known Glinka, I have believed in him as in God ", he wrote to Stassof. And although the " *kvass* patriotism " of the central idea of " A Life for the Tsar " remained distasteful to him, he now became enthusiastic about the music. Enthusiasm for Russian music in general followed. And with one of his flashes of critical commonsense he saw that " Russian opera of the future will need fantastic, legendary subjects as an outlet for all the wealth of Russian mythology ".

Naturally he must needs try to write an opera himself, choosing as his subject " Askold's Grave " in deliberate rivalry with Verstovsky, whose seven-year-old opera on the same theme was one of the most popular works of the day. He attempted to write his own libretto, came to grief, and in a sudden burst of lucidity saw the ridiculousness of embarking on a large-scale composition with no better equipment than his. " I'm obliged to laugh at myself . . . A man who has never heard a note of his own except on the piano, who has learned absolutely nothing, neither thoroughbass nor counterpoint nor instrumentation, and who is compelled to feel his way about in the dark like a blind man!" But this interval of commonsense was only temporary. Instead of taking Dargomyjsky's advice to " work hard ", sitting down and teaching himself a little elementary harmony, he flew from one grandiose plan to another. He drew up another opera scenario, actually commissioned a libretto on " The Merry Wives of Windsor ", brooded over oratorio settings of Goethe's " Der Gott und die Bajadere " and Metastasio's " Santa Elena al Calvario ". Naturally, none of them materialised. The mountain of poor Serof's creative genius refused to bring forth anything but mice—a few songs, a " Capriccioso quasi burlesco " for piano, a couple of sonatinas and a set of variations also for piano—mice that the composer himself afterwards decided were fit only to be drowned.

In 1845 Serof was unpleasantly awakened from his ambitious dreams by an unexpected and quite undeserved promotion. He was appointed assistant to the President of the Appeal Court at Simferopol in the Crimea. It was promotion, and his duties were practically non-existent. But to a man of culture it was dreary exile, despite one or two interesting new acquaintances, the brother of the anarchist Bakunin among them, and despite an affair with a married lady of mature years. Yet the three years of exile were not without benefit to Serof. He did at last learn something. For, perhaps from sheer boredom, he made up his mind to investigate the mysteries of counterpoint and, to that end, became the true inventor and pioneer of correspondence tuition courses, getting Stassof to arrange for him lessons from Joseph Hunke, a Czech musician living in Petersburg. The postal lessons did not last very long, but they were the only ones Serof ever had. Equally important, he gained some practical knowledge of the orchestra. Soon after his arrival in Simferopol he had completed a French operetta, " La Meunière de Marly ", which he considered quite as good as Glinka's " Ruslan ". Simferopol society being much impressed with his talents, perhaps taking him almost at his own valuation, he soon had his hands full with the composition of incidental music for amateur theatricals and the scoring of dance-music for the little orchestras of the theatre and *Kursaal.* True, he did not at first recognise his own music when the orchestra played it; but he was not the only composer who has learned to swim through being thrown into the water. From scoring dance-music he progressed to the scoring of Beethoven sonatas, and since his arrangements were played as entr'actes at the Alexandrinsky Theatre in Petersburg, we must conclude that by this time he had acquired reasonable competence. Nor did he abandon original composition. Before he left Simferopol he wrote an orchestral fantasy with a " programme " taken from Theocritus, which he sent to Stassof with the assurance that he would be " satisfied " if his friend could find in the piece but " one spark of real inspiration, one drop of truth and beauty ".

Although his post was almost a sinecure, Serof was already bent on leaving the government service; in the summer of 1848 he threw it up and returned to Petersburg. But faced with his father's wrath, even with the closed front door of the paternal residence, he was obliged to submit and accept a similar position at Pskof. Luckily his new superior was a Lvof, son of the late Director of the Imperial Chapel, and himself a keen amateur who sympathised with the young man. Pressed as lightly as before by his official duties, Serof devoted his time to the concoction of a violin sonata, which he afterwards induced Vieuxtemps to try over but not to play in public, and of fugues. (One would like to see those fugues.) At Pskof, too, he began another opera, based on Gogol's story "May Night" and actually completed it in 1850 during a year's leave which he spent in Simferopol. (Whither he was, no doubt, attracted by his lady-love.) But Stassof condemned the work, and Serof, alternating as ever between extreme self-confidence and profound self-dissatisfaction, threw the five-hundred page score into the flames. At least, he says he did; composers always appear to be rather proud of such conflagrations. But Hanna's prayer from the Third Act was afterwards given at a charity concert in Petersburg.

Why he was not content with burning his opera but must needs burn his boats as well is by no means clear. But in 1851, on his return to Petersburg, he defied his father, resigned from a service which paid him well and made the least possible demand on his time, and with no financial resources, no artistic reputation and no obviously marketable talents abandoned himself to picturesque starvation. What was the justification of this supreme gesture of heroic idiocy? The most important clue is to be found in some self-conscious phrases in a letter to his sister:

> For me the most important thing of all is—*life*. Let life only be stamped in sufficiently sharp outline and I rejoice, even when I feel it painfully and in the unhappiness of those dear to me. If that is peculiar, it is the peculiarity of an artistic nature, which always seeks joy in *spectacle, even if the spectacle be that of its own sufferings*.

Serof was genuinely very hard pressed for a long time and we must allow him the credit of sincerely believing himself to be a martyr in the cause of art. Nor was he sustained by Stassof's encouragement, for his friend went abroad that very year and did not return till 1854. At his wit's end, Serof took to the only thing he could do that would earn him a little money, the contribution of musical articles to the press. So far the only Russian who had written anything of the least importance on music was Alexander Ulybyshef, a wealthy nobleman who lived on his estate in the wilds of Nijni-Novgorod, studied Mozart and hated Beethoven. His great antagonist, Wilhelm von Lenz, a man of similar type, had not yet published his " Beethoven et ses trois styles ". Newspaper criticism of music in Russia was of the most contemptible kind; criticism in the true sense, even wrong-headed or pedantic criticism, was simply non-existent. It is easy, therefore, to understand the sensation caused by Serof's first articles on " Music and Virtuosi ", " Spontini and his Music ", " Mozart's ' Don Juan ' and its Panegyrists " and so on, when they appeared in the columns of the " Contemporary " and the " Pantheon ", long essays informed by wide learning and putting forward a definite, and at that period in many respects original, point of view. (For instance, that in *musical* drama it is always the *drama* that matters most—and Serof was as yet unacquainted with Wagner's theoretical writings.) But a critic, no matter how brilliant, is seldom a general favourite; Serof, with his fearless candour, his love of controversy and his tendency to heavy sarcasm, quickly made himself the most unpopular figure in the world of Russian music. It is characteristic that he attacked the anti-Beethovenian Ulybyshef at the very outset of his career.

In 1856 Serof's appointment to the musical editorship of a newly founded weekly, " The Musical and Theatrical Herald ", gave much needed scope to his extraordinary fertility. For he was astoundingly productive. In addition to his Russian articles he was writing in French for the " Journal de St. Petersbourg " and continuing his polemic against Ulybyshef in German in the " Neue Zeitschrift für Musik ", as well as giving courses of lectures. Yet all this industry was wretchedly paid and he was still, as he said, " literally without three kopeks in his pocket for a week at a time ". Nor was he helped materially by his father's death. Even his appointment to the " Musical and Theatrical Herald " seems to have made little difference to his financial position, for soon afterwards we find him reduced to the humiliation of re-entering the despised civil service, first in the Ministry of the Interior, then as a Post Office Censor at sixty rubles (say £3) a month. He remained in the service till 1869, two years before his death.

1858 was a most memorable year for Serof, a real turning-point in his life. Glinka's friend, Prince Sergei Golitsyn, who was arranging some Russian concerts in Germany, invited Serof to accompany him. In Dresden they heard " Tannhäuser ", and Serof to the end of his life never quite got over the experience. Two years before, in one of his first " Herald " articles, he had written that Wagner's operas were " the *forced, laboured* productions of a very gifted but *half-educated dilettante.*[1] The general impression one gets from his music is one of *intolerable boredom* . . . The *melodic* element in Wagner's operas is *very weak*. Most of his music is more or less dramatically true in declamation, but none the less a boring, wearisome sort of sing-song, against a background of forced, pretentious, unpleasantly original harmony and no less pretentious orchestration (*à la Meyerbeer* and *à la Berlioz*)". (It would be interesting to know how much of Wagner's music Serof was really acquainted with in 1856, when he wrote these lines.) But " Tannhäuser " changed all that. Though still conscious of " great shortcomings in Wagner's music ", as he privately admitted to his sister, he saw in " Tannhäuser " " the highest work of art yet produced by the human intellect ". And since he never did things by halves, he forthwith sent home to Russia

---

[1] Lest I should be thought guilty of spoiling a priceless tit-bit by underlining it, I must explain that the italics are Serof's own.

a proclamation that anti-Wagnerians were *ipso facto* " idiots " and " cretins ".

At Weimar Serof renewed his acquaintanceship with Liszt, spending a whole ecstatic month as his guest. Judging from a letter to von Lenz, Liszt in turn had a high opinion both of Serof's " musical sense " and of his transcriptions of Beethoven quartets for two pianos. (Serof had always been an industrious transcriber, chiefly for his own amusement.) Going on to Baden-Baden, Serof met Berlioz and effervesced again. As in the case of Glinka, he was not impressed by the other's personality, yet personal contact opened his eyes to the virtues of the " cold, egotistic Frenchman's " music, music which he found he had hitherto " not understood ". Apart altogether from the orchestral colouring, " in which he is the *teacher* of Liszt and Wagner ", Serof found one of Berlioz's compositions quite overpowering. He would have liked " to hear it again and again ". On the evidence of this work alone, Berlioz was " a master of the first rank ". The masterpiece in question was " Sara la baigneuse "!

Ever a lion-hunter, Serof also introduced himself at Baden to his first hero, Meyerbeer. And next year he made an even bigger bag. Being sent back to Germany on official business, he contrived to slip off to Switzerland and, uninvited, to visit the greatest of all his heroes at Zürich. Wagner's impression of him is tersely recorded in " Mein Leben ": " A curious, intelligent man ". But Serof returned to Russia the Perfect Wagnerite.

One of the principal tragedies of Serof's life was that this greatest of his enthusiasms cost him his oldest and best, if not his only, friend. With that terrible doctrinaire seriousness so characteristic of the Russian temperament, the friendship of Serof and Stassof was shipwrecked purely on differences of musical opinion. Because Stassof considered " Ruslan " one of the peaks of human creative genius and Serof thought the same of " Tannhäuser ", they found friendship no longer possible. From private sneers behind each other's backs, they gradually passed to open and bitter warfare in the press. Nor in this " falling out of faithful friends " was there ever " renewal of love ". Even over the grave of Serof's mother, in 1865, Stassof is said to have refused his old friend's proffered hand. Serof sneered at the " Ruslan-ists ", Stassof at the " *Zukunft*-ist ". Stassof was passionately patriotic; Serof was one of those Russians who believed that all good things came from the West. Stassof's idol was the young Balakiref, the through-and-through Russian, while Serof, though he at first paid tribute to Balakiref's talent, soon turned against " the mighty handful ",[1] attacking each new work of theirs as blindly and consistently as Stassof praised. But he had not even the satisfaction of alliance with the other enemies of the young native school, the chiefs of the newly founded Russian Music Society and St. Petersburg Conservatoire. The prime mover in the founding of both these closely connected institutions was Anton Rubinstein, a Westerner, a German Jew, apparently Serof's natural ally. In view of his high critical reputation, Serof expected to be invited to join the staff of the Conservatoire, if not the directorate of the Society. But Rubinstein, if a Westerner, was a Mendelssohnian Westerner. He had no use for the " music of the future " or its Russian champion. Ironically enough, not one member of the staff of the new Conservatoire was a true Russian. And the R.M.S. declined to perform Serof's " Christmas Hymn " for chorus and orchestra. It was enough to drive the poor man into the camp of Stassof and the Slavophiles. As it was, he so far forgot his boasted Hebrew ancestry as to nickname the Russian Music Society, the " Jewish Musical Association ". He was now the

---

[1] The phrase " mogutchaia kutchka " was first applied to Balakiref and his group by Stassof in 1867; their antagonists seized on it and used it as a term of contempt. " Kutchka " literally means " a little heap "; applied figuratively, a " knot " or " handful " of people. The usual translation, " invincible band ", is a little misleading.

"official opposition" with a vengeance, at war with both parties, the Western conservatives and the Slavophile progressives.[1] His own party, the Western progressives, as yet consisted only of himself. Six or seven years were to pass before the Slavophils would accept Liszt, nearly thirty before the survivors of their party accepted Wagner.

Ever since the unlucky "May Night" of ten years earlier, Serof had resigned himself to "being a Winckelmann", a critic and not a creator. Only once had he been tempted to embark on another opera, and he had quickly brushed the temptation aside. But in 1859 or 1860 the old craving for distinction as a composer reasserted itself, and not even the rebuff of the R. M. S. crushed it. First came a few choral works, then an opera. The performance of a fifth-rate Italian drama, Giacometti's "Giuditta", at the Marinsky Theatre—at least, the final scene, the return of Judith with the head of Holofernes—appealed both to his theatrical sense and to that queer whim of his that attached so much importance to his Jewish blood. (What did Wagner think of it, one wonders?) It is typical of this Perfect Wagnerite that he thought at first of treating his patriotic Jewish opera, not as a music-drama but as a conventional Italian opera! He even got an Italian, Giustiniani, to prepare him an Italian libretto, set that seductive last scene, and offered it for concert performance to a fashionable Italian singer, who promptly rejected it as "insufficiently effective". That cured Serof of Italianism and, with some assistance from two or three friends, including the poet Maikof, he turned Giustiniani's libretto into Russian, expanding the original three acts into five. In August, 1862, Serof wrote, "Thanks to Jehovah! the libretto is quite finished". And as the completed work was accepted by the Directorate of the Imperial Theatres a

---

[1] This musical antithesis of sympathies was rather curious, for in politics the rôles were reversed. It was the Slavophils who were reactionary and obscurantist, while the Westerners were liberal and "enlightened".

month later, it is evident that as in the case of Glinka's operas, libretto and music must have been written more or less simultaneously.

In March, 1863, while the rehearsals of " Judith " were in progress, Wagner came to St. Petersburg to conduct one or two concerts of the Petersburg Philharmonic Society—and startled the Russian musicians by turning his back on the audience during the performance. (Henceforth the Russian conductors likewise faced their orchestras.) Boswell never prostrated himself before Johnson more humbly than Serof before Wagner. He wrote propaganda articles, hunted out singers, translated texts, and followed Wagner about with dog-like fidelity as interpreter, guide and general factotum. Wagner rewarded the " very neglected, sickly and indigent-looking " little man with a few words of approval of the orchestration of " Judith " and a handsomely bound score of " Tristan ". One incident recorded by Wagner in " Mein Leben " is highly characteristic. Serof, in his articles, had been comparing Wagner with Rubinstein, very much of course to the disadvantage of the latter. Wagner, not wishing to incur Rubinstein's enmity, begged him to be a little more discreet. " At which he retorted with the vehemence of a man in pain, 'I hate him and I can't make any concession'."

But Serof's own day of triumph was at hand. At last, at forty-three, he was going to make his debut as a serious composer. (One can hardly count a few arrangements of Ukrainian folk-songs.) " Judith " had its first performance at the Marinsky Theatre on May 16th/28th, 1863. Valentina Bianchi sang the heroine; Sariotti, Holofernes. The work was magnificently staged and the not shockingly original music being effective in a crude, second-hand Meyerbeerian way, Serof scored an astonishing success. Serof the the idealist, Serof the Perfect Wagnerite, must have blushed if Serof the composer had not been completely incapable of recognising his works as anything but masterpieces or (in moments of despair) utter failures. And " Judith " was obviously not a failure. The only adverse criticisms in all Petersburg came from the Stassof-Cui group. And, the success continuing, Serof's financial difficulties were at last ended.

One speedy consequence of the new state of affairs was marriage—to a girl of considerably less than half his age, Valentina Bergmann, a brilliant pianist (and, in later life, an opera composer), who had been a student at the detested Conservatoire, from which he had easily enticed her. Valentina appears not only to have adored but to have understood him: in short, to have made him a perfect wife. She has left it on record that in the early days they danced a mazurka each morning before he started work.

The newly-married pair spent the early summer of 1864 in Vienna, or rather at Neuwaldegg near by, the bliss of their honeymoon being completed by a visit from Wagner. Wagner was jubilant on account of Ludwig II's famous letter, received only a few weeks before, " intoxicated with hope for the future and belief in the present ", as Valentina tells us in her " Memoirs ". But the rest of the journey was less happy. Serof was disappointed in his hope of getting " Judith " produced in Vienna. And worse was to follow. When, at Karlsruhe, he showed the score to Liszt, the latter, in playing through the first two acts, plainly showed his boredom and then, breaking off, said frankly that he did not care for the work. That was fatal. Serof's final breach with Balakiref had been caused by the younger man's criticism of his scoring, while on the other hand his old enemy Theophil Tolstoy's approval of " Judith " led to something like friendship. Liszt's adverse judgment sadly upset Serof. It was unpardonable. And to crown all, before his return to St. Petersburg, he lost his precious manuscript score.

Nevertheless Serof was now a prophet honoured in his own

country. With Dargomyjsky in semi-retirement, Tchaïkovsky and the " handful " still very little known, he found himself bracketed with Anton Rubinstein as one of the greatest living native composers. The success of " Judith " naturally encouraged him to try again. For the material of his second opera he went back to the " Askold's Grave " of his youth, though he now called it " Rogneda ". No opera by a Perfect Wagnerite can have been written in a more curious way. For on Serof's own confession, " the music did not arise from the words of the libretto, which as a matter of fact did not yet exist, but simply from the *situations* which were clearly defined in the composer's imagination. Consequently the words had to be fitted to completed or half-completed music ". Even the " situations " were conceived separately, each for the sake of its stage-effectiveness, rather than as a link in a connected chain. In " Rogneda " Serof practised everything that he had preached most energetically against in " Ruslan ", with a consistent inconsistency between critical theory and creative practice hardly equalled even by Cui. Almost at the last moment, failing a suitable soprano for the title-rôle, the part was rewritten for a contralto, Daria Leonova. Petrof sang Vladimir the Great. The complicated stage-settings necessitated forty rehearsals. But when " Rogneda " was given, on October 27th/November 8th, 1865, its success far surpassed even that of " Judith "; for that matter, of every previous Russian opera. It was given twenty successive performances to crowded houses, seventy performances at the Marinsky Theatre in the first five years. Press and public were almost unanimous. Only the " handful " growled, yet even of these the twenty-one-year-old Rimsky-Korsakof found " much in it that pleased " him, though he was ashamed to admit as much to his comrades; the young Tchaïkovsky thought " Rogneda " disappointing after " Judith "; while Dargomyjsky murmured, " Why shouldn't Serof's operas succeed? He has camels in one and real dogs in the other ". But Theophil Tolstoy announced that a new epoch in the history of Russian music had begun, and the Tsar expressed his pleasure by the grant of a pension. To crown Serof's joy, his wife bore him a son, Valentine, who was afterwards to win fame as a portrait-painter.[1]

Poised on the peak of artistic and social success, Serof spent a whole year in considering the field and subject of his next triumph. Should it be ballet? Ballet was very popular at the moment, and the incidental dances and processions in his operas were among their most successful features. So ballet it should be. He chose as his subject another of Gogol's short stories, " Christmas Eve ", composed two numbers which became popular as separate orchestral pieces, and then gave it up. Next he thought of a Gogol opera, " Taras Bulba ". But nothing came of that except a single " Cossack Dance ". Then various Polish subjects. But there had recently been another Polish insurrection and—" I don't want the public to hiss my music, as happened recently in Moscow during the Polish scenes in ' A Life for the Tsar ' ". All these projects were forgotten for a while in the excitement of founding a fortnightly paper, " Theatre and Music " which Serof himself edited, wrote almost single-handed, and signally mismanaged from the business point of view. But its vitriolic existence, begun in April, 1867, came to an end with the seventeenth number in December, and Serof turned once more to creative work.

Nothing is more extraordinary about this extraordinary man than the duality of the sincere, even fanatical idealist of the critic in him, who recked nothing of popularity, and the vulgar opportunism of the composer with his flair for giving

[1] Valentine Serof was commissioned by Diaghilef to make a pencil-sketch of Rimsky-Korsakof in March, 1908, just before the latter's death, for publicity purposes in connection with the Russian performances in Paris. Someone having remarked that it looked rather like an ikon, Serof said, " So much the better. Let the French pray to it ! "

the public what it wanted. Realism was now the fashion. Realism and "the people", the recently emancipated peasants. " Expression, truth to life . . . were the watchwords of our circle ", wrote Serof's widow. No matter that the critic Serof had been the bitterest antagonist of nationalism and Slavophil primitivism. (Though it was true he had lately adopted a milder tone toward both Glinka and Dargomyjsky.) The composer Serof, if he was to keep in the fashion, would have to choose a subject " from the life of the people ". He chose Ostrovsky's realistic peasant drama, " Don't Live as You'd Like To ", and even induced Ostrovsky to help him with the libretto. But the collaboration came to grief over the Fourth Act, with its " butterweek " or carnival scene. Ostrovsky wanted to treat this fantastically, introducing the characters of Russian mythology, but Serof insisted on austere realism, and found himself left to finish the libretto alone. (Incidentally, it was a phrase from this scene which suggested the title of the opera, " Hostile Power ".) As for the music, " the piano and writing-table were soon cluttered with all the available collections of Russian folk-songs ", his widow tells us. " The room was enlivened, to the joy of our little son, by the sounds of Russian dance-tunes. Serof sat in his study from morning to night buried in the study of Russian folk-music."

Several numbers from the new work were included in an orchestral concert entirely devoted to Serof's music, given in Moscow in the spring of 1868. " Judith " was also being revived there; Serof lectured at the University; and his friendly reception by Nicholas Rubinstein, brother of his Petersburg *bête noire*, excited his usual optimism to the wildest hopes. Rubinstein is going to depute to him all the " intellectual side " of his activities at the Moscow Conservatoire, he writes to a friend. He is accepted in Moscow as the great man he is, " as I have always expected in Petersburg and always in vain ". At the Conservatoire he is to have *carte blanche* in the teaching of theory and musical history; he will have great influence over the choice of the Music Society's programmes and will write descriptive notes for them; he is to be the critic of an important Moscow weekly. Rubinstein has even promised financial backing for the foundation of a paper of his own . . . But all these Alnaschar dreams came to nothing. Serof never even returned to Moscow again.

During the summer of 1868 Serof had the joy of superintending the rehearsals for the first Russian performance of " Lohengrin " at the Marinsky Theatre, St. Petersburg, a performance largely due to his own incessant propaganda. It took place on October 4th/16th, K. N. Liadof conducting, and scored only a moderate success. Dargomyjsky, Balakiref, Cui, Mussorgsky and Rimsky-Korsakof sat together in a box and sneered, and musical Petersburg as a whole was not deeply impressed for either good or bad. In an open letter to Wagner in the " Journal de St. Petersbourg ", Serof bewailed the " somewhat prosaic realism " of the production, which had destroyed the effect of " the tender, mysterious tones of the sentimental scenes " and the idealism of the Teutonic poetry. But on the whole he seems to have been fairly satisfied.

Suffering from *angina pectoris*, Serof was ordered abroad that winter by the doctors. The Tsar made him a present of fifteen hundred rubles to cover his travelling expenses, and he set out in the spring with his wife and little boy. Naturally the journey took the form of a Wagnerian pilgrimage. At Munich they heard " Tristan " and " Die Meistersinger " for the first time—the celebrated performances under von Bülow and Richter. Then they made for Tribschen, staying at Lucerne, but constantly visiting Wagner and Cosima von Bülow, whom they now met for the first time. And it is extremely probable that they made the acquaintance of the new Professor of Classical Philology at

Basel, a young man named Friedrich Nietzsche, who was also a frequent visitor at Tribschen that summer .

Returning to Petersburg, apparently in better health, Serof was flattered by an invitation at last to join the advisory committee of the Russian Music Society, from which Anton Rubinstein had just resigned. In the following May he was elected chairman, a post which he held to the end of his life. He also resumed work on " Hostile Power ". He had found another librettist for the last two acts, on whose suggestion he altered Ostrovsky's tranquil, realistic ending to melodramatic tragedy. And we hear of his playing excerpts from the music to Dostoevsky,[1] Theophil Tolstoy (with whom he had again quarrelled and made it up), Repin, Tchaïkovsky[2] and others of his circle. But " Hostile Power " was destined never to be finished, and for a reason thoroughly characteristic of Serof. An Italian opera company, including Adelina Patti, Pauline Lucca and Mario, visited St. Petersburg in the winter of 1870-71 and the Perfect Wagnerite forthwith, to the unspeakable delight of his enemies, became a Patti-worshipper. " Hostile Power ", though nearly completed, was laid aside in favour of a conventional Italian opera to be based on George Sand's " Consuelo "! " Consuelo " never got beyond the stage of rough sketches, but Serof wrote a coloratura " Ave Maria " for Patti, who returned thanks by singing it, once only, after his death. A quasi-Italian choral " Stabat Mater " dates from the same period. But we must place to the other side of the account the fact that, on his return from Vienna, where he had represented the Russian Music Society at the Beethoven Centenary celebrations in

---

[1] Although Dostoevsky was out of Russia from April, 1867 till after Serof's death !

[2] Tchaïkovsky himself told Mme. von Meck that he met Serof at about the time of the first performance of " Judith ". Laroche says he introduced them a year or two later than this, on an evening when " Dostoevsky talked a lot of nonsense about music, as literary men who know nothing about it, will ". But Tchaïkovsky never made any secret of his personal dislike of Serof's " moral character ". Serof, in Tchaïkovsky's opinion, was " not good-hearted ".

December, Serof instigated the first Russian performance of the " Missa Solennis ".

Serof's complaint was wearing him down but, in spite of his pain, he was full of plans for the future. When " Hostile Power " was finished,[1] he proposed to take up Gogol's " Christmas Eve " again, this time as an opera; and the Grand Duchess Helena Pavlovna, who admired his music, commissioned the poet Polonsky to prepare a libretto for him. Some of the numbers were actually composed and, with the two earlier dances, were posthumously arranged as an orchestral suite by Serof's widow. Then, after " Christmas Eve ", there was to be a " great tragic opera with a subject taken from the Hussite wars ". But in this, as in so much else, Serof's confident hopes were never realised. On the afternoon of January 20th/February 1st, 1871, he was discussing Emil Naumann's new book, " Die Kulturgeschichte der Tonkunst ", with the pianist Slavinsky and had just sung one of the music-type examples when " all at once a curious sort of smile passed over his face. His countenance was suddenly distorted ", says Slavinsky, " and as suddenly regained its normal expression; his eyes closed; his legs gave way under him; he slowly bent over and slipped to the ground ". It was the end.

* * * * *

One would like to think Wagner was quite sincere when he wrote that " for me Serof is not dead; his image lives on unchangeably in my mind; it is only that there is an end to the pains he took for me. He remains what he was—one of the noblest of men. His tender soul, his pure feelings, his lively and cultured mind made his friendship one of the most precious possessions of my whole life ". But Tchaïkovsky summed him up better when he wrote that " his

---

[1] It was actually completed and orchestrated by N. F. Solovief and performed in the spring, but won only a *succès d'estime*.

petty vanity and self-adoration, which often showed themselves in the most naïve way, were repugnant and incomprehensible in so gifted a man. For he was remarkably clever in spite of his small-minded egotism . . . . . . But one can forgive him all, on account of what he suffered before success raised him from poverty, and because he bore his troubles in a strong, manly spirit for love of his art ". With all his weaknesses and contradictions, Serof still contrived to be fanatically sincere. His bitterest enemies never seem to have questioned his sincerity, in spite of the numerous opportunities offered by his operas. " To write against one's own convictions, I consider the worst of all intellectual crimes, the the sin against the Holy Ghost ", he once wrote. As long as he kept off staved paper, he never committed it.

G. A.

BALAKIREF

MILY BALAKIREF

" But for Balakiref the fate of Russian music might have been far different from what we actually have to register."

" Had there been no Balakiref to act as leader, educator, champion, and helpmate, what would have happened to Cui, Mussorgsky, Borodin, Rimsky-Korsakof, and later to Glazunof, Liadof, Liapunof, and many other Russian composers? Most of them, no doubt, would have made their way independently. We cannot tell how; but we can confidently assert that, but for him, there would have been no new Russian school, and many a page telling of live, fearless and joyous activity and progress would be missing from the history of Russia's musical life."

" The importance of the part he played in the evolution of Russian music is so great as to preclude all possibilities of comparison and entitles him to the first place in the history of Russian music after Glinka."

These three quotations—from Stassof's " Art in the Nineteenth Century ", Findeisen's " Obituary of Balakiref " in the *Russian Musical Gazette*, and an article by Liapunof in the " Year Book of the Imperial Theatres ", respectively—make clear how great a debt of gratitude not only Russia, but the musical world at large owes to Balakiref, the head of the group of nineteenth-century composers, usually called the " new " or " national " Russian school, or " the mighty handful " (Kutchka)—a debt far more readily and generally acknowledged than the one we owe to him as a composer. The greater part of his output (not a large one) may remain neglected and the small portion of it that is generally known patently undervalued, but tribute is ungrudgingly paid to the loving labour he devoted to fighting the battle of Russian music, to training and guiding the young composers who, instinctively and inevitably, had mustered around him, and to propagating not only the music of his contemporaries, but musical culture in general.

And yet, to the present day, no reasonably accurate and complete biography of him, no adequate study of his personality as man and artist, no adequate critical survey of his output has appeared in his native country or in any other, nor is there any likelihood of one appearing in the near future. The difficulties in the way of making good the deficiency as regards his life and personality are great. Little information is available on certain periods and circumstances of his life. A considerable proportion of his correspondence with Stassof, Rimsky-Korsakof, and others still awaits publication. Most of the useful descriptions of his personality which those who knew him have left are scattered in Russian periodicals now practically unprocurable—the only one which happens to be widely known being that provided by Rimsky-Korsakof in his " Memoirs of my Musical Life ", which in Russia has been unanimously denounced as inaccurate and unjust in many important respects.

In due time, no doubt—and very probably on the occasion of the centenary of Balakiref's birth, January, 1937—this deplorable state of things will be made good, at least to some extent. Meanwhile the utmost that can be done is to outline the story of his life and to fill in a few gaps and correct a few errors in the current descriptions of him as man and artist.

The story of his life starts with a childhood spent in Nijni Novgorod, his native city, in which, but for his mother's mild but genuine interest in music, and the fact that one keen music-lover who maintained a private orchestra lived there, he would have had no opportunity to bring his inborn gifts into early play, or to acquire some kind of musical education. It continues with his debut in Petersburg at the age of eighteen, as pianist and composer—a brilliant success from the artistic and moral points of view, but not otherwise profitable to him. Then came a few years of hard work and struggle against poverty; success, recognition, leadership, against tremendous odds and at the cost of a tremendous expenditure of vitality; then defeat, a breakdown in health, a temporary withdrawal from musical life. A few years later he reappeared and resumed work where he had left off, but his disposition and outlook were so greatly changed as to appal those who had known him before. A long period of fruitful activities followed, but led to thorough disenchantment, seclusion except for a small circle of friends. He wrote a good deal of music, watched developments that were alien and distasteful to him, saw himself avoided or forgotten by most of his former friends and pupils, kept up a keen interest in the music he loved, and to the end remained a keen propagandist of it, and eager to respond to the love of those who loved him. All this is to be accounted for in a great measure by the idiosyncrasies of his personality—keen, enthusiastic, glowing, uncompromising, genuine to the core, utterly disinterested, so scrupulous that he would retain compositions for years and years before feeling that he had done his utmost with them, or would refuse posts and responsibilities which he felt he could not fill to his own satisfaction; so despotic and outspoken as to be endowed with an almost infinite capacity for giving or taking offence, fully aware of his own defects yet unwilling or unable to curb them, thoroughly exasperating in many respects, and yet most lovable and worthy of grateful admiration.

He was born on December 21st, 1836/January 2nd, 1837, at Nijni-Novgorod, an old Russian city on the confluent of the rivers Volga and Oka, built in the thirteenth century, and for many centuries an outpost on the Eastern frontier of

Muscovite Russia, a stronghold against Tartar invaders and the incursions of the aboriginal Mordivinians. It had been many a time ravaged by war, fires and pestilences. For centuries, too, the famous fair held there had attracted to it, yearly, representatives of all manners of Slavonic and Eastern races, whose native music must have left some kind of unconscious impression on the mind of the future author of "Islamey" and "Tamara". In ordinary times life in the city was quiet and even drowsy. There was no cultural life to speak of. According to statistics published in the 'eighties, nearly one-eighth of the population of seventy thousand inhabitants were factory workers.

His father was a state official of small means, a descendant of a very old family, members of which had been in the service of the Grand Dukes of Moscow for many generations. The direct line of descent, so far as known nowadays, leads back to Andrei Simonovitch Balakiref, who in 1613 received a grant of land for services rendered.

The only son, and the eldest of four children, Mily Balakiref, according to information recorded by Glinka's sister, Liudmila Shestakova, showed, at an early age, a definite disposition for music, a sensitive ear, and a good memory. His mother gave him his first piano lessons, and, when he had reached the age of ten, took him to Moscow so that he should receive lessons from the best piano teacher there, Alexander Dubuque, a pupil of Field. He had to return to school after the holidays, so that he took only ten lessons with Dubuque. He used to say that he had derived great and lasting benefit from them. His second teacher, in Nijni-Novgorod, was Karl Eiserich, of whom nothing is known except that he was the son of Karl Travtgott Eiserich (1770-1835, organist and composer), enjoyed a local reputation as a teacher, had been an orchestral conductor of a small theatre run by a local manufacturer for the benefit of his factory hands (a remarkably democratic initiative at the time), and afterwards fulfilled the same function at the home of a keen music lover and writer on music, Alexander Ulybyshef, remembered to the present day by his books on Mozart (1844—very useful spade-work, of which Otto John availed himself) and on Beethoven (1857—a far less successful effort).

It was through Eiserich that the boy heard on one occasion Chopin's E minor Concerto and the great Trio from Glinka's " Life for the Tsar "—memorable experiences, which sowed in him the first seeds of a lifelong devotion to the music of both these masters. Soon Eiserich introduced him to Ulybyshef, who decided to engage him as assistant conductor, pianist in ordinary, and coach. One of the first works which he helped to rehearse was Mozart's " Requiem ". Ulybyshef owned a good musical library. The repertory of the concerts given at his house included sonatas, chamber-music, and orchestral works by Mozart, Beethoven, Mendelssohn and Hummel among others. And so Balakiref was able to acquire a good deal of knowledge and of practical experience. He developed the habit of learning the technique of composition by studying live examples and not theoretical treatises—which, by the way, were not available in Russia at the time.

He eventually succeeded Eiserich as chief conductor, and by 1852 he had turned out a few compositions, including the first movement of a septet for strings, flute, clarinet and piano, which he never completed (this first movement, he said later, was written in imitation of Henselt's piano concerto) and a Fantasy for piano and orchestra—or, to be more accurate, only one movement of if out of several he had originally planned. The full title ran:

> Grande Fantaisie sur airs nationales (*sic*) russes pour la pianoforte avec accompagnement d'orchestre composée et dédiée à son maître Monsieur Charles Eisrich par Mily Balakireff, Op. 4.

At the end of the manuscript (now in a Moscow library) further linguistic acrobatics appear:

Finis del prima parte Auctor Milius Balakireff.

Of the other two works whose coming into being is suggested by the ascription of the Opus No. 4 to the Fantasy, nothing is known.

After completing his school curriculum (his mother had died meanwhile) he was sent to Kazan, where he entered the University to study mathematics—but not as a matriculated student, his father's means not permitting so great an expenditure. At Kazan there was no musical life to speak of, except for the occasional visits of a few artists such as Laskovsky, Seymour Shiff, and Anton Kontsky. Laskovsky was a composer as well as a pianist, and his music created a great impression on Balakiref.[1] From Seymour Shiff, according to brief recollections which he jotted down years later, he learnt much about music in general; and from Kontsky, much about piano playing:

Hearing that Kontsky intended to settle in Petersburg, where I was hoping to go, I planned to take lessons with him. But when I did go to Petersburg, I discovered more about his outlook on music, and this led me to change my mind. The people who go averring that I received lessons from Kontsky are thoroughly mistaken. We were just acquaintances.

A typical Balakiref utterance!

Balakiref also found himself in fairly great demand as a musician and teacher. The lessons he gave enabled him to eke out his slender means. He continued to study music

---

[1] In July, 1909—less than a year before his death, Balakiref wrote to a friend: "I longed to set his music going, but never succeeded, because in those days practically all music teachers were German, and the few who were Russians had not enough musical sense to acknowledge the merits of his works. I also wished to publish at least a selection of his best things in a worthy edition. But again I failed. Jurgenson was so prejudiced against them that all my efforts to persuade him were vain."

eagerly and to compose. He wrote one or two songs, and also a piano fantasy on motifs from Glinka's " A Life for the Tsar " which was, a little later, to win Glinka's enthusiastic approval. So a couple of years went by; and he remained facing the difficulty of deciding whether to take up mathematics professionally and keep music as a side-line, or to devote himself wholly to music, hoping against hope, under most unfavourable circumstances. Fortunately, Ulybyshef solved the problem by offering to take him to Petersburg and give him his chance. Naturally, he accepted with joy; and towards the end of the year 1855, just before his nineteenth birthday, he arrived at Petersburg with his protector and friend. On his way he had made a short stay in Moscow and met Nicholas Rubinstein, the pianist and composer (Anton Rubinstein's younger brother), and the future founder of the Moscow section of the Russian Music Society and the Moscow Conservatoire, whom he greatly admired, and who was prove a true friend to him.

Petersburg in 1855 was not a promising field for a young Russian composer. The only music that enjoyed real favour was Italian opera. The Russian Philharmonic Society gave only two concerts every year, and the programme of these consisted of " tableaux vivants " as well as of music. Chamber music was practised only in private circles, and the University concerts, founded a few years before by a University inspector named Alexander Fitztum von Eckstedt, were the only ones at which new orchestral works, Russian or foreign, could from time to time be heard. Glinka's " A Life for the Tsar " enjoyed a measure of popularity, but his admirable " Ruslan and Liudmila " had been a failure. A special concert of Dargomyjsky's works, given in 1853, had created a good impression, but in 1856 his opera, " The Russalka ", was to fail miserably. But Balakiref had vitality and courage to spare; and, as it happened, his debut was most auspicious from the artistic point of view.

One of Ulybyshef's first steps was to introduce him to Glinka, who heard him play the Fantasy on motifs from " A Life for the Tsar " and was absolutely delighted.

" My brother ", Liudmila Shestakova recorded, " invited him to call as often as possible, and every time insisted on his playing the Fantasy again. Before leaving for Berlin, in April, 1856, he said to me: ' If I am no longer there to take charge of the musical education of our Olia (my little daughter, Olga), promise me that you will allow no one but Balakiref to teach her music. He is the first man in whom I have found views on the art corresponding to my own. You can fully trust him; and, believe me, in time he will become a second Glinka ' ".

Glinka also gave two Spanish themes noted down by him to Balakiref, who used one in his Overture on a Spanish March Theme (composed 1857) and the other in a Sérénade Espagnole (composed 1890).

Balakiref appeared as pianist at a concert given at Kronstadt by Karl Schubert, the 'cellist, and Klamroth, on December 12th, 1855; and on February 22nd, 1856, he played at a University Concert the first movement of a new piano concerto of his in F sharp minor. A month later, he gave a concert of his own at which he played several compositions of his: The Fantasy on motifs from " A Life for the Tsar ", a Nocturne, and a Scherzo (later he was to consider that Nocturne one of his best works, but the Scherzo very feeble) and took part in the performance of the first movement of another work, an Octet (which he never carried further). He also played pieces by Glinka, Dargomyjsky and Laskovsky.

It was during the year 1856 that he became acquainted with Dargomyjsky, who was as greatly impressed by his personality and musicianship as Glinka had been, and was often to allude to him as " a musical eagle "; with Serof, who praised his gifts as a pianist and his early compositions (later, he was to become hostile to Balakiref and his group); with Lvof, who held a high social position and, although a mere amateur in the matter of composition, was very much in the limelight as the author of the Russian national anthem; with Prince Vassily Odoievsky and Count Vielgorsky, both of them very influential people and interested in music; with César Cui, who became the first of his comrades-in-arms (and often a most compromising one on account of his narrow, vehemently expressed views); and with the two brothers Stassof, Vladimir and Dimitri.

Vladimir Stassof (1824-1906) was primarily a historian and an art critic, but also a keen music-lover; and at an early date he blossomed into a critic and especially a propagandist of music. He had the utmost faith in the future of the Russian composers of his time, and was one of the very first to support them. The history of his career, from this particular point of view, begins with his relations with Glinka, whose acquaintance he had made in the early 'fifties. He was one of the first to espouse the cause of " Ruslan and Liudmila ". It is thoroughly characteristic of the attitude he maintained throughout his life that even with Glinka, he should have felt impelled to play the part of Mentor as well as that of champion—as shown by a letter of 1855 from Glinka to his sister:

> Stassof came to see me yesterday and urged me to go on working. He does not care whether I am in good health or not. The one thing that matters to him is that I should compose. But I do not agree: health means more to me than any music on earth.

He was to devote much thought and labour to supplying Balakiref, Mussorgsky, Borodin, Tchaïkovsky, and Rimsky-Korsakof with ideas or plans for descriptive symphonic works and with opera libretti. No doubt, at times, they may have found him a little trying; but they courted his advice, and valued it even when it was volunteered. His interest in their progress, his eagerness to serve them and guide them, were in themselves enough to constitute precious encouragements at a time when the encouragements they received were few and far between; and a good many of the ideas he thrust upon them bore fruit. In 1861, for instance, he suggested to Balakiref the notion of composing a tone-poem, based on the legend of Sadko, the merchant from Novgorod who, cast into the ocean as a sacrifice to the marine deities, ended by marrying the Sea-King's daughter—an idea which Balakiref did not carry out, and which was handed over first to Mussorgsky, also without result, and then to Rimsky-Korsakof, who composed a tone-poem and later, with Stassof's help for the libretto, a whole opera on the subject. He was to give Borodin the idea of " Prince Igor " and Mussorgsky the idea of " Khovanshchina "; and also to help Mussorgsky to build up the libretto of " Boris Godunof ". He never tired of calling attention to the work of the young Russian composers, of providing opportunities for them, of challenging and denouncing their adversaries and censors. It is becoming clearer every day that he was practically the only contemporary to have real faith in Mussorgsky and to encourage him. He was to do a great deal for Balakiref too, and remain faithful to him to the end of his life. The two had much in common—enthusiasm, an enquiring turn of mind, a good measure of intolerance, a great capacity for affection, and a great desire to teach and guide and fight for their ideals. It would, indeed, be more accurate to say that Stassof, rather than the narrow-minded and self-centred César Cui, was the first of Balakiref's comrades-in-arms, the associate leader of the new Russian school.

His brother, Dimitri (1828-1917), a barrister by profession, less bustling and less combative, less in the limelight because he did not issue articles and pamphlets on music, an excellent and most active musician, was one of the founders of the Russian Music Society, rendered yeoman service to music, and also proved a faithful friend to Balakiref, as well as to Mussorgsky and to many other composers.

And so, by 1857, Balakiref, aged twenty, and a newcomer in the Russian capital, having composed but a few works or first movements of works, none of them the least sensational in character (although the piano Fantasy was a brilliant, imaginative, skilfully carried out piece of virtuosity, and, like the first movement of the piano concerto, something altogether new in the Russian repertory), found himself thoroughly *lancé* in the Petersburg musical world—partly, no doubt, thanks to Ulybyshef's influence, but mainly on the strength of his talent, and of his charming, forceful, glowing personality. No doubt, having definite ideas on his art and being very independent by nature, he did not cotton to all his new acquaintances or go out of his way to curry favour with possible patrons. Lvof was very much an amateur; both he and Vielgorsky held " Ruslan and Liudmila " cheap —an opinion which Balakiref was unlikely to condone or to leave unchallenged. From Nijni-Novgorod where he had returned, Ulybyshef reminded him that a man such as Lvof could be most useful and was worth cultivating: " Do your utmost for him ", he wrote, " and you will be doing your best for yourself and also for me "—for, as he told Balakiref in another letter, he " loved him as his own son " and was most desirous that he should do well.

Balakiref much later, told his Russian biographer Timofeief a story to the effect that once he was able to delight and impress Lvof in a curious way:

> He showed me twenty-four Capriccios for solo violin which he had just composed. I remarked that it would be easy to provide these with piano accompaniments. So he started playing them, and I sat down at the piano and

extemporised accompaniments. Being already acquainted with Schumann's new harmonic style, I introduced some chords which surprised and pleased him. He asked me to repeat them, and, in order not to forget them, took a pencil and made marks on the keys I had been striking on the piano.

In the spring of 1857, Balakiref was engaged to play as soloist in Beethoven's E flat (the " Emperor ") concerto at one of the concerts of the " Concert Society ", founded by Lvof and run by Dimitri Stassof. It was a solemn and brilliant affair. The whole Imperial family attended and Balakiref was presented to the Tsar.

Obviously, he would have had every inducement to make a career as a pianist; but the prospect held no allurement for him. He did not enjoy playing in public and never courted success. Later in life he never appeared as soloist except on rare occasions, to earn a little money for himself or for his undertakings, or for special propaganda purposes—as when it became necessary to collect funds for the erection of the monument to Glinka at Smolensk.

At that time it seemed as though success was his for the asking. Despite his high cheek-bones, big mouth, and thick lips (features which suggested a partly Tartar origin, although no indication to that effect is to be found in his genealogy), he must have been most attractive with his light chestnut hair and beard, high forehead, beautiful and expressive eyes, mobile, kindly, virile physiognomy, and fundamentally honest, spirited, expansive disposition. It may be well to note here that nothing is recorded of his sentimental life except an infatuation, in the late 'fifties, for a beautiful society lady, Anna Kovalevskaya. He was to remain a bachelor to the end of his life. But he certainly was never insensitive to feminine charms, and far from unsuccessful with women.

Despite his growing popularity as man and musician, his position and prospects were highly unsatisfactory. In fact, those early years in Petersburg were a time of dire poverty. He depended for his daily bread on lessons (of which he gave, at times, as many as nine a day), not all of them regular and few, if any, well paid. He could neither sell his new compositions nor receive the money owing to him for the few he had already sold. In 1857 he fell ill, struck with some kind of typhus; and the following year he had another long illness, ending in encephalitis. The rest of the time he kept hard at work. In 1857-1858 he wrote the Overture on a Spanish March Theme and an Overture on three Russian Themes, the first example of his Russian " national " style, which was performed in March, 1859. On that occasion Serof praised him as " the best representative of the Russian school ", and pointed out that " had his name been Balacchirini or Balakirstein, the public would have been less indifferent to the merits of his overture ". In 1858-1859 he composed songs, of which he sold the copyright for fifteen rubles apiece (quite a reasonable price for the time) and began planning the incidental music for Shakespeare's " King Lear ", which was being played at Petersburg (by a German company, but with the negro actor Aldridge playing the title-part in English).

In 1858 Ulybyshef died, bequeathing to his young friend " whom he loved as his own son ", his musical library and a sum of a thousand rubles—which Balakiref had great difficulty in collecting. His letters to Stassof (in several of which he mentions the fact) show him depressed and worried at times, but more often teeming with energy; planning, among other things, a big choral symphony in the honour of the twenty-fifth anniversary of the first performance of " A Life for the Tsar " (this plan had to be shelved, but in 1904 Balakiref did write a choral cantata for the centenary of Glinka's birth). Referring to his schemes for " Lear " and the choral symphony, he wrote this characteristic sentence:

> I can do nothing quickly or to order, nor undertake to deliver at a given date. In order to compose properly, I need absolute freedom and peace of mind.

Sometimes, however, depression gained the upper hand. Apart from confessing that often he did not know where to turn for money, and referring to pessimistic moods " à la Byron ", he declared that his various troubles had rendered him " irritable, fretful, and suspicious ". Stassof did his utmost to cheer and stimulate him, urged him to work away, hunted up and copied for him old English tunes suitable for use in the " King Lear " music, and more than once succeeded in restoring his confidence in himself.

His interests in life were increasing steadily in other directions. Young composers had started mustering around him, receiving tuition from him; and he naturally and almost unconsciously slid into his predestined rôle as a leader.

The first to come to him (this happened early in 1856) was César Cui, his elder by two years, who had previously studied a while under Moniuszko, but knew very little, and who received from Balakiref a definite impulse to practise composition, as he says in his " Memoirs ". He was not without gifts, but had no great understanding of technique or capacity for learning. Balakiref helped him a good deal in matters of part-writing and especially scoring. He was, on the other hand, a born journalist and pamphleteer; and from the moment when he was given the post of music critic to a big Petersburg daily, he became the self-appointed spokesman and fighting-man of the group that by then had taken shape around Balakiref.

The second was Mussorgsky, whom he met in 1857, and who forthwith became his loving and diligent pupil. Balakiref loved him too, and never ceased to be concerned in his welfare. But he was disconcerted by Mussorgsky's tendencies, his lack of interest in traditional technique, and even in technique generally. He strove to bring him back to what he considered the one and only right path. Mussorgsky eventually rebelled, especially after Balakiref had repeatedly offended him by sharp criticisms, sometimes tactlessly proffered in public. But in the end, these misunderstandings were forgotten. After a long period of estrangement the two met again (in 1878, three years before Mussorgsky's death).

Mussorgsky, Balakiref wrote to Vladimir Stassof, showed no signs of vanity or obstinacy. He listened earnestly to what was said to him; he raised no protest against the suggestion that it was indispensable to know harmony, and he even did not object to the idea of studying under Rimsky-Korsakof.

This meekness on the part of the composer of " Boris Godunof " must have been the outcome of an ever present consciousness of the debt he owed to Balakiref—a debt which a couple of years later he generously acknowledged in his autobiography, paying tribute to " Balakiref's great heart and great mind, which had opened wide vistas to his own ".

With the advent of Rimsky-Korsakof in 1861, and of Borodin the following year, the Balakiref group or " Kutchka " (" mighty handful ") as it became known to history, was complete (it also comprised Apollon Gussakovsky [1841-1875], a composer whose music both Balakiref and Rimsky-Korsakof held in high esteem).

Nothing could have suited Balakiref better than to have all these young men to teach and to guide. His was the true spirit of an apostle, thoroughly disinterested and unsparing of effort. Despite his poverty, he was not concerned with receiving payment for the lessons he gave to worthy pupils. His lessons to Mussorgsky, for instance, were given free from the moment when Mussorgsky found himself in financial difficulties, and maybe even before. And in 1863, when Liudmila Shestakova's daughter (the "little Olia" whose musical education Glinka had recommended should be entrusted to none but him) died, he undertook in memory of her to give music lessons free to two promising young boys. With his knowledge, his infectious courage and enthusiasm, his readiness to help, he was the very man of whom the young Russian composers stood in need, and who would have been of great use to them even if the country had not been entirely devoid of resources for their technical education—schools, teachers, and text-books in the Russian language.

For a long time critics and historians have been spreading the legend of the "mighty handful" or "the great Russian five"—of five composers united by the strong bond of a common ideal, resolved to stand and fall together, advising and helping one another, and reacting upon one another. This legend was created partly by the writings of Stassof and Cui (and especially by the latter's book "La Musique en Russie", published in 1880 for foreign consumption), and partly by the practice which hostile Russian critics adopted of bunching Balakiref and his pupils together, so as to kill as many birds as possible with any stone they found an opportunity to throw.

Here is a case in point: Borodin recorded, in a letter to Stassof, that one day Mussorgsky, while playing at the piano a movement of a Schumann symphony, muttered: "Here begin the musical mathematics." This has enabled certain English critics of today gravely to proclaim that "the Russian five regarded symphonic working-out as mere mathematics". And as often as not Cui's personal views as expressed in his writings are believed to be those of the whole group and more especially of its leader, Balakiref.

The truth is that they had little in common beyond the fact that they were Balakiref's pupils—some of them amenable to his influence, others impervious to it—that they occasionally exchanged friendly advice and criticism, and that three of them (the exception being Cui) used in their music elements derived from folk-tunes, Russian or Eastern. To speak (as at least one French critic has done) of their " collective personality " is as fundamentally inaccurate as to speak of their " solidarity ". Balakiref was eager to advise and direct his pupils, and maybe over-eager that they should see things as he himself saw them. But he did not at all consider his group as standing in opposition to any other—except, as will presently appear, the " German clique ", which was up in arms against Russian national music—or as forming a closed circle. Indeed, a time was to come when Tchaïkovsky, whom writers often contrast with the " Five ", received from him as much advice, and very much the same kind of advice, as he was giving to his actual pupils.

The best known description of the line taken by Balakiref and his group in the early 'sixties is that given in Rimsky-Korsakof's memoirs. Here are its principal portions in slightly abridged form.

> He impressed me tremendously from the very first. A splendid pianist, with a boundless capacity for playing at sight and for extemporising, endowed with an intuitive feeling for good harmony and part-writing, he commanded an adequate technique of his own, partly inborn and partly acquired by practice. He knew a prodigious quantity of music of all kinds, and could remember, at any moment, every bar he had ever heard or read. He was incomparable as a critic of technicalities. He never failed to spot an error or shortcoming—having done which he would sit at the piano and start extemporising to show how the defect should be corrected. He was so despotic that he insisted upon our music being remodelled in exact accordance with his prescriptions; and often whole passages in

his pupils' compositions were not their work, but his. We simply couldn't help obeying. He held us absolutely spellbound by his talents, his authority, his magnetism. He appreciated even the faintest signs of talent; but anything he disapproved of he would tear to pieces and hold up to derision so remorselessly that often his victims, humiliated and angry, were led to renounce him for a time, if not for ever.

He criticised music bar by bar, seeing it in its details rather than as a whole. . . . Was he right in his methods? I think he was not. A gifted student of composition does not need much in the way of theory. It is easy enough to teach him enough harmony, counterpoint and form principles to set him on his feet. Balakiref proceeded according to his knowledge and capacities. He himself had never studied theory methodically, nor suffered from his lack of theoretical knowledge. He could not see that others might stand in need of such knowledge. I, for one, knew very little about the principles of scoring; but I felt sure that he knew everything on earth. In many respects he was as ill-informed as I was, but he skilfully concealed the fact from us all. He had a very good working knowledge of timbres and orchestral combinations, and his advice on such matters was invaluable to me.

The group favoured Glinka, Schumann and Beethoven's last quartets. Beethoven's symphonies, except the ninth, were considered relatively insignificant; Mozart and Haydn, antiquated and naïve; Bach, frigid and mechanical. Balakiref used to compare Chopin to a " nervous society lady ". Liszt's music was little known, and dismissed as jerky and perverse.

As soon as these " Memoirs " had appeared, a storm of protests was aroused in Russia. The best critics agreed in describing them as "entirely subjective" (the words run through the notices like a *leitmotif*); and, while acknowledging Rimsky-Korsakof's good faith, they all pointed out that he had written most of his "Memoirs" in 1893 only—over thirty years after the events—and had been led, partly by the change which had taken place in his own outlook, and partly, perhaps, by a certain shortness of memory, to overlook certain facts, colour certain others, and greatly to underrate the value to himself and to others of Balakiref's teaching and influence. It was under Balakiref's guidance that Rimsky-Korsakof wrote many of his finest works, they all remarked. Later, when he developed a belief in a more conventional discipline and strove to acquire technique as taught in Western schools of music, his change of front, Karenin pointed out, "led him to over-emphasise and parade, not without complacency, his gift for dispassionate self-criticism and also for criticising others".

This is true not only of his retrospective indictment of Balakiref's tuition, but of his very description of the circle. Other evidence is available and should be weighed against his. Cui, for instance, in his recollections, recorded that "Liszt and Berlioz were objects of great admiration, Chopin and Glinka of positive worship". Karenin informs us that the damnatory views on Bach's music registered by Rimsky-Korsakof were merely those of a certain Nikolai Borozdin a friend of Balakiref and Stassof, and the composer of a few songs (he was, apparently, no end of a wag, and the inventor of most of the nicknames in use in the circle). Balakiref may have seen for a while only the worst side of Liszt before knowing his music well; indeed, in a letter of 1858 to Stassof, he declared that "it would not be very flattering for his vanity to be considered the first in a company consisting of Liszt, Kontsky, and Anton Rubinstein". Others since have fallen into a similar error at a much later time, and with no valid excuse. But he soon acknowledged Liszt's genius and became one of his keenest champions. His admiration for Chopin is vouched for by the whole story of his life, and Rimsky-Korsakof's statement to the contrary appears to rest only on a casual remark of Balakiref's to the effect that " the public seemed to enjoy Chopin's facile and ladylike music more than his finest works ".

When speaking of Balakiref's intolerance and despotism as a teacher, Rimsky-Korsakof failed to remember a letter which he had received from him as early as 1862—that is, at the very beginning of his musical work under his direction. Balakiref, after offering suggestions for the working out of the finale of Rimsky-Korsakof's symphony, wound up as follows:

> But I do not know how you hear it all in your mind. Maybe if you write it out according to your own feeling, ignoring my advice, I shall nevertheless find it excellent. As I shall be giving you lots of suggestions, once and for all I advise you not to follow my prescriptions blindly, and to trust your own self rather than anybody else. You may rely upon my capacity as a critic and my capacity to understand music; but you must never regard my opinions as absolutely binding—otherwise you would eventually find yourself as badly off as in a Conservatoire.

And to Stassof he wrote, in June, 1863:

> By the time Rimsky-Korsakof matures, I shall be old, and he will have no further use for me.

Certainly Balakiref did not always practise what he preached. Although aware of his tendency to despotism and of other composers' right to use their own judgment, he would now and then lay down the law according to the whim of the moment. And then it was for the sore-tried pupil to take things philosophically and obey, as best he could, conflicting instructions. Thus Borodin, when composing his second symphony.

I had decided, he told his wife, that the second theme should reappear in full and in G major, but he advised me to repeat but partly, and in E flat. When I played it to him in that form, he asked me why I had not repeated the theme in full, and not in the unsuitable key of E flat! When I got back from him the score of my first symphony, it was besprinkled with notes all suggesting the very things that I had done at first, but altered in accordance with his advice.

No doubt he was not infallible, and his position was very much the same as Glinka's and Dargomyjsky's had been: he had learned all he could, as he could, and this he handed over to others. He was indeed " one who, placing himself in the midst of his pupils, sought diligently and was sometimes rewarded by finding ". (Arnold Schönberg's definition of the ideal teacher.) He is hardly to be blamed for not having acquired knowledge not available at the time in Russia. On the contrary, he is greatly to be admired for having contrived to learn as much as he did. The notion of learning the processes of composition from the study of actual works, new in Balakiref's time, has made great headway since. It was, for instance, the basis of Vincent d'Indy's admirable course of composition. It is strange that no fairer tribute should have yet been paid to the far-reaching intuition which led him to direct his pupils (as we know he did) towards Liszt's music, from which many composers besides the Russians—from Wagner onwards—have learned so much, and Beethoven's last quartets, then greatly neglected, and from which to this day so much remains to be learned. It is unlikely, by the way, that he should have held any of Beethoven's symphonies cheap: one of the works he gave

Mussorgsky to study in 1857 was Beethoven's second symphony.

In 1928 a new edition of the " Memoirs " appeared in Russia. It contains a long and illuminating preface by Andrei Rimsky-Korsakof, the composer's son, which is a model of understanding, fairness, and tact. The writer points out that at the periods during which the " Memoirs " were written, Rimsky-Korsakof suffered from acute depression and went through a succession of inner crises; and that both his reminiscences and his critical pronouncements were thereby affected:

> Had he written them during more auspicious periods, he certainly would have dealt otherwise with the history of his youth and of his association with Balakiref. As it is, one may rightly aver that the way in which Balakiref is treated in the " Memoirs " " is not altogether undeserving of reproof ".

But so far only readers who know Russian, and can gain access to the essays on Balakiref and the " Memoirs " scattered in practically unprocurable periodicals, are in a position to adjust the scale. Outside Russia the " Memoirs ", translated long before 1928, passed practically unchallenged. In fairness to Rimsky-Korsakof as well as to Balakiref, it is imperative that critical prefaces containing the gist of Andrei Rimsky-Korsakof's preface to the 1928 edition, and also adequate references to what other well-informed and unprejudiced Russian critics had to say on the matter, be added to all translated editions of the " Memoirs ".

In 1862 another big opportunity came to Balakiref the teacher and propagandist. This was the year in which Anton Rubinstein founded the Petersburg Conservatoire, the first institution of its kind in Russia. Three years before he had founded the Russian Musical Society, and so exercised a well-nigh all-powerful influence—being also supported by the

Court and by official circles. He was a determined adversary of " national " music. In 1855 an article of his, published in Germany, had proclaimed:

> Passions are not national, therefore there can be no national opera. Attempts to write national music are doomed to spell failure . . . Glinka's were failures.

He also feared that the " barbaric " tendencies of the new Russian school would frustrate his efforts to sow the seeds of musical culture as he understood it. Balakiref, naturally, was eager to uphold the cause of Russian music, and also dreamt of leadership on a big scale. It occurred to him to submit to Gabriel Lomakin, the conductor of Count Sheremetief's choir, the idea of founding a school of music where instrumentalists and singers would be educated free of charge and would provide an orchestra and choir for performances of music old and new, Russian and foreign. A concert was given on March 11th/23rd, 1862, in aid of the scheme; the programme consisted of classical music only (from Haydn, Mozart, Méhul and Pergolesi to Mendelssohn), and the foundation of the school was officially announced a week later. Work began soon afterwards with Lomakin as the head of the school and Balakiref as his assistant. The first batches of pupils were government officials, university students, tradespeople, workmen, and women belonging to an equally great variety of classes. Eagerness to join was so great that Sheremetief once remarked " This is like people rushing to church on a Sunday." The Tsarevich Nicholas, and afterwards the Tsarevich Alexander, granted their patronage to the school. The first attempts to build up an orchestra and choir were not very successful; but soon a methodical programme of tuition, including solfeggio and theory courses, set things right. Between 1862 and 1867, a dozen concerts were given, Balakiref sharing the conducting with Lomakin. The programmes included, besides a variety of classical works, music by Berlioz (various overtures, excerpts from " Lelio ", " Romeo et Juliette ", the " Damnation of Faust ", and the " Te Deum "), Schumann and Liszt (" Les Préludes ", both piano concertos, the " Mephisto Waltz ", and the " Danse Macabre " [1866, first performance in Russia]). The principal Russian works performed, apart from a good many by Glinka and Dargomyjsky, were Rimsky-Korsakof's First Symphony and Russian Overture, Mussorgsky's " Rout of Sennacherib ", Cui's Overture " The Captive from the Caucasus " (the scoring was mainly, if not wholly, Balakiref's work) and a choral excerpt from his opera " Ratcliffe ", and Balakiref's Overture on Russian Themes, Second Overture on Russian Themes (of which more hereafter), " Lear Overture ", and " Song of the Golden Fish "— the last-named, like the Russian Overtures, a landmark in the history of Russian music and one of the loveliest songs in the Russian repertory.

In the summer of 1862 Balakiref took a well-earned holiday in the Caucasus, finding sources of inspiration in both the splendid scenery and the Eastern music which he was ever hearing around him. He loved that admirable region, and revisited it more than once. Three masterpieces, the " Song of Georgia ", " Tamara " and " Islamey ", reflect his impressions of its character and atmosphere. And it was going down the Volga, on his way there, that he conceived the notion of preparing a collection of Russian folk-songs—which appeared in 1866 and was the first one to give genuine texts, suitably harmonised for performance at concerts or in other urban circles.

Although many of the works which he began at that time remained unfinished or were not finished until much later, this period was one of comparatively great activity in composition. He outlined a second piano concerto, but put it aside (towards the end of his life, forty years later, he took it up again and succeeded in finishing two movements of it; it appeared posthumously, with a finale written by Liapunof in accordance with very definite instructions from him). He also began a symphony which he was to finish only in 1898. In 1863 he started planning an opera, " The Fire-Bird ", the subject of which was the famous Russian fairy-tale illustrated by Stravinsky in a ballet nearly half a century later. The fantastic atmosphere of the tale attracted him, and he would have found plenty of use in it for Eastern themes collected in the Caucasus, but it lacked dramatic action and human passion; so he eventually gave it up, and nothing remains of the scheme but the memory of a few very lovely episodes which his friends used to hear him play on the piano, but which were never written down. According to Rimsky-Korsakof (who says that by 1865-1866 Balakiref was no longer keen on carrying out the scheme), episodes evoking the lions that kept watch over the golden apples, and the flight of the fire-bird, were particularly beautiful.

His ever growing interest in all things Slavonic led him to study the folk-songs of various Slav countries. Visitors from these countries were expected in Petersburg, and a concert was to be given in their honour under his conductorship. For this occasion he started writing an overture on Czech themes (which, contrary to his usual practice, he finished speedily) and advised Rimsky-Korsakof to write a Serbian Fantasy, for which he gave him " lovely themes ". These works were first performed on May 11th, 1867. Later, Balakiref remodelled the overture which became the tone-poem " In Bohemia ", published in 1906. When this appeared he wrote:

> With all my heart I hope that this work of mine will help to foster a love for the tunes of the Czech people, and so develop, maybe, an increased interest in that lovable little nation, which is so energetically resisting the attempts

of the Germans to absorb it. When the Germans took Prague, soldiers were sent to persecute the people until they promised to embrace the Roman faith.

(Letter to M. D. Calvocoressi, March, 1906.)

An important branch of his activities during that period was in connexion with Glinka's music:

> I shall never forget, Liudmila Shestakova says in her recollections, his devotion to my brother's memory. Whenever I planned a move to make his works known, Balakiref would pounce upon my ideas and carry them out with energy, patience and love, regardless of the hard work this entailed, and his indifferent health. " A Life for the Tsar " having been performed at Prague, it occurred to me to try to get " Ruslan " performed there. I asked him to go to Prague that very spring. He went, but without results, because the Austro-Prussian War was raging. The war ended, I made the journey myself and paved the way for his second visit (and for performances, under his conductorship of both " Ruslan " and " A Life for the Tsar "). At the end of 1867 I began to arrange for the publication of the full score of " Ruslan ". Balakiref undertook all the musical work it entailed—the preparation, checking and thorough revision of the manuscripts. Later he invited Rimsky-Korsakof and Liadof to help; and to my intense joy, the score appeared at last in 1878.

The letters Balakiref wrote from Prague to Mrs. Shestakova state that he had to fight against relentless opposition on the part of Smetana, the composer, who was at that time the chief conductor at the National Theatre, and who, " belonging to the pro-Polish party ", wished to exclude everything Russian. " But I am a doughty champion ", he added " and shall take the initiative in attacking ". After the first performance of " Ruslan " (on February 4th) he was able to announce to her that it had been a great success. He did not tell her, however, that on that night, the full score which he was to have used had mysteriously vanished—whereupon he burnt his boats and conducted the whole opera by heart. " A Life for the Tsar " was given under stormy conditions, for political reasons; and in compliance with police orders, no second performance of it took place.

Shortly after his return to Petersburg, Balakiref found his hands very full. The Free School was in a difficult situation, doing well from the artistic point of view, but badly from the financial. Lomakin in his " Memoirs " acknowledges himself to have been inadequate in administrative matters; but on the other hand, the school had found no support on the part of the Press or public. In November, 1867, the Home Secretary decreed that a council should be appointed to direct the policy of the school. Lomakin resigned and Balakiref accepted the post of director in his stead—a generous but unwise decision. He was not built for administrative work; he lacked the needful tact and tolerance and could not endure the atmosphere of officialdom, with its narrow horizon, formalism, procrastination, and cross-currents. His real troubles, however, were not to come for another couple of years. In fact, he found himself, for a time, nearer complete success than at any other period of his career.

He threw himself into his new duties with boundless energy and hopefulness. That same year Anton Rubinstein resigned his post as conductor of the Russian Music Society, and Balakiref was invited to succeed him, thanks to the recommendation of several members of the board, and, according to Rimsky-Korsakof, of Rubinstein himself. He was also in great request with organisers of other orchestral concerts, and so found ever widening scope for his activities as a champion of contemporary music. One of his first concerns was to get Berlioz invited to conduct six concerts of the Russian Music Society—the result being, Kashkin remarks, that he himself remained overshadowed by his French colleague during his very first season in his new capacity. But, then and later, he conducted many most interesting programmes both at the Russian Music Society and at the Free School, of which important works by Beethoven, Liszt, Berlioz, Schumann, and Russian composers were the main items.

Both his policy and his conducting were acrimoniously criticised in the Press. It is almost impossible to decide whether the latter criticisms were justified, at least, in a measure. Testimonies differ widely. Tchaïkovsky described his conducting as first-rate; Borodin praised it; Rimsky-Korsakof is less enthusiastic; Kashkin says:

> He was a forceful personality in life, but not at the desk. He would devote great attention to details, but it seemed as though he did not see the works whole; nor was his beat decisive enough, as though he was not altogether convinced that the music should be taken thus rather than otherwise.

He was becoming increasingly unpopular in the most influential quarters. The Grand Duchess Helena Pavlovna, the president of the Russian Music Society (the " Euterpe " of Mussorgsky's " Peep-Show ") was hostile to him. Rimsky-Korsakof avers that at one time she wished him well, and even offered to provide him with funds for a musical journey abroad " to study the ways of people " (possibly a two-edged suggestion), but that he offended her by the form he gave to his refusal. He also offended most of the members of the board and the orchestral players, Germans whom he annoyed by persisting in using at rehearsals only the Russian language which they did not, or would not, understand. Tactless articles by Cui had further spoilt matters, and onslaughts in the Press became more and more violent. In the spring of 1869, Balakiref had to resign.

Great indignation ensued among his friends and admirers. Tchaïkovsky wrote a scathing article in a big Moscow daily, inviting all Russian musicians to raise their voices in protest. Nicholas Rubinstein, also from Moscow, took sides by offering to come to Petersburg then and there, specially to play at one of the Free School's concerts (he gave there, on November 30th/December 12th, the first performance of Balakiref's " Islamey ").

Nothing daunted, Balakiref concentrated upon his work at the Free School, and resumed his fight against the Russian Music Society, when the pro-German conservatoire party triumphed. He organised, early in the season, a series of subscription concerts with the hope of cutting the grass under their feet. The Grand Duchess and the Press became more actively hostile than ever. The public continued not to respond:

> The Grand Duchess, Borodin wrote to his wife in October 1869, is furious; and last night the hall was far from full. Things are very hard for poor Mily: he receives no salary from the school, and he has to support his two sisters. And yet, I never saw him so buoyant and cheerful, so energetic and active. He even seems stronger physically. There's a true artist for you! How he will manage to solve those financial difficulties I do not know.

Serof (who long since had become a bitter foe to Balakiref, Stassof and their group) described Balakiref's failure as logical and justified. Three whole numbers of Famyntsin's gazette " The Musical Season " (founded in 1869, with financial assistance from the Grand Duchess) were devoted, Stassof records, to " throwing mud at him ". The financial deficit speedily increased, and Balakiref spent as much of his own slender earnings as he could afford, and more, in attempts to keep things going. But both the school and himself were heading towards disaster.

In 1870, his financial difficulties compelled him to take the strangest and most unexpected of steps—he became a railway official, and started work at the goods station of the Warsaw line. An acquaintance of his, named Le Dantu (or Le Dentu) who was a high official in the service, had found the job for him. In this capacity, he earned a monthly salary of eighty rubles (a trifle over £8), which he eked out by giving as many lessons as he could find time for—a desperate remedy to an all but desperate situation. That very year he had gone to Nijni-Novgorod to give a concert, hoping to make some money. But his native city had forgotten him, or was not interested: the result was so disastrous that in after years he always referred to the venture as " his Sedan ".

Gradually he developed a kind of apathy, became indifferent to the things that had most interested him—to his own creative work, and to the doings of his friends.

He soon began to withdraw from the musical world at large, and to live in isolation. His frame of mind at the time may be surmised from the fact that years later, he told his friend Liapunof: " Had not accidental circumstances cut short my career as a railway official, I might have got promotion, and a salary sufficient to enable me to cease giving lessons and to concentrate upon composing." Even more pathetic are his remarks to another friend of his old age, the composer Constantine Tchernof:

> We live not as we should wish, but as God ordains. He did not grant His blessings to my public musical activities; and although I was considered the best conductor, and the programmes of my concerts won nothing but approval, I had to resign and take up work as a railway official. I fulfilled my duties as such scrupulously for three years or so, never grumbling at my fate.

It is possible that these words, written in 1907, represent his feeling at the time they refer to: for in the early 'seventies, he underwent a violent mental crisis, and from a sceptic and atheist became a strict and even bigoted believer. The inner history of this crisis is not known, and may never be. What is clear is that it coincided more or less with a nervous breakdown which caused the greatest of anxiety to his friends. In April, 1871, Stassof wrote to Rimsky-Korsakof:

> I met Balakiref at Liudmila Ivanovna's yesterday, and seeing him impressed me most painfully. Outwardly he is in all respects the same as ever. His voice, his carriage, his face, his way of speaking are the same, and yet everything is different, and no trace remains of his former self. He kept silent most of the time, I simply couldn't make him talk. I've known him fifteen years, and never saw him thus. I felt I was confronting a coffin, so to speak, and not the live, energetic, restless Balakiref we knew, so eager to peer into everything new, to question and press everybody he met. Now nothing interests him. From our dull, trying, disconnected conversation only one fact emerged: our dear Liudmila tried hard to rouse him and adjured him to finish " if only for her sake ", the work he has in hand.[1] But the only reply she got was that if he was to finish any work it would certainly be not that one, but another. We asked if he was referring to his Concerto. He replied no, and no other scrap of information could we get out of him.

Rimsky-Korsakof's " Memoirs " record that at that time, he came very much under the influence of a professional soothsayer.

> She was, he told me, a fairly young woman with big black eyes. Filippof's wife described her as " a witch pure

[1] Probably " Tamara."

and simple "—so Balakiref, who at that time did not believe in God, believed in the powers of darkness! Liudmila Shestakova assured me that she was in love with him. His object in consulting her was to learn the fate of his concerts and the issue of his fight against the hated Russian Music Society. In the mirror she used, he told me, he saw the Grand Duchess and Napravnik and the members of the board; and she revealed to him their thoughts and intentions. He used to speak of all this of his own accord, yet reluctantly, in hushed tones, bit by bit, not clearly or coherently.

In June, 1871, Borodin wrote to his wife:

> I fear that his mind is not quite in order. Maybe it is only his wounded vanity reacting. He is so despotic by nature that he insists upon his will being a law unto all, even in the most trifling matters. He cannot understand that people are entitled to use their own judgment. He cannot endure the faintest sign of opposition to his tastes or caprices. He must impose his yoke upon everybody and everything. At the same time, he is quite aware that we have reached the age of reason, stand firm on our own feet, and do not require help. And this, obviously, irks him. Often he has said to Liudmila Shestakova: "Why should I go and hear their music? They are all so mature now that they have no use for me." He, on the other hand, is the kind of man who has use only for immature people, with whom he can take the attitude of a nurse to the children in her care. He has become unpopular with most of the people around him. If he goes on chiding and offending them, he might well find himself in isolation; and this to him, would amount to moral death. We are all very sorry for him, but what can we do? Even Liudmila Ivanovna has lost all the influence she used to have on

him. Maybe his unexpected conversion to pietism has something to do with it: he may find it irksome to consort with people who are not in sympathy with his views on the matter. He may fear merciless and tactless onslaughts—like Vladimir Stassof's, who, whenever he meets him, starts forthwith " demonstrating " to him that it is all nonsense, that an intelligent man such as he should not, etc. Moreover, he is being very much blamed for his indifference to musical matters. Mussorgsky is offended by his unjust and presumptuous remarks on " Boris Godunof ", he had no business to utter them, tactlessly and sharply, in the presence of other people. Rimsky-Korsakof is pained by his behaviour, and resents his indifference to " The Maid of Pskof ". Cui deplores his lack of interest in the doings of our musical circle. The time is not far back when he was the first to evince interest in the slightest novelties, even in their embryonic stages. There is no denying that the breach between him and us is growing wider and wider. It is most painful, and painful chiefly on his own account, because he himself is the only one to suffer: the other members of the circle, just now, are living in greater harmony than ever before.

In August, Borodin wrote to Rimsky-Korsakof:

I have just heard an appalling rumour—that Mily has lost his reason. Remembering his encephalitis of yore, his ever-recurrent headaches, his nervous irritability and his recent behaviour, I am prepared to believe the news, although it does not come from an altogether trustworthy source.

There was no truth in the rumour. He seems to have carried on with his railway work and his lessons without intermission, and there are no records of his condition having called, at any time, for special treatment or precautions. But thorough disenchantment, mental weariness, nervous depression, and concentration upon his new religious ideals combined to make him seek refuge in seclusion. The grief caused in 1869 by the death of his father may have been a contributory cause.

He gave up conducting in 1872, after having found it impossible, for lack of funds, to give the last of five subscription concerts announced for that season.

He retained, nominally, his directorship of the moribund Free School until 1874, when he resigned and Rimsky-Korsakof was invited to take the school's affairs in hand. But from 1872 to 1876 he remained invisible to all, or almost. A very few communications passed between him and members of his circle. In 1874, for instance, he sent to Rimsky-Korsakof, who was about to make his debut as conductor, his good wishes; and a year or so later, he wrote to him again, rebuking him because his programmes were too exclusively classical. In March, 1876, he did not trouble to attend the rehearsal of a concert where his " King Lear " Overture was to be played, and whose programme consisted exclusively of works by the members of the " handful ", Glinka, and Dargomyjsky. And during all that period nobody seems to have known how he was faring, or what was going on in his mind.

His Moscow friends seem to have shown their concern in his welfare more actively than the members of his own circle in Petersburg. Maybe it was easier for them than for the latter, from whom he had deliberately cut himself off, discouraging all their attempts to get into touch with him. But he remained well-disposed towards the Moscow group. He had been in friendly relations with Tchaïkovsky since 1868 (he was the only person in the world who could persuade Tchaïkovsky to accept criticism and be guided by it to the extent of remodelling or even destroying a work—as happened in 1869 to the Overture " Fatum ", later reconstituted, after Tchaïkovsky's death, from preserved orchestral parts); and he had kept in more or less close touch with him, with Nicholas Rubinstein and other Muscovites. As soon as the news of his retirement and difficulties had come, Rubinstein, greatly upset, wrote to him, offering him a chair at the Moscow Conservatoire with a guaranteed salary of three thousand rubles per annum. He refused it, expressing, Kashkin records, deep appreciation of the offer, but saying that he felt he lacked the needful systematic theoretical knowledge, " having never had any guide but instinct and practice ". (This, by the way, proves again how inaccurate the oft-repeated assertions are that he considered theoretical studies not only superfluous, but nefarious; on the other hand, it seems true that he detested the cut-and-dried, narrow methods in honour in Conservatoires). Rubinstein and his colleagues were greatly distressed, but Balakiref, despite the most pressing entreaties, persisted in his refusal.

Shortly afterwards, Kashkin continues, being at Petersburg, I heard from Stassof that although Balakiref refused to see any of his former friends, I might, being a Muscovite, gain access to his house. And, indeed, I was admitted: but I found him terribly changed. His whole person exhaled an atmosphere of deep dejection; and although his behaviour to me was the same as before, there was a painful constraint in his manners—as if he feared to touch upon a personal topic or to provoke questions on my part. I left with the impression that I had been seeing a cruelly stricken man.

After losing (for reasons which he never explained) his railway job, he had to depend exclusively upon lessons. Eventually, however, he was given a post as inspector of the musical classes at two Petersburg schools. And little by little, he shook off his depression, and started composing and meeting his friends again. In June, 1876, Borodin wrote to his friend Liubov Karmalina:

> Thanks to Liudmila Shestakova's tireless exhortations, Balakiref has started work afresh on his unfinished " Tamara ". God grant!

And again a few months later:

> Do you know the joyous news? Our dear, our peerlessly-gifted Balakiref has resuscitated for music! He is the same as before; he again champions the keys of D flat major and B minor [N.B.: These had always been Balakiref's favourite keys], and fusses about the tiniest details of the music with which a while ago he would have nothing to do. He bombards Rimsky-Korsakof with letters about the Free School, helps to devise the programmes of its concerts, is at work on his " Tamara ", and has just finished an arrangement for piano duet of Berlioz's " Harold " commissioned by a Paris publisher. In short, he is alive and kicking. Nevertheless, he does not yet appear at concerts or at theatres, and does not call on any of his friends except Liudmila Shestakova and the Stassofs. Nobody knows what has brought about this sudden change.

To this very day no definite reply has been found to this question. The likeliest is that time and nature had done their work; that Balakiref had recovered his health, and that his active disposition and inborn love for the art he had temporarily forsaken were asserting themselves. The influence of Liudmila Shestakova, that most lovable woman, with whom nobody could get acquainted without learning to regard her as a dear and trusted friend, must have helped con-

siderably. In 1883, sending her, on her namesday, a copy of
" Tamara ", Balakiref wrote to her:

At last my dream of many years has become reality, thanks to your wishes and insistence.

But even the prospect of finishing " Tamara " must have been, to a man of his stamp, less attractive than that of starting work on preparing for publication the full score of Glinka's " Ruslan and Liudmila "—a task which he actually began in 1876.

Thus he entered the second part of his artistic career, during which he no longer suffered from financial straits, but must have felt, not without bitterness, that he was no longer a leader, no longer able even to take a very active part in the musical life around him. Indeed, he was to see the coming of many things that were to be alien, and unbearable to him. His artistic conviction remained as strong as ever, his musical loves unchanged; and to the end of his life he was to have the joy of doing useful work for the music and memory of Glinka, of Berlioz, of Chopin. In 1881, he finished his masterpiece " Tamara " (which, together with " Islamey ", was to win for him international fame among the musical élite if not with the public at large); and after that, not only finished most of the works begun years before, but composed many new ones, some of them very lovely.

Yet one cannot help feeling that something had gone away from him which could never be brought back. The sphere in which he moved became narrower and narrower. Maybe his religious faith contributed to create in him a kind of detachment, and even, according to reports, something of that hardness of mind which is not uncommon in those who incline to view all things human *sub specie æternitatis*. It will be seen, however, that he remained as eager as ever to serve and love and help, and continued to assert his fundamental generosity and kindness as well as his incurable intolerance.

He lost most of his old friends, partly through circumstances, partly through his own fault. He found new ones, whom he valued and who learned to love him as those of his youth had loved him, and so did not feel altogether isolated and forgotten. But the story of the last period of his life is one of peace not unperturbed by tragic undercurrents, of glowing energy and beliefs, over which hung, perceptible at times, a mist of disenchantment.

Referring to 1876, and after, Rimsky-Korsakof writes:

> I found him very much changed. In every room in his home were holy images with a little lamp burning in front of each. He was ever attending services. He had given up wearing furs, smoking, and eating meat. He liked to eat fish, provided it had not been knocked on the head. His love for all living creatures had become so great, that if a noxious insect found its way into his room, he would catch it with care and throw it out of the window, wishing it 'God speed'. At the end of his talks on religion with people he was fond of, he used to press them to cross themselves. And if they demurred, he would insist: "Please do! For my sake, just this once! Why not try?" He believed in the supernatural efficiency of this symbolic gesture—believed that it might help to turn the minds of irreligious people who made it.

Tchernof relates how, one day, he availed himself of the temporary absence of a friend of his, an unbeliever, to enter his flat and place in every room a holy image, with a lighted lamp in front of it, thereby throwing that friend into fury.

An interesting point, to which Andrei Rimsky-Korsakof was the first to call attention, is that his religious preoccupations, while deeply affecting his outlook and manner of living, had no influence whatever on his outlook on art, determined no new phase of his evolution as a composer. He took up work at the point at which he had left off, and carried on in an unchanged direction.

Very little is known of his life during the next four or five years. His duties as a school inspector, his lessons, his work on " Tamara " (which proceeded very slowly) and on Glinka's " Ruslan " and the task of taking stock of all that had happened during his years of seclusion, must have filled most of his time. In 1881, he received from Moscow a new offer which would have tempted a less scrupulous or more ambitious man, and might well have tempted even him, because it would have given him great influence of a practical order, and not only mere prestige. Nicholas Rubinstein died in Paris, and the post of Director and Conductor-in-chief of the Moscow Conservatoire became vacant. The Moscow section of the Russian Music Society offered it to Balakiref, sending a deputation to Petersburg to that effect. He declined, suggested that Rimsky-Korsakof be appointed (this, Kashkin says, could not be done for various reasons, one of which was that in Moscow, Rimsky-Korsakof was not considered good enough a conductor—a remark which is worth weighing in conjunction with Kashkin's own reservations, already quoted, on the subject of Balakiref's merits as conductor). All efforts to persuade him remained fruitless: he declared that the duties entailed would be too complex and too heavy for him.

In 1882 Rimsky-Korsakof resigned his directorship of the Free School of Music (where he had been doing excellent work) and Balakiref resumed the post he had relinquished six years before—reappearing at the conductor's desk on February 15th that same year.

It was at that time that he resumed his friendly relations with Tchaïkovsky, his influence on whom, at a previous period, has already been referred to. It should now be marked that it was far greater, and far more readily accepted, than would appear from Tchaïkovsky's often-quoted letter of 1877 to Mrs. von Meck; and that the disparaging way in which he spoke to her of Balakiref:

> He has done a lot of harm. For instance, he made Rimsky-Korsakof waste his years of youth, telling him that there was no need to study theory, etc.

is in sharp contrast not only with his article of 1869, praising his influence on Rimsky-Korsakof, but with the warm respect, affection and gratitude in which he expressed himself when writing to Balakiref. He welcomed, after a period of doubt, the notion which Balakiref gave him of composing a " Manfred " Symphony. A letter of 1884 from Balakiref contains a remarkable list of " auxiliary sources " for this symphony, and so throws light on Balakiref's practical methods of studying processes of composition from live examples:

Auxiliary Sources

For the first and last movements:

" Francesca da Rimini "	Tchaïkovsky
" Hamlet "	Liszt
Finale of " Harold "	Berlioz
Preludes: E minor	Chopin
E flat minor	Chopin
C sharp minor No. 25 (published separately).	Chopin

For the Larghetto:

Adagio of Symphonie Fantastique	Berlioz

For the Scherzo:

" La Reine Mab "	Berlioz
Scherzo (B minor) of third Symphony	Tchaïkovsky

Of course, he did not suggest that Tchaïkovsky should imitate any of the works he mentioned. Not long before he himself had completed (probably with the help of similar " auxiliary sources ") his strikingly original " Tamara " which, ever since he had begun to play to his friends and pupils portions of it in the making, played a big part in forming, after Glinka's " Ruslan ", the characteristic style of Russian national-oriental music. In 1869, when urging Tchaïkovsky to go ahead with " Romeo and Juliet " (also Balakiref's idea in the first place) he had written to him:

> Determine your plan. Do not worry about the actual musical ideas. When your imagination is fired by the plan, put your goloshes on, take your stick, go for a walk, fix your mind on your plan, and before you reach the Szetensky Boulevard, some kind of theme will surely occur to you.

Tchaïkovsky finished " Manfred " in 1885.
" Some of my friends like it ", he wrote to Balakiref the following year " others do not, and allege that it does not quite represent my true self. I, myself, feel that it is my best symphonic work ". All this is worth remembering, not only because it shows the real value of that letter to Mrs. von Meck which provided Balakiref's detractors with a weapon long before Rimsky-Korsakof's " Memoirs " had appeared, but because the story of the genesis of " Manfred " is that of a unique case: Tchaïkovsky, at that time was the only one of the older and well-known Russian composers to receive advice from Balakiref and be influenced by it.

In 1882 Balakiref also revised his Second Overture on Russian Themes and gave it the title " Russia ", under which it is known nowadays. He also toyed with the idea of continuing work on his piano concerto.

The first performance of " Tamara " took place on March

7th/19th, 1882, at the Free School Concert. The work was received with great enthusiasm. Balakiref inscribed it to Liszt, whom he had never met, but for whom his admiration was ever growing greater. In 1883, on the recommendation of his friend Filippof, he was appointed Director of the Court Chapel, and so was able to give up, at last, all private lessons. In this new capacity, he worked enthusiastically and to excellent purpose, greatly extending the scope of both technical and practical classes (he entrusted the classes for instrumentalists and choir-masters to Rimsky-Korsakof), introducing valuable reforms in the matter of the younger pupils' and choir-boys' comfort and hygiene, enriching the Chapel's repertory with old traditional church chants in suitable choral arrangements devised by himself and his staff. All this left him practically no time for composing.

In 1884, Liapunof, twenty-five years old, came to Petersburg after having completed his curriculum at the Moscow Conservatoire. He was to be the first of the new friends who formed a circle around Balakiref—a very different one from the " mighty handful ": the other members were to be composers whose names are little known nowadays. One of them, Constantine Tchernof, better known as a critic, gave in his recollections of Balakiref a circumstantial description of the circle and its atmosphere. The reunions took place on Tuesday evenings. Balakiref was a kindly host, whose conception of hospitality was " Eastern in its thoroughness and wholeheartedness ", but also, it would appear, a bit fussy and trying at times. He did not like to mix his guests. The Tuesdays were for musicians only, and no ladies were admitted. Even his own niece, when she called on him of a Tuesday, had to leave before 8 p.m., when the guests were expected. Nor did he like his friends to call at odd times, unless specially invited. Once, Tchernof called on him unexpectedly, for some urgent reason, and found him with a roomful of lady guests, merrily chatting. Balakiref greeted him, introduced him, and this formality duly accomplished, said to him quite audibly: " Of course, you know that I am always delighted to see you on Tuesday nights, when you will always find me at your disposal."

One of the guests of later years was Balakiref's new publisher, Julius Heinrich Zimmermann, of whom he grew very fond, and who played no small part in encouraging him to compose steadily towards the end of his life.

God has blessed us, Balakiref wrote to Tchernof, with a publisher who greatly appreciates us: in this respect, we are far more fortunate than most of our competitors.

Every Tuesday music was played and discussed—mainly, but not exclusively, Balakiref's, Liapunof's and that of the younger members. All in all, the circle was a narrow one, the atmosphere not very stimulating; but it was one in which Balakiref felt happy, and could forget his disappointments, his fits of ill-humour, and also from time to time, actual affronts which he had every reason to resent bitterly.

In 1885, Mitrofan Belaief, the millionaire timber merchant, founded a publishing firm and instituted symphony concerts, both for the exclusive benefit of Russian composers. Rimsky-Korsakof, Liadof, Glazunof and others all mustered around him. Balakiref did not. The story of his early relations with Belaief is not quite clear. He began by asking him to support the Free School, and suggested that he should acquire the business of the publisher, Stellovsky, which was on the market at the time, and included most of Glinka's and Dargomyjsky's works. Belaief flatly refused to do either. Then Balakiref was antagonistic to the idea of all-Russian symphony concerts. He considered, very sensibly, that mixed programmes, including among other things some of the many great modern works from other countries, which the Russian public had no opportunity to hear, would prove more attractive, and therefore more useful for the special purpose of making new Russian works known to a wide circle of listeners. Belaief rejected this piece of advice, too. He also offended Balakiref deeply by refusing to purchase the publishing rights of "Russia", although he had considered this work not unworthy of receiving one of the prizes he had founded, anonymously, for Russian composers. Thereafter Balakiref would have nothing to do with him, and urged other people (Glazunof among others) to do the same. But, unavoidably, Belaief's circle grew, and Balakiref kept more and more aloof from its members.

One instance of almost incredible rudeness to him is recorded by Rimsky-Korsakof. In 1884, he had conducted, at Moscow and elsewhere, concerts to collect funds for a monument to Glinka at Smolensk. When the monument was unveiled, in May 1885, he conducted two concerts in that city. At one of the rehearsals, Sergei Taneief, the composer, so far forgot himself as to shout: " Mily Alexeievitch, we are dissatisfied with you!"

But as often as not, it was Balakiref himself who was the offender. In 1889 he created a sensation by refusing to attend the festivities on the occasion of Anton Rubinstein's jubilee, declaring, in a letter of protest to the organisers, that Rubinstein had done nothing but harm to Russian music.

In 1890 he broke with Rimsky-Korsakof, for some apparently quite trivial reason, disclosed only in the unpublished portion of his correspondence with him.

On the day of my jubilee (the twenty-fifth anniversary of his debut as composer), Rimsky-Korsakof relates, I was congratulated by deputations from the Conservatoire, headed by Rubinstein, and the Imperial Chapel, headed by Balakiref. By way of acknowledgement, I gave a dinner at my house. Balakiref refused my invitation in cutting, frigid terms. From that moment on, our relations became more and more distant, until they ceased altogether.

Early in the 'nineties, Balakiref began to arrange for a statue of Chopin to be erected in his native townlet, Jelazova Vola, near Warsaw. He organised festivities on the occasion of the unveiling in 1894, and took part, as a pianist, in concerts both at Jelazova Vola and Warsaw. It is characteristic of him that during his old age, he should have turned with renewed eagerness to commemorations of this kind—his very last public activities were to be in conjunction with the centenary of Chopin's birth, in 1910—and also devoted much time and labour to trying to keep alive, by performing their music or preparing it for publication, the memory of many of his friends of yore—especially Laskovsky, Gussakovsky, Henselt, Vielgorsky and Lvof.

This does not mean that he lived altogether in the past. The letters which various correspondents (including the author of this chapter) received from him during his last years on earth show him eager enough to keep in touch with current events and with new music. Often, it is true, this music disappointed him. It did not correspond to his conception of musical art. This is not in the least surprising. He, and (except for Mussorgsky) the other Russian composers whose whole-hearted admiration had gone straight to innovators such as Chopin, Berlioz, Schumann and Liszt, and whose music was to open so many thrillingly new vistas to Western musicians and listeners (Balakiref's exercised a great influence on Debussy's and Ravel's) were not, and had no desire to be, revolutionists. To be described as such would have shocked them greatly. Even Glinka, who showed the way with " Ruslan ", did not aim at being a reformer: he simply wished to compose music " which would make his beloved fellow-countrymen feel quite at home ". Balakiref rightly considered that Berlioz and Liszt were as much in line with tradition as, for instance, Beethoven in those last quartets of his whose significance Balakiref realised so well at a time when many people doubted it. But, as years flew by, music in its course outpaced him, as it did most of his Russian contemporaries. Rimsky-Korsakof, too, who prided himself on belonging to a circle more progressive than Balakiref's (the Belaief circle), was towards the end of his life, to speak with bitterness of the " unintelligible developments " exemplified in the music of Strauss, d'Indy and Debussy. Even if it were not quite usual for composers—who in the very nature of things should be self-centred artistically, and not too adaptable—not to see the merits of music differing in spirit from their own, no undue importance should be ascribed to points such as these. The fact that Balakiref, after having been the leader of the progressive party, came to be regarded as a leader of reaction, is not to be considered as a characteristic instance of the strange contradictions that were part and parcel of his nature: such has been the lot of many a reformer endowed with a perfectly consistent personality.

In 1895 Balakiref retired on a pension, and so was able at last to devote the whole of his energies to composing. He had been longing to do so, being weary of duties that were administrative rather than musical—but not before being able to hand over to Rimsky-Korsakof, the Chapel " perfectly organised, with all its duties, rights and prerogatives duly determined ".

In April, 1898, his first symphony was performed at a Free School concert, under his conductorship. This was to be his last appearance as a conductor. The symphony was received with enthusiasm. Wreaths of laurel and tributes of all kind —including a marble sculpture of Liszt's hand—poured upon him. He was in those days, Tchernof says, very efficient as a conductor, and very popular, exercising a magnetic influence over audiences. And Rimsky-Korsakof says that whenever the question arose of finding financial support for the Free School, his powers of persuasion proved unfailing, and contributions poured in " not for the sake of the school or of musical art, but just for the sake of Balakiref, to whom alone the school owed the possibility to carry on ". But after his complete retirement, his popularity soon waned, as will presently appear.

The symphony also had one or two performances abroad; but neither it nor any of his later works ever became popular.

Naturally, he felt this neglect deeply, and used to speak with bitterness of Russian critics and the Russian public. On the other hand, he found compensation in the fact that in other countries, a few critics and musicians—Bourgault-Ducoudray, Paul Dukas, Debussy, and Ravel in France and Mrs. Newmarch in England, among others—loved and praised his music, and that now and then a work of his was performed abroad.

In 1902 or thereabouts, a few of his French admirers conceived the notion of inviting him to conduct in Paris concerts of Berlioz's works on the occasion of Berlioz's centenary (December, 1903). He declined, on the plea that he feared the long journey would prove too much for him and that in Paris he might not be able to get the fare (especially the fish, he mentioned) to which he was accustomed. But the invitation—probably the only one he ever received from abroad—must have touched him doubly, because tributes to composers he admired meant more to him than any tribute to himself (to the present writer, who was engaged in arranging a performance of his second symphony in Paris, he once wrote: " I wish you would leave that for later and try to get Liapunof's symphony performed first "). The extent of his devotions to the cause of Berlioz may be gauged by the following story. When Weingartner and Charles Malherbe were preparing a complete edition of Berlioz's works, they applied to Balakiref for help with reference to the " Te Deum ". Balakiref was greatly upset when he found out that in the new edition, some instruments prescribed by Berlioz, but no longer in common use, were to be replaced by their current equivalents. He wrote to Malherbe that " his duty as a Frenchman was to ensure that the works of France's one and only composer of genius should appear in their genuine form " and wound up with the offer to forgo, if this was done, the fee agreed upon for his services.

A good part of his time during the same period was devoted to preparing a new edition of Glinka's works, including the full scores of both operas. And he took the lion's share in organising festivities to commemorate the centenary of Glinka's birth. Circumstances delayed the celebration, which took place in 1906 instead of 1904.

That same year, 1906, should have been marked by the celebration of the fiftieth anniversary of Balakiref's debut in Petersburg as a pianist and composer. Ceremonies of this kind were an invariable custom in Russia, and took place as a matter of course on the occasion of the twenty-fifth, thirty-fifth anniversary and so on of the débuts of even quite minor composers or other people whose activities were connected with music. Quinquagenaries especially were never neglected. That Balakiref's should have remained overlooked even by his former pupils and all the people who, at some time or other, had been indebted to him—only one Russian newspaper in Moscow, and Findeisen's " Musical Gazette " in Petersburg, belatedly calling attention to the fact—is truly incredible. Maybe he found solace in organising the " Glinka " music classes to the foundation of which in the city's elementary schools the funds left over from grants and subscriptions for the centenary celebrations were applied by the Tsar's order. His interest in these classes was so great that a few months before his death, being already very ill and unable to walk much, he had himself carried up to a schoolroom in which he carried out, for the last time, his duties as president of the examination board.

A concert of his works was announced for February 18th/March 3rd, 1909, but could not take place owing to the fact that practically no tickets had been sold in advance, and that long before the appointed date, it had become obvious that the hall would remain nearly empty. This final proof of the general indifference to Balakiref was not mentioned in the Russian Press, but Findeisen recorded it in an obituary notice written for a French periodical.

Ever since the late 'nineties, his health had been steadily deteriorating. He suffered from a disease of the heart. In 1908 he had the energy to finish his second symphony; and a little later he completed two movements of the piano concerto published posthumously with a finale set in order by Liapunof. Most of the year 1909 was devoted to plans and steps—his last public activities—in view of the centenary of Chopin's birth, for the celebration of which he arranged into an orchestral suite four of Chopin's pieces (Etude-Mazurka-Intermezzo-Scherzo). He also remodelled the orchestration of Chopin's E minor Concerto. He grew weaker and weaker. His doctor foretold that he would barely last the summer. He lived nearly another year, however, and had the joy of hearing of the success of the Chopin centenary celebrations, at which Liapunof conducted his contributions. But by the end of 1909 he had grown so weak that he had to keep to his room and none but his most intimate friends were allowed to see him. On May 16th/29th, 1910, at seven o'clock in the morning, he died painlessly.

He was buried in the Alexander Nevsky cemetery, close by the tombs of Glinka, Mussorgsky, Borodin and Stassof. According to his wish, there were no speeches at the funeral: " let the voice of the Church be the last one heard ", he had told Liapunof. A couple of years later a monument was erected over his grave. Liapunof and other faithful friends of his, it was said, had great trouble in collecting the necessary funds, which a special concert given by the Free Musical School, in whose foundations and work he had played so great a part, had failed to provide.

Since then his music has made little headway. Not only most of his orchestral works, but even the finest of his songs remain neglected, as well as the many piano pieces (beginning with a delightful piano sonata which appeared in 1905) which he composed late in life. Not all of these, it is true, represent him at his greatest. It is in " Tamara ", in " Russia ", in " Islamey ", in a few of the songs, and to some extent, in the symphonies that the essential Balakiref stands revealed. He has given us only a handful of first-rate works —not more than Borodin: but these are enough to testify to the rare quality of his imagination. His creative genius had its limitations, it is true. It lacked the capacity for renovations that usually goes with genius, but it was true genius none the less. That wonderful intuitive sense of music which had struck Rimsky-Korsakof in the 'sixties, enabled him to soar high and also to create a discipline of his own. The formal excellence of " Tamara ", " Russia ", or " Islamey ", can no more be explained in words than their deep poetic significance, and seems to have been achieved in defiance of all conventions. It was in no spirit of calculated nationalism that he brought to maturity the Russian (and Russian-Oriental) idiom which had begun to take form in Glinka's music: this idiom was the natural and necessary vehicle of his thinking. And so the few works which represent him at his best justify the assertion that Balakiref the composer stands as high as Balakiref the educator and leader.

M. D. C.

CUI
by Repin

CÉSAR CUI

César Cui is usually mentioned as the leader, jointly with Balakiref, of the Russian nationalist group or " mighty handful "(see Balakiref chapter, pp. 110-12). He earned this reputation owing to a variety of circumstances. He was the first of the composers who mustered around Balakiref; he enjoyed the prestige of having received lessons in theory from the famous Polish composer Moniuszko, of being, from 1864 onwards, the musical critic of a big Petersburg daily, and of having had an opera performed as early as 1869; he had appointed himself spokesman of the group, and by his articles and books published in Russia and elsewhere, he helped to draw attention to his comrades' music—and also to stimulate hostility against it by the caustic, tactless tone of his writings. He was born at Vilna on January 6th/18th, 1835, the son of a French officer who had remained in Poland after the Napoleonic wars, married a Lithuanian, and become a teacher of French at the Vilna high school; so that unless his mother was partly of Russian descent (a point on which no information has come forth so far), no single drop of Russian blood flowed in his veins. He showed an early disposition for music, received his first piano lessons from his elder sister and continued with two teachers, " neither of them capable instructors ", he says in his " Recollections ". The second, however, Dist by name, " was a fairly good violinist, and used to play with him de Bériot's fantasias on opera themes, which contributed to develop his sense of rhythm and musicianship ". Chopin's music—and especially the Mazurkas—was the first to fascinate him. Then his father presented him with the vocal scores of a couple of Italian operas, and these, too, aroused his enthusiasm (later he was to be a relentless foe of Italian opera). At fourteen he began composing Mazurkas and Nocturnes " in naïve imitation of Chopin ", songs, and other things. Dist found these attempts worthy of being shown to Moniuszko, who was interested and offered to give the boy free lessons in theory, harmony and counterpoint.

This tuition continued for seven months (Cui's " Recollections " do not confirm in the least the statement in Mrs. Rosa Newmarch's book " Russian Opera " that the lessons were neither systematic nor regular). But César, in 1851, was sent to Petersburg to enter the school for military engineers, and for four years he made little progress in music. In 1855 he received his commission and was transferred to the special school for officers to continue his studies. That was the time when he became acquainted with Dargomyjsky, Balakiref and Stassof, and so really entered the world of music. With the advent of Mussorgsky, Rimsky-Korsakof and Borodin, the little group of Balakiref's disciples was formed.

" Balakiref ", Rimsky-Korsakof says in his " Memoirs ", " regarded Cui as having a certain gift for opera, and left him a comparatively free hand. But there was no prospect of his ever becoming good at scoring; and so Balakiref was willing to score his compositions for him—e.g. the Overture of the opera ' The Captive in the Caucasus '. Cui also wrote a symphonic allegro under Balakiref's strict supervision. He and Mussorgsky badly needed all the help that Balakiref could give them. Both Balakiref and Cui, however, had a high opinion of their own value. They were the mature and great ones, whereas Borodin, Mussorgsky and I were the immature and small. Their views were commands and had to be obeyed. But they had not the slightest use for *our* views: and so our relations with them were the relations between pupils and teachers ".

In 1858 three songs by Cui were published, and he started

composing the opera in two acts " The Captive in the Caucasus ", on a libretto supplied by his comrade Victor Krylof (this was remodelled later and performed in 1881). That same year he married Malvina Bamberg, a singer and a pupil of Dargomyjsky. In 1859 a Scherzo of his was performed at a concert of the Russian Music Society; and he composed a light opera " The Mandarin's Son " (also on a libretto by Krylof), specially, he says, for his wife. This was privately performed at the Bambergs' house.

Then he started work on a more ambitious opera, " William Ratcliffe ", after Heine's tragedy of the same name. This, begun in 1861, was not finished until 1868. He had but little time to devote to composing. To eke out his slender income he had opened a small preparatory school for candidates to the School of Engineers, and was taking most of the classes himself—a heavy addition to his other professional duties. On February 14th, 1869, " William Ratcliffe " was performed at the Imperial Opera, with a splendid cast comprising Melnikof, Platonova and Leonova in the principal parts. It had no success with the public, the Press notices were condemnatory, and it was withdrawn after seven performances (it was to be performed at Moscow in 1900, and favourably received).

" The critics ", Cui says in his " Recollections ", " vented in their attitude towards ' Ratcliffe ' their resentment of my Press campaigns against routine in general and Italian opera in particular. They went to the extent of hissing me when I stood up from my seat to bow to the audience. But there was another reason for the failure. I had attempted to embody in ' Ratcliffe ' our ideals of opera, and it was the first gun in our fight for them (' The Stone Guest ', ' The Maid of Pskof ', and ' Boris Godunof ' were performed later). It gave the audiences, instead of the usual arias, narratives in free form; it gave them choruses with a certain amount of symphonic working out; and it gave them a *leitmotif* for

'Ratcliffe' himself, which was developed and modified in accordance with changes of situation and mood—in those days hardly anything was known of Wagnerian tendencies".

By that time he had been four years the musical critic of a big daily paper, and had indulged in violent denunciation against not only Italian opera, but Rubinstein and the reactionary Russian party, and also (the point is worth noting with reference to the remark about Wagnerian methods just quoted) against Wagner. His notice of "Lohengrin", on the occasion of the first Petersburg performance (October, 1868), was derisive in tone. In 1874 he was to blame Mussorgsky severely for "having resorted to so cheap a device as the *leitmotif*".

As will presently be shown, these ideas, in the main, were current at the time in Balakiref's circle; but Cui deluded himself as to the extent to which "Ratcliffe" embodied the group's ideals of opera.

During these years and after he made steady progress in his military career. He became a recognised authority on fortification, was given professorships at the Artillery and Engineering Academies, wrote various technical manuals, and rose to the rank of Lieutenant-General of Engineers. Despite those manifold activities he found time to compose steadily. In the early 'seventies he wrote a number of fine songs and a four-act opera, "Angelo", on a libretto derived from a drama by Victor Hugo. This was given at Petersburg in 1876, successfully enough, and later at Moscow. He took part in the composition of the "collective" opera "Mlada" (see chapters on Mussorgsky and Borodin). His preference for non-Russian subjects is evinced in the list of his other operas: "The Saracen", after Alexandre Dumas (Petersburg, 1889); "Le Flibustier", on a French libretto by Jean Richepin (Paris, 1894); and "Mademoiselle Fifi", after Maupassant (unpublished and never performed). But in 1900 he set to music Pushkin's dramatic scene "A Feast in Time of Plague" (one act; Moscow, 1902). And the subject of his last opera, "The Captain's Daughter", was also taken from Pushkin and thoroughly Russian.

His output comprises over two hundred songs, many of them beautiful (a number of them were composed on French texts, a few on Polish texts, and three on German texts), four orchestral suites, and a good many instrumental pieces of small or moderate compass. He reached the age of eighty-three, outliving all the other members of the group and remaining, even in his advanced years, remarkably alert, active, and youthful-looking. He was eighty when he undertook to finish Mussorgsky's opera "Sorochintsi Fair", which was performed at Petersburg, in his arrangement, in 1917.

Perusing his book "La Musique en Russie" (written in French and published in Paris in 1880) it is easy to determine his actual relation to the national Russian school, whose faith and ideals he professed to proclaim and explain. He describes the members of that group as reformers of opera generally rather than as intent on evoking Russian history, legend, and on using a characteristically Russian musical idiom. It is true that he begins with a few remarks on the advantages to be derived from the use of the modes, rhythms, and colours of folk-music, and on the excellence (according to him) of the prosody of Russian folk-songs. He was mainly interested in prosody, declamation, realism in dramatic expression and characterisation.

"After Beethoven, Schumann, Liszt and Berlioz", he wrote, "it is reasonable to admit that symphonic art has reached perfection, and that no means could be new enough to carry it farther and give it greater freedom. Opera, on the contrary, is still in a very imperfect, transitional state. The ideal of the new Russian school is: pregnant, specific characterisation not only of each character, but also of the period and atmosphere of the drama and of every single point in it. All these principles are very similar to Wagner's, but Wagner's way of carrying them out is in many respects deplorable ".

And his conclusions are that the masterpiece of the Russian school is Dargomyjsky's " Stone Guest ", and that the Russian school has stirred artistic problems of vital interest and " alone reacted against the encroachments of a perilous musical lethargy ". All this may, more or less, accord with the views of the group in the 'sixties and 'seventies. No doubt most of its members, including Vladimir Stassof, talked a certain amount of hot air on opera reform, and on other topics too. Most of them were hostile to Wagner's music. The leader of the opposition to him seems to have been Stassof, who in 1868 wrote to Berlioz:

> Tonight " Lohengrin " will be played for the first time at the Petersburg Opera. Possibly part of the audience will like this brutal, heavy-handed music. But *we all* do not believe that Wagner is a prophet: we hold that he marks a retrogression from Weber's music. We find in him a lack of taste and measure, vulgarity, noisy scoring, no gift for the recitative, horrible modulations.

But the spirit which led to Cui to find fault with Rimsky-Korsakof's " Maid of Pskof " for being " symphonic rather than dramatic, poor in melody, and lacking in warmth and vitality "; with Borodin's symphonies for " the restlessly changing rhythms and time-signatures in them—a process which can be excellent in vocal music but in symphonic music makes for obscurity "; to be so horrified with the greater part of " Boris Godunof " that his notice of it after its first performance amounted to a stab in Mussorgsky's back; and, generally speaking, to raise almost as many objections against the works of his comrades-in-arms (except Dargomyjsky's and Balakiref's) as against those of his pet aversions, Tchaïkovsky and Rubinstein—that spirit was entirely Cui's own.

This narrowness of outlook is no less manifest in his music, which betrays most of the time the weakness of both his technique and his imagination. The lack of vernacular elements in his musical idiom is, of course, of no importance whatever. It has nothing to do with his almost total lack of originality (all his critics in turn have pointed out how very reminiscent his style is of Auber's and Schumann's) and of that power to characterise which he himself regarded as the first requisite for an opera composer. Even in the matter of prosody, he did not always succeed in practising what he preached—as more than one of the critics he had irritated was able to show in notices of his operas. Now and then, it is true—and especially in the early days—he evinced a measure of originality in thematic inventions, and so exercised a slight, and very occasional, influence. Rimsky-Korsakof mentions a few instances in his " Memoirs ". But all this amounts to very little indeed. And the crowning irony is that nowadays he should be found worth remembering, not for his activities as a champion of the group, not for the example he set in his works on reformative lines, but for his works on a small and unambitious scale—songs and piano pieces which show that his lack of fundamental, far-reaching originality was compensated, in a measure, by a genuine sense of grace and delicacy in lyrical melody.

To sum up: the legend of his leadership does not resist investigation. Modern Russian criticism has adopted the view that Stassof rather than Cui, should be regarded as the leader, after Balakiref, of the group; and history, no doubt, will confirm it. Meanwhile it is becoming clearer every day that Cui has fallen into his right place—that of a minor poet, less original and imaginative than Liadof, less spontaneous and warmhearted than Gretchaninof, less closely related to the Russian school than either of them, but still distinguished in his own way.

Did he, when in his late maturity he concentrated almost

exclusively upon composing brief lyrical works, realise that such was to be his ultimate fate? It is difficult to tell. He lived to the ripe old age of eighty-three, and in his seventies remained surprisingly youthful-looking and alert. There is little evidence as to his views and feelings at that time, when, the only survivor of the group, he was able to witness the fortune of all the music its members had turned out, and compare it with the fortune of his own big works. In all likelihood he took things philosophically. He certainly did not seem embittered; but he must have remained as uncompromising as ever. As late as 1911 he took up his pen to perpetrate a parody of Debussy's music which he entitled " L'après-midi d'un faune qui lit son journal ". And at the age of eighty he undertook the task of completing Mussorgsky's " The Sorochintsi Fair ", which was performed in his arrangement at Petrograd in October, 1917, but later superseded by N. Tcherepnin's version. He died at Petrograd on March 1st/14th, 1918. The event passed practically unnoticed in the turmoil and anxieties of the moment. In recent years nobody, whether in Russia or elsewhere, has attempted a reassessment of his music.

M. D. C.

BORODIN
by Repin

ALEXANDER BORODIN

ALEXANDER Borodin was born at Petersburg on October 31st/ November 12th, 1833. Misinformation as to this date arose forty years later in the following curious circumstances. On October 31st/November 12th, 1873, he wrote to his wife " today is my fortieth birthday ". But that same day an old servant of his mother, Catherine Beltzman by name, came to him with what she called a " birthday surprise ": to wit, the information that he was thirty-nine years old and not forty. Borodin, delighted, accepted the news without ever troubling to verify it; and thus it came to pass that on his tombstone and until 1933, in all the literature referring to him the year of his birth was given as 1834. Investigations carried out by Mr. Serge Dianin, the son of his pupil, friend and executor, Alexander Dianin, brought the truth to light again.

This little story is thoroughly characteristic of one aspect of Borodin, the man—genial, easy-going, always ready to believe the best, and never inclined to ascribe undue importance to unessentials. But there is a strong contrast between this particular aspect (very much emphasised by Rimsky-Korsakof in his " Memoirs ") and the earnestness and purposefulness of Borodin the worker, scientist, and composer, who left his mark on the social and scientific fields as well as in the musical, and whose cheerful, serene, robust philosophy is reflected, not only in his attitude to life and his activities, but in his correspondence—one of the most valuable sources of information for investigators wishful to discover the truth about Russian musical life in his time.

He was the illegitimate son of Prince Luke Ghedeanof, a descendant of the old Kings of Imeretia in the Caucasus (the name Ghedeanof is the Russian form of the Georgian, Ghedeanishvili), and Eudoxia Kleineke (*née* Antonova; she belonged to the middle classes; Kleineke, her second husband, was an army doctor). He was registered, for propriety's sake, as the son of one of his father's serfs, Porphyri Borodin. Prince Ghedeanof, in 1833, was sixty-one years of age, Eudoxia Kleineke twenty-four. He died in 1840, and the care of the child was left to her alone. She was an intelligent and cultured woman, in easy circumstances, and brought him up with loving solicitude. His first years were spent under feminine influences only: that of his mother, of his governess, and of a cousin, Mary, who was his first playmate. He was delicate in health (at a time it was feared that he might become consumptive), gentle, very sensitive, dreamy in disposition, but an eager and quick learner. He soon became proficient in English, French and German, and later, in Italian. He showed a keen interest in music and in the natural sciences. He received his first musical impressions from concerts given by military bands. He used to scrape acquaintance with the players, examine the instruments and try to find out how these were played. At the age of nine he "fell in love" with a grown-up woman, Helen by name (who was, Stassof records, as full-sized as he was frail), and composed a polka which he inscribed to her. According to Findeisen, this little piece, preserved in manuscript, is far more striking for its originality than for its childishness; certain features in it bring Glinka's music to the mind, and others foreshadow the mature Borodin.

After this feat a music-teacher was found for him—a member of a military band, who taught him the flute. A little later he and one of his playmates, Michael Shchiglef, took piano lessons with a certain Porman, and eagerly started discovering Haydn, Beethoven and Mendelssohn, whose works they played in arrangements for piano duet. They started learning without help, to play, Shchiglef the violin, and Borodin the 'cello, in order to play chamber-music (later Borodin took lessons with a 'cellist named Shleiko). They attended orchestral concerts at Pavlovsk, Karl Schubert's symphony concerts at the Petersburg University and so greatly increased their musical knowledge. In 1847 Borodin, without having been taught even the rudiments of composition, turned out a concerto for flute and piano, and a trio for two violins and 'cello on a theme from Meyerbeer's " Robert le Diable " (neither of these has been preserved).

At the same time he was eagerly studying chemistry; he rigged up a laboratory in his own room and spent much time carrying out experiments and manufacturing fireworks. Other hobbies of his were modelling, galvanoplasty and painting (with pigments manufactured by himself). His interest in the natural sciences grew steadily. In 1850 he matriculated at the Academy of Medicine and Surgery. He made steady progress in all branches but devoted particular attention to botany and chemistry, ultimately specialising in the latter branch, partly under the influence of his master, the admirable chemist Zinin. It is characteristic of him that simultaneously he should have devoted ever-increasing energy to musical study and practice. " Mister Borodin ", Zinin used to say, " please don't think so much of ballads, when here I am, believing in your future and trying to train you to succeed me. You can't hunt two hares at the same time ". But Borodin did hunt both hares successfully. His concern at the moment was not with " ballads ", but with studying the fugue—again a significant trait, for we now see that of all the nineteenth-century Russian composers, he was the only one endowed with an inborn sense of polyphony (on which more hereafter)—and with chamber music. He, Shchiglef, and a new friend, Vassilief, who played the violin, clubbed together to secure the services of a viola player, and thus constituted a string quartet. In order to attend practice meetings Borodin had to trudge nearly seven miles with his 'cello, not being able to afford cab fares. Neither fatigue nor bad weather ever discouraged him. And that this enthusiasm was general is proved by the story which Braudo records, that on one occasion the players kept on practising for twenty-four hours on end.

Vassilief had a brother who sang. Another of Borodin's friends, Gavrushkevich, used to give chamber concerts at his home. So the young student had plenty of opportunities of getting acquainted with a variety of music. He also composed a few songs and instrumental works (unpublished) and outlined another few (in most of these, both Braudo and Findeisen see affinities with Glinka, and forecasts of his own mature style). And, year after year, he shone among his fellow-students at the Academy, and passed all examinations with flying colours. In 1856 he was appointed assistant to the professor of pathology and therapeutics. The next year he was sent to attend a medical congress at Brussels—the city where he was to score his first successes outside Russia as a composer. Soon afterwards he presented to the Academy his thesis on " The analogies between arsenious acid and phosphorous acid "; and in May, 1858, he received his degree of doctor of medicine. He had previously made a stay at a military hospital as house physician. His experiences there—especially when having to dress the wounds of serfs cruelly mauled by floggings—reacted upon him deeply; and in the end rather than remain a practising physician he devoted himself entirely to research work.

Throughout his life his dual activities pursued their parallel course; but years were to elapse before he actually came to the front as a composer. In 1859 an event took place which had a great influence on the further course of his life, and contributed not a little, in various ways, to the maturing of his musical outlook. He was sent on a journey abroad to continue his scientific studies. He spent the winter at Heidelberg, the following summer in Italy and Switzerland, and paid a short visit to Paris before returning to Heidelberg. This journey led to his having many new musical experiences and meeting the girl who was to become his wife. Her name was Catherine Protopopova. She was an excellent pianist, and had devoted the proceeds of a recital given by her in Moscow to come to Heidelberg for a cure. There she stayed in the same boarding-house as Borodin. She played to him music by Chopin and Schumann, of which he knew very little and which impressed him deeply. They went to concerts and had long talks about music. Their friendship increased by leaps and bounds, and soon turned into deep, genuine love. They became engaged. In 1861 they went to Mannheim to hear Wagner's " Flying Dutchman ", " Tannhäuser ", and " Lohengrin "—works which, naturally, interested Borodin, but did not attract him or influence him as the German chamber music and the Italian operas which he heard elsewhere did.

His output during those years consisted: on the scientific side, of eight papers on chemical subjects, published in Russian, French, or Italian periodicals; on the musical side, of several chamber music works (not all of them finished, none of them published), the principal of which were a string sextet written at Heidelberg " in very Mendelssohnian style, to please the Germans ", he himself records, a piano trio, and a fantasia for two violins and 'cello on the theme of a Russian folk-song.

And so, returning to Petersburg shortly before his twenty-ninth birthday, he stood splendidly equipped as a scientist; and as a composer, an eager amateur, knowing nothing of technique but the little he had managed to learn for himself, benefiting by a useful knowledge of a few classics and a certain amount of experience of orchestral and chamber music playing. It is more than likely that he also had a working knowledge of Glinka's music. But his natural affinities with this master originate mainly, it would seem, in some obscure instinct which led him to use the "Russian" forms of expression discoverable in his early works; and also, for sure, in the latent influence of his Eastern heredity on his father's side (all his biographers have drawn attention to the strong resemblance between the father and the son). He is said to have been interested in the Russian elements in quintets by Gebel which he heard at Gavrushkevich's house.[1] But there is no indication whatever that, like Glinka, he consciously longed to write "truly national" music. He had met Mussorgsky in 1856, and again in 1859; and it has been suggested that Mussorgsky's ideas may have had some influence on him. It is hardly needful to point out that at the time there was nothing about the very young, very callow Mussorgsky likely to impress the older, far better grounded and more cool-headed Borodin. This is clearly shown by Borodin's own accounts of the meetings (see pp. 180 and 186). And if we were to admit that any influence from outside contributed to Borodin's genius evolving in a certain direction and not otherwise, it is of Balakiref's, and not Mussorgsky's, that one would naturally think. For it was Borodin's good fortune that, shortly after returning to Petersburg, he met Balakiref and became his pupil.

"Until then", Balakiref wrote to Stassof after Borodin's death, " he regarded himself as a mere amateur, and ascribed no importance to the impulse that drove him towards musical composition. I believe I was the first to tell him that composition was his real business. He eagerly started work on his symphony in E flat major. Every bar of it was criticised and overhauled by me—which may have contributed to develop his critical sense, and finally determined his musical tastes and sympathies ".

Balakiref's methods of tuition were considered in the chapter devoted to him (pp. 113 sq.); and the excerpts from

---

[1] Gebel, Franz Xaver, was a German who had settled in Moscow in 1817, and contributed to develop there a taste for chamber music.

a letter written by Borodin to his wife there quoted show how trying his " criticising and overhauling " could be. But Borodin, being blessed with a sense of humour as well as with a philosophical disposition, did not allow himself to be perturbed; he took Balakiref's good advice to heart and was never put off by his whimsies.

The composition of the symphony proceeded speedily for a while and by December, 1862, a rough draft of the first movement was completed. That same month Borodin was appointed assistant professor of organic chemistry at the Academy. He soon won great popularity, not only for the value of his teaching, but for his cheerfulness, thoughtfulness, kindness, and eagerness to help.

" When working in his laboratory ", one of his students, who afterwards became a professor at the same Academy, wrote " we felt as if we were in our own home. Even while at work he never forgot music. He would hum tunes, talk with us of new works, technique, or tendencies. And, after he had withdrawn to his private flat, we often heard the sound of the professorial piano ".

In April, 1863, his marriage with Catherine Protopopova took place. It was to be a very happy union, for their love endured in all its freshness; they had many tastes and inclinations in common, and understood one another perfectly. That year he started research work on the results of the solidification of various aldehydes which led to important discoveries (made by him in 1873, simultaneously with another chemist in France, but independently); and he was appointed lecturer at the Petersburg Academy of Forestry. In 1864 he rose to the rank of titular professor at the Academy of Medicine.

In 1865 he met for the first time Rimsky-Korsakof, whose musical studies under Balakiref had been interrupted by his having had to go for a world cruise in his capacity as a naval officer.

This was the beginning of a close and enduring friendship (Rimsky-Korsakof records in his " Memoirs "). I soon became a regular visitor to his home. I heard him play portions of the symphony he was composing. These delighted me, especially when I came to understand the first movement, which at the first hearing merely bewildered me. He knew almost as little as I did about orchestration generally, but a little more of its practical side, since he could play the flute, the oboe, and the 'cello. I often found him at work in his laboratory, whence he would lead me to his rooms. But even in the midst of playing or talking, he would jump up all of a sudden and fly to his retorts and burners to make sure that all was well —filling the air, as he went about, with incredible sequences of ninths and sevenths, bellowed at the top of his voice. His wife was a very charming and cultured woman, who worshipped his talents.

The symphony made slow progress and was finished in 1867 only. The first performance—Borodin's debut as a composer before the Petersburg public—took place at a concert of the Russian Music Society, conducted by Balakiref, on January 4th/16th, 1869. According to Balakiref:

> The first movement was coldly received, the Scherzo very warmly, the composer being cheered and an encore called for. The last two movements went splendidly. At the end Borodin had to take several calls. The critic T. Tolstoy, who loathed the new Russian music, spoke to me of the finale in tones of praise, and was obviously perplexed by the success of the symphony.

Borodin, greatly delighted, realised where his true path lay, and started forthwith planning his second symphony.

Little of the audience's interest in at least three of the four movements of the symphony was reflected in the Press notices. Indeed, the work was freely described as freakish and amateurish. As it has reached us not in its primitive form, but with emendations carried out later by Borodin in the light of his further experience and of advice given by colleagues and friends (even the first published text, in piano duet, differs in various particulars from the full score published later), it is difficult to say how far, in 1869, it showed signs of immaturity. As it now stands, its motley style reveals a measure of inexperience in the art of conceiving and selecting, but not so its execution from the technical point of view. Much in it is thoroughly characteristic of the composer's genius at its best: the vigour, warmth and imaginative quality of the music, the subtlety and boldness of the melodic, rhythmic, and harmonic invention, the surety of touch, and the genuineness of the tone throughout. It was, as will presently appear, one of the very earliest works to gain fame for Russian music in other countries.

The year 1867 was also marked by a particular venture. In the course of October the Moscow newspapers announced the production at the Grand Theatre of " ' The Bogatyrs ' (' The Valiant Knights '), a farcical opera in five acts, the music original and parodied from various operas, by ***, arranged for orchestra by Messrs. Merten and Büchner (the second conductor of, and the first flute in, the Theatre's orchestra)". The performance took place on November 6th, without success. And it was only a few years ago that the anonymous composer and parodist was discovered to be Borodin, who, availing himself of a libretto by Victor Krylof that was a skit on Serof's " Judith " (produced in 1863, and very much despised by the Balakiref circle), turned out a score that is regarded by the best contemporary Russian critics (Gliebof, Lamm and Popof among others) as containing—apart from really ingenious and telling adaptations of music by Meyerbeer, Rossini, Offenbach, Verdi, Serof, and others—a good deal of original music in which Borodin gave of his best as a humorist. The original music he wrote amounts to over two-fifths of the whole score (one thousand two hundred and forty-six bars against one thousand five hundred and thirty-six of parodies and adaptations). One can imagine him heartily enjoying the relaxation that kind of work brought him.

After 1867 Borodin turned his attention not only to planning a second symphony, but to songs and to opera—in which his first venture was with a libretto derived, on Balakiref's advice, from Mey's tragedy " The Tsar's Bride ". But he soon gave up the idea (which Rimsky-Korsakof took up later) in favour of " Prince Igor ", a subject suggested to him by Stassof in 1869. This stimulated his imagination strongly; yet he made but slow progress with it, experiencing great difficulty in building up the libretto, constantly altering his plan, composing the music fitfully and at long intervals. He followed, in short, the same haphazard course of procedure as Glinka with " Ruslan ", or Mussorgsky with " Khovanshchina "—the consequences being apparent in the structure and quality of the libretto but hardly, if at all, in the music.

Of the half-dozen songs composed by Borodin between 1867 and 1870, four—" The Sleeping Princess ", " The Sea ", " The Song of the Dark Forest ", and " The Queen of the Sea ", none of them as generally known as they deserve to be—are among the finest written not only in Russia, but anywhere at that time or after. Thorough originality of texture, lyrical beauty and expressive power of melody, and above all, lofty spirituality informing the picturesque treatment, reveal the essential Borodin in full.

The Russian critics of the period saw little of all this. Speaking of the " Sleeping Princess ", one of them—whose views may be taken to represent fairly accurately the trend of official opinion, wrote:

> It seems as though the composer always aimed at grating upon the listeners' feelings in some way or other. The

title of one of his songs " Dissonance " [N.B., another of those composed during the same period, the sixth being " My song is fierce and bitter "] appears to be his motto. Incredible as it may seem, this relentless foe of music is not ungifted. Perhaps his proclivity to ugliness is the " fierce and bitter " fruit of his inadequate technical schooling.

Giving up " Prince Igor " for a time, Borodin concentrated upon his second symphony, the first movement of which he finished in 1871. But in 1872 he had to put it aside for a time in order to take part in a curious collaborative work. S. A. Gedeonof, the director of the Imperial Theatres, commissioned from Cui, Borodin, Mussorgsky and Rimsky-Korsakof an opera-ballet, " Mlada ", to be composed collectively. The fourth act was allotted to Borodin, but the scheme fell through, owing to its expense, and he reverted to the second symphony and to " Igor ", the symphony providing an outlet for many musical ideas conceived for " Igor ", but which could not be included in its scheme. " It is not impossible ", Gerald Abraham remarks (*Musical Quarterly*, January, 1931), " that this great symphony was the result of his despair at being unable to realise the ' Igor ' of his dreams. Perhaps, in a sense, it *was* the ' Igor ' of his dreams ". This remark is justified by the epic character of the symphony.

It was first performed on February 26th, 1877, Napravnik conducting. The performance was most unsatisfactory—partly, Rimsky-Korsakof says, because Borodin had given the brass, in consequence of his imperfect knowledge of the limitations of valve-instruments, parts impossible to perform in the prescribed quick *tempi*. Unavoidably the symphony fell flat. The mistakes were corrected for the second performance, which Rimsky-Korsakof conducted a year later. But the work was to win golden opinions abroad before finding favour with the Russian public. Nowadays, it is regarded as a masterpiece and a landmark in the history of the symphony in modern times.

That same year Borodin finished a string quartet, of which he had begun to think in 1875—the earliest example of first-rate chamber music to be written by a Russian composer, and, in the opinion of many competent judges, the very finest in the output of the whole school.

His scientific and educational activities during all that period were many and fruitful. He played an important part in founding medical courses for women, and took charge of some of these in addition to his other duties. He organised his own laboratory on a new basis, rendering it available for students and meeting all the expenses thereby entailed out of his own pocket. All this work left him little time for music.

"I am never able to concentrate upon composition", he wrote to a friend in 1876, "except during my summer holiday, or when some ailment compels me to keep to my rooms".

The difficulty of concentrating upon composition was increased by his nervous, absent-minded disposition, and also by his untidiness and lack of method. There seems to be no evidence that these manifested themselves in his scientific pursuits, but they certainly affected conditions in his home—in which, moreover, his privacy was often encroached upon owing to his obliging, hospitable nature.

Apart from his countless duties at the Academy, Rimsky-Korsakof writes in his "Memoirs", and all his professional committees, his time was taken up by society ladies in need of his help for various charity affairs. And his home was ever invaded by students in need of advice or assistance, or by relatives, poor, or ailing, or simply on a visit to town. He had to look after them, see them into hospital, provide them with food and lodging. At times they were so many that they slept on sofas or on the floor.

Often he was debarred from using his piano for fear of waking them. The house was also full of cats, chiefly strays, which his wife had collected and taken under her special protection.

In 1878/1879, I arranged to have portions of " Prince Igor " performed at a Free School of Music concert. But to get the music delivered proved a heart-breaking task. When asked if he had written anything, he would reply, " I have "—but what he had actually done was to write a batch of letters. " Have you transposed such and such a number?" I inquired one day. " I have indeed ", he replied with perfect gravity, " I have transposed it from the piano to my writing-table ". The day of the concert was near, and the situation most serious. I offered to help him with the scoring of the Polovtsian Dances and the final chorus. He brought the unfinished scores to my house, and Liadof, he, and I, sharing the work, completed that of the Dances, working far into the night. To save time we wrote in pencil. Borodin then daubed the sheets with liquid gelatine so that the pencil should not rub off, and hung them on lines to dry. They went to the copyist the next day. The final chorus I scored practically alone, Liadof being unable to attend. Thus, thanks to the existence of the Free School of Music concerts, certain parts of " Igor " received their final form.

But before further referring to the erratic course and final fate of " Igor ", it is necessary to mention a journey which Borodin made to Germany in 1877 to visit the laboratories of the principal universities there, in view of a pending reorganisation of the chemistry section of the Petersburg Academy, and also in connexion with his own investigation of important problems of organic chemistry—the determination of the presence and transmutations of nitrogen in the organism (these researches of his were eventually crowned with success; and the method invented by him is still in use). He went to Jena, and thence to Weimar, where he had the joy of meeting Liszt, who welcomed him warmly. His descriptions, in his letters to his wife, of his sojourn in Weimar, " a Venusberg in which Liszt was Venus ", of Liszt and his *entourage*, and of the musical events which he witnessed or took part in are as graphic and lively as they are instructive; and only lack of space prevents extensive quotation from them here. It must be noted, however, that Liszt said to Borodin with reference to his two symphonies: " Do not worry about the boldness of your forms and modulations. Do not listen to those people who would deter you from following your own way. You are on the right path. Similar advice was given to Mozart and to Beethoven, who wisely ignored it. Despite the adage that ' there is nothing new under the sun ', your second symphony is entirely new: nobody has done anything like it. And it is perfectly logical in structure."

It is undeniable that Liszt was often profuse in his encouragement to very mediocre composers. Without going into this complicated question, one may recall the encouragement he gave to many composers who afterwards rose to fame, and the steps he took for making their music known. His praise of, and active interest in, the works of Balakiref, Borodin, Mussorgsky, and other Russians, was particularly precious when these composers were inadequately appreciated in their own country and unknown, or almost, elsewhere. It was certainly owing to his influence that Borodin's first symphony was performed at Baden-Baden in 1880—an event which inaugurated the series of the composer's successes abroad. And after again meeting Liszt in 1881, Borodin expressed his appreciation of him in the following characteristic terms:

> Liszt is a real Balakiref, a great-hearted man indeed—such friends are really " friendly friends ".

Upon returning to Russia Borodin, proceeding far more speedily than was his wont, finished the splendid string quartet in A major which he had first planned in 1875 " to the great distress of Stassof and Mussorgsky " he notes in one of his letters.

Whether this distress was due to any other reason than eagerness to see him proceed with " Igor " rather than turn his attention to other plans does not appear. By 1875 he had left " Igor " almost untouched for nearly five years, after a first spurt of energy during which he had eagerly studied not only the old Russian epic, but all possible sources of information and examples of folk-music, outlined a libretto, and also begun composing the music. But towards the end of 1874 he resumed work on it, and during the following year he composed several numbers, including the Polovtsian Dances. In June, 1876, he wrote to his friend Liubov Karmalina:

You ask me for news of " Igor ". Whenever I have to mention this opera, I cannot help laughing at my own self. I feel rather like the old wizard, Finn, in " Ruslan ", who, wrapt in his love for Naina, does not realise that time is flying and starts acting only when he and his beloved one are stricken in years. . . . So far I have written the equivalent of one act and a half—out of four. I am pleased with what I have done, and so are my friends. One number performed at a Free School of Music concert was a great success, which is encouraging. So far I have felt shy of letting it be known that I am engaged on an opera. My real business, after all, is scientific work; and I feared lest by concentrating too much on music I discredit that work. But now, everybody knows; and I am, so to speak, in the same position as a girl who, having thrown her cap over the mill, has secured a certain amount of freedom: willy-nilly, I must finish " Igor ". . . . A remarkable fact is that all the members of our circle approve of what I have written so far; the ultra-realist Mussorgsky, and Cui, the reformer, Balakiref, our master, and Stassof, the doughty champion of all that is novel and great, unite in praise of it.

A few months earlier he had informed his wife that " Rimsky-Korsakof and Mussorgsky were especially taken with the wild Eastern dances ". How the performance of these dances and of a choral finale had become possible only by Rimsky-Korsakof's persistence and help has already been told.

The year 1880 was marked by the composition of the orchestral tone-picture " In the Steppes of Central Asia " and the publication (by Rahter at Hamburg) of a little work of a very peculiar kind " Paraphrases for piano duet, on the theme of the Chopsticks-Polka ", by Borodin, Rimsky-Korsakof, Cui, and Liadof. " In the Steppes " was written on the occasion of the jubilee of Tsar Alexander II to accompany one of the series of historical *tableaux vivants* included in the programme of the festivities. It is altogether lovely, thoroughly characteristic of Borodin and, although an occasional piece, brief and utterly simple, contributed as much to his fame abroad as any of his other orchestral works, not even excluding the gorgeous " Igor ".

The first notion of the " Paraphrases " arose from the fact that one day an adopted daughter of Borodin asked him to play piano duets with her, but had to confess that all she could do was to play the " Chopsticks " with one finger of each hand. Borodin extemporised a polka to fit in with this (and also, apparently, a " Doggy's Waltz " which has not been preserved). This gave Rimsky-Korsakof the idea of writing, jointly with Borodin, a set of variations on the same basis. Cui and Liadof were persuaded to join in the fun. Shortly after the " Paraphrases " had appeared, Liszt praised them in a letter to a Russian friend. Excerpts of this appeared in a Petersburg paper, to the great indignation of the critics, who started proclaiming that Liszt could never have written such a letter and that the composers of the " Paraphrases " had hopelessly compromised their reputations. Liszt retorted by composing a little Prelude to Borodin's Polka " for the second edition of the ' *marvellous* ' work "; and this was published in facsimile in the second edition.

Borodin contributed, besides the Polka, a miniature " Funeral March " and " Requiem ". The perfect ease and aptness with which he combined the earnest, tragic themes with the " Chopsticks " is as much an object-lesson as are the theme-combinations in the first string quartet, the Polovtsian Dances, or " In the Steppes ". Both those little pieces also show Borodin's exceptional gift for musical humour and farce. His intimate friends have told many stories of the amusing parodies of the music of his colleagues he used to indulge in. The verdict of modern Russian criticism on the high standard achieved in the music of the unpublished " Bogatyrs " has been alluded to above. The most typical examples of comic music in his published output are a " Serenade of four swains to a lady " and the parts of the jesters, Eroshka and Skula, in " Igor ". These teem with examples of real spontaneous musical humour and wit, as distinct from the facile and often stereotyped approximations, or counterfeits, which are usually accepted as such.

How far Borodin's scientific occupations, and the other causes which prevented him from devoting more time and labour to music, affected his achievements as a composer is a many-sided problem on which a few suggestions will presently be offered. But one remark may be made forthwith: in all likelihood careful investigation will lead to the conclusion that of all his rare gifts, those which he exploited the least thoroughly were his sense of polyphony and his sense of musical humour and farce. There can be, of course, no reply to the question whether, by greater concentration on polyphonic methods, Borodin, advancing further along that particular line, might have sped the evolution of contrapuntal style, and alone among the nineteenth-century Russians given us live and original works in that style. All told, he seems, in his mature instrumental works, to have thoroughly found himself and the means of expression that best suited his genius. But if he had had more opportunities to write humorous works, and especially operas, he might have struck new paths while raising the art to a level seldom reached before or after.

The year 1880 was marked by performances at Moscow of his second symphony, and at Baden-Baden of the first. The Moscow audience gave the new work a fairly warm welcome, but the Press notices were not favourable. At Baden-Baden, Borodin scored a big success, which was the first of a long series of triumphs for his music abroad. At Petersburg, performances of excerpts from "Igor" and of his string quartet contributed to spread his reputation. Soon afterwards he wrote a second string quartet (inscribed to his wife, and not published until after his death) more intimate and purely lyrical in style than the first. But his creative energies began to slacken. His health began to fail him. That of his wife, never good, had grown steadily worse and caused him continuous anxiety. The Petersburg climate proving too severe for her, she was compelled to live in Moscow, where he went to see her as often as possible—which, of course, meant still less time for composition. In 1884 he had a severe illness—a bout of cholera, Rimsky-Korsakof told Stassof. He soon rallied, but a period of mental numbness followed. He felt his disability keenly, and often would wake up at night, groaning, "I cannot compose! I cannot compose!"

Eventually he took heart again, stimulated by cheering news from Belgium. Countess de Mercy-Argenteau, a keen champion of the Russian composers, arranged for three concerts of their music to be given at Liège. His first symphony, " In the Steppes ", and songs of his were performed there with great success. The symphony was also performed at Verviers. Borodin was almost as surprised with the news as he was delighted. " Russian music ", he wrote to the Countess, " is not of the kind that makes for success ". That this sentence expressed his actual feeling is shown by a remark which he made a few months later: " ' Igor ', being fundamentally a national opera, can hardly interest anybody but us Russians, who love to go back to the springs of our history and see our past depicted on the stage ". But there was no mistaking the fact that his music had created a deep impression. In the spring of 1885 he decided to visit Belgium on the occasion of the International Exhibition at Antwerp. He was warmly welcomed, invited to conduct concerts (an invitation which he declined, having little experience in the art); and he witnessed the success of his music. The following Christmas he made a second journey to Belgium together with Cui, whose opera " The Captive in the Caucasus " was to be performed at Liège. Successful performances of works of his, including excerpts from " Igor ", took place at Liège and Brussels. Arrangements were made for publishing his music in Belgium and in France, for translating his songs, and (as soon as it would be ready) " Igor ". By way of tribute to the Countess, he wrote a " Petite Suite " (seven pieces) for piano, and a song, " The Enchanted Garden ": and as a tribute to the Belgium conductor Jadoul, a Scherzo in A flat major—which, for some unfathomable reason, is never heard nowadays in its orchestral version, and hardly ever in the piano version, which he turned out simultaneously.

Despite the new incentive, " Igor " made but little progress. Some time before, Rimsky-Korsakof had written to Kruglikof, the Moscow critic: " Alas! I can foresee that it is to me that the task of finishing ' Igor ' will befall." And according to a letter from Stassof to the same correspondent, a little later, when Rimsky-Korsakof offered to set in order and finish the opera, " Borodin, strange to say, was not annoyed but delighted ". And upon his return from Belgium, instead of concentrating upon " Igor ", he began planning and writing a third symphony.

The year 1886 (in which the last of his scientific papers, and the first one to appear since 1880, was published, embodying the results of his studies on the determination of nitrogen and its transformations in the organism) was a sad and trying one for him. His wife was struck by a serious illness. His mother-in-law, whom he dearly loved, also fell ill, and died soon afterwards. In the autumn, however, he conquered his depression and resumed work with a will. On February 14th/26th, 1887, he wrote to his wife:

> My beloved, I shall not be able to come to see you during Carnival week. I was asking myself whether to come to Moscow for a very short spell, but now I find I have to appear before a magistrate as a witness. Tomorrow we are having a dance. It will be " grandement beau. Il y aura de la bougie ", as is said in Murger's " La Vie de Bohème ". I shall say no more about it and leave the description of the festivity to the more expert pen of your other correspondents.

The dance was one given by the Academy professors. Borodin, who had spent the day working at his third symphony, attended in Russian national costume, and was in high spirits. In the midst of the rejoicings he collapsed, and within a few seconds died of a burst aneurism, without even uttering a sigh.

He was buried in the Alexander Nevsky cemetery, close by Mussorgsky's tomb. Themes from his compositions and formulæ of chemical bodies studied by him stand inscribed on the monument erected over his grave in 1889. His wife survived him only by a few months, dying in July, 1887.

Rimsky-Korsakof and Glazunof undertook the task of finishing and orchestrating " Prince Igor ", except in respect of the third act, for which it proved needful to compose a certain amount of music. Their work consisted mainly in setting in order and co-ordinating the numbers, carrying out Borodin's intentions from sketches or from memory (Glazunof had often heard him play the overture and other unwritten portions) and providing transitions and complements. All this they did with thorough tact and understanding. And so, thanks to their admirable labour, " Prince Igor ", of all Russian operas the most directly in line of succession to Glinka's " Ruslan ", musically speaking (which it greatly surpasses in unity of style and continuity of musical interest), was published in 1888. Glazunof also finished and prepared for publication two movements of the third symphony. Among the other posthumous works, apart from the second string quartet, a song " To the shores of my distant fatherland ", composed in memory of Mussorgsky in 1881, deserves special mention.

Tributes to Borodin's scientific career were paid by Dianin and others in obituary articles. An important obituary by Stassof on his life and music was expanded, in 1889, into a volume, biographical and critical, in which a number of his letters were printed and a few musical articles contributed by him to Petersburg journals reprinted. After that, while his music continued to make headway, slowly but steadily, very little original literature, biographical or critical, appeared for many years. But of late, valuable contributions in both fields have been made by Russian writers such as Khubof, Gliebof and Braudo among many. (The present writer has drawn extensively from the last-named author's excellent biography, published in 1922.) A complete edition of Borodin's letters, with notes and comments by Serge Dianin, the son of Borodin's friend and pupil, is in course of publication; and the same author is at work on a big biography. In other countries useful studies of Borodin's music have been appearing. This beginning of a new period of Borodin research and criticism testifies to the significance ascribed nowadays to the music of a composer whom the majority of writers had long neglected as much as they had Mussorgsky.

Surveying his life, musical output, and the part played by this output in the further evolution of the art, one is inevitably led to begin by quoting Sir Henry Hadow's verdict.

> No musician has ever claimed immortality with so slender an offering. Yet if there be, indeed, immortalities in music, his claim is incontestable.

And this in turn leads to considering the question how much truth there may be in the epithet " amateur " which critics, in Russia and elsewhere, have freely applied to him at some time or other. The epithet is true so far as it means that he did not take up music as a profession, devote the whole of his time to it, or expect any advantage, financial or other, from it. But no evidence of amateurishness could be found in the music of his maturity. There is no need to prove the point by a discussion of technicalities. It is enough to ask, with Khubof, whether " a mere amateur could have written the first Russian national works to gain an international reputation?" Borodin himself, fortunately, was allowed to see the coming of a recognition whose significance was unmistakable. A few months before his death he wrote to his old friend, Gavrushkevich:

> I have been fairly fortunate as a composer, especially abroad. My symphonies have enjoyed unexpected successes, the first establishing my reputation in several countries, the second mainly in Belgium. My " Steppes "

have made the round of Europe. My first quartet pleased not only many European audiences, but also American. During the past season it was played four times at the Buffalo Philharmonic Concerts. My songs, too, are going well. . . . But ware the evil eye!

Since then nearly half a century has elapsed, and Borodin's music has proved its artistic value by continued progress, its seminal value by exercising widespread and beneficial influence on many a composer, and not in Russia only. So the question whether he was an amateur is of purely academic, not critical, æsthetical, or even practical interest. The only critical and practical conclusion is that if Borodin (and the same is to be said of Mussorgsky) was an amateur, then the musical world could do with a good many more amateurs of the same kind.

M. D. C.

MODEST MUSSORGSKY

MODEST Petrovitch Mussorgsky was born on March 9th/21st,[1] 1839, in the village of Karevo, in the Toropets district of the Pskof Government, where his father was a well-to-do landowner. (The estate in 1851 covered more than forty square miles.) The father, Peter Alexeievitch Mussorgsky, was the illegitimate son of an officer of the Preobrajensky Guards, by a serf-woman. But his parents married after his birth and he was legitimised in 1820 and even posthumously entered in the register of the nobility of the Pskof Government. After a few years of government service in Petersburg, he retired to his estate and married a young lady of romantic temperament who wrote bad verse and bore him four sons, of whom the composer was the youngest. The two eldest died in babyhood but the third, Filaret, born in 1836, survived his famous brother by nearly twenty years.

We know very little of Mussorgsky's early years, our only sources of information being an autobiographical sketch written in 1881 (probably at the request of Hugo Riemann, the German musical lexicographer), a list of his compositions drawn up for Liudmila Shestakova in 1871, and some very brief reminiscences by his brother Filaret, written down at the request of V. V. Stassof. And none of these sources is completely reliable. According to Mussorgsky's autobiography, written in the third person, " under his nurse's influence, he became familiar with Russian fairy-tales, and it was mainly this contact with the spirit of the life of the people which impelled him to improvise music before he had learned

[1] Not, as he believed and as his biographers have in consequence repeatedly asserted, on March 16th/28th.

MUSSORGSKY

even the most elementary rules of piano-playing. His mother gave him his first piano lessons and he made such progress that at seven he played small pieces by Liszt, and at nine played a concerto of Field's before a large audience in his parents' house. His father, who worshipped music, decided to develop the child's ability—and entrusted his further musical education to Herke[1] in Petersburg ". (This was in August, 1849, and the boy's general education was continued first at a preparatory school, then with a " crammer ".) " The teacher was so satisfied with his pupil that when he was twelve he made him play a Concert Rondo by Herz at a private charity concert. The young musician's performance was so successful that Professor Herke, severe critic as he was, gave him a copy of Beethoven's Sonata in A flat. At thirteen young Mussorgsky entered the Cadet School of the Guards and was honoured by the particularly kind attention of the late Emperor Nicholas." Filaret, who was also at the Cadet School, says his brother was a good scholar, popular with the other boys, and that he was specially interested in history and German philosophy. But the atmosphere of the Cadet School was by no means conducive to study, while its moral influence was thoroughly bad. According to another cadet of nearly the same period, who knew Mussorgsky in later years, " The cadets considered study beneath their dignity. The same view was taken by the head of the School who, whenever he saw Mussorgsky working at his desk, would say, ' *Mon cher*, what sort of officer will you make?' The General objected to his pupils' drinking vodka like the common people, or coming back on foot when they were drunk. But he was genuinely proud when one of them was brought back in a carriage and pair, overcome by champagne ".

During his first year at the School, Mussorgsky wrote a " Porte-Enseigne Polka ", dedicated to his school-fellows.

[1] Anton Herke, a pupil of Henselt's.

He knew nothing of the rules of composition, for Herke taught him nothing but piano-playing. But his proud father, with Herke's help, had the piece printed by the publisher Bernard, to the composer's later regret. This was the only one of his son's compositions Peter Mussorgsky ever saw, for he died the following year (1853). In his autobiography Mussorgsky goes on to claim that he " associated a great deal with the religious instructor, Father Krupsky, thanks to whom he acquired a profound knowledge of the very essence of ancient Greek and Catholic church-music ". (In another draft, he adds " Lutheran-Protestant ".) But according to Krupsky's own account, the good priest simply encouraged the boy, who was in the school choir, to study the works of Bortniansky and his contemporaries; that is to say, dull and feeble Russian church-music written only half-a-century earlier. The lessons with Herke also came to an end in 1854.

In 1856, when Mussorgsky left the Cadet School and entered the Preobrajensky Guards, a year after his brother, he says he " tried to write an opera based on Hugo's ' Han d'Islande '—but nothing came of it, nor could have come of it ". In September or October of that year, being orderly officer of the day at the Second Military Hospital—and bored—he got into conversation with the equally bored young doctor who was also on duty. They liked each other and chanced to meet again the same evening at the house of the chief medical officer who, having a marriageable daughter, entertained frequently. They met two or three times more at his house—successfully evading the marriageable daughter. But, their host going away, they saw no more of each other for three years. However, the young doctor, whose name was Borodin, has left us a graphic word-sketch of the seventeen-year-old Mussorgsky:

> A smallish, very elegant, dapper little officer: brand-new, close-fitting uniform; shapely feet; delicate, altogether

aristocratic hands. Elegant, aristocratic manners; conversation the same, somewhat through his teeth, interspersed with French phrases, rather affected. Some traces of foppishness, but very moderate. Unusually polite and cultured. The ladies made a fuss of him. He sat at the piano and, coquettishly throwing up his hands, played excerpts from " Trovatore ", " Traviata ", etc. very pleasantly and gracefully, while the circle around him murmured in chorus, " Charmant! Délicieux! " and so on.

The following spring Mussorgsky made other interesting acquaintances. Through a fellow-officer he was introduced to Dargomyjsky, whose " Russalka " had been produced the year before, and to the fiancé of one of Dargomyjsky's pupils, a young Engineer officer named Cui, who was dabbling in composition and even thinking of writing an opera. A little later, through these new friends, he came into contact with that young Balakiref, to whom Glinka had taken such a fancy. And, Balakiref falling ill that summer, Mussorgsky was introduced in his sick-room to two of his other visitors, the brothers Stassof. Apparently the contact with these vital personalities, two of them only a year or so older than himself, awoke in him a desire to increase his rather scanty knowledge of music and even to compose. To that end he induced Balakiref in the autumn or winter of 1857 to give him lessons on musical form and analysis. As Balakiref said himself, after Mussorgsky's death, " not being a theorist, I could not—unfortunately—teach Mussorgsky harmony, as Rimsky-Korsakof teaches it now. But I used to explain the form of a composition to him. We played through all Beethoven's symphonies in four-hand arrangements as well as many other compositions by Schumann, Schubert, Glinka and others. I explained to him the technical construction of the pieces we played, and he himself analysed their form. However, as far as I remember, there were not many paid lessons;

for some reason or other ", probably Balakiref's absence from Petersburg during the spring and summer of 1858, " they came to an end and changed into friendly conversations ".

The first fruits of this rather vague and superficial study were a charming, but suspiciously Balakirefian, little song, " Where art thou, little star?" and a " Souvenir d'enfance " for piano, dated October 16th/28th, 1857. A little later we find Mussorgsky apologising to Balakiref that an *allegro*, which has " wearied him to death " is not ready and his letters during 1858 mention another *allegro* and scherzo (for a Sonata in E flat, from which he gives musical quotations) and an Introduction to " Œdipus ", all of which have disappeared. Notwithstanding his intention, avowed to Balakiref, " not to write oriental music ", he made a piano arrangement of the Persian Chorus from " Ruslan ". In his spare time he studied harmony on his own. " I'm awfully keen to write respectably ", he confided to Balakiref.

His attitude to Balakiref—his senior by only two years, it must be remembered—was already rather rebellious. He recognised the other's greater knowledge and ability, and he was boyishly eager to learn from him. But at the same time, as he acknowledged later, his *amour propre* again and again goaded him into conflicts with a man who, even at twenty-one, was extraordinarily sure of himself. Mussorgsky's nature was dangerously weak; as he admitted, he was easily influenced by bad companions. But like so many weak people, he had a strong vein of sheer contradictoriness. His declaration against " eastern music " is probably a case in point: for he *was* writing " eastern music " in his two Scherzos a few months later.

Little as we know of Mussorgsky's musical development at this critical period, our information about him personally is even more inadequate. All we know definitely is that he began to suffer from some nervous disorder, resigned his commission on July 5th/17th, 1858, using as a pretext the fact that his regiment was about to be moved from Petersburg where his mother and friends were, and went immediately afterwards to Tikhvin with his brother to take a cure.[1] But a certain amount of light on his condition at this time is thrown by a confession to Balakiref, made the following year:

> I was oppressed by a terrible disease, which came on very badly while I was in the country. This was mysticism, mixed up with cynical thoughts about God. It developed terribly when I returned to Petersburg. I succeeded in concealing it from you, but you must have noticed traces of it in my music. I suffered dreadfully, becoming awfully sensitive (morbidly so). Then, either through various distractions or because I indulged in fantastic dreams, this mysticism gradually began to disappear. Having recovered my mental equilibrium, I took steps to destroy it . . . I am now very far from mysticism—I hope, for ever; for moral and intellectual development are quite incompatible with it.

The compositions in which he fancied these " traces " were discernible, the finale of the E flat Sonata and another Sonata in F sharp minor, have disappeared, though a letter written in August to Balakiref, who had not yet returned to Petersburg, gives us a hint as to the direction Mussorgsky's thoughts were taking. He is translating Lavater, he says—" his writings on the condition of the soul after death, a very interesting subject; and besides, the visionary world has always attracted me ". All the time, " I think, think, and think ". His head is full of plans. " It would be fine if only I could carry them out." Then, too, he had been studying

---

[1] Mussorgsky, with that light-hearted disregard for accuracy which is so characteristic of Russian autobiographers, has misled everybody by placing these events in 1859.

Gluck's operas and Mozart's " Requiem " and was delighted with his discovery of Beethoven's " Moonlight " Sonata . . . But all this was only on the surface. As far as we know, he confessed to no one what was troubling his depths.

On Balakiref's return from Nijni-Novgorod, Mussorgsky evidently worked with him again, and no longer at such mere scholastic exercises as the two sonatas must have been. At any rate, if still exercises, the compositions were preserved and one of them was performed soon afterwards. First came a song, " Meines Herzens Sehnsucht ", dedicated to Cui's bride. (They were married in October, with Mussorgsky as best man.) Then in November two Scherzos, one in B flat, orchestrated with Balakiref's assistance, and another in C sharp minor, both with decidedly Balakirefian trios. And in January, 1859, Mussorgsky completed a first version of the Temple Scene from " Œdipus ", for double chorus and piano. The incidental music to Shestakof's translation of " Œdipus " was no doubt one of numerous plans which he had mentioned in the letter to Balakiref. Another cherished idea was the composition of an opera based on Gogol's story, " St. John's Eve ".

In the course of that winter, if not earlier, Mussorgsky made the acquaintance (through Dargomyjsky, whose pupil she was) of Maria Shilovskaya, one of the most famous society beauties of the day. Then about twenty-nine, Maria enjoyed a double reputation, as a lady of numerous lovers and as a very good amateur singer. Her husband, S. S. Shilovsky, was one of the wealthiest men in Russia and at his country-house of Glebovo, near Moscow, he sometimes arranged performances of entire operas in which his wife sang, Constantine Liadof, conductor of the Marinsky Theatre and father of the composer, Anatol Liadof, being brought from Petersburg to conduct. Maria was one of the only three women towards whom Mussorgsky's attitude was, in Stassof's phrase, " something like love ". But considering that

Mussorgsky had a horror of marriage; that his few attempts at the musical expression of amorous passion were quite unsuccessful; that the most important female friendships of his life—with Liudmila Shestakova, Nadejda Opotchinina and Daria Leonova—seem to have been quasi-filial, at any rate merely platonic; and that we have nothing but Stassof's word for it that Mussorgsky was " something like in love " with Maria Shilovskaya and the opera-singer, Latysheva—in view of all this, it seems not unreasonable to assume that Mussorgsky's attitude to women was a little abnormal. As far as Maria Shilovskaya is concerned, all we know is that in May, 1859, Mussorgsky, with Dargomyjsky and others, was invited to Glebovo for a performance of " A Life for the Tsar ", in which she sang the part of Vania; and that he was her guest on one or two later occasions.

From Glebovo Mussorgsky, in June, went on to Moscow, a visit that was one of the profoundest experiences of his youth. Balakiref had been there the year before and in the Kremlin had " felt with pride that he was—*Russian* ". His enthusiastic letter had excited Mussorgsky's anticipation, and he was not disappointed. " The Kremlin, the marvellous Kremlin!", he wrote. " St. Basil's worked on me so pleasantly and yet so strangely that it seemed as if at any moment a boyar might appear in long smock and high cap." Not only St. Basil's, but the Red Square, the Spassky Gate, the Cathedral of the Archangels with the tombs of the dead tsars, the bell-tower " Ivan the Great ", built by Boris Godunof, all fired his imagination and his patriotism. Nor was he blind to other aspects of Moscow: " the world has never produced such rogues and beggars ". " Moscow has taken me into another world ", he tells Balakiref, " the world of antiquity, a dirty world, but one that none the less affects me pleasantly—I don't know why . . . You know I have been a cosmopolitan, but now—I have undergone a sort of re-birth; I have been brought near to everything Russian."

But these emotions produced no premature, unripe musical fruit. Mussorgsky's immediate musical inspiration came from quite a different source. His first composition after his return to Petersburg was a Schumannesque " Impromptu passioné ", suggested by the problem-novel " Who is to Blame?", by the celebrated socialist, Alexander Herzen. (The piece is dedicated to Nadejda Opotchinina, a woman of thirty-eight with whom—and her six brothers—he was later on terms of intimate friendship.) He even sketched out a definitely anti-patriotic piece, a sort of cantata, " Shamil's March ", in honour of the famous Caucasian chief who had just surrendered to Russian arms. It was at this period that he announced to Balakiref his emancipation from " mysticism ". That autumn, too, he met Borodin again. It was a single chance meeting at the house of an acquaintance, for Borodin was just going abroad for three years. But they remembered each other and played Mendelssohn's " Scottish " Symphony as a piano duet. (The Mussorgsky of this period regarded Mendelssohn-worship as a sort of disease which one was bound to have—and get over; he admired Schumann; but had no use for Chopin.) From Mendelssohn they turned to Schumann's symphonies, which Borodin did not know but of which Mussorgsky spoke with enthusiasm. And then Mussorgsky confided to the other that he too was a composer. " I confess ", said Borodin years afterwards, " that at first I was incredulous when he told me he intended to devote himself seriously to music. I took it for boasting and was inwardly rather amused ". But then Mussorgsky played one of his scherzos and compelled his listener to wonder: " Do I believe—or don't I?" According to Borodin, Mussorgsky now looked " much more mature; he had begun to fill out and his military air had disappeared. He still had the same elegance in dress, manners and so on, but there was no longer the slightest trace of foppishness ". If Borodin had stayed in Russia a few months longer, his doubts might have been finally dispelled by Mussorgsky's public debut as a composer, a debut made under the most distinguished auspices: the orchestral Scherzo in B flat was played with some success at a symphony concert of the newly-founded Russian Music Society on January 11th/23rd, 1860, Anton Rubinstein conducting. But apparently some circumstance annoyed the sensitive youngster, for when a second such opportunity presented itself, Mussorgsky, as we shall see, declined it.

The year begun so happily was not a happy one, however. Mussorgsky was tormented by a second nervous crisis, one rather different in nature from the first, as appears from a letter to Balakiref (February 10th/22nd):

> Thank God, I'm beginning to get better after severe, frightfully severe, mental and physical sufferings. Do you remember how once when we were reading " Manfred ", two years ago, I was so magnetised by the sufferings of that lofty nature, that I told you I should like to be a Manfred (I was a perfect child at the time)? Fate, it seems, was kind enough to fulfil my wish. I became literally " manfredised ", my mind killed my body. Now I'm obliged to have recourse to every sort of antidote. Dear Mily, I know you love me; for God's sake, try to keep me in hand. For a time I shall have to give up my musical concerns and every kind of intellectual work in order to get better. My recipe is—everything for the benefit of the physical side and as far as possible to the prejudice of the mental. I clearly see now the causes of my nervous disorder; it is not simply a consequence of onanism (that is almost a secondary reason), but chiefly: youth, excess of enthusiasm, awful irresistible desire for universal knowledge, exaggerated inward criticism, and idealism carried so far as to embody my dreams in shapes and actions. At the present moment I see that as I am

only twenty, owing to my onanism, my physical side is not sufficiently developed to keep pace with my strong mental growth; consequently my mental power has stifled the power of physical development. I shall have to help the latter; distractions and as much quietness as possible, gymnastics and bathing ought to save me.

But it was not till May that he went into the country, spending the summer months again with the Shilovskys at Glebovo. " My illness lasted almost till August, so that I could work only fragmentarily at music; during the greater part of this time, from May to August, my brain was weak and in a state of violent irritability." Nevertheless he had completed a little piano piece, " Ein Kinderscherz ", done some work towards another sonata, and revised and added to the " Œdipus " music. One new chorus for " Œdipus ", he told Balakiref, marked the end of his " mysticism ". " Thank God, Mily, I'm now completely recovered "—this was September 26th-October 8th—" I'm going to put all my musical sins in order. A new period of my musical life has begun ".

He apparently proposed to begin it with a setting of the witches' sabbath scene on the Bare Mountain " from Mengden's drama ' The Witch ' " (a work of which nothing whatever is known). " The libretto is very good. As I already have some materials, the thing ought to turn out very well." One wonders if these " materials " were originally intended for the " St. John's Eve " opera of 1858. But instead of getting on with it,[1] he persisted, probably in obedience to Balakiref's wishes, in trying to compose big works in the classical forms. In December, 1860, he began an Allegro in C major for piano duet, probably a sketch for the first movement of a symphony; the following month wrote the scherzo (also for

[1] On the strength of a letter of 1867, long supposed to have been written in 1862, everyone has believed that this " Witch " music was actually composed and that it formed the first version of " Night on the Bare Mountain ". Some of the material probably originated at this time, but there is no proof that it did.

four hands) and planned the slow movement of a Symphony in D, which was to be dedicated to " the Wednesday fellowship ", that is, to the circle which met weekly at Balakiref's. Balakiref, who had no very high opinion of his pupil's intellectual or musical ability, drily informed a friend that " Mussorgsky now looks well and jolly. He has written an *allegro* and thinks he has already done *quite a lot* for art in general and Russian art in particular ". And Mussorgsky's increasing sensitiveness to the other's attitude comes out in a letter written in January ,1861, where, after defending himself against a charge of being attracted by " commonplace people ", he petulantly tells Balakiref that " it is time to leave off treating me as a child who has to be kept in leading-strings ". Yet there is something childlike, if not childish, in the tone of his complaint. His touching humility was already becoming shot through with an equally pathetic vanity. Mussorgsky is a model case for the study of " inferiority complex ".

Early in the winter there had been a chance of having the Temple Scene from " Œdipus " performed by the R.M.S. but such was the prejudice against Anton Rubinstein in the Balakiref circle, so fearful was Mussorgsky of a " collision " with him, that he broke off negotiations. However, in April, 1861, the chorus (with some pieces by Cui, Balakiref and Dargomyjsky) was performed at a concert in the Marinsky Theatre, under Constantine Liadof. But the year was completely barren from a productive point of view, its only fruit being an " Alla marcia notturna ", a mere " exercise in instrumentation " as it is marked on the score. Mussorgsky had family worries. The Imperial Ukase of February 19th/March 3rd, 1861, ordering the gradual emancipation of the serfs during the next two years, seriously affected all but the wealthiest members of the land-owning class in Russia. Mussorgsky himself seems to have been prepared to accept this impoverishment cheerfully. As Filaret self-revealingly observed, Modest " throughout his life showed a peculiar affection for the peasants, considering the Russian *mujik* a genuine human being (in which he was sadly mistaken)". Modest could willingly endure losses for the sake of " the people ". Unfortunately Filaret, who had the sole management of the Karevo estate, was typical of the majority of his class not only in his contempt for the sub-human *mujik* but in his incompetence in practical matters. During the summer of 1861, Mussorgsky, judging by his letters, had his hands full with the concerns of the family estate—though as a business man he must have been even more helpless than Filaret. And in the winter of 1861-62, just after the Balakiref group had acquired a recruit in the person of the seventeen-year-old Rimsky-Korsakof; and just at the time when Balakiref was planning the foundation of his Free School of Music, Mussorgsky left Petersburg and joined his brother at Karevo. Soon after, their mother gave up her town house and followed him.

Nor was Mussorgsky in any hurry to return to Petersburg. From Karevo he went in the spring to a friend's estate at Volok, in the Pskof Government, still thinking about his D major Symphony, of which he now wrote the slow movement and began the finale, but reflecting rather ruefully that " although I haven't run away from work, I have—with my Russian indolence—done little ". Nor was he over-confident of his talent, " though I don't doubt its existence ". Yet these months in the country gave him at least one experience which he recoined in terms of music. One day he chanced to notice a band of peasants making their way with difficulty through deep snowdrifts in brilliant winter sunshine. " It was at once beautiful, picturesque, serious and amusing. Suddenly there appeared a group of peasant girls, singing and laughing as they came along on a strip of hard snow. This picture impressed itself on my mind in a musical form. The first melody, rising and falling *à la Bach*, at once came into my head; the happy laughter of the women suggested to me the theme on which I afterwards based the *trio*. But all this was conceived *in modo classico,* in accordance with my musical preoccupations at that time." This " Intermezzo in modo classico " is therefore the first instance of that *pantomimic* element which is one of the most characteristic features of Mussorgsky's music. But for the present, in spite of his improved health, Mussorgsky was troubled by no imperious flow of inspiration. He plodded along with his pseudo-classical Symphony, arranged Beethoven's Quartet, Op. 130, for two pianos, read and went for long walks in the snow with his host.

We know nothing definite of Mussorgsky's doings after his return to Petersburg. He rather vaguely informed Liudmila Shestakova later that during this year he " set his brains in order and stocked them with useful information ". At any rate the months passed quite unproductively. The troublesome Symphony appears to have been abandoned, perhaps destroyed, for it has totally disappeared. At the end of October, 1862, Rimsky-Korsakof left them, being ordered abroad on a long cruise, his place in the circle being almost immediately taken by Borodin, who had just returned from *his* travels, a married man already beginning to make a name for himself in the scientific world. Borodin now met Balakiref for the first time, and at Balakiref's once more encountered Mussorgsky. Korsakof had already begun a symphony, and Balakiref and Mussorgsky played " the absent one's " finale to Borodin. He has recorded that Mussorgsky's playing had now changed in style. " I was struck by the brilliance, intelligence and energy of the performance." In the summer of the following year we get another glimpse of Mussorgsky from the correspondence of Balakiref and Stassof, an extremely unflattering one which shows that the " setting in order " of his brains had not made a profound impression on his friends. He and Stassof had attended the first performance of Serof's "Judith" together, and both wrote long letters about it to Balakiref in the Caucasus. Stassof in the course of his letter remarks of his companion that "his thoughts agree with mine, yet I didn't hear from him a single idea or a single word of really deep understanding . . . Everything about him is flabby and colourless. He seems to me to be a perfect *idiot* . . . I believe if you withdrew your tutelage, took him from the sphere where you have held him by force and set him free to follow his own devices and his own tastes, he would soon get overrun with weeds like all the rest. There's nothing inside him". To which Balakiref tersely agreed: "Mussorgsky is almost an idiot".

Meanwhile the "idiot" had once more gone into the country to contemplate the problems of the family estate. (One can hardly imagine him solving them.) He detested the "lavatory atmosphere" of Toropets, the provincial capital near Karevo, with its conservative landowners drinking and bemoaning their "lost rights" and their "utter ruin". But "bored and sad and vexed" as he was, he set to music the Harper's Song from "Wilhelm Meister" ("An die Türen will ich schleichen"), and set it daringly with an unresolved final discord. And a little later, during a second visit to Volok, he composed two more songs, one of which, a setting of a translation of Byron's "Song of Saul before his Last Battle", shows that Mussorgsky was approaching artistic maturity. These three pieces, the Goethe song, "King Saul" and the piano "Intermezzo", which he was already thinking of orchestrating, mark the beginning of the period of transition.

Unfortunately at this very moment when his creative talent was at last ripening, material circumstances compelled Mussorgsky to abandon his independence and enter Government service. In December, 1863, he was posted to the Engineering Department of the Ministry of Communications with the rank of "collegiate secretary" and on January 20th/February 1st, appointed assistant head clerk. Yet the period was by no means an unhappy one. Indeed he afterwards spoke of the years 1864-65 as among the happiest of his life. Ever since his return to Petersburg in the autumn he had been living "communally", in the manner then fashionable among the young liberal intellectuals, with five other young fellows of congenial tastes, three of them brothers, of whom we know nothing but their names. No doubt the free and easy atmosphere of the "commune", which none the less allowed each member a sanctum of his own to work or read in, was the more pleasant to Mussorgsky by contrast with the over-bracing air of the Balakiref circle. Mussorgsky needed the occasional relaxation provided by the company of congenial "commonplace people", despicable weakness as it was in Balakiref's eyes. At any rate, Mussorgsky enjoyed the atmosphere of the commune and found that it assisted his productiveness. Whereas in the Balakiref circle he was considered the least significant member, he must have cut a much more imposing figure in the commune and he at once gained confidence to embark on a big work. Almost simultaneously with the beginning of his communal life he began to plan an opera on the subject of "Salammbô", which had appeared only two or three years before. He at once (October, 1863) began to concoct his libretto, beginning with the first scene of Act IV (Mathô in the dungeon) and also completed the second scene of Act II (the theft of the zaïmph) before the end of the year. It was a curious piece of work, that libretto. Some of its verses were Mussorgsky's own; but he patched into it any suitable passage he could find in Heine or Maikof or Zhukovsky, and cemented the whole together with liberal stage-directions taken directly from Flaubert's pages. He appears to have been taken up more with the possible stage-pictures and crowd effects than with the music. Yet much of the music, when it was written, was fit to be transferred wholesale to the pages of " Boris Godunof ".

According to his brother, Mussorgsky also busied himself at this period with the translation of celebrated French and German criminal cases, though whether for his own amusement or to earn a little money, Filaret does not say. But music was naturally not neglected. March, April and May of 1864 each brought forth a new song, each song (it is hardly too much to say) a step nearer the mature Mussorgsky: settings of Koltsof's " The Winds Blow " (a musical foretaste of the " revolt " scene at the end of " Boris "); Pushkin's " Night ", a masterpiece of pure lyricism; and a " first attempt at the comic ", as a note on the manuscript records, Nekrassof's " Kalistratushka ". Then he turned again to " Salammbô ", compiling the libretto of the scene of the sacrifice to Moloch, and composing a " Song of the Balearic Singer " and the music of the dungeon scene. It really seemed as if " Salammbô " would materialise into a completed whole. Yet during the whole of the following year he appears not to have touched it at all.

In the spring of 1865 Mussorgsky received a severe shock from the death of his mother. He had worshipped her, and the wound to his affectionate, childlike nature must have been particularly deep. Just before her death, perhaps during her illness, he had dedicated to her an attempt to rival Glinka in a setting of Lermontof's " Prayer ". And of the handful of little pieces, none of them of any importance, which he wrote in the course of the year, three are dedicated " to the memory of my mother ": the two piano pieces, " From Memories of my Childhood " and the " Cradle Song " from Ostrovsky's play, " The Voevoda ". Mussorgsky seems to have tried to drown his sorrows by all-too-familiar means and these excesses told heavily on a constitution undermined in the ways we have already noticed. Filaret felt obliged to rescue him from the commune and bring him under his own immediate care. "In the autumn of '65", Filaret told Stassof, "he fell seriously ill. A terrible disease *(delirium tremens)* was coming on, in consequence of which my wife induced Modest to leave the 'commune' and—at first this was against his will—to make his home with us." So Mussorgsky lived with his brother till the autumn of 1868. And the pitying gods gave him, in 1866, a new friend in Liudmila Shestakova, Glinka's sister. Her only child, Glinka's pet Olga, had died in 1863 and for three years she had quite withdrawn from the world of music. It seems that she returned to it so that history might repeat itself, for she had mothered her brother when he was left almost helpless by his " dear mamma's " death; and now, a woman of fifty, she was little by little to take precisely the same place in the life of the twenty-seven-year-old Mussorgsky.

In the domestic atmosphere of Filaret's home, Modest again began to devote his leisure hours to the opera he had neglected for a whole year. For a while his time was once more quietly divided between the ledgers of the Engineering Department and the score of " Salammbô ". In February, 1866, he wrote a chorus of priestesses "consoling Salammbô", in April, a male chorus, " The War Song of the Lybians ", in June, another version of the same number. And there he stopped, this time finally. Another idea was already enticing him aside. In March his old piano teacher, Herke, had given the first performance in Russia of Liszt's " Danse macabre " for piano and orchestra, at an R.M.S. concert, Anton Rubinstein conducting. This piece of musical diabolism seems to have reminded Mussorgsky of his old idea of writing music for the Bare Mountain scene of Mengden's " Witch ", and so indirectly to have given the death-blow to " Salammbô ". A month or so later we find him sending a note to Balakiref, whom he " hasn't seen for a long time " and with whom he " wants to discuss all sorts of things ", announcing that he has " begun to sketch out the witches ", but is " not satisfied yet with Satan's cortège ". Again in August: " I'm thirsting to talk to you about the witches ". But nearly a year was to pass before he seriously set to work at the music. The latter half of 1866 saw the production of nothing but a few songs, though of these few four are outstanding. Two—" Hopak " and " Yarema's Song "—are from the " Haidamaki " of the Ukrainian poet, Shevtchenko, the other two—" Darling Savishna " and " The Seminarist "—are settings of Mussorgsky's own words. And with these latter two masterpieces of naturalism, both written in September, 1866, the tragedy of the village idiot in love with the village beauty (based on an incident Mussorgsky had actually observed) and the sharp-edged comedy of the student-priest with the wandering thoughts, he definitely enters the ranks of those composers who have said something in music which no one else could have said. The fact that we know so little about his artistic development at this crucial period is peculiarly tantalising. But any attempt to describe its inner history, the finding of his own personality and the break away from Balakirefian leading-strings, would be merely imaginative fiction. An honest biographer must content himself with the dull but necessary cataloguing of compositions. The various elements had already shown themselves separately: the sympathy with the peasants as " real human beings ", the pantomimic possibilities of music in the " Intermezzo ", the humorous possibilities in " Kalistrat ", flagrant disregard of musical convention in the Harper's Song, leaning toward naturalistic *parlando* recitative (literal musical translation of the speaking voice, as it were) in a little piece " The Outcast " for voice and piano, written in 1865. Now all these different elements were crystallising into some sort of unity to provide a medium of expression for a man who, with all his weaknesses, partly perhaps because of them, was a subtle psychologist with peculiarly keen insight into the weaknesses of human nature.

At least, into those of the Russian nature, which was practically the only kind he knew. It must be remembered that, whereas every other Russian composer of importance except Balakiref travelled extensively, Mussorgsky never left Russia in his life—and only once went farther from Petersburg than Moscow. Nothing, therefore, shook his conviction, expressed in more than one chauvinistic letter of this period, that the Russian was far superior to all " Germans, Jews, Czechs and Poles ". In this, as in more important matters, Mussorgsky was simply taking the colour of his surroundings, as a few years before he had faithfully echoed the opinions of Balakiref and Cui. Even his mature artistic tendencies were largely conditioned by the surrounding intellectual atmosphere. The young Russia of the sixties, of the age of reform, was full of " facing the facts " and " going to the people ", contemptuous of beauty and art-for-art's-sake. We shall never know the real extent of Mussorgsky's debt to the " commune ".

On March 6th/18th, 1867, Mussorgsky for the third time had one of his compositions performed publicly, though strangely enough this was the first occasion on which Balakiref had included anything of his in the programmes of the Free School concerts. The new work was a setting of a translation of Byron's " Destruction of Sennacherib " for chorus and orchestra, written in January and dedicated to Balakiref.[1] The composer himself spoke of it as a " chorus *à la magyar* "! But this small artistic success was outset by a material misfortune. A month or so later Mussorgsky was dismissed from the Engineering Department. Not for any fault of his own, apparently, for he had only recently been promoted, but simply owing to a reduction of staff. One consequence, of course, was that he had more time to devote to music. He left Petersburg for his brother's little estate of Minkino—

---

[1] Another version, made six or seven years later and orchestrated by Rimsky-Korsakof during Mussorgsky's lifetime, was dedicated to V. V. Stassof.

they had been obliged to sell Karevo—and stayed there from June till November. It was a comparatively fruitful period for, in addition to a number of piano arrangements of Beethoven's quartets and several songs (among them, the " Hebrew Song " and " The Magpie "), he revised and orchestrated the " Intermezzo in modo classico ". More important still, he at last wrote out his long projected " witches ", which he now decided to call " St. John's Night on the Bare Mountain ". This " musical picture "[1] was appropriately finished on St. John's Eve (June 23rd/July 5th) after eleven days of feverish work. " Something boiled in me, so that I simply didn't know what was being created ", according to his own account. This was the first work on a fairly large scale he had so far managed to finish, and he proudly announced the fact in a letter to Rimsky-Korsakof, who was just then busy with his own " musical picture ", " Sadko ": " The general character of the thing is warm; it doesn't drag; its structure is concise without any German padding, which makes it remarkably refreshing . . . I feel that ' St. John's Night ' is something new and is bound to produce a favourable impression on intelligent musicians." He is quite aware that there are things in it for which " Cesar " (i.e. Cui) " would send me to the Conservatoire " for lessons in respectable composition, and other things " for which they would turn me *out* of the Conservatoire ". Nevertheless, " I'm not going to start altering it; with whatever shortcomings it was born, it will have to live—if it does live—though at the same time a great deal might with advantage be made clearer ". And to another friend, Nikolsky, after a lengthy description of the work, he writes: " I chatter rather a lot about my ' Night ', I suppose for this reason: that I see in my sinful pranks an original Russian

---

[1] According to Rimsky-Korsakof's " Memoirs ", this was a " fantasia for piano and orchestra ", but Mussorgsky himself says nothing of the pianoforte. Possibly Rimsky-Korsakof's memory was at fault. It was probably this 1867 version which was given in London on February 3rd, 1932, and there was no piano in that.

production; not a mass of Teutonic profundity and routine, but, like 'Savishna', produced from our native fields and nourished with Russian bread." Unfortunately Balakiref, to whom the masterpiece was dedicated, though presumably an "intelligent musician", was *not* favourably impressed. He disliked it and demanded that the "glorification of Satan" should be written in "F sharp major *à la* Liszt's 'Divina Comedia'". But Mussorgsky replied to his criticisms in a tone which shows to what extent he had now emancipated himself from the other's overbearing personality: "Although I'm ashamed to confess it, I was hurt by your opinion of my witches. I considered, consider and shall go on considering it a good piece of work. I have produced some individual trifles, but this is the first individual *big* thing I've done. Whether you agree to give my witches or not" (i.e. at a Free School concert) "I shall not alter either the general plan or the working-out. Every author remembers the mood in which he wrote a work and this feeling, or the recollection of a former mood, greatly strengthens his confidence in his personal judgment. I've done my job as well as I was able. I will change nothing but the use of the percussion, which is bad."

But if Balakiref was a severe critic, with a poor opinion of Mussorgsky as a composer, he was a none the less warm-hearted friend, as appears from other passages in this same letter of Mussorgsky's:

> Your friendly appeal is so strongly put that it would be ungracious of me to refuse to reply to it . . . But this is how things are, my dear Mily: if I were so placed that I had nothing to eat and could see no hope for the future, it would be different. But as it is, I don't consider myself *justified* in frightening my friends . . . My means are diminished, it's true, but not so much as to make it impossible for me to live independently. Being accustomed

to comfort, and to some extent to luxury, my present circumstances disquieted me about the future and it isn't surprising that I made a wry face. Anyone else would have done so in my position . . . But I not merely ask but implore you not to worry on my account, and to set at rest the minds of those dear to me; for their fears for me weigh heavily on me and are not justified by my position.

And he goes on to explain how he proposes to cut down expenses by staying a month longer in the country and only spending the period from October to April in " Peter ", and states his intention of trying for another Government post in the New Year when the annual changes in the personnel of the Ministries take place. The end of the letter, after the firm stand about " St. John's Night ", is particularly affectionate. He once more signs himself " Your Modest " as in earlier days, not, as he had done more recently, " Modest Mussorgsky ".

But it was now to the youngest member of the " mighty handful ", Rimsky-Korsakof, that Mussorgsky confided his more intimate aspirations. Korsakof and he corresponded eagerly, describing their new compositions in detail, with liberal musical quotations and much self-satisfaction. Rimsky-Korsakof's return to Russia, and hence to the weekly meetings of the circle, had coincided with Mussorgsky's removal from the commune to his brother's house, but their more intimate friendship naturally took some little time to develop.

" St. John's Night " was immediately followed by a number of Mussorgsky's most individual songs: " The Street Arab ", " A Worldly Story (The He-Goat)", " The Classicist " (a lampoon on the conservative critic, Famintsyn), " The Carousal ", " Gathering Mushrooms ", " On the Don " and " The Orphan ". And at some time—just when it is impossible to say—during the same year (1867) the publisher Johansen, brought out " Darling Savishna " and the " Hopak ", the first of Mussorgsky's serious compositions to appear in print. (Most of his other separate songs were published soon after, during the period 1868-71.) After this spate of songs, he was ready to try his wings in a longer flight, the direction of which is hinted at in the dedication of two more songs, " Yeromushka's Cradle Song " and " Child and Nurse ", written in the spring of 1868: " To the great teacher of musical truth, A. S. Dargomyjsky ".

The hitherto rather contemptuous attitude of the whole Balakiref circle toward Dargomyjsky had suddenly changed to one of interest and even respect. Up to now he had been the chief of the " Russian invalids " and they had vied with each other in inventing nicknames for him. (And Mussorgsky, in particular, had a talent for nicknames.) It was only, apparently, in February, 1868, that they learned of Dargomyjsky's daring experiment in setting to music Pushkin's " little tragedy ", " The Stone Guest ", just as it stood, without any of the customary " adaptation for musical purposes ". Naturally the boldness of the idea and of the treatment, the abandonment of all key-signature, the passages in the whole-tone mode and so on, interested them all; they had not expected such enterprise from " Dargopekh "; and through the spring they gathered weekly at his house to hear and perform the work as it progressed, Mussorgsky doubling the rôles of Leporello and Don Carlos.[1] Both Cui and Rimsky-Korsakof began to consider the composition of " dramatically truthful " operas. But to none can " The Stone Guest " have been as interesting as to Mussorgsky, who had been experimenting on such similar lines in his songs. He now considered the possibility of doing something on a large scale in the same vein. His success in handling the humorous and satirical in his songs no doubt decided his choice of a comic subject, and it finally fell

---

[1] According to the singer Platonova, Mussorgsky " had not much of a voice ; but hoarse and colourless as it was, it became powerful when he sang Varlaam in ' Boris '—and charming when he represented the Pretender dreaming of Marina, or Marina herself ".

on Gogol's comedy "The Marriage". Like Dargomyjsky, Mussorgsky determined to set the text without any modification, though this was prose, while "The Stone Guest" is in verse. He set out boldly. "In my *opéra dialogué* I shall try as far as possible clearly to note down those changes of intonation, which occur in the course of conversation apparently for the most trivial reasons and on the most insignificant words, in which in my opinion lies the secret of Gogol's humour."

Mussorgsky began "The Marriage" in "Petrograd" (as, like a good Slavophil, he had begun to call the capital) on June 11th/23rd, took the score with him to Shilovo, Filaret's other little estate in the Tula Government, and finished the First Act there, with piano accompaniment only, on July 8th/20th, twenty-seven days' work in all. It was written in the rough, contrary to his usual custom, "since I have no piano; I shall put it in order in 'Peter'". He was living in a peasant's hut, drinking milk and staying out in the open air all day; "they only pen me up at night". But having finished the First Act, he stuck fast and began to "think about it"—a fatal step for any Russian! "I'm thinking about the Second Act of 'The Marriage' . . . and observing characteristic old women and typical peasants—both may come in useful", he writes to Liudmila Shestakova. "How the Russian nature teems with fresh traits which art has so far left untouched, oh, *how* many and what splendid ones! Some of these things which life has brought me I have already turned into musical forms for those dear to me. If God gives me life and strength, I shall have much more to say; after 'The Marriage' the Rubicon will be passed, but 'The Marriage' is a cage in which I shall stay of my own free will until I'm disciplined . . . I'll tell you what I'd like to do: to make my characters speak on the stage as living people really speak . . . and my music must be an artistic reproduction of human speech in all its finest shades. That's my ideal (Savishna, The Orphan, Yeromushka, Child and Nurse)." But that he was not quite sure of his success appears from a letter written the very same day to Rimsky-Korsakof: " I've been looking through my work—in my opinion, it's fairly interesting—however, who knows?" And from a batch of letters to Nikolsky, Cui and Rimsky-Korsakof a fortnight or so later, we learn that the Second Act is " only in his thoughts " so far; it is too soon yet to start writing. " I've written a whole act of musical prose—in my opinion successfully. But I don't know how the other three will turn out. I know they've *got* to be good, but I don't know whether they *can* be. However, the thing must be finished and judged afterwards. But through the fog of uncertainty I see one point of light—there will have to be a total abandonment of the existing opera-tradition." And he winds up with a shower of *obiter dicta*: " Now my dear Korsinka, listen to one thing: the act of creation bears within itself its own laws of taste. Their verification is—inward criticism; their application—a matter for the artist's instinct . . . The artist is a law unto himself ".

Filaret Mussorgsky's increasing financial difficulties had obliged him to sell his town house, and Modest on returning to Petersburg took up his quarters with his old friends the Opotchinins, or, at least, with Nadejda and her eldest brother Alexander, the head of the Archives of the Engineering Department. From this time onward Filaret seems almost to have faded out of Modest's life, the break being so complete as to suggest a quarrel. At the end of the year Modest managed to get an appointment as assistant head clerk in the Forest Department of the Ministry of State Property. But for three months he was his own master. They were eventful months. To begin with, there was the private performance of the First Act of " The Marriage " at Cui's on September 24th/October 6th. A week or so later, the first Russian performance of " Lohengrin ", which

Dargomyjsky and the " handful " attended in a body—and greeted with mockery. In November, the private performance of the nearly complete " Stone Guest ". In Dargomyjsky's work, Mussorgsky took his two usual rôles, in his own that of the " hero " Podkolessin, while Dargomyjsky sang the part of Podkolessin's malicious friend. The circle as a whole were rather flabbergasted by " The Marriage ". They admired the boldness of the experiment, the composer's skill in characterisation and his handling of recitative, but they were severely shocked by his harmonies. Borodin expressed the general opinion when he wrote to his wife that the thing was " extraordinarily curious and paradoxical, full of innovations and in places of great humour, but as a whole—*une chose manquée*—impossible in performance. Besides, it bears marks of too hurried labour ". Even Dargomyjsky thought the composer had " gone a little too far ". Stassof alone was " enraptured " by it, according to Rimsky-Korsakof. It is strange that the man who had so far shown no sign of acknowledging Mussorgsky to be anything better than a " perfect idiot " should now be the only member of the circle to approve what all the others looked upon as slightly idiotic![1] Stassof's *volte-face* with regard to Mussorgsky is even more remarkable than that of the " handful " as a whole toward Dargomyjsky. Yet from this time onward, we find Stassof taking an ever closer interest in Mussorgsky's work, an interest which led to a much more intimate friendship. As for the " Marriage ", whether Mussorgsky himself recognised it as *une chose manquée* or whether a new idea had driven all thought of it from his head, it is impossible to say. At any rate, he dropped it, as he had dropped " Œdipus " and " Salammbô ". Nor need we regret it, for the idea which had supplanted it was that of " Boris Godunof ", in which his own peculiar, uncompromising realism was to be

[1] Mussorgsky afterwards gave him the score of " The Marriage "—" my student work ".

blended with the more lyrical idiom of his comrades to form an unapproachable masterpiece.

The subject of Pushkin's early pseudo-Shakespearian drama was suggested to Mussorgsky, one evening that autumn, at Liudmila Shestakova's, by their friend Nikolsky, Professor of Russian Literature at the Alexandrovsky Lyceum, historian, editor of the first edition of Glinka's " Memoirs " and a well-known Pushkin scholar. Mussorgsky at once became enthusiastic over the idea. Liudmila Shestakova gave him a copy of the play, interleaved with blank pages, on which he could work out the libretto; for there was no more talk of setting whole plays just as they stood. (In fact, Mussorgsky " edited " Pushkin's play quite as drastically as Rimsky-Korsakof afterwards " edited " his own opera.) Stassof helped with all sorts of historical and archæological information. And already in November we find the Russian Music Society, now conducted by Balakiref, announcing among other events of the forthcoming season the performance of " excerpts from the opera ' Boris Godunof ' by Mr. Mussorgsky "! That was a little premature, for the opera did not yet exist and the promise was not fulfilled. But Mussorgsky began the composition with unusual industry, finishing the vocal score of the opening scene on November 4th/16th, the coronation scene and the scene in Pimen's cell a month later.[1] But at that point he entered the Forest Department and consequently had much less time to devote to composition. And there were other distractions: the first performance of Borodin's First Symphony, the death the very next day of Dargomyjsky, who had taken the keenest interest in the opening scenes of " Boris ", the first performances of Cui's "William Ratcliffe"

[1] As originally planned, "Boris" consisted of seven "pictures", divided into four "parts", not acts: these three and four others—the inn scene, the scene of Boris with his children, a scene before St. Basil's Cathedral, which has no place in the final form of the opera, and the scene of the *duma* with Boris's death. The opera was given in this form at Sadler's Wells in 1935.

and Rimsky-Korsakof's " Antar ", all events which naturally loomed very large in the eyes of the Balakiref circle. The inn scene of " Boris ", though not dated, must have been composed at about this time; the scene in the Tsar's apartment was finished by the end of May, the scene before St. Basil's a month later; and on July 18th/30th Stassof wrote to his brother Dmitri that " Mussorgsky has definitely completed ' Boris Godunof ' ", and proceeded to go into raptures about the death-scene. The orchestration was begun at the end of the summer and completed on December 15th/27th—a few weeks, incidentally, after Leo Tolstoy had written the last lines of " War and Peace ". " Boris " was the first big score Mussorgsky had managed to complete. Indeed, " Boris " was the only big work he ever did finish.

We again have singularly little information about Mussorgsky's life during this important year. " Boris " and the Forest Department (where he was soon promoted to the rank of " collegiate assessor ") can have left him little spare time. But we get a very revealing glimpse of his " difficult " temperament in the postscript to a note to Balakiref. The authorities of the detested Conservatoire had sent the members of Balakiref's circle complimentary tickets for their chamber and orchestral concerts. It was a friendly gesture and Borodin, at any rate, accepted the tickets in the same friendly spirit. Not so Mussorgsky. " I received the tickets for the *musical slum* concerts and decided to send them back at once to the musical slum." As a rule affectionate and easy-going, he was suspicious and quick to imagine an insult where none could possibly have been intended. On another occasion, not having received from Cui a prompt reply to a letter, he exploded to Korsakof: " *Cesare* has insulted me. When I don't receive an answer, having a suspicious nature, I suspect something wrong. And when I suspect that, I worry. And when I worry, I get in a bad temper." In June, 1870, he gave acid expression to his hatred of " official art" and its representatives in a song, "The Peepshow", a collective lampoon on Zaremba of the "musical slum", Theophil Tolstoy, Famintsyn, Serof and the Grand Duchess Helena Pavlovna, patroness of the R.M.S. "The Peepshow" was only the second of Mussorgsky's compositions to be dedicated to Stassof. Hitherto the bulk of his dedications had been to one or another of the Opotchinins, more rarely to his comrades of the "handful", and latterly to Liudmila Shestakova. The growing warmth of his friendship with Stassof is very noticeable, too, in the tone of his letters.

At this period Mussorgsky was in collision with other than musical officialdom. The censorship first forbade the publication in Russia of "The Seminarist", on the ground that it was slightly blasphemous, and then seized an imported edition which had been printed in Leipzig. The composer was allowed only ten copies for presentation to his most intimate friends. They were given to Liudmila Shestakova, Rimsky-Korsakof, his fiancée Nadejda Purgold, Nadejda's sister Alexandra, their uncle Vladimir Purgold, Balakiref, Nikolsky, Cui, Stassof, and Borodin.

Mussorgsky had met the Purgold girls at Dargomyjsky's in the course of the "Stone Guest" performances, in which Alexandra had sung Donna Anna and Laura, and Nadejda ("Dear Orchestra" and "Excellent Orchestra", as Mussorgsky used to call her) had been the pianist. Many years afterwards, Nadejda recorded her impressions of the thirty-three-year-old Mussorgsky. "Mussorgsky's personality was so unusual that, once having seen him, it was impossible to forget him. He was of middle height and well-built. He had elegant hands, beautifully brushed wavy hair, and rather large and somewhat protuberant eyes. But his features were very plain, particularly the nose, which was reddish—owing, as Mussorgsky used to explain, to its having been frost-bitten once on parade. Mussorgsky's eyes were by no means expressive; one might almost have called them glassy. On the whole, his face was not very mobile or expressive; it was as if it concealed some mystery. Mussorgsky never raised his voice in conversation, but rather lowered it to a *mezza voce*. (I remember how he used to make a witty or piquant remark as if to himself; or, with his tongue in his cheek, abuse one of his friends when it was obvious that he was really praising him.) His manners were elegant, aristocratic; he had the air of a cultured man of the world. Mussorgsky's personality produced an impression on both of us. And no wonder. There was so much in it that was interesting, peculiar, talented and enigmatic. His singing delighted us. He had a small but pleasant baritone and his power of expression, his perfect understanding of every shade of feeling, the simplicity and sincerity of his interpretation, without the least exaggeration or affectation—all this had a fascinating effect. I was later convinced of the many-sidedness of his talent as a performer; he was just as good in lyrical and dramatic as in comic things. In addition he was a fine pianist; his playing was marked by brilliance, strength and elegance, combined with life and humour. He sang things like ' The Peepshow ', ' The Street Arab ', ' The He-Goat ', ' The Classicist ', and so on, with inimitable humour. On the other hand, his performance of the parts of Ivan the Terrible and Tsar Boris was full of deep dramatic feeling. Mussorgsky was an enemy of every sort of routine and commonplace, not only in music but in every phase of life, even in trifles. He disliked using ordinary simple words." (Except, apparently, to children—whom he treated simply and naturally as equals, winning their confidence with surprising success.) " He always contrived to twist and alter even surnames. The style of his letters was unusually individual and piquant; they glittered with wit, humour and bull's-eye-hitting epithets. In later years this individual style became an affectation, particularly noticeable in his letters to V. V. Stassof. However, this affectation and unnaturalness sometimes showed itself in those later years not only in his letters but in the whole of his behaviour." That is very true. Mussorgsky's fantastic letters—sometimes exasperatingly fantastic, with their puns and roundabout phrases and distortions of names—defy adequate translation.

Mussorgsky had frequently performed "Boris" to his small circle of intimate friends; and in the summer, at Stassof's summer villa at Pargolovo, he played it through to larger and more mixed audiences who were rather puzzled, he says, by the *mujiks* (i.e. the opening scene). Some took it for a comic scene; others recognised the underlying tragedy. But at last in July, 1870, six months after he had finished the full score, Mussorgsky approached the Director of the Imperial Theatres with a request for its production. The Director, S. A. Gedeonof, son of the Gedeonof who had occupied the same position in Glinka's time and brother of Michael Gedeonof, to whom Glinka had dedicated "Ruslan", told Mussorgsky that he could put on nothing new that year but gave him permission to submit the score to the selection committee a month or two later. Although he speaks of "frightening them with 'Boris'", Mussorgsky seems not to have had any doubt about the acceptance of his work. He was even looking round for another opera subject and had already been borrowing from Nikolsky books on the sectarian Old Believers—pointing to the idea of "Khovanshchina". Cui suggested a play of Ostrovsky's; he himself contemplated for a time another comic subject from Gogol but rejected it on the ground that there was not enough in it of "Mother Russia in all her simple-hearted breadth"; and Stassof sent him the complete scenario of a four-act opera, "Bobyl", for which he actually composed a conjuration scene, the music of which was used later in "Khovanshchina".

But Mussorgsky could whip up little interest in this work. He turned once more to his vivid little sketches of children and in the period September-December, 1870, wrote four songs to words of his own, " In the Corner ", " The Cockchafer ", " With the Doll " and " Going to Sleep ". These with the " Child and Nurse " of two years before and two more written in 1872, were published as a cycle " The Nursery ". The dedication of " In the Corner " marks the beginning of Mussorgsky's friendship with the brilliant young architect and water-colour painter, Victor Hartmann, who had attracted general attention that year by his work exhibited at the Petersburg All-Russian Exhibition. Stassof took a fancy to him and drew him into his circle, and a warm friendship soon sprang up between him and Mussorgsky.

In February, 1871, Mussorgsky suffered a bitter disappointment. The opera committee of the Marinsky Theatre by six votes to one rejected " Boris Godunof ". The committee consisted of the conductors Napravnik, Voiatchek, Papkof and Betz, the violinists Maurer and Klamrodt, and the double-bassist Ferrero. One wonders which of the seven had the insight to slip that white ball into the ballot-box. Could it have been Napravnik? He was the likeliest. And the reasons for the six black balls? According to Rimsky-Korsakof who, writing thirty or forty years later, has given the constitution of the committee wrongly, " the modernism and unusualness of the music flabbergasted them . . . Among other things, they complained of the lack of a female rôle of any importance. Many of the committee's quibbles were simply ridiculous. For instance, the double-basses *divisi* playing chromatic thirds in the accompaniment of Varlaam's second song badly shocked the double-bassist Ferrero, who could not forgive the composer for employing such a device ". But, contrary to his usual habit of taking offence at official views, Mussorgsky began to recast his work in the hope of inducing the committee to change its mind. He restored the figure of the seductive Marina, whom he had entirely left out of his first draft, and at once wrote the

first scene of what is now the Third Act (often spoken of as
" the Polish act "), finishing it in April. The composition
of this scene " boiled ", as he used to say, giving him no sleep
for two nights running on one occasion. (" I love it when
composition goes like that ", he told Stassof.) Yet he wrote
no more for three or four months, when, instead of continuing
the Polish act, he set about the entire rewriting of the scene
of Boris with his children.

Mussorgsky spent the greater part of his spare time that
summer with Rimsky-Korsakof and the latter's brother, Voin,
making frequent expeditions together to Pargolovo, where
Stassof and the Purgolds had summer villas. Finally, at
the beginning of September, " Korsinka " and Modest
decided to share apartments, taking a furnished room in a
house in Panteleïmonskaya Street. " I shall never forget
that time ", Stassof wrote in 1905, just before his death,
" when they, both still young, lived together in one room . . .
I used to visit them early in the morning, find them still
asleep, wake them, haul them out of bed, make them wash
and hand them their stockings, trousers, dressing-gowns or
jackets, and slippers. Nor how we used to drink tea together,
eating a snack of bread and butter with Swiss cheese. . . .
And directly that was over, we would turn to our chief and
favourite occupation—music . . . and they would show me
with delight and great excitement what they had written
during the last day or two. How jolly it all was! What
good times those were—but how long past! " The two
composers had only one writing-table and one piano. " How
did we manage not to interfere with each other?" writes
Rimsky-Korsakof. " Like this. In the morning until
noon Mussorgsky used the piano and I copied or orchestrated
something I had fully thought out. At noon he went off to
his duties at the Ministry and I had the piano. The evenings
were a matter of mutual arrangement. Besides, twice a week
I went to the Conservatoire at 9 a.m., and Mussorgsky often

dined with the Opotchinins, and things worked out most satisfactorily. We both got through a lot of work that winter, constantly exchanging ideas and plans." Korsakof was finishing his " Maid of Pskof ", in which Mussorgsky had helped with the libretto; Mussorgsky was making drastic changes in the scene in Pimen's cell, rescoring it, and composing the second scene of the Polish act, to the great approval, as he tells Stassof, of " the Corsican admiral " (Rimsky-Korsakof). Borodin, too, was charmed with the second version of " Boris " as it had shaped itself so far— " simply magnificent ". " As an opera ", he considered it " stronger than ' The Maid of Pskof ', though the latter is richer in purely musical beauties ". Only Balakiref still thought as poorly of Mussorgsky as ever; and in his distraught condition, for he was on the verge of his breakdown, he uttered the most biting criticisms of " Boris " " in the presence of people who on no account ought to have heard them ", as Borodin wrote to his wife.

Both " Boris " and " The Maid " were performed several times at the Purgolds' that winter, Mussorgsky singing the rôles of Ivan the Terrible, Tokmakof, etc. in his friend's opera. He invites Stassof to one such performance in a characteristic, though unusually coherent note:

> Most delightful *généralissime*, to-morrow, Saturday, beginning at 9.30 p.m. we are going to pull " Boris " by the hair. Naturally we shall meet, naturally we shall have a talk, naturally it will be pleasant for me to see the dear *généralissime*, naturally it's always pleasant for me to see him, naturally I may be too late with the information—naturally I finish the letter.—Mussorianin.

During the first three months of 1872 Mussorgsky was occupied with the orchestration of the scene with the children and the two scenes of the Polish act; and on April 3rd/15th Balakiref, after " editing " the piece a little, condescended to play the polonaise at one of his Free School concerts. (Coming at the end of the programme, it was actually the last thing he conducted before his withdrawal.) The finale of the First Act had already been given at an R.M.S. symphony concert, under Napravnik, on February 5th/17th. Simultaneously with this work on " Boris ", Mussorgsky was busy with his share in Gedeonof's projected " Mlada ". He and Rimsky-Korsakof divided the Second and Third Acts between them, an arrangement which would hardly have been possible had they not been living together. Mussorgsky composed a " March of the Princes " and a market-scene, but it appears that, like Borodin, he proposed to adapt previously written music for the rest of his contribution. He once more laid violent hands on his old temple chorus from " Œdipus ", already adapted once to fit into " Salammbô ", this time with the idea of using it for a scene of fisticuffs! Having a witches' sabbath to deal with, he was able to resuscitate his unfortunate " St. John's Night ", adding choral parts to it. But even before the project fell through, Mussorgsky was in revolt against the stupidity of the libretto and alarmed lest " the virgin purity of our circle " should be sullied by such hackwork.

Dropping " Mlada ", he concentrated again on " Boris ", adding the revolution scene in the forest near Kromy, an episode which does not occur in Pushkin's play. He had originally intended to insert this before the scene of Boris's death, but on Nikolsky's advice put it last of all, a stroke of dramatic genius which made Stassof furious with himself for not having thought of it. The complete work was tried out at the Purgolds' on April 8th/20th; and a month later, even before the new scene had been orchestrated, it was again submitted to the Directorate of the Imperial Theatres. The committee reconsidered it and—rejected it for the second time. Most composers would have accepted such a defeat as final. But Mussorgsky was encouraged by the interest of some of the artists of the Opera, who had heard the run through before the committee. According to his not altogether reliable autobiography, there was yet another performance before " an enormous company " at the Purgolds', the " enormous company " including Petrof, Platonova, F. P. Komissarjevsky (the famous father of two still more famous children—Vera and Theodore) and N. A. Lukashevitch, artistic director of the Imperial Theatres. And, solely on the initiative of these artists and in defiance of the advisory committee, it was resolved to give three scenes from " Boris " in a benefit performance for G. P. Kondratief, the stage-manager of the Marinsky Theatre.

In the meantime Mussorgsky was already looking round for another subject. As in 1870, he had no sooner submitted " Boris " to the Directorate than he began to think of its successor. Even before he finished the full score of " Boris " on June 23rd/July 5th, he had accepted Stassof's suggestion of the subject of " Khovanshchina ". A week or two later, he made a list of books on the period, the beginning of the reign of Peter the Great, marking them as " Materials for ' Khovanshchina ': a National Musical Drama in Five Parts by M. Mussorgsky ",[1] and a few days afterwards dedicated " to Vladimir Vassilievitch Stassof, my labour (according to my ability) inspired by his love ". He was in a melancholy mood, acutely conscious that " the bright days of our circle are over; its present is gloomy ". He blamed no one for the fact, yet it was clear that the ill-fated " Mlada ", their one grand collective effort, had marked the end of the Balakiref circle. Their leader had just entered upon his strange hegira. Rimsky-Korsakof, now a professor at the " musical slum ", had married Nadejda Purgold only a week or two before—Mussorgsky officiating as best man— and gone abroad with his bride. Borodin was busy, Cui never very sympathetic. Mussorgsky drew all the more closely to

[1] Mussorgsky himself never called " Boris " anything but an " opera "—*tout simple*.

Liudmila Shestakova and to the Stassof-Hartmann-Repin circle. Writing of the break-up of the old group to Liudmila, he told her: " It remains for you, my dear, to collect the remnants of the shattered, sacred army; and if pitched battle with the host of Philistines is impossible, we must still fight on to the last drop of blood." But it was chiefly on Stassof that he leaned, the Stassof who until recently had considered him a " perfect idiot ". His letters to Stassof, with their proud self-confidence and their humble, childlike affection, remind one of his earliest letters to Balakiref, though the pride is now more confident, the affection warmer. And one seldom or never hears the old note of revolt and resentment which Balakiref had so often provoked. " You are necessary to me, not because you are dear to me, but because you expect much of me. But I demand still more—and so you lead me on as a magnet would. . . . Without you I should soon be done for." Again, explaining his dedication of a work as yet non-existent, he says characteristically, " I like to look forward, not backward. I dedicate to you all that period of my life which will be occupied by the composition of ' Khovanshchina '. There would be nothing absurd in my saying: ' I dedicate to you both myself and my life for that period ', for I still vividly remember how I *lived* ' Boris ', in ' Boris '; and the time I lived in ' Boris ' has left precious and indelible marks on my mind. Now the new work, your work, is in full swing; I am already beginning to live in it. How many rich impressions, how many new lands to discover! Splendid!—So I beg you to accept ' all my disorderly being ' in the dedication of ' *Khovanshchina*', *which originated with you yourself.—* Mussorianin." But Rimsky-Korsakof and his friends took the view that Stassof was Mussorgsky's evil genius, musically, who encouraged him in his " eccentricities " and fed his vanity by accepting his " illiterate " blunders as strokes of genius.

During the summer and autumn, while gathering materials for " Khovanshchina ", Mussorgsky poured out to Stassof a wealth of views on the value of technique and the function of art in general. "*Tell me* why, when I listen to the conversation of young artists—painters or sculptors—I can follow their thoughts, their intellectual make-up, and seldom hear anything said about technique—unless it's quite unavoidable. Yet when I'm among our musical fraternity, I seldom hear a vital thought; one might as well be on a school-bench—it's all technique and the ABC of music." And again, towards the end of a letter mainly devoted to " the colossus Darwin": " The artistic representation of beauty alone, in the material sense, is vulgar puerility—artistic childishness. *The most subtle traits* of man's nature and *humanity in the mass*, the investigation of these little known regions and their conquest —that is the artist's real vocation. ' To new shores!' Fearlessly through storms, over shoals and sunken reefs, ' to new shores '! Man is animal and social, and he can't be otherwise; in the human masses, as in individuals, there are always the subtlest traits, elusive traits that no one has ever touched; to observe and study these by reading, by observation, by conjecture, to study *all this intensively* and with it to feed humanity as with some health-giving food, as yet untasted... There's an undertaking! Joy of joys! In our ' Khovanshchina ' we'll have a shot at it, won't we, my dear soothsayer?" And one or two meetings with Tchaïkovsky, who came to Petersburg twice that autumn to interview the Theatre Directorate about his " Opritchnik ", still further embittered Mussorgsky against " the admirers of absolute musical beauty ". He tells Stassof he has " experienced a strange *feeling of emptiness* in conversation with them ", and goes on to give an acidly amusing account of Tchaïkovsky's listening with disapproval to " The Nursery " and excerpts from " Boris ", " blowing bubbles which burst with dull, sluggish, unlovely sounds. From the sum of the sounds (there weren't many) from the bursting bubbles, I gathered: ' gifted '... (who—you know), ' but gifts dissipated ... would be a good idea to set about . . . a symphony . . . (*en forme*, of course) '. The gifted one thanked Sadyk Pasha " (his nickname for Tchaïkovsky) " and that was that ". And not only Tchaïkovsky but Rimsky-Korsakof had now to be reckoned among those " admirers of absolute beauty " whose views gave Mussorgsky the sense of having " lost someone near and dear ".

This spate of theorising was not accompanied by much productive work. From June, 1872, till June, 1873, Mussorgsky completed nothing but the last two songs of " The Nursery " and made a few alterations in the vocal score of " Boris ". There is a tide in the affairs of Russians when they can do nothing but spin theories and dissect themselves, and Mussorgsky seems to have been caught in such a flood. At any rate, for all his study of the " Khovanshchina " period, he made little progress with the work. Indeed, it is pretty clear that he studied the period a great deal too much, reading both at home and at the Petersburg Public Library, and completely muddled himself with the wealth of available material. Stassof had suggested the subject and the possible treatment of certain characters but not, as far as one can gather, a definite scenario such as he had drawn up for " Bobyl " and Borodin's " Prince Igor ". Which was unfortunate. For instead of systematically preparing one for himself and then basing his libretto on it, Mussorgsky evidently devised the libretto a bit at a time; writing some of it down and carrying the rest in his head; altering and adding to such plan as he had, as he went along; composing the music in the same piecemeal fashion; and hoping vaguely that it would all fit in and come right in the end! One is vividly reminded of Glinka with his " Ruslan " and its committee of librettists. And, of course, Borodin was at this very time writing " Igor " in a state of chaos only less confusing because the subject was more limited. Mussorgsky frequently discussed the work with Stassof, but as for the rest of the circle,

" none of us ", says Rimsky-Korsakof, " knew the real plot or plan, and from Mussorgsky's account—very flamboyant, florid and complicated, in accordance with his usual way of expressing himself at that time—it was difficult to understand the plot as a coherent whole ".

In the meantime, the prospect for " Boris " was brighter. The three scenes (the inn scene and the whole of the Polish act) given, with Act Two of " Lohengrin " and the First Act of " Der Freischütz ", in Kondratief's benefit at the Marinsky Theatre on February 5th/17th, 1873 (a few weeks after the first performance of " The Maid of Pskof "), had won complete success, a success celebrated by a champagne supper at the Rimsky-Korsakofs'. Though given only two rehearsals, the excerpts had the advantage of a first-rate cast. Petrof sang Varlaam, Platonova Marina, and Komissarjevsky Dmitri. Napravnik conducted, and on the following day Mussorgsky wrote him that " *only you* could have interpreted the scenes from ' Boris ' with such fire and artistry ... You saw deeply not only into all the details of the orchestral performance, but into all the finest shades of the scenes and of the declamation; in all your observations I perceived your sincere desire for the success of the work; I considered, and still consider, your observations an honour and reward for my student labour; only an artist of great talent could have understood the composer's intentions so exactly and with such artistic truth. Notwithstanding the ovations, neither in thought nor imagination have I once taken the credit to myself ... All the honour and glory I ascribe to you, Eduard Franzovitch, and to our dear comrades the artists and to the splendid orchestra. I tell you frankly that I bless your name for enabling me to continue my studies ". Such humble and effusive gratitude would have come not unnaturally from many a composer of nearly thirty-six, seeing his work on the stage for the first time. But the tone of this letter to one of the constituted authorities contrasts strangely with Mussorgsky's usual attitude to such authorities, particularly with the arrogance of a letter to Stassof a few weeks earlier: " No one has seen my inner self more easily, and consequently more deeply than you; no one has pointed out my path more clearly. You are dear to me—you know that; and I to you—I feel it. If our mutual attempts to make a living man in living music are going to be understood by *living* people; if the *vegetating* men fling lumps of mud at us; if the musical Pharisees crucify us—so much the better. The more mud, the faster our cause will advance. *Yes, judgment is at hand*! It's jolly to think of our standing on the place of execution, thinking *about ' Khovanshchina '* and living in it, while they are judging us for ' *Boris* '; daringly cheerful, we gaze into the musical distance which beckons us onward . . ."

One immediate result of this fragmentary performance was that the publisher Bessel, who had already issued some of Mussorgsky's songs, agreed to publish the vocal score, even though there seemed to be no hope as yet of a complete production in the usual way. Bessel's paper, " The Musical Leaflet ", announced on March 25th/April 6th, that he had acquired the copyright of the work, and that the vocal score arranged by the composer himself, " including scenes which, owing to the length of the spectacle, will not be performed on the stage ", would be available to subscribers at ten silver rubles and to non-subscribers at fifteen. The subscription list would not be open long and the score was to appear in the autumn. Actually it remained open till the end of the year, and the score was not published till January, 1874, a week or two before the first performance. Bessel later agreed to pay Mussorgsky 600 rubles (say £60) for the rights, half in the first season the opera was performed, the other 300 in the second season, though his accounts show that he actually paid the composer only 250 each year.

In June, 1873, Mussorgsky began to share rooms with a

young family connexion of his, Count Golenishchef-Kutuzof, later well known as a poet. Mussorgsky, who introduced him to the Stassofs, took a very exaggerated view of his talent, even placing him above Nekrassof and Mey. " Since Pushkin and Lermontof I have never come across stuff like some of Kutuzof's." With his " artistic nature and sympathetic mind ", the young man made an admirable companion for Mussorgsky. The composer badly needed some such companion; for, as he confessed to Stassof, he had been experiencing " fits of dementia such as he had had some years before ", fits which were really the consequence of drinking bouts. Stassof observed that he was " considerably altered—sunken, grown thin and more silent; but fortunately he composes as before ".

In fact, he at last began the music of " Khovanshchina " and was able to inform Dmitri Stassof's wife at the end of July that " the introduction to ' Khovanshchina ' (dawn in Moscow, matins at cockcrow, the patrol and the taking down of the chains) and the first beginnings of the act are ready, but not written down "—the piano score of the introduction is dated September 2nd/14th of the *following* year—and went on to announce that he was " now living in ' Khovanshchina ' as I lived in ' Boris ' ". He made no attempt to work more or less systematically as he had done in the composition of " Boris ", however. That was hardly possible with the course of the action as yet by no means decided; apart from the fact that the beginning of the composition of " Khovanshchina " appears to have coincided with a fresh outburst of dissipation. All he seems to have been at all clear about was the culmination, the self-immolation of the Old Believers. Accordingly, he began with the music of the opening scene, which might have served as the prelude to almost anything, and that of the last act. Then we find him working at situations in the Second and Third Acts. Martha's song in Act III, based on a folk-tune, was actually finished in August and *sent to the engravers*; and Bessel's " Musical Leaflet " in November, announcing its separate publication, uttered a preliminary fanfare heralding the entire opera. But there the publisher was a little too optimistic. Work was already slowing down to a standstill and, but for a few spasmodic efforts—and no doubt, a good deal of sketching and brooding—seems not to have been seriously resumed for nearly a year. At one moment Mussorgsky was eager only to get " Khovanshchina " finished, slashing out whole scenes and characters with the sole object of reducing the scheme to manageable proportions, so as to be free to press on to other subjects " each better than the rest ". The next, he had relapsed into apathy. And drunken apathy at that.

That summer Victor Hartmann died suddenly in Moscow, a heavy blow to Mussorgsky, as is evident from his grief-stricken letters, and one made all the heavier by self-reproach. For he tormented himself with the thought that, on the occasion of their last meeting, he had treated a heart-attack of his friend's with callous indifference. We may safely conclude that his grief did not make him more abstemious. Besides, Stassof was in Western Europe; and, out of his care, Mussorgsky quickly took the downward path. " It was really incredible ", says Repin, " how that well-bred Guards officer with his beautiful manners, that witty conversationalist with ladies, that inexhaustible punster, directly he was left without Stassof, quickly sank down, sold his furniture, even his elegant clothes, and took to haunting cheap restaurants where he settled down into the familiar type of ' has been '. . . . Was it really he? The once well-dressed, irreproachable society man, scented and fastidious? How many times had Stassof, on his return from abroad, to dig him out of some cellar, nearly in rags, swollen with drink! . . . . He would sit with disreputable companions till two in the morning, sometimes till daybreak ". Golenishchef-Kutuzof seems to have been powerless to keep a grip on him, even if he tried. Yet all this did not prevent his promotion in the service, for he received another step in December; though it is true he complains to Liudmila Shestakova of a " vulgar intrigue " against him at the Ministry.

Mussorgsky had already heard through Bessel that Liszt had seen his " Nursery " songs and expressed his approval of them. (" What will Liszt say when he sees the piano score of ' Boris '! ") And now Stassof wrote from Germany pressing him to join their family party, go to Weimar and make Liszt's acquaintance personally; even offering to pay his expenses. In vain. Mussorgsky wired, " Impossible ", and wrote excuses—he couldn't leave his office-chief in the lurch, for the latter's eyes were bad. " To turn my back on sacred, most vital life in order to pour over rubbish. Awful! For that's the truth." And still more awful if it was not the whole truth. Perhaps Stassof doubted, for he wrote again more urgently, imploring Mussorgsky to resign from the service altogether rather than not come. But now the excuse was that he could not leave " Khovanshchina ". " I have never felt more robust than at the present moment." He was enjoying that " tranquillity indispensable *for creative labour* ". As for seeing Liszt, it was " IMPOSSIBLE ". And having dismissed that topic in a few lines, he goes on with pages of details of his opera.

Mussorgsky may have had an inkling, too, that wires were being pulled on his behalf in the region of the Imperial Theatres, though he gave no hint of this to Stassof. Actually, he was on the eve of the greatest triumph of his life. On October 22nd/November 3rd, he was able to send Bessel an excited note: " *The Director has sanctioned ' Boris '.* I beg you to get the *Clavierauszug* ready *by the end of November.* That is indispensable—or it'll be all up ". What had produced this dramatic change of front on the part of the Directorate? According to the picturesque account given to Stassof by the singer Platonova it was entirely *her* doing:

she refuses to renew her contract unless Gedeonof will give 'Boris' for her benefit performance; Gedeonof, beside himself with despair, bullies Ferrero, the chairman of the committee; Ferrero is stubborn; Gedeonof, white with rage, announces that he will override the committee's repeated decision and personally take the responsibility of authorising " Boris ", in spite of the fact that he has " no sympathy with innovators ". He is even prepared to risk dismissal on account of his action—all rather than lose the precious Platonova. . . . Unfortunately, for romance, a letter of Platonova's to Gedeonof, written months before all this was supposed to have happened, shows that she only asked for the right to produce " a new opera " for her benefit; and even that point was not included in her contract. However, the truth appears to be that she and Lukashevitch did somehow persuade Gedeonof to disregard his advisory committee. Napravnik having refused to take the rehearsals, according to Platonova, " because he had so much else to do ", private rehearsals were held under Mussorgsky himself, the chorus being trained separately by the harpist Pomazansky. Orchestral rehearsals began in the theatre on January 9th/ 21st, 1874, and the first performance took place on January 27th/February 8th.[1]

According to Stassof: " It was a great triumph for Mussorgsky. The old men, the indifferentists, the routinists and the worshippers of banal operatic music sulked and raged (that, too, was a triumph); the pedants of the Conservatoire and the critics protested with foaming mouths. Through some stupid intrigue, four wreaths from youthful admirers of Mussorgsky were not presented to him during the first performance, and the poor girls had to send them to his house. On the other hand, the younger generation exulted and at once raised Mussorgsky on their shields . . . With their fresh,

[1] The second was given a week later, and there were eight more in the course of the season.

still unspoiled feelings, they realised that a great artistic power had created a wonderful national work, and they exulted and rejoiced and triumphed." Rimsky-Korsakof said long afterwards: "We all triumphed." Yet this cup of supreme joy was not without drops of bitterness—mostly distilled from the absurd consequences of the affair of the wreaths. Actually, it appears, the four girls had not complied with the regulations; but like Stassof, who ought to have known better, they scented intrigue and foolishly wrote to the "St. Petersburg Vedomosteï" blaming Napravnik. Mussorgsky, fearful lest this should result in the withdrawal of his opera, hastened to apologise to Napravnik privately and to "explain" in the columns of the "Vedomosteï". His explanation naturally made matters worse, vastly amusing his enemies, and Laroche of the "Golos" maliciously hinted that the composer was delighted at "the opportunity to talk about himself in a great newspaper". Worse than all, his own friend, Cui, the critic of the "Vedomosteï", not only made a playful allusion to the affair of the wreaths, but criticised the opera itself by no means flatteringly. The recitatives in the inn scene were "not melodic". "No inspiration is needed for the writing of that sort of recitative, only routine, practice." (Which, of course, hit Mussorgsky in a very tender spot.) "The two chief faults of 'Boris' are: the chopped recitative and the disconnectedness of the musical thought, making parts of the opera rather like a potpourri. These faults are by no means due to Mr. Mussorgsky's lack of creative power. By no means. Think of the two crowd scenes and the inn scene, with the melodic character of the recitatives; how smoothly and naturally the music flows. Besides, Mr. Mussorgsky is capable of striking, graceful prettiness, as in Theodore's story of the parrot, the Tsar's reply and the end of the love-duet. The shortcomings of the work are due to immaturity, to the fact that the composer is insufficiently self-critical, to that unfastidious, self-satisfied, hasty writing which has led to such lamentable results in the cases of Messrs. Rubinstein and Tchaïkovsky." Poor Mussorgsky exploded at once to Stassof: " My dear *and ever dear* généralissime *in spite of everything and everybody*. I was angry, as a loving woman must be angry; I fumed and raged... Now I am grieved and indignant, indignant and grieved. What an awful article of Cui's! To begin at the end: no well-bred man would dare to refer to women as Cui has done in his senseless witticisms. *Shame on him* who, in print, publicly, jeers at women who have won nothing but sympathy (I hear) for their bold and fearless conduct... The tone of Cui's article is execrable... And that attack on the composer's *self-satisfaction*! The fools have little of that modesty and humility which have never deserted me, and will not as long as the brains in my head are not altogether done for. Behind this insane attack, this deliberate lie, I see nothing—as if the air were full of soapy water dimming every object.—*Self-satisfaction*! ! ! *Hasty composition*! *Immaturity*! ... whose? ... whose? .... I should like to know."

The production of " Boris " thus had the double effect of deepening Mussorgsky's pride and of badly wounding it. Rimsky-Korsakof wrote twenty years later in his " Memoirs " that " generally speaking, from the time of the production of ' Boris ' Mussorgsky began to appear among us less often than before, and a change in his manner became noticeable: a certain mysteriousness, even superciliousness, began to show itself. His self-esteem increased enormously and his veiled and complicated way of expressing himself, which was always characteristic of him, developed beyond all bounds. It was often impossible to understand his accounts, his arguments, and his would-be witty remarks ". Korsakof then goes on to speak of his all-night brandy-drinking in restaurants, alone or with strange companions, which he dates from this period; though, according to Repin, it had actually begun some months before. (Incidentally, Rimsky-Korsakof mentions that Mussorgsky used to refuse wine when dining with his older friends.) " What was the reason of Mussorgsky's moral and intellectual downfall? It was due in great measure to the initial success of ' Boris ', which inflated his pride and ambition as a composer; and then to its failure "—that is, its infrequent performance. (It was given only once or twice a year after October, 1876, and then with such drastic cuts that Stassof was moved to public protest.) And, not altogether logically, Korsakof goes on first to blame Stassof for feeding Mussorgsky's vanity and then to point out that the composer's low companions, " people immeasurably his inferiors ", were, no doubt, the more attractive to him since they freely and generously gave him that admiration which was denied him in official musical circles. No doubt Rimsky-Korsakof was right, but his attitude to his unfortunate friend does seem more than a little Pharisaical.

In May, 1874, Mussorgsky wrote two songs of the cycle " Sunless ", to words by Golenishchef-Kutuzof, the other four following later in the year, and in June composed his well-known memorial to his friend, Hartmann, the set of " Pictures from an Exhibition " for piano. The exhibition was an actual, not a fictitious one, the memorial display of Hartmann's sketches, water-colours and stage-designs organised by Stassof at the Academy of Arts, four or five months before. The " Pictures " were written very quickly; " Hartmann is seething as ' Boris ' seethed ", the composer tells Stassof—" seething " was a favourite expression of his —" I hardly have time to scribble on the paper ". Just a week after the completion of this tribute to one dead friend, he lost another, even dearer—that Nadejda Opotchinina to whom he had dedicated so many of his earlier compositions. Now he wrote, or at least began to write, a passionate, deeply-felt epitaph for her, " Evil Death ", the words of which testify to the maternal-filial nature of their relationship. It breaks off—and was never finished. None of Mussorgsky's letters to Nadejda have been preserved and to none of his correspondents does he even mention her death. That little mystery is characteristic of the whole part she played in his life. No one doubts that it was a very important one, but no one really knows anything about it.

One can understand that Mussorgsky's mood at this time was in tune with the pessimism of Golenishchef-Kutuzof's words in the " Sunless " songs and in the powerful " ballad ", " Forgotten ", inspired by Vereshchagin's ghastly picture. But it is certainly a little surprising to find him, less than a month after Nadejda's death, announcing to Liubov Karmalina his intention of writing a comic opera based on Gogol's story, " The Fair of Sorotchintsi "! And this with " Khovanshchina " still in confusion and making very slow progress. He ingeniously excuses this digression as " economy of creative power ". He has been working at " two heavyweights: ' Boris ' and ' Khovanshchina ' ", so that the composition of a comic opera will be a complete and refreshing change. " The materials of Ukrainian folk-song are so little known that lay connoisseurs look upon them as imitations (of what?) dug up wholesale." And anyhow, " creative moods are elusive and more capricious than the most capricious of coquettes; one must catch them as they come, wholly surrendering oneself to the decrees of caprice ". Gogol was always Mussorgsky's favourite author. Reckoning up great Russian artists on one occasion, he wrote, " Glinka and Dargomyjsky, Pushkin and Lermontof, Gogol and Gogol, and again Gogol (there's no one to balance him) ". But the immediate impulse to the composition of "The Fair", according to Stassof, was the idea of writing a Ukrainian part for the great Ukrainian bass, Petrof—the same Petrof who had sung the leading rôle in the first performance of " A Life for the Tsar " in 1836, and who had recently sung Varlaam in the first performance of " Boris " nearly thirty-eight years later; " the titan ", in Mussorgsky's own words, " who has borne on his Homeric shoulders almost the whole of our dramatic music ".

Mussorgsky set about the composition of " The Fair " in much the same haphazard way as he had started " Khovanshchina ", though Gogol's story provided him with a firm, general outline such as the other work never possessed. There was no proper libretto, not even a written-down scenario for the First and Third Acts till three years after this. Apparently it was all carried in that so often fuddled head. For some of the music Mussorgsky proposed to draw on earlier works, the ill-fated " St. John's Night on the Bare Mountain ", the market-scene from " Mlada ", and others. But for the time being he seems to have done very little, for in September, 1874, his interest in " Khovanshchina " began to revive. He at last finished the introduction and in November " Mussinka ", informing Liudmila Shestakova that he is " cruelly tired with office-work, being now without an assistant "—he was made senior head-clerk of his department a few months later, adds in a postcript that " ' Khovanshchina ' is going well, though I haven't much time and I get very weary ". Yet he willingly gave his services as accompanist at the charity concerts organised by Borodin and the Stassofs in aid of poor students at the Army Medical Academy, the Medical and Surgical Academy, the women medical students, and the rest of Borodin's lame ducks. (All accounts agree that Mussorgsky was an excellent accompanist.)

In February, 1875, with the grim " Trepak ", dedicated to Petrof, he began a new song-cycle to Golenishchef-Kutuzof's words. Two more numbers, the " Cradle Song " and " Serenade " came later in the spring. But by then he was " working manfully at ' Khovanshchina ' once more ", as he informed Liubov Karmalina. He had abandoned " The Fair ". " I've given up the Little Russian opera. And for this reason—the impossibility of a Great Russian's pretending to be a Little Russian, and consequently the impossibility of mastering Little Russian recitative, all the nuances and peculiarities of the musical rise and fall of Little Russian speech." On July 30th/August 11th, he finished the First Act of " Khovanshchina ", " in Petrograd, at P. A. Naumof's flat opposite the garden of the Academy of Arts ", as he noted with Pepysian precision on the manuscript.

But that inscription is not without interest, even importance. How did Mussorgsky come to be " at Naumof's flat "? The date marks the end of his life with Golenishchef-Kutuzof, who married a few months later, very much to his friend's annoyance. (They quarrelled bitterly when Kutuzof announced his intention of marrying, though they were reconciled later.) But the actual circumstances of Mussorgsky's removal are wrapped in a certain amount of mystery. According to the account Mussorgsky sent to Stassof in Paris, Kutuzof had gone away, forgetting to leave him a key, and so obliged him to take refuge with Naumof. But according to Naumof himself, a retired naval officer with a passion for the arts, but very doubtful morals, Mussorgsky was turned out of his old quarters through being hopelessly in arrears with his rent, and wandered the streets of Petersburg that night with empty pockets and a bag containing his few possessions, till, finally, sitting down in despair to rest on a stone lion ornamenting one of the big houses on the Neva bank, he bethought himself of Naumof, who lived not far away. At any rate, Naumof gave Mussorgsky a home and treated him with kindness. And in the flat " opposite the garden of the Academy of Arts ", the composer not only finished the First Act of " Khovanshchina " but worked most industriously at the Second. " ' Toward new shores ' ", he writes to Stassof, " and no turning back; I've put to sea—and I shan't fail! . . How many unseen, unheard of worlds and lives reveal themselves!" Yet, although he was writing pages of lovely music, he was *not* travelling " toward new shores "—except in imagination. If anything, " Khovanshchina " was a retrograde step from " Boris ", just as " Boris " itself was less adventurous than " The Marriage ".

Still, he had reason to consider himself an advanced progressive by comparison with some of his old friends; for instance, Rimsky-Korsakof, who was now busy teaching himself scholastic counterpoint. " I met the Roman ",[1] he tells Stassof in the letter just quoted from. " I hear he has written sixteen fugues, each more complicated than the rest, and nothing more . . . ." Then, alluding to César Cui, who had just finished the Third Act of his " Angelo ", " I haven't been at his place—I'm not to be caught, I'm afraid; i.e. I'm afraid of the Third Act. And I didn't bother the Roman about Caesar. (Rome mixed up in it again!) When will these people leave their *fugues and obligatory three acts* and take a peep into sensible books—and converse in their pages with sensible people? Or is it already too late? A contemporary *human being* has no use for their sort of art; that isn't the artist's real job. *Life,* wherever it shows itself; *truth,* no matter how bitter; bold, sincere speech with *people à bout portant,* that's what I'm after—and that's where I'm afraid of missing the mark ". A couple of months later— only just recovered, it is true, from a fortnight of bronchitis— he expressed himself to Stassof even more bitterly about his old friends: " When I think of certain artists, I feel not merely distress but a *slushy sensation.* All they long to do is —to *drizzle* drop by drop, and all in such precious, equal little drops; it amuses them, but to a real human being it's distressing and boring . . . Without thought or will, they've chained themselves up with the fetters of tradition; they are only proving the law of inertia, while they imagine they're really doing something. All this wouldn't be so bad, though

---

[1] " Rimlianin " : a play on Rimsky-Korsakof's name. " Rimsky " is the Russian adjective, " Roman ".

rather antipathetic, if only they'd never seized a different sort of flag and never tried ' *to raise it proudly before humanity* '. As long as they were held in Balakiref's iron grip, they breathed deep breaths with his powerful lungs (though not quite as his heroic breast did), setting themselves the tasks of heroes. Balakiref's iron grip relaxed—and they felt tired and in need of rest. And where do they seek this rest? In tradition, of course: ' as our forefathers did, so will we.' They have put away the glorious standard of battle in some secret hiding-place . . . They have rested and relaxed. *Without a standard*, without desire, neither seeing nor wishing to see into the distance, they plod away at things already done long before and which nobody wants them to do again . . . The ' mighty handful ' have degenerated into soulless traitors . . . I don't believe you'd find people more indifferent to the essence of life, more useless to contemporary creativeness, *in the kingdom of the clouds*." Remembering this outburst, it is difficult to suppress an ironic smile when the following year we find him meditating the addition of a quintet to the Second Act of " Khovanshchina " and deciding to leave it till his return to Petersburg when he " will write it under R. Korsakof's guidance, as the technical requirements are awkward: alto, tenor and three basses ". For it was solely against Cui and Rimsky-Korsakof that his anger was directed. " It seems that Borodin has not turned traitor ", he remarks to Liudmila Shestakova at the end of a later, even more bitter outburst against the other two. It was only Borodin's imperturbable good humour that exasperated him. " *Oh, if only Borodin could lose his temper!* " Even with the two " traitors ", however, there seems to have been no complete rupture of relations. At least, no permanent rupture, though their relations were evidently very severely strained during the winter of 1875-76. But in the following summer we find Mussorgsky helping Rimsky-Korsakof with his collection of folk-songs. Mussorgsky still saw them from time to time at Liudmila Shestakova's and occasionally at Rimsky-Korsakof's own house. But he was wounded and resentful. He not only despised them for their " surrender to tradition " but was conscious that they now looked down on him as a sort of musical illiterate. What would he have felt had he suspected that, towards the end, even his beloved *généralissime* would notice a " falling off " in his powers and find his last compositions " confused, forced, sometimes even incoherent and banal ". Mercifully, Mussorgsky never knew.

But if the " traitors " had " abjured the covenant of art—*to speak truthfully with people* ", there was all the more reason why he should bear witness to it. The Second Act of " Khovanshchina " was " ready ", though in rather a rough state, by the end of 1875. During 1876 he pressed on, not quite so energetically, with Act III. And in April he presented Golenishchef-Kutuzof's young wife with the manuscript of the Persian dances from Act IV, apparently as a token of reconciliation. He was much occupied, too, in helping Liudmila Shestakova to organise the celebrations of the jubilee of Petrof's stage-career in April. Was it that event, one wonders, the emotional excitement of ovations and a *tusch* at the Maryinsky Theatre, the laurel-crowning of a bust at the Conservatoire, and all the rest of it, which turned his mind back to his own projected tribute to the " titan "? Or was it simply that he had lost his way in the jungle of " Khovanshchina "? At any rate, a month or so after this he recommenced work on " The Fair of Sorotchintsi ", not putting " Khovanshchina " aside to concentrate on it, but trying—he who found it difficult enough to finish a single opera—to write two operas at once. His muddled state of mind is reflected in a letter to Stassof, who had evidently been reproaching him for idleness: " For some rather long time Mussorianin has been subject to doubt, suspicion, conjecture . . . Mussorianin is working—*only for work* he needs quiet. 'Khovanshchina' is too big, too extraordinary a task . . . *I have stopped work—I have been thinking things over,* and now, and yesterday, and for weeks back, and to-morrow, do nothing but think—the one thought to go forth as a conqueror and say to people a *new* word of friendship and love, *frank, single-hearted, and traversing the whole breadth of the Russian land,* the true-sounding word of one who is a humble musician but a fighter for the true conception of art." Could anyone but a Russian have written those sentences? They might almost have been spoken by one of Dostoevsky's Marmeladofs or Lebedefs. Still, that summer (incidentally the summer of the first Bayreuth Festival) on leave at Tsarskoe Selo, given the rest and change he needed, Mussorgsky worked industriously at both his operas. " The air is wonderful; we walk three or four miles a day; but my nerves torment me sometimes. However, I suppose I must resign myself to that for the rest of my life. All the same, work has been going ahead better—that is, as it ought to go with real work, not mere cooking up." And on his return to Petersburg, Stassof was able to report to Golenishchef-Kutuzof: " Mussorianin has composed a lot of wonderful stuff this summer."

Unhappily this burst of energy exhausted itself almost at once. We hear nothing at all of " Khovanshchina " throughout the whole of 1877, very little in 1878. Mussorgsky had again flown off at a tangent. " You know that before ' Boris ' I did some little pictures of popular life " (" Savishna " and the other songs of that period). Now he wanted to make another " prognostic "—" *living,* not classical, melodies ". Only they were to be genuine melodies this time, not merely accurate declamation as in the " Marriage " period. " I'm working at human speech; I've hit on a sort of melody shaped by that speech, the incorporation of recitative in melody . . . . I should like to call it ' intelligently justified ' melody." Accordingly the first few months of

1877 were marked by a new crop of songs, most of them to words by Alexei Tolstoy, but also including the fourth and last of the " Songs and Dances of Death ", " The Field Marshal ". More surprisingly, he began noting down Caucasian and other melodies for use in yet another opera, " Pugatchevshchina ", to be based on the history of the Pugatchef rebellion, perhaps on Pushkin's story, " The Captain's Daughter "! But apart from the writing down of a " Hebrew chorus ", " Jesus Navinus (Joshua)", rearranged from the old " Salammbô " music a year or two before and now completed and dedicated, as a friendly gesture, to Rimsky-Korsakof's wife, the summer was entirely devoted to " The Fair of Sorotchintsi ", for which Mussorgsky had at last drawn up a rough scenario. He was again at Tsarskoe Selo; but for some reason he broke off his correspondence with Stassof. " Have heard hardly anything of Mussorgsky ", the latter tells Golenishchef-Kutuzof in July. " However, they say he has been composing." Again in August: " I've heard nothing of Mussarion all the summer." And finally in November, when the composer had returned to Petersburg: " Mussorgsky has written a lot of rubbish for ' The Fair of Sorotchintsi ' this summer, but has now decided to throw it all away ... During the last few weeks he has written a couple of gypsy choruses (also for ' The Fair ')." But Petrof's death in March, 1878, seems to have damped the composer's enthusiasm for this work in turn.

The scanty particulars of Mussorgsky's life during the latter part of 1877 suggest that he had been drinking even more than usual. It is significant that his musical and intellectual friends appear to have seen very little of him. But early in 1878 we hear of his visiting the Rimsky-Korsakofs, listening rather disapprovingly to " May Night ", and taking part just as of old in domestic performances of the newly composed Prologue to " The Maid of Pskof ". A little later Stassof saw him at Liudmila Shestakova's, " looking almost like a respectable person "; and he was promoted again in May.

In the summer, staying at Peterhof with Liudmila, Mussorgsky once more met Balakiref, who was just beginning to show himself in the musical world again. Balakiref's impression of him after six years, given in a letter to Stassof, is very interesting: " I don't mind telling you that I was pleasantly surprised. No swagger or anything in the way of self-adoration; on the contrary he was very modest, listened seriously to what was said to him and didn't protest at all against the necessity of *knowing harmony*, didn't even jib at the suggestion that he should work at it with Korsinka. All this pleasantly—even *very, very pleasantly*—surprised me, and of course I was very delighted." And then comes a very characteristic touch, Balakiref's cool resumption of the old relation of master and pupil. " For the present I've set him to a good piece of work; he has taken the score of his *witches' sabbath* to revise and rewrite. There are so many good and beautiful things in it that it would have been a pity to leave it in its present disorder."[1] But less than a fortnight after this, Mussorgsky was at Liudmila's for several days running, " looking awful ". And Stassof was obliged to tell Balakiref frankly that " Mussorgsky is going to the dogs ", modestly saying nothing of his own attempts to save him. One consequence of the renewal of Mussorgsky's friendship with Balakiref was his transfer in October from the Forest Department, where he had evidently been unpopular for some time, to the Inspection Commission of Government Control, of which the Director was Balakiref's friend, T. I. Filippof, the folk-song enthusiast. (According to N. S. Lavrof, Filippof

[1] Apparently this was the 1872 (" Mlada ") version, of which Liapunof showed Calvocoressi the manuscript in 1912. It was covered with Balakiref's blue-pencillings and such remarks as " horrible ", " senseless " and " transfer to the beginning ". But Mussorgsky did leave it " in its present disorder " and Balakiref evidently kept the score. The orchestral piece generally known as " Mussorgsky's ' Night on the Bare Mountain ' " is to all intents a composition of Rimsky-Korsakof's, based on Mussorgsky's materials.

"was indulgent to the point of unfairness . . . He forgave Mussorgsky absolutely anything, though the latter did no work and very often arrived in a state of intoxication after sleepless nights. Filippof never reprimanded him for it, and admitting this indulgent attitude said ' I am the servant of artists!' ") But Balakiref wrote sadly to Stassof that " Mussorgsky is such a physical wreck that he can hardly become more a corpse than he is at present ". In November he was " very ill ", though able to attend a revival of " Boris " at the Marinsky Theatre on December 10th/22nd, and take several calls.

In January, 1879, Rimsky-Korsakof at a concert of the Free School of Music conducted the first performance of the scene in Pimen's cell, which had always been omitted from the stage-productions of " Boris ". " At the rehearsals ", he rather maliciously recollects in his memoirs, " Mussorgsky tried to be original. Under the influence of wine, or simply for the sake of showing off, of which he had become increasingly fond, he often did try to be original; his conversation was frequently muddled and incomprehensible. At these rehearsals he listened with exaggerated attentiveness to the performance, constantly going into raptures over the playing of individual instruments, often in the most commonplace and indifferent passages, sometimes bowing his head pensively, sometimes haughtily raising it and shaking his hair, sometimes throwing up his hand with a theatrical gesture—always a favourite trick of his. When at the end of the scene the gong was struck *pianissimo*, imitating the monastery bell, Mussorgsky made the player a deep and respectful bow, crossing his hands on his breast ".

Up to now Mussorgsky had never in his life been further afield than Moscow, but during the summer of 1879 he made an extensive tour of Southern Russia. It came about in this way. Daria Leonova, the contralto, who had interested Glinka in the last years of his life, was now coming to the end of a successful if not brilliant career. Goodhearted, boastful, badly trained but with much natural talent, not very well educated, she was now a woman of fifty. She had left the stage of the Imperial Theatres some years before and, after touring in the Far East and in America, was now giving recitals in Petersburg and the Russian provinces. Mussorgsky had known her for years; as early as 1868 he had orchestrated the accompaniment of his " Hopak " for her; and they had a number of mutual friends. She included some of his songs in her repertoire, and on more than one occasion he had played her accompaniments at charity concerts. Now in June, Leonova proposed that he should accompany her (in both senses) on a three months' tour of the Ukraine, the Crimea and the Don and Volga towns. Mussorgsky was sorely in need of money, for his new official post was only temporary, and in any case his constitution was now so thoroughly ruined that there was little prospect of his being fit for work in a government department much longer. In this tour he joyfully saw a chance of making money. " Mussorgsky is in raptures about his proposed journey; he expects to make something like 1,000 rubles (!!!) ", Stassof informed Balakiref. His departmental chief, Filippof, far from putting obstacles in the way, approved of the tour. But Stassof was very annoyed at the idea, while Balakiref wrote in alarm to Liudmila Shestakova imploring her to use her influence to keep Mussorgsky from going. " On the one hand you will rescue him from the shameful rôle he wishes to play, and on the other our friend Modest and Leonova are running a big risk "—financially. For there was some suspicion that they were both being exploited by Leonova's husband, a notoriously bad character. However, they set out at the end of July, the middle-aged ex-*prima donna* and her drink-sodden genius of an accompanist, and Mussorgsky was at first in the highest spirits at the change of scene, the escape from the never-ending treadmill of St. Petersburg, with its days of routine drudgery and its nights of sordid dissipation. They gave their first concert at Poltava, and the receipts were good, though less than they had expected. But, as Mussorgsky wrote to Naumof, " the artistic triumph was *irrevocable* ". After Poltava, they visited Elizavetgrad (where Mussorgsky made a solemn pilgrimage to Petrof's birthplace and met young Felix Blumenfeld and his brother), Nikolaef, Kherson, Odessa, Sevastopol, Yalta, Voronezh and Tambof, returning to Petersburg early in November. It was the same story everywhere: artistic triumph, and entertainment by " the best families " in each town, but less decisive financial success. And even their artistic triumphs were marred by minor humiliations. At Voronezh they had to appear as a sort of variety turn, sandwiched into the middle of a theatrical performance. And while Mussorgsky proudly informed Liudmila Shestakova that " our repertoire includes Glinka, Dargomyjsky, Serof, Balakiref, Cui, Borodin, R.-Korsakof, Fr. Schubert, Chopin, Liszt and Schumann ", he omitted to mention that it also included, doubtless by way of concession to provincial taste, a certain amount of Meyerbeer and Gounod. Leonova sang Mussorgsky's own " Orphan ", " Hopak ", and " Forgotten ", and Martha's song from the Fourth Act of " Khovanshchina ". And as Mussorgsky also appeared as a supporting soloist, as well as playing Leonova's accompaniments, the good amateurs of Poltava and Odessa and Sevastopol had opportunities of being surprised by " ' The Coronation of Tsar Boris, with the pealing of bells and acclamations of the people ': picture from the opera ' Boris Godunof ' ", " ' Triumphal March of the Preobrajensky Company of Tsar Peter's Poteshnye ': from the new opera " Khovanshchina ' ", " The Glorification of Tchernobog and Witches' Sabbath on the Bare Mountain ': musical picture from a new comic opera, ' The Fair of Sorotchintsi ' ", and similar curiosities of piano literature, brilliantly performed by the composer himself. At some of the later concerts he also played or improvised what he described as a " grand musical picture: Storm on the Black Sea "—according to Rimsky-Korsakof, at whose house he played it on his return to Petersburg, " a rather long and confused fantasia ". This was never written down, but two other slighter impressions " from the southern shores of the Crimea ", " Gurzuf " and a " Capriccio ", a pair of rather trivial piano pieces, were published the following year. For Leonova, during the tour, he also set a Russian translation of the " Song of the Flea " from Goethe's " Faust ", one of his least distingushed songs, though unfortunately one of the best known. Yet he was still writing to Liudmila Shestakova, from Yalta, the old refrain, " ardently *toward new shores* . . . to seek those shores . . . that is the all-absorbing task ".

Mussorgsky's artistic and business partnership with Leonova continued in a still more curious form on their return to the capital. Leonova naturally possessed the secret of " the only true method of voice production " and she now proposed to set up a school of singing—which, by the way, produced only one fairly notable pupil. For this she needed a *maestro*, a musician who not only could accompany but who knew a little more than she did about the technicalities of music, apart from singing. Mussorgsky was glad to earn a pittance even in this way; according to Rimksy-Korsakof, " he spent quite a lot of time at these classes, even teaching elementary theory and, by way of exercises for the pupils, composing trios and quartets with fearful part-writing ". " Mussorgsky's assistance served Leonova to some extent as an advertisement ", he adds. " Of course, his employment was not very enviable, but he was unconscious of this—at least, he tried not to be conscious of it." Under the circumstances there is peculiar pathos in a note addressed to Stassof in January, 1880, thanking the *généralissime* for some " good news ": " Notwithstanding little misfortunes, I've never given way to faint-heartedness—nor shall I. My motto, as you know is: 'Dare! Forward to new shores!' It has remained unchanged. If destiny allows me to widen the beaten track toward the vital aims of art, I shall rejoice and be triumphant; the demands of art from the contemporary worker are so enormous, that they are quite capable of swallowing up the whole of a man. The time for writing *at leisure* is gone; to give people the whole of oneself—that's what is needed now in art."

But for the help of his good friends, Mussorgsky's position would have been pitiable in the extreme. At the beginning of 1880 he was obliged to leave the civil service and, but for Leonova's pittance, would have been destitute. Stassof appealed to his circle of friends to club together and help him, and Balakiref suggested the organisation of a concert in his aid. But the good Filippof with other friends came to the rescue with an offer of a pension of one hundred rubles a month, on one condition: that he was to finish the long-neglected " Khovanshchina ". (This was probably the " good news " mentioned in the note to Stassof, quoted above.) Desperately trying to reduce the chaos of the libretto to order, Mussorgsky made the whole still more incoherent by further drastic cuts; among other things, an entire scene in the " German quarter " of Moscow disappeared. Already at a Free School Concert on November 27th/December 9th Rimsky-Korsakof had performed the chorus of the Streltsy and Martha's song, both orchestrated by Mussorgsky himself, as well as the Persian Dances which, owing to pressure of time, Korsakof had to orchestrate for him—characteristically taking the opportunity to " edit " them into the bargain. And so " Khovanshchina " might have been finished after all, but for the untimely assistance of another group of friends whose identity has not been disclosed. " It appears ", Stassof wrote to Balakiref on February 12th/24th, " that some other people are helping

Mussorgsky at the rate of eighty rubles a month on condition that he finishes his 'Fair of Sorotchintsi' within about a year". There is a strange irony in these two groups of friends cancelling each other out, except as regards the material assistance. For, compelled to the end to work at both operas side by side, Mussorgsky was prevented from finishing either.

At first, as is evident from Stassof's statement, "The Fair" won the preference. It appears that this second mysterious group pressed Mussorgsky to arrange some excerpts from it for piano solo and sell them to the publisher Bernard. (The popular little "Hopak" first appeared in this form.) Unfortunately Bernard paid Mussorgsky very little for the pieces and, losing two or three of the manuscripts, obliged the composer to write them out again. However, in the summer, Leonova insisted on taking Mussorgsky with her to her summer villa at Oranienbaum, and there on May 29th/June 10th he at last finished the vocal score of Act III of "Khovanshchina". The first scene of Act IV was completed on August 5th/17th, and proudly shown to Filippof who came to see him. And he worked a little at Act V. But even now Mussorgsky could not concentrate. He began a "suite for orchestra with harps and piano, on motifs I have collected from various good pilgrims of this world: its programme is from the shores of Bulgaria, through the Black Sea, Caucasus and Caspian to Burma". A little later he tells Stassof he has "done the Fair Scene for 'Sorotchintsi'". As for "Khovanshchina", it is practically finished—"but the instrumentation—O gods!—time!" A professor of Petersburg University, who frequently saw Mussorgsky at Oranienbaum that summer, has recorded that "his appearance vividly recalled Repin's celebrated picture" (painted only a fortnight before his death). "He was always dressed very shabbily and a mutual acquaintance told me later that he often had to buy secondhand clothes for the unfortunate composer." Yet he still used to play brilliantly at Leonova's weekly musical evenings.

It must have been at about this time that, apparently in reply to Hugo Riemann's request for biographical particulars for his " Dictionary ", Mussorgsky wrote that curious autobiographical sketch in which he describes his career in the most glowing colours as a sort of march from triumph to triumph; claims to have known Turgenef, Pisemsky, Shevtchenko and other distinguished writers with whom there is no other reason to believe he was ever acquainted;[1] refers to the previous year's tour as " a real triumphal progress of two great Russian artists "; announces that his two new operas " are already in the press "; and makes various other curious and vainglorious statements. A pitiful document, considering the conditions amid which it was written. But it concludes with a profession of his artistic faith which could hardly be bettered: " Mussorgsky cannot be classed with any existing group of musicians, either by the character of his compositions or by his musical views. The formula of his artistic *profession de foi* may be explained by his view of the function of art: art is a means of communicating with people, not an aim in itself. This guiding principle has defined the whole of his creative activity. Proceeding from the conviction that human speech is strictly controlled by musical laws *(Virchow, Gerwinus)* he considers the function of art to be the reproduction in musical sounds not merely of feelings, but first and foremost of human speech. Acknowledging that in the realm of art only artist-reformers such as Palestrina, Bach, Gluck, Beethoven, Berlioz and Liszt have created the laws of art, he considers these laws as not immutable but liable to change and progress, like everything else in man's inner world."

Mussorgsky was yet to enjoy one or two tastes of public

---

[1] It appears from the draft that he also thought of including Dostoevsky but, on reconsideration, crossed him out.

success. In October his old " Procession of the Princes " from " Mlada ", recently furbished up with a new trio " *alla turca* " and re-titled " The Taking of Kars ", for that same series of " living pictures " which inspired Borodin's " In the Steppes of Central Asia ", was performed at an R.M.S. concert under Napravnik. And on February 3rd/15th, 1881, when Rimsky-Korsakof conducted " The Destruction of Sennacherib " at a Free School concert, Mussorgsky was present and appeared on the platform to acknowledge the applause.

Eight days later he came to Leonova, she tells us, " in a state of extreme nervous excitement ", and informed her that he no longer had any means of subsistence, " that there was nothing left for him but to go and beg in the streets ",—which can hardly have been literally true. That evening, after accompanying one of Leonova's pupils at a party, he had a fit—apparently of alcoholic epilepsy. A doctor who happened to be present attended to him and he appeared to be better. But leaving with Leonova in a *droshky*, he implored her to allow him to spend the night at her house. She gave him a room and " he slept the whole night in a sitting position ". Next morning he appeared in the dining-room, said he felt perfectly well—and immediately fell in another fit. Two others followed later in the day and Leonova sent in alarm for Stassof, Filippof and his other friends. Only Liudmila Shestakova was too ill to come; she never saw him again. On the 14th/26th Mussorgsky was moved, much against his will, to the Nikolaevsky Military Hospital in one of the suburbs. " The doctor says now that they weren't heart-attacks, but the beginning of *epilepsy* ", Stassof informed Balakiref. " I've been with him to-day and yesterday (Borodin and Korsakof were there yesterday and the day before, many other friends as well): he looks as if there were nothing the matter with him "—relatively, of course—" and now recognises everybody, but he talks the devil knows what gibberish and tells the most impossible stories. They say that besides the epilepsy and the attacks, he is also a bit mad. He is done for, though the doctors say he may linger on for a year—or only a day ".

After a fortnight or so the patient appeared to be better, though " terribly weak, changed and grown grey ". He was pleased to see his friends and sometimes conversed with them quite normally, suddenly breaking off into insane ravings. Then in the lovely spring weather he was able to sit up, dressed in Cui's dressing-gown, with his papers and a few books about him. (Among them, his old copy of Berlioz's " Instrumentation ".) And so Repin painted him. An awful, unforgettable portrait, and to most people the most familiar of all the pictures of Mussorgsky. Ten days later (March 15th/27th) a number of his friends came to see him as usual and stayed talking with him for some time. At five o'clock next morning, according to the two attendants, he cried out twice—and died.

Mussorgsky was buried on March 18th/30th, two days after his death, in the Alexander Nevsky Cemetery, where Dostoevsky had been laid only a few weeks before. There was a certain irony in the tributes from the official institutions he had hated so bitterly, and one wonders what he would have said in earlier years if he had known that the " musical slum " would one day honour him with a wreath. He might have been more pleased to be assured that the four survivors of the " mighty handful " would stand together round his grave, and that four years later at the unveiling of a monument to him, the same four would hold the corners of the sheet that covered it.

Stassof hastened to produce his memorial biography, a labour of love, if not an altogether reliable source of information. And in a similar well-intentioned spirit—though, as we see it to-day, a somewhat wrongheaded one—Rimsky-Korsakof, the " traitor ", undertook to reduce to order all that chaos of precious material which had so long baffled Mussorgsky himself.

* * * * *

Mussorgsky's art is essentially that of "a man of the 'sixties ". The phrase conveys little, perhaps, to the average Western reader. But to a Russian it is as familiar and as precise in meaning as the words " Elizabethan " or " Victorian " to an Englishman. " The 'sixties " mark an epoch in Russian history; and " the men of the 'sixties ", alternately worshipped as heroes and derided as back-numbers, seem a race apart. Coming after the appalling despotism of Nicholas I, the reign of Alexander II (at least, in its first half) appeared almost millennial. With the freeing of the serfs, which altered so much and seemed to have altered so vastly much more, Russia took one of the greatest of all her clumsy strides from feudalism toward the modern Western state. The freed *mujik* was suddenly elevated to a pedestal and sentimentally worshipped—particularly by aristocrats like Tolstoy and Mussorgsky who saw that he was free from the vices of their class and were wilfully, happily blind to those of his own. To all that was young and generous and intelligent in Russia it was a dawn as blissful as that which intoxicated the young Wordsworth.

But the expression of this exuberant emotion took a surprising form. Just as the business-like Western, in such moments of spiritual intoxication, turns his back on harsh reality and kicks up his heels in the most fanciful antics, the enthusiasm of the dreamy Slav takes the form of fiery determination to be practical. (The 1860's help us to understand the 1920's.) He works himself up to the facing of facts and the grappling with them, enthusiastically resolves to put behind him the seductions of mere sensuous beauty to which he is generally so susceptible. Mussorgsky's art is a manifestation of both the spiritual and intellectual exuberance, the intense aspirations of the period (toward the brotherhood of man, and so on), and a relentless determination to be truthful at all costs, a contempt for that which is merely beautiful. And at its best, when these two elements are in perfect equilibrium as in " Boris ", Mussorgsky transcends " the 'sixties " and rises to universality as completely as Shakespeare transcends the Elizabethan age. If Mussorgsky is in every fibre a Russian " of the 'sixties ", he is so only as Shakespeare is, through and through, an Elizabethan Englishman.

Leaving aside all technical, purely musical considerations, the head and front of Rimsky-Korsakof's offending against " Boris " is that he has completely altered its values. It is as if Rubens had repainted a Pieter Breughel. The " truth " is carefully toned down, the beauty made correspondingly more luscious. It is all very splendid—but it is the negation of that which is Mussorgsky's special, and still unique, contribution to music in general and to opera in particular. It parallels Dryden's " Tempest ", Cibber's " Richard III ", " Othello "-with-a-happy-ending; and Korsakof's justification is precisely that of the " practical men of the theatre " who made the crudities of Shakespeare tolerable to polite English audiences of the Augustan age. But if Rimsky-Korsakof is to be indicted for his well-intentioned crime, practically the whole of musical Russia must go into the dock with him for aiding, abetting and approving. For not only the rank and file of professional musicians and cultured amateurs, but critics of the high standing of Findeisen and Karatygin long agreed in preferring the Korsakof version to the original. The resuscitation and revaluation of the genuine " Boris " is principally due to the efforts of a few critics in France, Russia following suit only after the Revolution. Professor Paul Lamm of Moscow must be given the highest praise for his recent admirable edition of the authentic texts of Mussorgsky's complete works.

Apart from his harmonic forthrightness and his consistent

refusal to " manufacture " music by conventional technical processes, the most striking of Mussorgsky's musical innovations are in the field of naturalism—truth to the spoken word, truth to plastic movement (the " writing " themes in " Boris " and " Khovanshchina ", the " Promenade ", the two Jews and so on in the " Exhibition Pictures ")—a naturalism equally effective in comedy and tragedy. In all this, particularly as regards the musical opportunities offered by humour, Mussorgsky was indebted to Dargomyjsky for a number of hints; he would hardly have taken quite the course he did, but for Dargomyjsky. Yet his actual musical style owes little to the older man, even in " The Marriage " or the most naturalistic of the songs. (And neither Dargomyjsky nor anyone else has possessed anything like Mussorgsky's ability to get inside the minds of children.)

Even if we object, on general æsthetic grounds, to Mussorgsky's musical prose in his less inspired moments, when he is content to give a mere literal translation of word and gesture into tone, we are left with an extraordinary wealth not only of inspired " translation ", of sheer lyrical loveliness and of racy, vital melody, but—the seal of Mussorgsky's genius—of dramatic points produced by non-naturalistic means: the moving innocence of the " Tsarevitch " motif at its first appearance in " Boris " (cut even from Mussorgsky's own version of 1874) where it accompanies Pimen's words, " All steeped in blood and lifeless lay Dimitri "; the brass chords in the second scene of the Prologue, just before Boris's words " Now let us pay a solemn tribute to the tombs of Russia's rulers ", chords (particularly the unexpected D major) almost as thrilling as those of Mozart's trombones in " Don Giovanni "; the music which accompanies Golitsyn's departure into exile in " Khovanshchina " (based on that of Marfa's divination), so simple and beautiful, yet loaded with an intolerable weight of tragic destiny; the irony of the lovely snatch of folk-song sung by Shaklovity over the body of the murdered Khovansky; the equally effective, but more brutal irony of the banal march of the Preobrajensky Guards in the last Act of the same opera. There is no end to these strokes of dramatic genius, astounding in their simplicity, each as definite and final as an overwhelming line of Shakespeare's.

What Mussorgsky's operas do on the large scale is done in miniature by his songs. They cover an even wider field of emotion and experience, and explore each corner with even greater daring. Things like " Savishna ", " The Magpie ", " The Peep-Show " and the " Nursery " cycle are unique in song-literature; and each is an adventure along a different line from the others. A man who had written nothing but the " Songs and Dances of Death " and " Sunless " would have to be given an important place among the world's song-composers. Nor have even twentieth-century musicians given us anything quite like the " Pictures from an Exhibition " for piano .... And we owe all this to a poor, drink-sodden, inefficient little Government clerk, more than half a child to the end of his life, a naughty child, vain, affectionate, lovable —a pitiable creature who happened also to be a genius.

G. A.

TCHAÏKOVSKY
by Kuznetsof

Page 249

PETER TCHAÏKOVSKY

In the year 1833 a thirty-eight-year-old Inspector in the Department of Mines, Ilia Petrovitch Tchaïkovsky, took as his second wife a girl in her early twenties, Alexandra Assière, the daughter of a French emigrant of whom we know nothing except that he was epileptic. (It is possible that the French grandfather of the composer of " 1812 " was, like Cui's father, part of the jetsam left in Russia from the wreck of Napoleon's army.) Ilia Tchaïkovsky, an official of very moderate ability and intelligence, was, in 1837, put in charge of the important mines at Votkinsk in the Viatka Government; and the following year Alexandra bore him a first son, Nicholas. (He already had a daughter, Zinaïda, by his first wife, a German.) On April 25th/May 7th, 1840,[1] came a second son, Peter, or " Pierre " as his mother called him. In less than two years a daughter, Alexandra, arrived; in 1844, another son Hippolyte; finally, in 1850, twins, Anatol and Modest.

Peter's education began at the end of 1844, when his mother engaged a young French governess, Fanny Dürbach, for Nicholas and her niece, Lydia, who was also a member of their household. He insisted on sharing their lessons, and at six is reputed to have been able to read French and German fluently. At seven he was writing verses in French. For the rest, he was slovenly, imaginative and excessively sensitive. Mlle. Dürbach, who outlived her famous pupil, told Modest half a century later that " Peter's sensitiveness was simply boundless and one had to handle him very carefully. A mere

[1] This not unimportant date is given incorrectly in the abridged English edition of Modest Tchaïkovsky's " Life and Letters " of his famous brother.

trifle would wound him. He was a 'porcelain' child. There could be no question of punishing him; he would take to heart the least criticism—a single word of reproof, such as other children would take no notice of—and be alarmingly upset by it... One day, turning over the pages of his atlas and coming to the map of Europe, he at once began to cover Russia with kisses and spat on the other parts of Europe. When I told him he ought to be ashamed of himself ... and reminded him that he was spitting on his Fanny, since she was a Frenchwoman, he replied: 'There's no need to scold me. Didn't you see that I covered France with my left hand?'.... Left to himself, he preferred to play the piano, or read or write poetry". His governess preserved some of the precocious verses in his old exercise books, one or two in Russian, the rest in French—religious, patriotic and dreadfully sentimental.

Neither Mlle. Dürbach nor either of the boy's parents was musical, but at five he began to have lessons from a Russian girl. We know nothing of her, except that in three years her pupil could read at sight as well as she could, which may or may not be a tribute to her ability as a teacher. Even before these first piano lessons he had shown intense delight in the tunes played by an "orchestrion"—airs from "Don Giovanni" and the operas of Bellini and Donizetti, which he managed to pick out on the piano—and his governess has recorded that music always had an extraordinarily exciting effect on his nervous system. Once, after a party, at which there had been music, she found him sitting up in bed, his eyes feverish and glittering, crying, "Oh, this music, this music! Take it away! It's here in my head and it won't let me go to sleep!" A Polish visitor having introduced little Pierre to Chopin's mazurkas, the boy taught himself to play two of them.

In 1848 Ilia Tchaïkovsky retired from the government service with the rank of major-general, and the family left

Votkinsk first for Moscow, then for St. Petersburg. Fanny Dürbach was dismissed and Nicholas and Peter were sent to a school where they were absurdly overworked. Peter also had a few music-lessons from a rather better teacher, and was taken more than once to the opera, though the only work he remembered was " A Life for the Tsar ". But within a month or two, both boys had measles, which affected Peter's health so seriously that he was forbidden all work for nearly six months. By that time (June, 1849) his father had obtained a private appointment as manager of some mines at Alapief, and the family (except Nicholas who was left at school in Petersburg) moved to that small provincial town. Peter's education was put into the indifferent hands of his half-sister, and he quickly grew morose and idle, making his mother " cry with vexation ", as she wrote to Mlle. Dürbach. Only with the arrival of a new governess, Anastasia Petrova, did he begin to behave himself. But his musical education was quite neglected, as his parents considered that music had an " unhealthy " effect on him. But he used to amuse himself with improvisation; by his own account, his head was at that time always full of musical sounds.

In August, 1850, Peter's mother took him to Petersburg, where he entered a preparatory school. The memory of the October day when she left him—and he had to be separated from her literally by force—remained with Tchaïkovsky to the end of his life. So, perhaps, did the effect of the year or so of agonising homesickness which followed. Peter with his brother, who was being prepared for the School of Mining Engineers, boarded with family friends, but nothing seemed to compensate the moody, sensitive child for the loss of his parents. It was not till May, 1852, when his father retired on his savings and pension, and the family settled in Petersburg, that the boy's life became a little happier. At the same time he entered the School of Jurisprudence, the School which had produced Serof and Vladimir Stassof, though music was no longer cultivated in its classrooms as in their days. But this period of happiness was shortlived. The mother's death from cholera in July, 1854, broke up the Tchaïkovsky household, for the older half-sister was already married. Ilia made his home in 1855 with his brother, and the children were sent to various schools. In 1858, in consequence of the loss of badly-invested savings, however, he was obliged to re-enter the civil service as Director of the Technological Institute. Seven years later—at seventy—he married for a third time.

Curiously enough, Peter's very first attempt at definite composition dates from the month of his mother's death, for in July, 1854, he wrote to a now-forgotten poet, V. I. Olkhovsky, about a libretto for a one-act lyric opera " Hyperbole ", which he thought of composing—naturally, without the faintest idea of how to set about it. And the following month, at Oranienbaum, the fourteen-year-old wrote his first known composition, a little " Valse dédiée à m-lle. Anastasie ", i.e. to Anastasia Petrova, his former governess. None of Peter's comrades at the School of Jurisprudence were musical, but his mother's sister, an amateur singer of some ability, introduced him to a good deal of the popular operatic music of the day. Again it was " Don Giovanni ", of which she had a vocal score, which made by far the deepest impression on him. In later life, Tchaïkovsky always attributed his real initiation into the world of music to Mozart—and to " Don Giovanni " in particular. The boy appears to have had an extraordinarily good soprano voice; he had a few singing lessons from Lomakin, who, a few years later, was to join Balakiref in founding the Free School of Music; and his aunt encouraged him to tackle the florid bravura airs of Rossini and the other Italians. As a pianist he was still merely an exceedingly diffident amateur, willing to play for dancing, however, and fond of improvisation when assured that he was quite alone. But he does not appear to have written anything between

1854 and 1860, with the exception of a setting of a poem by Mey, which, according to Modest, was " a purely amateurish affair without the least trace of talent ". He had a few lessons from one Bekker, more from a German, Rudolf Kündinger, who as he confessed later " had no real faith in Peter Ilitch's gift for music ". As for his studies at the School of Jurisprudence, Tchaïkovsky distinguished himself in no way, except as a particularly bad mathematician. Neither his professors nor his fellow-pupils made any deep impression on him, though he was friendly with Apukhtin, who soon acquired some reputation as a minor poet. The most intimate of Tchaïkovsky's school-friends was V. S. Adamof, afterwards a brilliant jurist, fond of music, but no musician. On May 13th/25th, 1859, Tchaïkovsky left the School and entered the Ministry of Justice as a first-class clerk.

The new official must have been one of the most inefficient members even of the Russian civil service of that period. He quite forgot afterwards what his duties had been! Tchaïkovsky always had a habit of absent-mindedly tearing little bits off concert-programmes and the like, and chewing them; and there is a legend that on one occasion he partly devoured an official document in this way. Nor was he dreaming, as far as we know, of an artistic career, fond though he was of music. It was just that he was an idle young man-about-town, a frequenter of the theatre (particularly the ballet and the Italian opera), egotistical and slightly patronising toward his father and the other elder members of his family. The high-water marks of his musical taste were " Don Giovanni ", " Der Freischütz " and " A Life for the Tsar ". For the last year or two he had been intimate with an unpleasant character named Piccioli, an Italian singing-master who " dyed his hair and painted his face " and was reputed to be a good deal older than the fifty years which he modestly claimed. Just what part Piccioli played in Tchaïkovsky's private life we shall never know, but musically he was a violent admirer of the works of his fellow-countrymen—and nothing else. He equally detested Beethoven and Glinka. It was perhaps under his influence that Tchaïkovsky wrote his first printed composition: "*Mezza Notte:*" *Romance pour soprano ou ténor avec accompagnement de piano*, a setting of Italian words to quasi-Italian music. The song, printed in 1860 or 1861, probably at the composer's expense, and issued by Leibrock's music-shop, the " Musée Musical ", was unknown till 1926, when a copy was found in Jurgenson's archives.

It may have been this effusion which suddenly gave Ilia Tchaïkovsy the notion that his son might do something as a musician after all. " At supper they spoke of my musical talent ", Peter wrote in March, 1861, to his sister Alexandra.[1] " Father declared it was not yet too late for me to become an artist. If only that were really true! But it's like this: even if I actually had any talent, it can hardly be developed now. They've made an official of me, though a bad one; I'm doing my best to improve and attend to my duties more conscientiously; and at the same time I'm to study thoroughbass! "

One consequence of his sister's marriage was that he began to take an interest in the twins, ten years younger than himself, whom he had hitherto ignored. They worshipped him and he now became extremely fond of them, trying (as he said) " to give them a substitute for a mother's love and care ". During his first trip abroad, his letters home were full of enquiries about " Modi " and " Toly ". During this expedition (July-September, 1861) he visited Berlin, Hamburg, Brussels, London (which he found " very interesting, but gloomy ") and Paris, which delighted him. But the trip was spoiled by " painful misunderstandings " with his travelling-companion, a friend of his father's for whom he

---

[1] She had recently married L. V. Davydof, son of a prominent Decembrist, who had been a friend of Pushkin's, and had gone to live in the Kief Government.

had to act as interpreter. In a letter to his sister, after his return, he says: " If ever I started on a colossal piece of folly, it was this journey... I spent more money than I ought to have, and got nothing useful for it. D'you see now what a fool I've been? But don't scold me. I've behaved like a child—that's all... You know I have a weakness; directly I get any money I squander it on pleasure; it's vulgar and stupid, I know; but it seems to be a part of my nature... What can I expect from the future? It's terrible to think of it. I know that sooner or later I shall no longer be able to battle with life's difficulties; till then, however, I intend to enjoy it and to sacrifice everything to that enjoyment. I have been pursued by misfortune during the last fortnight; official work —very bad... P.S. I've begun to study thoroughbass and am making good progress. Who knows? Perhaps in three years' time you'll be hearing my operas and singing my arias." Six weeks later he writes again that " with my fairly respectable talent (I hope you won't take that for bragging) it would be foolish not to try my fortune in this direction " (i.e. music). " I am fearful only of my own backbonelessness. In the end my indolence will conquer; but if it doesn't I promise you that something will come of me. Fortunately, it's not yet too late."

These " studies in thoroughbass " were private lessons from the pedantic Polish theorist, N. I. Zaremba, the *bête noire* and butt of Balakiref and Mussorgsky. But the twenty-one-year-old dilettante, after beginning to study " very superficially, like a true amateur ", was inspired by Zaremba to work diligently, as Rimsky-Korsakof did only later and as Mussorgsky never did, cutting adrift from all his old friends except Apukhtin and Adamof and devoting himself to his harmony-exercises and the twins. (Both his other brothers had left Petersburg, Nicholas following his father in the Mining Department, Hippolyte entering the navy.) In 1862 an " unjust " promotion over his head extinguished whatever flickering enthusiasm Tchaïkovsky had managed to work up for his official duties. And in September the Russian Music Society opened its new Conservatoire of Music, with Anton Rubinstein as its principal. Zaremba became a member of the staff—he succeeded Rubinstein as head of the Conservatoire in 1867—and Tchaïkovsky followed his teacher, attending two classes a week, for he now added strict counterpoint to his harmony studies. He had already " come to the conclusion that sooner or later I shall exchange the civil service for music. Don't imagine that I dream of ever becoming a great artist. . ." (Though he *was* dreaming of it, even boasting to Nicholas that " even if I don't turn out to be a Glinka, you will be proud one of these days to be my brother ".) " I only want to do the work for which I feel I have a vocation. Whether I become a celebrated composer or a poor music-teacher—it's all the same... My conscience will be clear... Of course, I shan't resign my post till I'm quite sure that I'm not an official but an artist ". However, it took him less than six months to come to that conclusion, for in April, 1863, he decided to resign from the Ministry of Justice and concentrate on his musical studies. It was a risky step, for his father was by no means well off and could give him nothing but board and lodging, a small bed-sitting-room. But he cut down all his amusements and renounced the theatre; Rubinstein got him a few private pupils; and he looked forward to obtaining perhaps an assistant professorship at the Conservatoire before long. He was confident, he told Alexandra, that by the time he had finished the course he would be at least a good musician, able to earn a living. " The professors are satisfied with me and say that with the necessary zeal I shall do very well indeed. I don't say that boastfully—it's not my nature—but frankly and without false modesty. I dream of coming to you for a whole year, when my studies are finished, and composing a big work in your quiet surroundings. Then—out into the wide world."

At the very beginning of his Conservatoire days, in the piano-class of Mussorgsky's old teacher, Herke, Tchaïkovsky had made the acquaintance of Hermann Laroche, a German-Russian lad five years younger than himself, afterwards notorious as a critic, " a Russian copy of Eduard Hanslick " as Rimsky-Korsakof said. Laroche was a bitter antagonist of the Balakiref group, but he became Tchaïkovsky's intimate and lifelong friend. From the first, Tchaïkovsky attached great importance to his judgment, and we are indebted to Laroche for most of our information concerning Tchaïkovsky's Conservatoire period.

In September, 1863, the once foppish Tchaïkovsky, now long-haired and distinctly shabby, began to study form with Zaremba and entered Rubinstein's instrumentation class. Zaremba had never been more than a mere teacher to him; he was antagonised by Zaremba's contempt for Mozart and Glinka, while Zaremba's own gods, Beethoven and Mendelssohn, never had much attraction for Tchaïkovsky. But with Rubinstein, a much younger man, still only in his early thirties, it was different. Tchaïkovsky disliked his compositions and made fun of his bad Russian, but according to Laroche he was completely under his spell as a man and teacher and would take any amount of trouble to please him, sometimes sitting up all night over the scores he had to submit. But he seldom, if ever, earned much reward in the way of praise, for Rubinstein was a hard taskmaster and he failed to see that Tchaïkovsky was specially gifted. To the end the man whose praise Tchaïkovsky would have valued more than that of anyone else, disliked Tchaïkovsky's music. Just before he came under Rubinstein's direct influence, he and Laroche also made the acquaintance of Rubinstein's enemy, Serof. Tchaïkovsky attended the rehearsals of " Judith ", which he still admired long afterward, but he soon took a dislike to Serof personally. Among other new friends of the same period were Alexandra's two musical sisters-in-law, Elisabeth and Vera Davydova, who, with their aged mother[1] came to live in the northern capital.

In addition to his more serious studies, Tchaïkovsky took a few organ lessons and learned the flute in order to play in the Conservatoire orchestra. With the same orchestra he had his first experience of conducting. According to Laroche: " He declared that having to stand at the raised desk in front of the orchestra produced such a nervous terror that he felt all the time his head must fall from his shoulders; in order to prevent such a catastrophe, he kept his left hand under his chin and conducted only with his right. Incredible as it seems, this illusion lasted for years."

In the summer of 1864, during a holiday in the country, Tchaïkovsky wrote his first orchestral work. Rubinstein usually gave his composition pupils a biggish holiday task and Tchaïkovsky was told to write an overture. Now Tchaïkovsky, though he disliked what little he knew of Liszt and Wagner, had been attracted to programme-music by the overtures of the now-forgotten Henri Litolff, a composer who was also admired by Balakiref and Borodin. Accordingly, instead of a harmless academic piece in sonata-form, his exercise took the shape of a highly-dramatic concert-overture[2] with a programme based on Ostrovsky's tragedy, " The Storm ", a play which had appeared three or four years before and completely enthralled him. This in itself was enough to annoy Rubinstein. And it was scored for a very " modern " orchestra, including harp, *cor anglais* and tuba—extravagances of which Anton strongly disapproved. Amusingly enough, Tchaïkovsky was in such a hurry for Rubinstein to see it that he posted the score to Laroche with a request that *he* would take it to Rubinstein. And so it came

---

[1] Mme. Davydova, a Frenchwoman, had been frivolous and coquettish in her younger days and evidently made amorous advances to Pushkin, when he was her husband's guest at Kamenka. The poet alludes to her very disrespectfully in some of his verses.

[2] Published posthumously as Op. 76.

about that it was Laroche who had to bear the brunt of the outraged purist's wrath. The next composition of which we hear is an orchestral " Dance of the Serving Maidens " (afterwards used in the opera " The Voevoda ") which was played at Pavlovsk during the summer of 1865, by Johann Strauss, the Strauss of the " Blue Danube ".

Tchaïkovsky spent that summer with his brother-in-law Davydof, on the latter's estate of Kamenka in the Kief Government. Kamenka had poetic and historical associations that might well have stirred an imaginative man. It had been a favourite meeting-place of the Decembrist conspirators, and Pushkin had stayed there forty-five years before and written part of his " Prisoner of the Caucasus " under its hospitable roof. But Tchaïkovsky had learned his lesson. He annoyed Rubinstein with no Pushkinian symphonic poem. Two overtures were written that summer, besides a translation of Gevaert's recently-published " Traité d'Instrumentation " for Rubinstein, but they were both perfectly innocuous works, in C minor and F. Tchaïkovsky returned to Petersburg in August with his two overtures (of which only the second was orchestrated, so far) and a Ukrainian folk-song, which he had heard sung every day by women in the garden at Kamenka and which he proceeded to use in the slow movement of a String Quartet in B flat.

Tchaïkovsky's position was anything but pleasant that autumn. His eyes were giving him a great deal of trouble, while his rooms were uncomfortable and he kept flitting from one apartment to another. Nor was he by any means as confident as he had been two years before of his ability to earn a living on leaving the Conservatoire. He even thought—and some of his friends encouraged the idea—of returning to the civil service. But an unexpected way out presented itself. Rubinstein's younger brother Nicholas—a man only five years Tchaïkovsky's senior, assisted by a still younger man, the twenty-nine-year-old publisher Jurgenson, was founding a

Conservatoire of Music in Moscow. He wanted a Professor of Harmony, but being unable to pay more than a miserable pittance—fifty rubles (say £5) a month!—sounded Anton as to the capabilities of any of his senior students for the post. Anton recommended Tchaïkovsky and in November the latter accepted.

But the rather callow professor of twenty-five did not leave the Petersburg Conservatoire under the happiest auspices. True, his Quartet was played at a pupils' concert. But he must have been dissatisfied with it, for he destroyed all but the first movement and used his folk-song a few months later in a " Scherzo à la russe " for piano, his Op. 1, No. 1. The Overture in F, which the Conservatoire orchestra played under his baton, pleased him better, for in February he rescored it for a larger orchestra and it was played publicly in both Petersburg and Moscow. But his leaving cantata, a modest attempt to rival Beethoven in setting Schiller's " An die Freude " for chorus and orchestra, was a failure. (The subject was Rubinstein's choice, not Tchaïkovsky's, and a quarter of a century later the composer very firmly refused to allow Jurgenson to publish the work.) The cantata was performed at the prize distribution on December 31st, 1865/January 12th, 1866—just twelve days after the first performance of Rimsky-Korsakof's First Symphony—in the presence of the directors of the Russian Music Society, the Director of the Imperial Chapel and the conductors of the Imperial Theatres, but in the absence of the composer. Tchaïkovsky's nerve had given way at the last moment and he could not bring himself to face the customary *viva voce* examination in public. Rubinstein was not only so annoyed that he at first threatened to withhold the diploma, but afterwards declined to perform the cantata at an R.M.S. concert unless it was drastically revised. Indeed, the unlucky cantata had the distinction of being condemned by *all* parties, one not easily achieved in Petersburg in those days. A work which compelled Anton Rubinstein, Cui *and* Serof to agree must, one feels, have possessed very unusual qualities. Only the unhappy composer's bosom friend thought otherwise. In his first letter to Tchaïkovsky in Moscow, Laroche said: " I tell you frankly that *I consider yours the greatest musical talent in Russia today.* Stronger and more original than Balakiref, loftier and more creative than Serof, incomparably more cultured than Rimsky-Korsakof " (who, after all, was not yet twenty-two, had had *no* musical education, and had produced nothing but that one Symphony!) " *In you I see the greatest—or rather the only—hope of our musical future!* You know quite well I'm not a flatterer; I never hesitated for a moment to tell you that your ' Romans in the Coliseum ' was a wretched piece of triviality and your ' Storm ' a museum of anti-musical curiosities. Besides— everything you've done so far, the ' Characteristic Dances ' and the scene from ' Boris Godunof '[1] not excepted, is in my opinion only preparatory, experimental school-work. Your own real creations may not appear for five years or so. But these ripe and classic works will surpass everything we have had since Glinka."

Tchaïkovsky arrived in Moscow still depressed by the fate of his cantata and at leaving the twins; lonely; and more than a little homesick. But he was greeted with warmth and kindness by at least two of the strangers he had come to live among. One of Laroche's friends, N. D. Kashkin, likewise a professor at the new Conservatoire, afterwards a critic, took to Tchaïkovsky at once. While Nicholas Rubinstein, an uncompromising idealist who concealed an extremely forceful personality under an air of aristocratic languor, but " a very good and sympathetic man " with " none of his brother's unapproachableness " (as Tchaïkovsky told the twins), overpowered the fledgling professor with kindness. He not only

---

[1] Nothing whatever is known of Tchaïkovsky's " Boris " and the " Romans in the Coliseum ".

insisted on taking him into his own house (which at first had to serve also as the Conservatoire building!) but " looked after him as if he were his nurse ", lending him a dress-coat, forcing on him a present of half-a-dozen shirts, taking him to a tailor to be measured for a frock-coat—all within a week or two of his arrival. Yet, as a composer, Tchaïkovsky's Moscow life began as unhappily as his Petersburg life had ended. Immediately on his arrival he had begun the orchestration of the C minor Overture written at Kamenka the previous summer; the work helped him to kill his melancholy. But when it was finished Nicholas Rubinstein condemned it. The score was sent to Anton with no better result and the work had to wait till 1931—thirty-eight years after the composer's death—for its first performance.[1] Tchaïkovsky himself afterwards admitted that it was " awful rubbish ", but he used some of its material again in the First Act of his opera " The Voevoda ". He appears to have made up his mind to write an opera on this subject, another of Ostrovsky's tragedies, within a few weeks of his arrival in Moscow and at first decided to prepare his own libretto. But a year or more passed before anything was done. In the meantime he busied himself with the rescoring of his F major Overture, with which he made a very successful public debut in Moscow at the end of March. Nicholas Rubinstein conducted.

Early in February he was able to write to Alexandra that he was " gradually beginning to get used to Moscow, though loneliness often makes me miserable. My classes are very successful, to my great surprise; my nervousness has completely vanished and I'm gradually acquiring the proper professorial air. My homesickness is also wearing off, but Moscow is still a strange town for me, and it will be a long time yet before I shall be able to think without dread of having to stay here for long years, perhaps for ever ". Still,

[1] The score was found among S. I. Taneief's papers in 1922 and has since been published.

his life was by no means unrelievedly gloomy. He could laugh heartily over " Pickwick "; his nerves were steady; and he was having his leg pulled a good deal about a pretty girl at a friend's house. And at Easter he was able to spend a few days in St. Petersburg.

In March Tchaïkovsky began his First Symphony. Though not programme-music, it was given a title, " Winter Daydreams ", and the first two movements had sub-titles. The composition worried him excessively, for the fate of his cantata and the C minor Overture had shaken his faith in his own powers. He began to suffer from insomnia and " throbbing sensations in the head "; his nerves were completely upset; and he was haunted by a conviction that he was going to die and leave the Symphony unfinished. Working feverishly far into the night, in an attempt to outwit destiny, he naturally made matters worse. To crown everything he was disappointed of another summer at Kamenka, owing to the state of the roads, and obliged to console himself with a holiday at Miatlef, near Petersburg. At the end of June he had a very serious nervous breakdown, suffering from hallucinations and " an inescapeable sense of horror ", indeed, dangerously near the borderline of insanity. Nevertheless, he recovered sufficiently to return to Moscow by the end of August.

In Petersburg he had shown his unfinished Symphony to Anton Rubinstein and Zaremba, who had promptly condemned it. But in Moscow brighter prospects were opening up. The Conservatoire was flourishing. Not only was it to be housed in a building of its own—though not the present Conservatoire building—and the staff increased, but Nicholas Rubinstein had been able to double Tchaïkovsky's salary. After the banquet which followed the official opening of the new building on September 1st/13th, Tchaïkovsky, " feeling ", says Kashkin, " that the first music to be heard in the new Conservatoire should be Glinka's, went to the piano and played the ' Ruslan ' Overture from memory ". The next month he composed a " Festival Overture on the Danish National Anthem " in celebration of the visit to Moscow of the Tsarevitch with his bride, the Danish Princess Dagmar. (It is amusing to learn that the composer promptly sold the jewelled cuff-links with which the Tsarevitch acknowledged the musical compliment, to one of his colleagues, the pianist, A. I. Dubuque.) By November the Symphony was finished and the scherzo played in Moscow almost immediately; and the adagio and scherzo were given in Petersburg at an R.M.S. concert on February 11th/23rd, 1867. Anton Rubinstein had flatly refused to play the whole of the Symphony, and the reception of these excerpts in both Moscow and Petersburg was distinctly cool. However, the two movements were almost the last things Anton Rubinstein conducted for the R.M.S. Shortly afterwards he resigned from both the R.M.S. and the Conservatoire, being succeeded at the latter by Zaremba and as conductor by Balakiref.

During the winter Tchaïkovsky made the acquaintance of Ostrovsky, whom he so much admired. The dramatist, who lived in Moscow, agreed to help him with the libretto of " The Voevoda " and did actually give him the libretto of the First Act in the spring of 1867. But the composer having lost the manuscript, Ostrovsky had to rewrite it from memory and then seems to have lost patience. He was doomed to have bad luck with composers! At any rate, nearly the whole of the libretto was Tchaïkovsky's own. But the composition of the music must have gone very smoothly, for the score was finished by the end of the year. Foiled through lack of funds in an attempt to spend a holiday in Finland, Tchaïkovsky and Anatol spent the summer at Hapsal with the Davydof ladies, pleasant weeks which the composer commemorated in a set of three piano pieces (one of them the popular " Chant sans Paroles "), " Souvenir de Hapsal ", Op. 2, dedicated to Vera Davydova. Already he talked happily of being " weary of life ", though he wished to escape from it not into extinction but into vegetation. " In those moments when I am too lazy not only to talk but even to think ", he writes to Alexandra, "*I long for a quiet, heavenly, happy existence*, and I can't imagine such an existence except in your immediate neighbourhood. You may be sure that one of these days you will have to devote part of your maternal care to your tired old brother. Perhaps you may think such a frame of mind leads to thoughts of marriage. No... my weariness has made me *too lazy*... to take upon myself the responsibility of a wife and children. Marriage is out of the question for me ". Yet when he went back to Moscow, he was by no means averse to the pleasures of social life. His letters speak of " coming home slightly drunk ";[1] " spending two evenings running at the English Club " (the most fashionable and dissipated club in Moscow, where Nicholas Rubinstein spent night after night, playing for high stakes) and regretting that he cannot afford to become a member; " coming home late with an overloaded stomach five days running ". In December, Laroche joined the staff of the Moscow Conservatoire and perhaps exercised a steadying influence on Tchaïkovsky.

That winter—the winter, incidentally, of Berlioz's visit—brought a definite increase to Tchaïkovsky's reputation. Nicholas Rubinstein played the dances from " The Voevoda " in December and the whole of the G minor Symphony, which was dedicated to him, for the first time on February 3rd/15th, 1868, both with great success. Sixteen days later Tchaïkovsky made a rather disastrous first appearance as a conductor, directing his " Voevoda " dances at a charity concert in such a state of utter demoralisation that the players were obliged simply to ignore his beat. He told Kashkin that he had had a recurrence of his former strange illusion that his head would fall off unless he held on to it tightly, a

---

[1] His diary in later years has an endless succession of entries, tersely recording : " Drunkenness ".

sensation which would certainly account for occasional lapses of attention. Laroche vividly recollected years afterwards how the unhappy composer had stood " with the baton in his right hand, while his left firmly supported his fair beard ". Tchaïkovsky was so terrified that he made no attempt to conduct again for nearly ten years. Yet in another respect this charity concert had important consequences, for it assisted indirectly in Tchaïkovsky's *rapprochement* with the group of " Petersburg amateurs ", the " mighty handful ", of which under slightly different circumstances he might so easily have become a member.

In his student days in Petersburg, Tchaïkovsky had known no musical people socially. Under Zaremba's wing he had been shepherded into the new Conservatoire and, but for the passing acquaintance with Serof, had met no musicians outside Conservatoire circles. The Conservatoire, staffed entirely by teachers of foreign blood, had given him a sound education, a hearty contempt for those who had not had a sound education, and a warm dislike of people who were constantly attacking " Germans " and " Jews ". His idol was a German Jew and his bosom-friend a German-Russian. Added to this he was always quick to suspect hostility to his own work even where none existed, and Cui, the journalistic mouthpiece of the " handful ", had dismissed his leaving cantata with contemptuous sarcasm. It is not unnatural that although he had never met any of the " handful ", he regarded them as a hostile group, while, according to Rimsky-Korsakof, they on their side considered him " a mere child of the Conservatoire ". Yet whereas his own loved and respected teacher, when conductor of the R.M.S. concerts, had repeatedly refused to play his music, the " hostile " Balakiref in his very first season had written asking to see the score of the " Voevoda " dances. At first Tchaïkovsky was—characteristically—so suspicious of his good intentions that he had actually refused to send it without a formal request signed by all the directors of the Society. Having received that, in January, 1868, he had sent off the " Dances " to Petersburg with a humble request for " a word of encouragement ". " It would be extremely gratifying to receive such from you." Then at the already mentioned charity concert in February, Rimsky-Korsakof's " Serbian Fantasia " was played for the second time that winter in Moscow and dismissed as " colourless and impersonal " by the critic of " The Entr'acte " (who praised Tchaïkovsky's " Dances "). This judgment provoked Tchaïkovsky, who had liked the " Fantasia ", into making his debut as a musical critic. In another Moscow paper he put the " Entr'acte " critic very firmly in his place, warmly praised the " Fantasia " and referred flatteringly to Rimsky-Korsakof's Symphony and his talent in general. And on February 21st/March 4th, Balakiref belatedly acknowledged the receipt of the " Voevoda " dances, regretting that it was now too late to play them that season. " As for the word of encouragement .. encouragement is suitable only for the little children of art, whereas your score shows me that you are a mature artist worthy of *severe criticism*. When we meet, I shall be very glad to give you my opinion; but it would be impossible in a letter, for the letter would grow into a whole essay—and from my unskilled pen that would be deadly. It would be far better to play through the piece together at the piano and criticise it bar by bar." Tchaïkovsky made no comment on this, but a lively correspondence sprang up as to the possibility of Nicholas Rubinstein's playing at a Free School concert for Balakiref. When Tchaïkovsky visited Petersburg for a few days in the spring he naturally called on Balakiref and met the other members of his circle. " He showed himself to be a pleasant companion, with a sympathetic personality ", says Rimsky-Korsakof. " His manner was simple and natural and he always appeared to speak with warmth and sincerity. On the first evening of our acquaintance Balakiref got him to play the first movement of his G minor

Symphony, which pleased us very much. Our former opinion of him changed to a more favourable one, though his Conservatoire education still placed a considerable barrier between him and us." This favourable impression was mutual, though Tchaïkovsky was drawn more particularly to Rimsky-Korsakof, whom he soon began to call by his nickname " Korsinka ", rather than to the other members of what he called " the Jacobin Club ".

Another indirect link with the " handful " had been forged the previous year in a rather curious way. Begitchef, the Intendant of the Imperial Theatres in Moscow, an elderly Don Juan, had " adopted " (and afterwards married) a lady with a past as colourful as his own—no other than Dargomyjsky's pupil, Mussorgsky's old friend, Maria Shilovskaya. Of her two sons by her first husband, who died in 1870, one (Constantine) became Tchaïkovsky's librettist, the other (Vladimir) a favourite pupil and beloved friend. Vladimir Shilovsky was consumptive, and in the summer of 1868 Begitchef took the lad to Paris to consult a specialist. Tchaïkovsky accompanied them and completed the scoring of " The Voevoda " in Paris.

Returning to Moscow in September, he began the composition of a symphonic fantasia, " Fatum ", and completed the rough sketch by the end of October. In the meantime choral rehearsals of " The Voevoda " had begun at the Grand Theatre. But a third-rate Italian opera company, run by a certain Merelli, happened to be visiting Moscow and drawing crowded houses, chiefly owing to the superb art of the leading soprano, Désirée Artôt. The Opera chorus and orchestra were so much occupied by their work with the Italians that Tchaïkovsky, seeing that his own work was going to be very perfunctorily prepared, asked that the production should be postponed till the visitors had gone. But before the Italians left, they—or at least one of their number—had done him still further injury.

Désirée Artôt, a pupil of Pauline Viardot-Garcia and a lady five years older than Tchaïkovsky, has the distinction of being the only woman who is known to have made any impression on him, other than a Platonic one. The progress of the affair may be traced from Tchaïkovsky's letters to Modest and Anatol during the period September/November: " Artôt is a charming creature; she and I are good friends." " I am very busy writing choruses and recitatives to Auber's ' Domino Noir ' for Artôt's benefit." " I've become very friendly with Artôt and she seems to like me. I've seldom met such a nice, good, sensible woman." " I've not written to you for a long time, but various circumstances have made it impossible for me to write letters, for all my leisure has been devoted to a being of whom I am very fond." He dedicates a piano piece to her (the Romance, Op. 5) and on Boxing Day/January 7th, 1869) announces to his father his intention of marrying Désirée next summer " if nothing happens to prevent it ". At the same time there are all sorts of obstacles: Désirée's mother is against the match; Nicholas Rubinstein and his other friends are doing their best to stop it, lest it should interfere with his career as a composer and reduce him to the rôle of " prima donna's husband "; the ardent lover himself " doesn't want to sacrifice his future to her. . . On the one hand I love her with all my heart and soul, and feel I can't live any longer without her; on the other, calm reason bids me stop and think ". He would like his father's views on the matter—and Ilia, like the old Micawber he was, replied in a bless-you-my-children strain. And the next we hear is in the course of a letter to Anatol only a few weeks later: " At the moment I'm in a great state of excitement. ' The Voevoda ' is going to be performed. Everyone is taking the greatest pains ", etc. etc. " I've already begun another opera. . .but I want to keep it a secret for a while. How surprised people will be to find half the opera already done in the summer ", and so on. And only then: " As for the love-affair . . . it's very doubtful whether I shall enter Hymen's kingdom. Things are beginning to go rather awry. I'll tell you more about it later. No time now." As a matter of fact, Désirée was already betrothed to the Spanish baritone Padilla-y-Ramos, whom she married the following September. But although her brief return to Moscow later in 1869 caused Tchaïkovsky some painful hours, considering his sufferings from much less important troubles he seems to have borne his disappointment extraordinarily well. Indeed, Kashkin hints that his friend was in love with the artist rather than the woman, and says that the initiative in the affair was taken by Artôt.

"The Voevoda" had its first performance on January 30th/February 11th, 1869, and scored an apparent triumph, the composer receiving no less than fifteen calls. Yet the opera was repeated only four times more; Laroche criticised it adversely, thereby causing a quarrel which lasted for some months; and a few years later Tchaïkovsky himself destroyed the score. (The "Dances", however, had already been published separately as Op. 3, and sixty years or so later the whole opera was almost entirely reconstructed from existing parts by S. Popof.) On February 25th/March 9th Nicholas Rubinstein also played "Fatum" (another work destroyed in the 'seventies but posthumously reconstructed and published as Op. 77) at a Moscow R.M.S. concert. Tchaïkovsky immediately sent the score to Balakiref with a request that he would accept the dedication if he liked the piece. Balakiref accepted the dedication, almost without looking at the score, which had been borrowed first by Rimsky-Korsakof and then by Borodin. "But in any case, whether I like it or not, I'll play it at the next concert", he assured the composer. He was as good as his word. "Fatum" was performed at a Petersburg R.M.S. concert on March 17th/29th, just a week after Korsakof's "Antar". But Balakiref did *not* like it. In some embarrassment he tried to write to Tchaïkovsky about it, but the letter " grew into a whole essay " and was never sent. The letter he did send after a fortnight or so was quite frank enough, however: " Your ' Fatum ' has been played .... There was little applause, which I ascribe to the hideous din at the end ..." But finally, after a good deal of typically Balakirefian advice: " I write with perfect candour, feeling quite sure that you won't change your intention of dedicating ' Fatum ' to me. Your dedication is precious as a sign of your sympathy—and I have a soft corner in my heart for you." To which Tchaïkovsky replied on May 3rd/15th: " It was very wrong of me not to write before and, by my silence, perhaps to give you reason to think I had taken offence at your letter criticising ' Fatum '. In the depths of my heart I quite agree with your remarks about this concoction, though I admit I should have been very happy if you could have found something to praise in it—if only a little. Your letter is all fault-finding—though quite justifiably. I admit I was not delighted with your criticism, but I wasn't in the least offended. I paid homage to the sincere straightforwardness which is one of the most delightful traits of your musical personality. Of course I shan't withdraw the dedication, but I hope somewhen to write something better for you." And he goes on to express the intense indignation he and Nicholas Rubinstein were feeling at the treatment Balakiref had received from the Grand Duchess Helena Pavlovna, treatment which resulted in his leaving the R.M.S. Nor was this indignation expressed only in private; Tchaïkovsky wrote a very outspoken article on the subject for the " Contemporary Record ". At the end of the letter he tells Balakiref: " I am now occupied with the instrumentation of my opera ' Undine '; one act is already finished; the other two will be scored in the summer."

This " Undine ", to a libretto based on Zhukovsky's poem, was the " secret " opera that Tchaïkovsky had mentioned to Anatol in January. It was duly completed at Kamenka in

July, and Begitchef took the score to Petersburg. But there the composer was doomed to disappointment. Gedeonof already had two new operas—by nonentities—on his hands and Tchaïkovsky was informed that "Undine" could not be produced that season. In the meantime he concluded a commission from Jurgenson, the arrangement of fifty Russian folk-songs for piano duet. He had done the first twenty-five during the autumn of 1869, taking the melodies from Villebois's collection—and altering them according to his fancy! Now, with Balakiref's permission, he took the second batch from the latter's collection, treating them a little more respectfully and winning the other's approval for at least a few of his arrangements. Of the whole fifty, only one had been collected by himself—a lovely melody he had heard sung (to ribald words) that summer at Kamenka, by a carpenter working outside the room in which he was orchestrating "Undine".

Balakiref appeared in Moscow in August, perhaps hoping (like Serof the year before) that Nicholas Rubinstein would be able to help him in some way. "I confess", wrote Tchaïkovsky, "that his presence weighs on me", as indeed it had begun to weigh on Mussorgsky and Rimsky-Korsakof. "He expects me to spend the whole day with him, and that bores me. He is a very good fellow and very well-disposed toward me but—I don't know why—I can never feel absolutely at home with him. I particularly dislike the one-sidedness of his musical opinions and the acerbity of his tone." Nevertheless, it was during this visit that Balakiref induced Tchaïkovsky to write a concert-overture on the subject of "Romeo and Juliet". For a month or so Tchaïkovsky was empty of ideas and the other eagerly sketched out a beginning, of which Tchaïkovsky made no use. Towards the end of October, however, he was able to report that "my overture is going ahead fairly quickly; already the greater part is fully sketched out and if nothing hinders me

I hope it will be ready in a month and a half ". A fortnight later he sent Balakiref the chief themes—and the dedication of what he hoped was the promised " something better ". Balakiref was delighted with the *cor anglais* love-theme, but critical of other points. When he and Rimsky-Korsakof visited Moscow in January, Tchaïkovsky " of course, saw them every day. Balakiref is beginning to admire me more and more; Korsakof has dedicated a very good song to me. They are both pleased with my overture ". In fact at this period Tchaïkovsky was, so far as his residence in Moscow permitted, a member of the " Balakiref circle ".[1]

With " Undine " still unproduced, Tchaïkovsky was already thinking of a third opera. In January, 1870, he began one on a subject " Mandragora " and wrote one number, an " Insects' Chorus " (afterwards sung at an R.M.S. concert as a " Chorus of Elves "), but abandoned the work in consequence of Kashkin's criticism. He turned instead to Lajetchnikof's tragedy, " The Opritchnik ", but for a time that also stuck at the first chorus. The failure first of " Romeo and Juliet " on March 4th/16th and then, a fortnight later, of five excerpts from the First Act of " Undine ", only confirmed him in his conviction that " nobody takes any interest in what I write " and discouraged him from working at " The Opritchnik ". He " yearned so for sympathy and appreciation ", and the only encouraging word came from the " handful ". " At our meetings we keep on playing the score of ' Romeo ' that you sent us ", wrote Balakiref, " and we are all delighted with a great deal of it. Stassof (Vlad.) is extraordinarily pleased and says our army has now been reinforced ". Balakiref insisted on despotically supervising the work of the recruit, as of the rest of his forces; but far from resenting his advice as to the improvement of parts of " Romeo ", Tchaïkovsky acted on it and largely rewrote the

[1] Simultaneously with " Romeo and Juliet "—in November/December, 1869—Tchaïkovsky wrote his first songs, the half-dozen which make up Op. 6.

work on the lines suggested, during the summer in Switzerland. In the meantime he had suffered a fresh disappointment. In the middle of May the Opera Committee—that famous Opera Committee which nine months later was to reject " Boris "—turned down " Undine ". Four or five years later Tchaïkovsky himself destroyed the score, after using some of the numbers in other works, but at the time he felt himself to be the victim of terrible injustice. He left Petersburg to join Vladimir Shilovsky in Paris with a heart full of bitterness.

Shilovsky was very ill, but Tchaïkovsky got him away from Paris to Bad Soden, near Frankfurt-am-Main, in June. " We lead a monotonous existence and get very bored ", he wrote to Modest, " but for that very reason my health is excellent . . . I'm very lazy and haven't the slightest wish to work ". At the Beethoven Centenary Festival at Mannheim, he heard the D major Mass for the first time and thought it " a creation of the highest genius ". (But Tchaïkovsky always respected Beethoven a great deal more than he loved him.) At Wiesbaden he found Nicholas Rubinstein " in the act of losing his last ruble at roulette . . . but firmly convinced that he's going to break the bank before he leaves ". The outbreak of the Franco-German War in July sent them all scuttling over the frontier into Switzerland, to escape the expected French invasion! After six weeks at Interlaken, where his " astonishment and admiration in the presence of these sublime beauties of Nature passed all bounds ", Tchaïkovsky wandered back to Moscow by way of Munich, Vienna and Petersburg.

Having orchestrated the new version of " Romeo and Juliet ", which was published in Berlin by Bote and Bock the following year, he resumed work on " The Opritchnik ". But he was disappointed of a Petersburg performance of " Romeo ", since, owing to financial difficulties, the Free School was unable to give any concerts that winter. " I so badly want to hear my overture under your direction ", he had written to Balakiref, " that I would come to Petersburg —though for one day only. Of course, this expedition must remain a secret between you and me, for it's really ludicrous to go four hundred miles to hear one's own things!" Two or three years later he wrote to Bessel in exactly the same strain: " I tell you quite as a secret that I'd like to be present at the first symphony concert in Petersburg, so as to hear my Symphony. As I don't on any account want people to know about this, I must ask you to give me your word of honour not to betray me . . . For Heaven's sake, not a word, or my whole joke will be turned into a terrible piece of unpleasantness." And there were other occasions when Tchaïkovsky attended performances of his own works in this furtive way.

Early in 1871 Tchaïkovsky, hoping to raise a little money, decided to give a concert. The desire to arouse interest by a new work of his own, combined with lack of funds to engage an orchestra, more or less obliged him to write a string quartet —in spite of his lack of interest in chamber music—and the Quartet in D, Op. 11, was the result. For the chief theme of the slow movement, the all too famous *andante cantabile*, Tchaïkovsky took the folk-song he had heard at his sister's in the summer of 1869. But the Quartet, written rather hurriedly in February and played at the concert on March 16th/28th, was only an interlude in the composition of " The Opritchnik ". The period as a whole was a rather disturbed one. In the summer Tchaïkovsky made quite a round of visits—to his elder brother, to Anatol in Kief, to Kamenka, to the home of a friend (N. D. Kondratief) at Nizy in the Ukraine (where he finished his text-book on harmony), and to Vladimir Shilovsky at Ussovo. On returning to Moscow he at last managed to break away from Nicholas Rubinstein's too hospitable roof. Rubinstein was the exact counterpart of Balakiref in well-meaning despotism as in other respects, and he had insisted on having Tchaïkovsky's company constantly and in arranging every detail of his life for him—to all of which Tchaïkovsky had meekly, though unwillingly, submitted. But he now took a three-roomed flat of his own and engaged a manservant. From about the same time dates the beginning of his more or less regular work as one of the musical critics of the "Moscow Gazette", which continued till 1876. Laroche having returned to Petersburg, his post as critic was nominally filled by N. A. Hubert, but the work was actually shared by Hubert, Tchaïkovsky and Kashkin.

In the autumn the correspondence with Balakiref was as lively as ever. And now there are references to other members of the circle, besides Tchaïkovsky's favourite "Korsinka". "Make Borodin hurry up and finish his splendid symphony" (i.e. the B minor), he writes to Balakiref. While Balakiref is "*very* anxious to perform your D major chorus" (the "Chorus of Insects"), and shortly afterwards sends a detailed plan for converting this solitary chorus into a "lyrical and descriptive" cantata, "Night", with "an instrumental scherzo in the style of 'Queen Mab', depicting the hum of gnats, etc.", fantastic choruses of spirits, and an orchestral epilogue depicting dawn and sunrise. To which Tchaïkovsky replies: "I like your idea for a cantata, 'Night', very much and shall certainly make use of it, though not in the immediate future. At the moment I am employing all my few free hours on my *opera*, '*The Opritchnik*', which I am very anxious to finish during the present winter. I dare say this unlucky opera will share the fate of my 'Undine', but none the less I want to finish it, so I can't begin another composition yet for a while." He is also very anxious to know at which Free School concert his chorus will be given. "Who knows whether I may not manage to skip over to 'Peter'?" Balakiref replies that it will be done on December 18th/30th, and "we shall all be very glad to see you".

But before that date Tchaïkovsky had left Russia and was on his way to Nice! The episode is curious and not easily explicable, considering his anxiety to finish " The Opritchnik ". " I must tell you that at Shilovsky's urgent desire I am going abroad for a month ", he writes to Anatol on December 2nd/14th. " I shall start in a week or two. But as no one in Moscow—except Rubinstein—must know anything about it, they must all be made to think I've gone to Sasha's ", i.e. to Kamenka. After a month at Nice, where even the " many pleasant hours " were shot through with melancholy—" I have grown old and can enjoy nothing more. I live on my memories and hopes. But what is there to hope for?"—he returned to Moscow, worked during February and March at a Festival Cantata commissioned for a forthcoming Polytechnic Exhibition, while his Petersburg friends were busy with " Mlada ", and completed " The Opritchnik " by the beginning of May.

In the meantime Balakiref had disappeared from the scene and nine years were to elapse before they resumed contact. It is idle to conjecture how Tchaïkovsky would have developed if he had stayed under Balakiref's influence, but it is interesting to note that he remained an ally of the " mighty handful " until the " handful " itself began to disintegrate. As we shall see, the link was not immediately broken—though weakened—by Balakiref's disappearance. Tchaïkovsky was never more completely a nationalist than in the work he wrote during the summer of 1872, the Second Symphony, with its first and last movements based on folk-songs. (The second, a march, was taken from the ill-fated " Undine ".) The Symphony was begun at Kamenka in June, continued at Nizy and Ussovo, and orchestrated in the autumn after the composer's return to Moscow.

Tchaïkovsky's letters that winter are full of familiar refrains: " Nothing particular happens to any of us . . . . We go to the Conservatoire as usual; sometimes we meet in the old way for a general 'booze'; and are just as bored as last year. Boredom consumes us all, and the reason is that we are growing old. Yes ... every moment brings us nearer the grave. ... As for myself, I have only one interest in life: my success as a composer." His sight was giving him trouble and as usual his nerves were bad, " often getting out of order for no obvious reason ". He was also worrying about " the not very consoling fate of my compositions. The Symphony, on which I build great hopes, will probably not be performed before the middle of January at the earliest ". However, at Christmas the even greater worry as to the fate of " The Opritchnik " was removed. Tchaïkovsky was summoned to Petersburg and the Opera Committee accepted the work unanimously.

It was during this visit to Petersburg that Tchaïkovsky so exasperated Mussorgsky by his " admiration of absolute musical beauty " and by his " blowing bubbles ". Tchaïkovsky frankly expressed his dislike of " The Nursery ", though he admired the lyrical " parrot " episode in " Boris ", while Mussorgsky was secretly scornful of Tchaïkovsky's avowed attempt to reconcile artistic sincerity with the demands of the public taste in " The Opritchnik ". But that was only Mussorgsky's attitude, not that of the circle as a whole; we must remember that at this period Mussorgsky was beginning to be quite equally contemptuous of Rimsky-Korsakof. The others were delighted with the Second Symphony, particularly the finale;[1] Rimsky-Korsakof's wife undertook the piano-duet arrangement of the Symphony; while even Balakiref made a single, fleeting appearance specially to hear Tchaïkovsky's String Quartet. And before leaving Peters-

[1] Cui attacked the Second Symphony when it was played in Petersburg. And he attacked " The Opritchnik ", comparing it unfavourably with " Boris ". But he had also handled " Boris " very roughly. Cui's critical method was peculiar to himself. Having belaboured his antagonists with tremendous enthusiasm, he would turn round and knock down a few of his friends just to show that he was quite impartial.

burg, Tchaïkovsky asked Stassof to suggest a subject for a symphonic fantasia. Stassof suggested three—Shakespeare's " Tempest ", " Ivanhoe " or Gogol's " Taras Bulba "— giving him a detailed programme for " The Tempest " which the composer accepted in every detail, dedicating the resultant work to the critic.

The Second Symphony was played in Moscow on January 26th/February 7th, 1873, with such success that it was repeated at another concert the same season. Then Tchaïkovsky was commissioned to write incidental music for the production in May of Ostrovsky's fantastic play, " Snow Maiden ", work which he completed rather hurriedly during the spring, patching in bits of odd material from earlier, discarded works. (The overture, for instance, was originally the introduction to " Undine ", while another number from " Undine " was used for Lel's third song.) He again spent the summer abroad, returning to Russia early in August to spend a couple of weeks with Shilovsky at Ussovo. Shilovsky had to go to Moscow for a short time, and, for the first time in his life, Tchaïkovsky found himself alone in the heart of the Russian countryside. Years afterwards he described the peculiar delights of those few days: " I found myself in a mood of serene exaltation, wandered in the day through the woods, walked each evening in the deep valley, and at night, sitting by the open window, listened to the solemn silence all around, broken now and again by some indefinite sound of nature. During those two weeks, without the least labour— just as if I had been guided by some supernatural power—I sketched out my ' Tempest '." The piece so fluently written, actually in ten days, was orchestrated in the autumn and given its first performance in Moscow on December 7th/19th. There was again a triumph. And a second String Quartet, in F major, Op. 22, written early in 1874, scored an immediate success.

The tide of Tchaïkovsky's fortune seemed to have

definitely turned. He had been moaning to the publisher Bessel in October: " It's useless for you to hope that ' The Opritchnik ' will be put on next season. It will never be given at all, simply because I'm not known personally to the ' great ones ' of this world in general and to those of the Petersburg Opera in particular. Isn't it perfectly absurd that Kondratief[1] should have chosen Mussorgsky's ' Boris Godunof ' for his benefit, although it's been rejected by the Committee? And Platonova also is interested in this work, while no one wants to know anything about my opera, which has been accepted." But almost immediately news came that " The Opritchnik " was to be produced in the spring. Like every other Russian opera composer of the period, Tchaïkovsky had to run the double gauntlet of the Censorship (which cut the figure of Ivan the Terrible out of the *dramatis personæ*) and of Napravnik with his blue pencil. At first he accepted all Napravnik's suggestions with surprising humility, but as the rehearsals went on—he stayed in Petersburg with his father while they were in progress—he became more and more annoyed by Napravnik's drastic surgery. To make matters worse, he was a prey to self-dissatisfaction, disliking his work a little more at every rehearsal and writing to his friends in Moscow that he would prefer them not to come and hear it as " *there's nothing good in the thing* ". At the same time, he was careful enough to get tickets for them, and one imagines he would have been rather badly hurt if they had taken him at his word. Actually the *première* (April 12th/24th) was attended by Nicholas Rubinstein and almost the whole of the Moscow Conservatoire staff. But even the brilliant success of the first performance, followed by a supper at which the Petersburg and Moscow branches of the Russian Music Society combined to do him honour, did not end Tchaïkovsky's torment of dissatisfaction. Within three days

[1] G. P. Kondratief. Not to be confused with Tchaïkovsky's friend, N. D. Kondratief.

he fled to Italy and wandered from Venice to Rome, from Rome to Naples, Naples to Florence, in utter wretchedness. Venice he found " gloomy ", Rome " uninteresting ". " At Naples it came to such a pass that every day I shed tears from sheer homesickness. . . . But the chief source of all my misery remains in Petersburg. ' The Opritchnik ' torments me." Yet he had no sooner returned to Petersburg in May than he thought of a fresh opera, began it the next month, and actually completed it, orchestration and all, in the course of the summer.

The history of this work, " Vakula the Smith ", is curious, that of its composer's behaviour in connection with it still more so. Three or four years before, Polonsky had been commissioned by the Grand Duchess Helena Pavlovna to prepare for Serof a libretto on Gogol's " Christmas Eve ". But Serof having died with the work hardly begun, the Grand Duchess had decided to offer two prizes for the best settings of the libretto. In the meantime she herself had died in 1873 and the competition was now being run by the R.M.S. The closing date was fixed for August 1st/13th, 1875; the first prize work would be performed at the Marinsky Theatre; but naturally no unsuccessful setting of the libretto would stand any chance of production. Considering that last fact, it is understandable that Tchaïkovsky did not wish to enter unless he was practically certain of winning. In itself there was nothing very despicable, if not particularly creditable, in his preliminary manœuvres to discover whether Rimsky-Korsakof, Anton Rubinstein or even Balakiref was competing. But this was only the first of a series of incidents, impossible to explain away and difficult to excuse, unless on the grounds that an artist is justified in sticking at nothing in order to succeed, and that Tchaïkovsky " felt he might go out of his mind if ' Vakula ' failed ". He had begun his opera and completed it so hurriedly under the impression that the competition closed in August, *1874.*

Now discovering that he was a year too soon and that he would have to wait all that time before the fate of his work was decided, he sounded Napravnik and G. P. Kondratief as to the possibility of having *his* " Vakula " produced at once, regardless of the other competitors! He naturally received a sharp rap over the knuckles from Napravnik and the Grand Duke Constantine Nikolaevitch, the chairman of the jury, and wrote expressing his regrets for his " stupid mistake " and repudiating " ulterior motives ". But Tchaïkovsky's indiscretions did not end there. Instead of keeping the authorship secret as he was in honour bound to do by the terms of the competition, he had the overture publicly performed in Moscow in November, 1874—and conducted by Nicholas Rubinstein, *one of the judges.* Although the score submitted had to be in a copyist's hand, it bore a distinguishing motto in the composer's own handwriting, well known to almost every member of the jury. And just before the actual judging, Tchaïkovsky sent Rimsky-Korsakof, one of their number, a quite unnecessarily flattering letter, in which he naïvely stresses his anxiety to win! Indeed, the whole affair was scandalous in the extreme. All Petersburg knew that Tchaïkovsky was the winner before the jury themselves were supposed to have learned the names of the competitors. Rimsky-Korsakof consoled himself afterwards with the reflection that " no harm was done, since Tchaïkovsky's opera was undoubtedly the best of those sent in ". But the affair was hardly the less discreditable on that account. The second prize, incidentally, went to Serof's old pupil, Solovief.

In the meantime, Tchaïkovsky was busy with a new composition, the famous B flat minor Piano Concerto, written (not without considerable labour) during November and December, 1874, and orchestrated a month or so later. The Concerto was a source of fresh pain to his morbidly sensitive nature, for Nicholas Rubinstein, to whom it was originally dedicated and for whom it had been specially written, abused it roundly and, according to the composer himself, with unnecessary brutality. " Deeply offended . . . I left the room in silence and went upstairs. I could not have spoken a word for rage and agitation." He altered the dedication, offering it to Hans von Bülow, whom he had never met but whom he knew to be interested in his work, and it was years before he completely forgave Nicholas Rubinstein. At the same time Laroche had just been abusing his " Tempest " after its performance in Petersburg! True, the Stassof-Rimsky-Korsakof group were writing him letters of sympathy and congratulation, and even Cui had been moved to public praise of " The Tempest " and the Second String Quartet. But that did not satisfy his craving for praise from his Moscow friends. In these moods he felt that they were " mere professional colleagues ". " I have clear proofs that not one of them gives me the tenderness and affection that my spirit needs." He already felt " often drawn towards a monastic life, or something of the kind. . . . In my nature there is so much fear of mankind, so much unnecessary timidity and mistrust—in short, a host of characteristics which make me more and more misanthropical. . . . All through the winter I've been depressed, so depressed that I've often been brought to the verge of despair and obliged to long for death ".

The summer—divided between Ussovo, Nizy and Verbovka, another property of the Davydofs', near Kamenka—brought relief. Tchaïkovsky wrote his Third Symphony, " commenced June 5th/17th at Ussovo, completed August 1st/13th, 1875, at Verbovka ", as a note on the score records. And he began a ballet, " The Swan Lake ", commissioned by the Imperial Theatres. The successful production of both the new Symphony and the Piano Concerto in Moscow in November, with the favourable result of the opera competition, dispelled his depression altogether, and he was in exceptionally high spirits during a visit to the West with Modest that winter. It was during this visit, in Paris, that he saw

"Carmen" for the first time, with Célestine Galli-Marié in the title-rôle. (He had already known the vocal score.) "Peter Ilitch had never before been so completely carried away by any piece of modern music as by ' Carmen ' ", says his brother. " Bizet's death, three months after the first performance still further strengthened his almost unhealthy passion for the opera. . . . I had never before seen Peter Ilitch so excited after a dramatic performance." In Paris, also, the composer began his third and last String Quartet (E flat minor, Op. 30), dedicated to the memory of his colleague, the violinist Laub, who had died the previous March. But his chief preoccupation was the finding of a new opera subject, " one concerned with real human beings, not lay-figures . . . in close touch with our life and time . . . a simple, realistic drama ", as Modest says. In short, something of the " Carmen " type.[1] " I am working at full steam to finish the Quartet ", he writes to Modest on February 10th/22nd, 1876, after his return to Moscow. " After that "—the Quartet was performed about five weeks later—" I shall rest for a while, i.e. do nothing but finish my ballet ". (That also was done by the end of March.) " I shan't start on anything new till I've decided on an opera. I'm still wavering between ' Ephraim ' "—a libretto concocted by Vladimir Shilovsky's brother, Constantine—" and ' Francesca da Rimini ', but I think it's going to be the latter ". It *was* the latter. Only, instead of an opera, " Francesca " became an orchestral piece, sketched roughly during the summer in Paris.

For in the summer Tchaïkovsky was again in the West, first taking a cure at Vichy, then going to Bayreuth in August for the famous first performance of the " Ring ", which he was to report for the " Russian Gazette ". Among the other

---

[1] Again, only six months before his death, he advised Modest to "find or invent a *not fantastic* subject—something in the style of ' Carmen ' or ' Cavalleria Rusticana ' ".

Russian musicians present were Nicholas Rubinstein (who shared rooms with Tchaïkovsky), Cui and Laroche; he also made the acquaintance of Liszt " who received me with extraordinary kindness " and called on Wagner, who apparently did not receive him at all. As for the " Ring " itself, Tchaïkovsky was obviously confused and oppressed by it all. He found the music of " Das Rheingold " " incredible nonsense ", though with " delightful moments ". There might be a lot of fine stuff in the " Ring " but it was all much too long-drawn. " To be sure there are beautiful passages, but as a whole it's deadly boring. The ballet ' Sylvia ' is a thousand times finer." " After the last chords of ' Götterdämmerung ' I felt as if I'd been let out of prison." " Bayreuth has left me with a disagreeable memory ", he wrote to Modest, " although my artistic pride has been flattered more than once. It appeared that I'm by no means as unknown in the West as I'd supposed ". Tchaïkovsky never grew to like Wagner's music, except " Lohengrin ", which he thought by far his best work, and though his published reports from Bayreuth show that he tried to be fair to it—no mean virtue in a Russian critic of those days—his impressions are all curiously blurred. It was with profound relief that he escaped to Nuremburg and Vienna, and then made for the seclusion of Verbovka.

From Verbovka in August he announced to Modest a project which, when actually carried into effect, was to have the most disastrous consequences. " I have now to surmount a very critical moment of my life. Later I will write you about it in more detail; in the meantime I will tell you only that *I've decided to marry.* That is irrevocable. . . ." And again, three weeks later, from Moscow: " My reflections have resulted in the firm determination to marry someone or other." A week later still: " How delightful to come home in the evening to my pleasant little room and settle down with a book! At this moment I hate, probably not less than you do, that beautiful unknown being who will force me to change my way of living. Don't be afraid; I shan't hurry in this matter." In October he reassured his sister: " Please don't worry about my marriage . . . which won't come off before next year. During the next few months I shall only look round and prepare myself a little for matrimony, which I consider necessary for various reasons. Rest assured that I shan't plunge heedlessly into the abyss of an unlucky union." According to Kashkin, with whom he discussed the matter in confidence more than once, what Tchaïkovsky needed was not a mate but a companion and housekeeper. He was lonely and needed " some elderly spinster or widow " who would " understand " him, " without any pretence of ardent passion ".

It was during this period (October/November) that he wrote " Francesca da Rimini ", finishing the score on November 5th/17th. Nineteen days later " Vakula the Smith " was produced in Petersburg at the Maryinsky Theatre. This time Tchaïkovsky himself was satisfied with his work; even Cui assured him it was bound to be a brilliant success; but the public thought otherwise. In spite of the admirable production, " Vakula " was a failure, and immediately afterwards came news of the failure of " Romeo and Juliet " simultaneously in Vienna (under Richter) and Paris (under Pasdeloup). A little balm to poor Tchaïkovsky's soul was provided by a meeting with Leo Tolstoy, whose novels he enthusiastically admired, but by whom he was definitely unimpressed in the flesh. However, Tolstoy, whose reactions to music were very naïve, wept at the *andante cantabile* of his D major Quartet, and—" I never felt so flattered in my life and so proud of my creative power as when L. Tolstoy, sitting beside me, listened to my *andante* while the tears streamed from his eyes ". But Tchaïkovsky seems to have met his trio of reverses with quite unusual buoyancy, a buoyancy reflected alike in the light-hearted

"Rococo Variations" for 'cello and orchestra, in his eager badgering of Stassof to provide him with a plan for an operatic "Othello", and in an unusually playful letter to Modest (January 2nd/14th, 1877): "Dear Mr. Modest Ilitch! I don't know whether you remember me, but I'm your own brother and Professor at the Moscow Conservatoire. I have also written several compositions: operas, symphonies, overtures, etc. Once upon a time you honoured me with your personal attention", and so on in the same vein. In February he actually plucked up courage to conduct his "Slavonic March" at the Moscow Opera House, apparently with sensations less alarming than in the old days, for he forthwith announced his intention of taking every opportunity to conduct, with a view to a foreign tour on which he would have to direct his own compositions. But he wisely left the first performance of "Francesca" a few days later in the safe hands of Nicholas Rubinstein.

But the year 1877, so happily begun, was remarkable for much more than Tchaïkovsky's nervous reappearance at a conductor's desk. Considering all it brought him—the beginning of the extraordinary connection with Nadejda von Meck, the tragic, mysterious marriage with its so nearly fatal sequel, the composition of two of his best works—it might well be considered the most important of his life. Certainly the note of subjective emotion, which had hitherto been seldom if ever noticeable in his music, became after this ever more and more insistent, sharply differentiating his work from that of all his Russian contemporaries.

Nadejda von Meck was in 1877 a widow of forty-six, cultured, much travelled, a lover of music in general and of Tchaïkovsky's music in particular. Her husband had died only the year before, leaving her eleven children (of whom seven were still living with her) and a very large fortune. Eccentric as she was, her enormous wealth enabled her to gratify the most extravagant of her numerous whims. After her husband's death she entirely shut herself up in her family circle. Tchaïkovsky himself never saw her except at a distance and they never exchanged a word of conversation. On one occasion when they met by accident, both were overcome by confusion and passed on hurriedly. Although Tchaïkovsky's niece, Anna Davydova, married her son Nicholas in 1884, Alexandra Davydova and her husband never met their daughter's mother-in-law. Yet she gave Tchaïkovsky his financial independence and for fourteen years they carried on a constant, voluminous and extremely intimate correspondence, often dreadfully gushing on her side but (one feels) none the less sincere; profoundly revealing, if less perfectly sincere, on his. History records no stranger, more freakish friendship. Already towards the end of 1876, through one of her house-musicians, the violinist Kotek, a friend and ex-pupil of Tchaïkovsky's, Nadejda had commissioned him at an absurdly generous fee to arrange some of his smaller pieces for violin and piano. And the epistolary acquaintanceship thus begun ripened rapidly. On February 15th/27th she says she would like to tell him of her " fantastic enthusiasm " for him, assuring him that it is " ideal, abstract, lofty and noble ". " You may call me a fool or a lunatic, but you must not laugh at me. All this would, perhaps, be ridiculous if it were not intended so seriously and sincerely." Two or three weeks later, after asking for his photograph, she writes: " In my opinion it is not personal intercourse which draws people together, but similarity of opinions, feelings and sympathies, so that one person may draw near to another, though (in a sense) a stranger. . . . All I have heard of you—both good and bad—gives me such extraordinary pleasure that I lay my warmest sympathy at your feet. I am happy at the thought that the man and the artist in you are so preciously and harmoniously united. There was a time when I was very anxious to make your personal acquaintance; but now the more you fascinate me the more I fear your acquaintanceship; I prefer to think of you from afar, to hear you speak in your music and to share your feelings through it." Tchaïkovsky completely understood this " fantastic feeling " of hers and reciprocated it, recognising her as a kindred spirit in more respects than one. " The circumstance that we both suffer from one and the same malady would alone bring us nearer to each other ", he told her. " This malady is misanthropy; but a quite peculiar form of misanthropy, for it does not spring from either hatred of or contempt for mankind. Those who suffer from this complaint do not fear the evils which their fellow-creatures may bring upon them, but they fear the disillusionment . . . which generally follows upon every intimacy. There was a time when I was so possessed by this fear of mankind that I became almost insane . . . I had to fight it out with myself, and God alone knows what this conflict cost me! . . . Work saved me. . . . Those few successes which I have been allowed have given me consolation and encouragement, so that the longings which used often to drive me to hallucinations and insanity, have almost entirely lost their power over me. . . . I'm not at all surprised that, in spite of your love of my music, you don't wish to make my acquaintance. You are afraid you will fail to find in my personality all those qualities with which your idealising imagination has endowed me. And in that you are quite right." As for the music itself: " Whether I write well or ill—at any rate, I write from inward necessity. I speak the language of music because I always have something to say."

As if to mock Tchaïkovsky's boast of conquered " longings " and depression, they returned with renewed force that spring. He was heavily in debt but when, early in May, Mme. von Meck wrote commissioning an original piece at a ridiculous fee, he declined to accept the commission. It would have been a merely manufactured piece and he declined to offer " false coin in exchange for true ".

However, " at the present moment ", he adds—this is on May 1st/13th, " I am completely absorbed in my symphony, which I began in the winter ", the Fourth Symphony. " I should like to dedicate it to you, for I believe you will find in it an echo of your most intimate thoughts and feelings... I am in a very worried and irritable state of mind, unfavourable to composition, which is all to the disadvantage of the symphony." A week later he wrote to another friend: " I am very much changed, especially in mind, since we met last. ... Life is terribly empty, boring and trivial. I am seriously considering matrimony as a lasting tie. The only thing that remains unalterable is my delight in composition. ... But for my work at the Conservatoire, which I dislike more and more every year, I might perhaps be able to accomplish something really valuable." Ten days later still, at the singer Lavrovskaya's, " the conversation fell upon opera texts. ... Suddenly Lavrovskaya remarked, ' What about " Eugene Onegin "?'. The idea struck me as very curious and I said nothing. Later, however, lunching alone at a restaurant, I remembered ' Onegin ' ... and found the idea by no means so absurd ... I soon made up my mind, and set off at once in search of Pushkin's works. ... I was delighted when I read the poem. I spent a sleepless night; result—the scenario of a splendid opera on Pushkin's text. The very next day I went to Constantine Shilovsky and he is now working like the wind at my scenario." Tchaïkovsky completed the sketch of the Fourth Symphony but postponed the orchestration till the end of the summer, in order to concentrate on " Eugene Onegin ". At the beginning of June, with an extraordinary secret on his mind, he went to stay at the Shilovskys' great house at Glebovo, where eighteen years before Mussorgsky and Dargomyjsky had come " with *tutta la compania* " to hear " A Life for the Tsar " performed privately in such splendour, and perhaps to flirt with Constantine's mother. (Maria may have been still at

Glebovo, for she did not die till 1879.) At Glebovo
" Onegin " went rapidly ahead. Tchaïkovsky was " in love
with the image of Tatiana "—he was working at the " letter
scene ", with which he began the opera—" under the spell
of Pushkin's verse, and writing the music under an irresistible
compulsion. I am quite buried in the composition of the
opera ". By June 23rd/July 5th, two-thirds of the work
was sketched out. But on that date he could keep his secret
no longer.

He announced in a series of letters to his family that he
had been engaged for nearly a month and proposed to get
married, as secretly as possible, in a week or two. " Please
don't worry about me ", he wrote to Anatol. " I've thought
it over well, and I am taking this important step with a quiet
mind. You will see that I really am calm when I tell you
that—with the prospect of marriage before me—I have been
able to write two-thirds of my opera." (Ten days later, he
says he " would certainly have been able to do more, but for
my agitated state of mind ".) " My bride is no longer very
young "—actually, twenty-eight—" but otherwise suitable
in every way. . . . She is poor and her name is Antonina
Ivanovna Miliukova ". (In another letter he adds that
" she is rather pretty, of spotless reputation . . . and
moderate education, but apparently good and capable of loyal
attachment ".) " Ask Father not to say a word about it to
anyone." In a letter to Nadejda von Meck (July 3rd/15th)
he gives a more detailed account of how his engagement had
come about and quite a different impression of his own attitude
to the affair. The girl, whom he had met some time before
at the Conservatoire but remembered only vaguely, had sent
him a love-letter, a letter " so warmly and sincerely written
that I decided to answer it, which I had always carefully
avoided doing in previous cases of the same kind. Without
going into details, I will tell you only . . . that I finally
accepted my future wife's invitation and visited her. Why

did I do that? It now seems to me that some mysterious power drew me to this girl. When we met, I repeated that for her love I could return only sympathy and gratitude. But later I began to consider how thoughtlessly I had acted. If I didn't love her . . . why had I gone to see her, and how would it all end? I saw that I had gone too far and that if I now suddenly turned from her, I should make her really unhappy and drive her to a tragic end. I was faced with an unpleasant alternative: either I must keep my freedom at the cost of a human life, or I must marry. There was nothing for it but to choose the latter course. So one fine evening I went to her, told her frankly that I couldn't love her, but that I would be her faithful and grateful friend; I described my character in detail, my irritability, the unevenness of my temperament, my misanthropy—and my material position. Then I asked her if she would be my wife. Her answer, of course, was that she would. The fearful torments I have suffered since that evening are not to be described. Which is very natural. To feel for thirty-seven years an innate antipathy for the married state, and then suddenly through the force of circumstances to be driven into it, without being in the slightest degree captivated by one's bride—is fearful. In order to get used to the idea and pull myself together a little, I decided not to abandon my original plan and to go into the country for a month. I did so. The quiet country life amid those very dear to me had a beneficial effect. I quieted myself with the reflection that no one can escape his destiny and that there was something fatalistic in my meeting with this girl. . . . God knows, I have the purest intentions with regard to my life-companion. If we are both unhappy, it won't be my fault. My conscience is clear. If I marry without love . . . it is because I could do nothing else ". To Kashkin, years afterwards, Tchaïkovsky gave a still more circumstantial, though slightly different, account which strangely links this personal tragedy with his greatest opera.

He had *ignored and forgotten Antonina's* first letter (in April, before " Onegin " was thought about), he told Kashkin, but when the second came, threatening suicide if that too were ignored, he was almost superstitiously impressed by the parallel between real life and the situation which had chiefly attracted him to Pushkin's poem: the letter scene. " I was in love with Tatiana and furious with Onegin for his coldness and heartlessness."   And here was a Tatiana in real life. Could he behave like Onegin, worse than Onegin? (His reasoning may have been fantastic but it was highly characteristic of the man, Kashkin says.) Then having agreed to this Platonic marriage, vaguely hoping, he says, that somehow everything would turn out for the best, he went to Glebovo, plunged happily into " Onegin "—and almost put the thought of Antonina from his mind! " Only somewhere deep within me stirred an uneasy expectation of something I didn't want to think about." But a letter from Antonina brought him back to unpleasant reality.

He went to Moscow, lying to Shilovsky that he was obliged to visit his eighty-three-year-old father in Petersburg, and on July 6th/18th was married. His father sent his blessing, but Anatol was the only member of the family who went to Moscow for the ceremony, while none of his Conservatoire colleagues knew anything about it till after. The unhappy bridegroom at once found that he had bound himself for life to a woman who would always be a stranger to him, intellectually and in every other respect. Still: " I sincerely wished and tried to be a good husband." After a week in Petersburg, they paid a visit to Antonina's mother, then separated for about a month, he going to his sister at Kamenka (lying to his wife that he was obliged to take a cure in the Caucasus), she to Moscow to prepare their home. " A few days longer and —I swear I should have gone mad." But Kamenka soon exercised a calming effect; he " again breathed freely "; after a couple of weeks he felt " decidedly better . . . *convinced* that I shall now triumph over my rather difficult and critical situation. I must fight down the feeling of *estrangement* from my wife and think of her good qualities ". " I feel so much better that I have begun the instrumentation of *your* Symphony ", he wrote to Nadejda von Meck. And he also completed the draft of " Eugene Onegin " and began to orchestrate that, too. By the time he rejoined his wife in Moscow he had finished the scoring of the first movement of the Symphony.

His first impression of his new home was favourable. It was " nice and comfortable ", he thought. He appeared at the Conservatoire, obviously battling hard with his nerves, but avoided conversation with his colleagues, rushing home the moment his classes were over. On one occasion only did the newly-married pair appear together socially one evening at Jurgenson's, when Antonina was introduced to her husband's friends. She struck them all as pleasant but " unreal ", " a sort of conserve ", as Nicholas Rubinstein said—while her husband hardly left her side, nervously interfering when she tried to converse and completing her unfinished sentences for her. But this strained position lasted barely a fortnight. Tchaïkovsky made up his mind that suicide was the only way out, and sought some method of suicide which might be disguised as a natural death. One bitterly-cold night, he told Kashkin later, he waded into the river " almost up to his waist ", hoping to catch pneumonia, and told Antonina, on his return, that he had been fishing and fallen in accidentally. But his robust physique defeated him. Finally, having induced Anatol to send a faked telegram in Napravnik's name, he fled to Petersburg on September 24th/October 6th " in a state bordering on insanity ". Anatol met his brother at the station and hardly recognised him, " his face had so changed in the course of a month ". Anatol took him straight to a hotel, where, after a terrible nerve-storm, he lay unconscious for nearly forty-eight hours. The verdict of the doctor, a mental specialist, was that nothing but complete change would save his reason; there must be no renewal of conjugal relations and it would be advisable for Tchaïkovsky never even to see his wife again. Anatol at once hurried to Moscow to break the news to Antonina, and Nicholas Rubinstein, who accompanied him, told her everything with brutal frankness. But she received the news with perfect calm, even indifference; said she would " bear anything for Peti's sake "; poured out tea; and when left alone with Anatol merely remarked pleasantly, " Well, I never expected that Rubinstein would drink tea with me today ". In later years she used to write her husband long but quite meaningless letters, and she died in a lunatic asylum many years after him; so it is not impossible that the seeds of insanity were already present in her mind in 1877.

What was the reason of Tchaïkovsky's nervous collapse? Neither was to blame for the disaster, Modest says in his biography of his brother. Certainly not Antonina Ivanovna, against whom Peter himself never uttered a word of reproach. It was simply that " having entered into closer relationship, they both discovered with horror that between them lay an abyss of misunderstandings which could never be bridged over ". It is clear that some of these " misunderstandings " were intellectual and spiritual. But it is equally clear that there was a physical factor. No one who has studied the evidence can doubt for a moment that Tchaïkovsky's sexual constitution was abnormal. That he was completely homosexual is more doubtful. But, in spite of the popular belief, there is an infinite number of conditions between complete homosexuality and perfect normality. When in 1905 the German sexual pathologist Magnus Hirschfeld published in his " Geschlechtsübergänge " a photograph of Tchaïkovsky *with Alexander Ziloti*, among other celebrated cases, he was no doubt blundering libellously; Ziloti simply happened to be a favourite pupil of the composer. But there are other cases where Tchaïkovsky certainly showed an unusual amount of affection toward males—to Vladimir Shilovsky, to his nephew Vladimir Davydof, even to Anton Rubinstein. The case of the fourteen-year-old Volodia Sklifasovsky is not untypical. Tchaïkovsky met this boy on the Marseilles-Constantinople boat in 1889 and, although their acquaintance lasted only a few days, " wept bitterly " on parting with him. On the other hand, he once wrote to Anatol that " there is a certain need for tenderness and care which only a woman can satisfy. I am sometimes overpowered by a mad longing to be caressed by a woman's hand ". In any case, whatever the extent of his abnormality, Tchaïkovsky's self-control was such that his reputation has remained almost unspotted.

After the marriage *débâcle*, Tchaïkovsky and his brother made first for Clarens on the shores of Lake Geneva. They had money for only a few weeks' stay, but Peter was far too upset to be able to return to Moscow and he was literally at his wits' end. It was at this juncture that Nadejda von Meck, who had already paid his debts to the tune of three thousand rubles, induced him to accept an annuity of six thousand rubles (rather more than £600), thus freeing him from all financial anxiety and enabling him, on his recovery, to devote the whole of his time to creative work. Deeply touched, Tchaïkovsky wrote that in future every note from his pen should be dedicated to her. It was the beginning of an entirely new phase of his life. Early in November the brothers left for Italy—Milan, Florence, Rome, Venice—Peter still ill, terribly depressed and with fearfully exacerbated nerves, unable to bear the least noise, furious even with the newsvendors who cried news of Turkish successes in the Russo-Turkish War. One night he drank two bottles of neat brandy in a vain attempt to induce oblivion, and lay sleepless till morning, fully conscious but " in a condition more awful than anything I ever experienced before or since ", he told Kashkin.

Yet even before leaving Clarens he had finished the orchestration of the First Act of " Onegin ", and in Venice he began the scoring of the Second. Early in December Anatol had to return to Russia, and Peter accompanied him as far as Vienna, where he was bored by " Die Walküre " and Brahms's " cold, obscure, pretentious " First Symphony, but quite enchanted by Delibes' " Sylvia ". He always preferred French composers, above all Bizet and Delibes, to their infinitely greater German contemporaries. (Presumably the explanation lies in his own French blood, which from this period onward left ever deeper marks on his own music.) With his young servant Sofronof, sent from Russia to take Anatol's place, he returned to Venice and then moved on to San Remo, finishing there the score of the Fourth Symphony, " the best thing I've written up to now ", on the 26th/ January 7th, 1878. The score was sent to Russia and performed with very mild success at an R.M.S. Concert in Moscow six weeks later. The Symphony off his mind, he resumed the scoring of " Onegin " and finished that work, too, on January 20th/February 1st. In San Remo he was joined by the other twin, Modest, with the latter's pupil.

And it was from San Remo that he sent Mme. von Meck that long letter, scathingly attacking Balakiref and the rest of the " handful ", except Rimsky-Korsakof, which has too often been quoted as an expression of his final judgment of the Petersburg group. It may have been a sincere statement of his view at that time, unbalanced as he was. But apart from its inaccuracies on points of fact, it contrasts curiously with many statements in other letters. He speaks of Rimsky-Korsakof's Quartet, Op. 12, for instance, as " permeated with a character of dry pedantry "—which is certainly true. Yet fifteen months before he had told Rimsky-Korsakof himself that the first movement is " simply delightful . . . a model of purity of style ", the slow movement " rather dry, but on that account very characteristic—as a reminiscence of the

Zopf period ", the scherzo " very lively and piquant; it must sound very beautiful ", and criticising only the finale. If this letter to Rimsky-Korsakof is not to be dismissed as mere insincere flattery, either Tchaïkovsky must have changed his mind (as he rarely did) about a work which, in his own words, " improved with closer acquaintance ", or the later letter to Mme. von Meck must be accepted only as the reflection of a mood of " mental and physical illness ". There is a peculiar irony, moreover, in his references to Balakiref as a man of enormous talent whose career was already over with little accomplished. For Tchaïkovsky, as we shall see, was once more to fall to some extent under Balakiref's influence for a time. And some of Balakiref's most important works were written long after Tchaïkovsky himself was in the grave.

In February the party moved to Florence, in March back to Clarens, where Tchaïkovsky began two large-scale works, his Piano Sonata and the Violin Concerto, completing both, orchestration and all, by the end of April at home at Kamenka. In May, Nadejda von Meck offered him the temporary use of her great house at Brailof. In her absence the entire establishment was placed at his disposal. It was " a wonderful dreamlike life ", and in these luxurious surroundings he completed his most important piece of religious music, the setting of the Liturgy of St. John Chrysostom, which as literature he considered " one of the greatest works of art in existence ". Tchaïkovsky's attitude to the Orthodox Church resembled Rimsky-Korsakof's in one respect; he could not accept its dogmas but, as an artistic experience, he found in its services " one of my greatest joys ". At Brailof, too, he brooded over other opera subjects—" Romeo and Juliet " or even another " Undine "—and wept over " Onegin " as he played it to himself. The summer passed in a round of visits to Brailof, Nizy, Kamenka and Verbovka (where in August he sketched out an orchestral Suite, Op. 43, " in Lachner's manner "). In September he returned to Moscow just a year after the catastrophe and resumed his Conservatoire work, though determined to resign as soon as he decently could and, opening the door unlocked by Mme. von Meck, to make the fullest use of his freedom. But it was impossible to do anything for the moment, for Nicholas Rubinstein was still in Paris conducting concerts of Russian music (including Tchaïkovsky's " Tempest " and the Piano Concerto) at the International Exhibition, a commission which Tchaïkovsky himself had been offered and refused the previous winter and which Rimsky-Korsakof had been extremely anxious to get. When Tchaïkovsky did announce his intention to Rubinstein, he was amusingly disappointed at the latter's failure to explode with indignation, or even to try to persuade him to change his mind. " It turned out quite otherwise. He listened to me laughingly as one listens to a headstrong child, and expressed no regret." (Rubinstein had already frankly revealed his disbelief in the seriousness of Tchaïkovsky's breakdown and accused him during the past winter of running away from life and its difficulties.) " He only remarked that the Conservatoire would lose *a lot of its prestige* with the withdrawal of my name—a polite way of saying that the pupils wouldn't lose much through my resignation. He is quite right, for I'm really a bad, unintelligent teacher—and yet I had expected more opposition from him."

After a few weeks in Petersburg and at Kamenka, the now free composer went to Italy at the end of November. Mme. von Meck had taken a suite of rooms for him in Florence and there he finished his orchestral Suite. But he was eager to press on with a new opera, based on Zhukovsky's translation of Schiller's " Jungfrau von Orleans ", and needing more quiet than he could find in Florence, returned at the beginning of 1879 to the Villa Richelieu at Clarens. On this occasion he prepared his own libretto, work which gave him infinitely more trouble than the writing of the music, but the whole opera—one of his feeblest works, though certainly free from the " Russianism " he feared might have crept into it—was completed on February 21st/March 5th. By that time he was in Paris. To flee to Clarens for peace and then to Paris for " brilliance, noise and distraction "—that was typical of Tchaïkovsky. But even in Paris he avoided calling on acquaintances—Turgenef, Saint-Saëns and others. " Every new acquaintanceship ", he wrote, " every fresh meeting with someone unknown has always been for me a source of fearful moral suffering . . . springing possibly from a shyness which has increased to a mania, perhaps from complete lack of any need for human society, perhaps also from inability, without an effort, to say things about oneself that one doesn't think (which is unavoidable in social intercourse)—in short, I don't know what it is. As long as I was not in a position to avoid such meetings, I went into society, pretended to enjoy myself, constantly played a part (as one must)—and suffered the most fearful torments. . . The society of a fellow-creature is pleasant only when long-standing intimacy or community of interests makes it possible to dispense with all effort ". But Tchaïkovsky liked the atmosphere of Paris; he was happy in reading Rousseau's " Confessions " and finding his own image (he says) reflected in so many of their pages; but then he heard his " Tempest " feebly applauded and feebly hissed at a Châtelet Concert—and hurried back to Russia. Though not before the ever-sincere one, the despiser of Liszt's " Jesuitry ", had sent Colonne a curious letter regretting that his " state of health had prevented his expressing his gratitude personally ", and beginning with the rather strange statement that " by chance, I came to Paris on the very day you were kind enough to perform my ' Tempest ' ". Tchaïkovsky never shirked a convenient lie—and often naïvely confessed to one. He told Jurgenson, for instance, how he once got rid of an unwelcome acquaintance encountered on a train-journey, by saying that he was travelling with a lady. But the lie to Colonne seems so unnecessary!

On March 17th/29th Tchaïkovsky heard the first performance of " Eugene Onegin ", given by the students of the Moscow Conservatoire. Even Anton Rubinstein came specially from Petersburg to hear the work, though as usual he was little impressed. The success as a whole was purely one " of esteem ". The summer, devoted to the adding of a sixth movement to the orchestral Suite and to the scoring of " The Maid of Orleans ", was again divided between Kamenka, Brailof and Simaki. This last-named estate was a smaller property of Mme. von Meck's, not far from Brailof, where Nadejda herself came in August. This proximity to his benefactress disturbed Tchaïkovsky terribly and one day " something very painful " happened; they met by accident in the woods. " It was very upsetting. Although we were face to face only for a brief moment, I was none the less very confused. I raised my hat, while she seemed to lose her head entirely and didn't know what to do."

At the end of November Tchaïkovsky again escaped with joy and relief from the native land of which he thought with such passionate love whenever he was far from it. After a week or so in Paris (where he finished the sketch of his Second Piano Concerto in G, a work of which none of our concert pianists has apparently ever heard) and a few days in Turin, he reached Rome in the second week of December. There he received the news of his father's death. He wept. But he seems to have been far more upset by the fact that no one in Moscow had wired him " a few words of appreciation " after the first performance of his Suite. " The sole interest which binds me to life is—my activity as a composer. Every first performance of my works marks an epoch for me. . . My nerves are upset and I'm as sick as a dog." In Rome he revised the Second Symphony and composed the " Italian Capriccio ", based on folk-melodies and opening with a trumpet-call heard each evening from the cavalry barracks near his hotel. The scoring was finished in the summer at Kamenka.

Shortly after his return to Petersburg in March, 1880, Tchaïkovsky made the acquaintance of the twenty-two-year-old Grand Duke Constantine Constantinovitch, son of the music-loving Grand Duke Constantine Nikolaevitch, and himself a passionate admirer of Tchaïkovsky's music. The young prince afterwards corresponded with the composer and some of Tchaïkovsky's later songs are settings of the Grand Duke's verses. The summer passed uneventfully, divided as usual between Kamenka, Brailof and Simaki. At Simaki Tchaïkovsky began to learn English, studying to such purpose that he afterwards managed to read " David Copperfield " and his favourite " Pickwick " in the original. (Among the occasional English phrases sprinkled through his diary, one notes the Wellerian " wery ".) He seems to have been suffering at this period from a mild attack of Rimsky-Korsakof's malady, a fever for revising his earlier works and for projecting monographs on composers, histories of music, and so on. Hitherto he had always sneered at those composers who worked only when they were in the mood, instead of regularly like craftsmen, " like cobblers "; but he now recognised the danger of continually trying to " meet inspiration half-way " and of becoming a mere composing-machine. Accordingly, we find a considerable falling off in the quantity of his production during the next year or two. Nevertheless, at Kamenka in October he wrote two biggish works in a great hurry, the " 1812 " Overture commissioned for the forthcoming Moscow Exhibition (" very noisy . . . written without much enthusiasm . . . and probably of no great artistic value ") and the Serenade for Strings, Op. 48 (" written from an inward impulse " and always rather a favourite work of the composer's). The two compositions have nothing in common but the employment of folk-songs. Three of Tchaïkovsky's works were heard for the first time in December and January —the Serenade, the " Italian Capriccio " and the Liturgy of St. John Chrysostom—and on January 11th/23rd, 1881,

"Eugene Onegin" was given in Moscow, this time by professionals, though still without marked success.

At about this period a very queer bird of passage flew into Tchaïkovsky's life for a time. A year or so before he had received a letter from an unknown young man named Tkatchenko, a Ukrainian who had proposed to become his servant in return for music-lessons. His letter was "so intelligent and sympathetic" that Tchaïkovsky had entered into correspondence with him, warning him, however, that it was too late at twenty-three to begin the study of music. After a silence of nine months, Tchaïkovsky received another communication in December, " returning all my letters, so that they should not fall into strange hands after his death. He bade me farewell and said he had decided to take his own life.... The letter was evidently written in great despair, and touched me very much ". Tchaïkovsky wired to a friend in the town where Tkatchenko lived, asking him to find and if possible save him; then sent money and invited the would-be suicide to come to Moscow. He arrived and made " a sympathetic impression " on Tchaïkovsky. He was " nervous, morbidly modest, broken in spirit, yet intelligent ", but had been obliged to earn a living as a railway guard. " Poverty and solitude have made him misanthropical." Tchaïkovsky pitied him and, since he was so anxious to become a musician, sent him to the Conservatoire where for a week or so he studied with enthusiasm. Then one day " he came ' to talk to me on a serious matter '. The longer I listened to him, the more I was convinced that he is mentally and morally deranged... He has taken it into his head that I've *not helped him for his own sake,* but so as *to acquire the reputation of a benefactor...* He explained that he was not disposed to be the *victim* of my weakness for popularity, and that he categorically declined to recognise me as his benefactor, so I was not to reckon on his gratitude ". To which Tchaïkovsky replied that he had better get on with his work and not worry about his "benefactor". But this grotesque, thoroughly Russian episode did not come to an end for nearly three years, when Tkatchenko again sent back Tchaïkovsky all his letters, obviously with the same meaning as before. At first Tchaïkovsky was worried; but he knew his man by this time, ignored the threat—and a week or so later received a "sarcastic" epistle asking for money (which was not sent) and saying nothing about the letters. "He is a man to be pitied, but not very sympathetic", was Tchaïkovsky's final comment on his protégé. Even before this, he had induced Jurgenson to take into his business another young man of similar type, a certain Klimenko, "a crazy fellow" who soon gave Jurgenson no end of trouble.

On February 13th/25th, 1881, "The Maid of Orleans" was produced at the Marinsky Theatre, Petersburg, after prolonged battles with the Direction, the singers and that knight of the baton and blue pencil, Eduard Napravnik, to whom the work was dedicated. Tchaïkovsky was recalled no less than twenty-four times, but the critics unanimously damned the thing and it was withdrawn from the repertory. The day after the production Tchaïkovsky left for Italy. Within two or three weeks he was lunching with the young Grand Duke Constantine and his cousins in Rome, and the three princes proposed to take him with them to Athens and Jerusalem. But the news of the assassination of Alexander II put an end to this plan by sending them back to Russia. Hardly more than a week later Tchaïkovsky learned of another death which affected him more closely. Nicholas Rubinstein, who was to have joined him at Nice, died in Paris on March 11th/23rd (just five days before Mussorgsky), and Tchaïkovsky hastened there, "suffering less, I must confess to my shame, from the sense of fearful, irreparable loss than from the fear of seeing poor Rubinstein's body". He was also worried by the news that Nadejda von Meck had suffered very heavy financial losses, caused by the extravagance of her son, Vladimir, and that his allowance might therefore be endangered. But for the time being she insisted on continuing it, and in spite of this possible embarrassment Tchaïkovsky declined " most emphatically " the Directorship of the Moscow Conservatoire, offered him in succession to Rubinstein.

He spent almost the whole of the summer, from May to October, at Kamenka. Alexandra was ill and away with her husband, so that Peter was obliged to act as " head of the family " and look after the children, of whom he was very fond. During the whole of this period he felt no desire to compose and even began to wonder whether he had not written himself out. He wiled away the time by studying the music, rites and ceremonials of the Orthodox Church and by editing for Jurgenson the works of Bortniansky, which he detested. But apparently he was glad to earn a little money by this means. Indeed, he was so worried about his financial position—with how much justification, it is difficult to say—that he secretly wrote to the young Tsar asking for help, and received a present of three thousand rubles. In November he left again for Rome, where he almost immediately received news of the first performance of his Violin Concerto, totally ignored for two years. Neither Auer, to whom it was originally dedicated, nor Tchaïkovsky's more intimate friend Kotek, would have anything to do with it. But now Brodsky had chosen it for his debut in Vienna, where it aroused a storm of criticism. Hanslick's notice was particularly devastating; according to his brother, Tchaïkovsky " was never able to forget it to the end of his life and even knew it by heart, just as he remembered a criticism of Cui's dating from 1866 ". (This must have been Cui's attack on his leaving cantata, " An die Freude ".)

In Rome, Tchaïkovsky began to compose again, embarking on a work for a combination—piano, violin and 'cello—which he had more than once declared was " torture " to have to listen to. He was now drawn to it, not because he had overcome his antipathy, but principally because he wished to dedicate to the memory of Nicholas Rubinstein a work of more or less intimate nature with an important piano part. But he informed Nadejda von Meck that he had reconciled himself to the combination solely in the hope of pleasing her, whom he knew to be a lover of piano trios![1] The lengthy variations which form the second part of the Trio are, in a sense, " enigma " variations, for not only had the theme a private association with Rubinstein but each variation refers to some episode in Rubinstein's career, though the details have never been revealed. The Trio, dedicated " To the Memory of a Great Artist ", was completed by the middle of January, 1882.

Tchaïkovsky's health was, for the time being, much better and he had nothing to worry about but affairs in Russia—the Nihilists (" who ought to be exterminated "), his sister's illness and the poor success of his operas. " But what angers me fearfully, and hurts and mortifies me ", he wrote to Jurgenson, " is the fact that the Theatre Directorate which wouldn't spend a kopeck on ' The Maid of Orleans ' has granted thirty thousand rubles for the production of Rimsky-Korsakof's ' Snow Maiden '. Isn't it also unpleasant to you that this subject has been torn from us and that Lel will now sing new music to the old words; that they have, as it were, taken by force a piece of myself and are going to offer it to the public in a new dress? I could cry with mortification ". He spent the greater part of February and March at Naples with Modest, happy but inactive, tormented not by nerves but by organ-grinders, mice—of which he was terrified—and the ubiquitous Neapolitan beggars.

At Kamenka, where he again spent practically the whole

---

[1] It is true she had suggested in October, 1880, that he should write something for her private trio, of which the pianist at that time was none other than Claude Debussy. (Debussy visited Moscow in the summer of 1881, but Tchaïkovsky was at Kamenka and they never met).

of the summer, he began in May to work—though with little enthusiasm—at a new opera, "Mazeppa", based on Pushkin's poem, "Poltava". About a year before K. Y. Davidof—the 'cello virtuoso and head of the Petersburg Conservatoire, not one of his brother-in-law's family—had given him Burenin's libretto on this subject, but it had not appealed to him. Even now he took it up only for want of something better and made very heavy going of the composition. "Never has any important work given me such trouble as this opera", he writes in September. And again at the end of October, when the actual composition was finished and he was merely orchestrating: "'Mazeppa' progresses at a snail's pace, though I work at it several hours a day." And he was unable to decide whether this was due to loss of powers or to increasing severity of self-criticism.

The Art and Industrial Exhibition in Moscow that summer also brought several first performances of his works: the Second Piano Concerto, with Taneief as soloist, the "1812" Overture, specially written for the Exhibition, and the Violin Concerto, again with Brodsky, now heard for the first time in Russia. One Exhibition concert was entirely devoted to his works. This drew him to Moscow for a few days and as usual the city ("for which I feel such keen affection, although I can't live in it") brought on a terrible fit of depression dispelled only by return to Kamenka. "The fact is", he wrote to Modest, "that life is impossible for me, except in the country or abroad. Why this is—God knows, I don't understand—but I'm on the verge of insanity. This indefinable, horrible, torturing malady of not being able to spend a single day, a single hour, in either of the Russian capitals without suffering, will one of these days be the cause of my promotion to a better world. . . I often think that the whole of my discontent is due to the fact that I am very egotistic, that I am unable to sacrifice myself for others, even those near and dear to me. Then it occurs to me that I certainly shouldn't have willingly submitted to moral torments if I didn't regard it as a sort of duty to come here now and again so as to give pleasure to others".

That autumn Tchaïkovsky renewed his correspondence with Balakiref after the ten years' break. About a year before, Tchaïkovsky had written him with regard to the new edition of " Romeo and Juliet " but without receiving a reply. Now Balakiref wrote, without the slightest reference to his little delay, expressing pleasure that the other had not forgotten him and characteristically announcing: " I've got a programme for a symphony, which you'd carry out splendidly." To which Tchaïkovsky replied in terms difficult to reconcile with the San Remo letter of 1877: " It would have been strange if I had ' *erased you from my affectionate memory!*' Apart altogether from the sincere respect for you, both as man and musician, which I should have felt even if fate had never brought us into contact—would it be possible for me not to value the innumerable tokens of friendly sympathy you have shown me? I can tell you without any exaggeration that if another ten or twenty years passed without my seeing you, it would be just the same. I should never forget you or cease to think of you with affection as one of the most brilliant, absolutely true and gifted artistic personalities I have ever met. I thank you cordially for your intention to suggest a subject for a symphonic poem. . . When I am in Petersburg, of course I will come and see you." But since that might not be for some months, " won't you outline the proposed subject by letter? I'm very interested. I can promise definitely that, if my mental and physical health allow, I shall carry out the task you set me with the greatest readiness ". (Although he had written no programme-music since " Francesca " five or six years before.) That was enough for Balakiref. He at once replied, not only disclosing the proposed subject, Byron's " Manfred ", which he had suggested to Berlioz sixteen years earlier, and detailing the four-movement programme with a Berliozian *idée fixe*, which in the end Tchaïkovsky followed almost exactly, but characteristically laying down a key-scheme for him as well. But Tchaïkovsky did not at first care for the subject and said so frankly. There, for the time being, the matter rested. But he took the opportunity to tell Balakiref he could not agree that " The Tempest " and " Francesca " were, as Balakiref considered, the " apogee " of his work. On the contrary, in his own view they were " really extremely cold, false and weak ".

In January, 1883, Tchaïkovsky joined Modest in Paris, intending to spend the rest of the winter in Italy. (On the way he heard " Tristan " in Berlin—it was just a month before Wagner's death—and " had never been so bored in his life ".) But while in Paris he received two commissions which had to be executed at once. The coronation of Alexander III was to take place in Moscow in May and Tchaïkovsky had already been instructed to arrange the " Slavsia " from " A Life for the Tsar " to be sung by a chorus of thousands of students as a greeting to the Tsar and Tsaritsa, as they entered the Kremlin. Now he received the libretto of a coronation cantata, " Moscow ", from the Coronation Committee, with a request that he would set it by the middle of April, and another commission from the city of Moscow for a march to be performed at a fête in the Sokolniky Park the week after the coronation. As an intensely loyal subject, and in gratitude for the Tsar's secret gift of three thousand rubles, he undertook both works but refused to accept any fee for them. All the work was done in Paris and Tchaïkovsky returned to Russia only on the eve of the coronation. During the summer and autumn, he wrote his Second Orchestral Suite, Op. 53, not because he was " inspired " but because he was tired of waiting for inspiration; it was confessedly a product of mere *cacoëthes scribendi.* That finished, he "feverishly" resumed his English study in his "impatience to be able to read Dickens fluently".

Tchaïkovsky was now definitely established in the favour of the Imperial family; "Eugene Onegin" was Alexander III's favourite opera; and Vsevolojsky, the new Director of the Theatres, being extremely well-disposed toward him, "Mazeppa" was produced almost simultaneously in both capitals—in Moscow on February 3rd/15th, 1884, in Petersburg four days later—winning in both cases mere *succés d'estime.* Tchaïkovsky attended the Moscow performance but, too nervous to go to Petersburg, left the next day for Paris, not even waiting in Moscow to hear Erdmannsdörfer conduct his Second Suite for the first time that very evening. The young Tsar attended the Petersburg *première,* staying to the end, and expressed his "extreme surprise" at the composer's absence. Jurgenson wrote to the fugitive, bluntly telling him that "Mazeppa" had failed and that he himself was largely to blame through his non-attendance. To which the composer humbly replied that he "knew better than anyone how he paralysed his success owing to his unfortunate temperament". Napravnik wrote him in much the same strain. Then came the news that the Tsar had conferred on him the Order of St. Vladimir (Fourth Class) and the unhappy runaway, who believed the failure of his opera to be far worse than it actually was, was hauled home from Paris to receive the decoration.

Well dosed with bromide, he was presented to the Tsar and Tsaritsa at Gatchina on March 7th/19th. "Both were most friendly and kind. I believe that anyone who has even a single opportunity to look into the Emperor's eyes will remain for ever his passionate admirer, for it is difficult to give any idea of the charm and sympathy of his whole manner." Tchaïkovsky had always been a very mild liberal in politics, a detester of nihilists and a believer in the "very gradual" abolition of autocracy and substitution of parliamentary government " when everyone would feel happy ". But by 1885, " although not yet one of the ultra-conservatives ", he had " become very doubtful of the perfect utility of these institutions ", i.e. parliaments. He was " firmly convinced that the welfare of the majority depends not on *principles* and *theories* but on those individuals who happen to be at the head of affairs. . . Now have we such a *man* in whom we can trust? I reply: Yes—the Sovereign. He has fascinated me —as a personality; but apart from that, I think the Tsar is a good man. I like his caution in introducing the new and doing away with the old ".

In April, 1884, Tchaïkovsky began two new works, the Concert Fantasia for piano and orchestra, Op. 56, and the Third Orchestral Suite (with its famous variations) which he dedicated to Erdmannsdörfer in gratitude for that conductor's success with the Second Suite. The new Suite was originally conceived as a Symphony and its original first movement became the second movement of the Concert Fantasia, both works being written in a rather laboured way. The composer spent September at Pleshcheevo, a smaller property which Nadejda von Meck had bought after the sale of Brailof, necessitated by her losses, and there made the acquaintance of " Khovanshchina " in which he found " what I expected—very peculiarly conceived realism, wretched technique, poverty of invention and some clever episodes in an ocean of harmonic absurdities and mannerisms ". Which is rather strange, for the " Khovanshchina " that Tchaïkovsky knew, as tidied up by Rimsky-Korsakof, is a singularly respectable piece of work, as Tchaïkovsky would have seen if he had not been blinded by preconceived ideas.

On October 19th/31st, at the Tsar's command, " Eugene Onegin " was given for the first time on the Imperial stage in Petersburg. (It had already been given in Petersburg by amateurs.) It had a poor press. But the public liked it, the Tsar was known to have given it the *cachet* of his approval, and from the second performance twelve days later the work enjoyed enormous popularity. There is a pleasant irony in the fact that the one opera which Tchaïkovsky wrote almost without any thought of its production, indeed loving the characters so intensely that it was distasteful to him to think of their being vulgarised by a stage performance, brought him wide popularity and swelled his bank-account. He attended the first two performances and, according to Modest, became much more sociable again at this period. He no longer avoided people and shirked public duties, but revived old friendships and made many new ones. At any rate it was during this visit to Petersburg that he renewed personal contact with Balakiref and Stassof. With Balakiref he plunged into discussions of religion and of church-music, the Emperor having hinted that he would like Tchaïkovsky to write for the Church. On the eve of his departure for Switzerland, Tchaïkovsky sent Balakiref a note in which he speaks of being " deeply touched by our conversation of yesterday ". " How good you are!" he goes on. " What a true friend you are to me! How I wish that that transfiguration which has been effected in your soul might be vouchsafed also to mine. I can say without the slightest infringement of the truth that I *thirst* more than ever for peace and support in *Christ*. Pray that I may be strengthened in my faith in Him." One wonders if he complied with Balakiref's request: " If you have a free half-hour today, don't refuse to hurry for a few moments to Glinka's sister, Liudmila Ivanovna Shestakova, who lives near you. . . . She is ill and confined to her house and your visit (even if a very short one) would give her *enormous pleasure*, and besides it's always nice to give pleasure to others. She has chosen your ' Romeo and Juliet ' Overture for performance at the unveiling of the Glinka monument at Smolensk. Please don't refuse my request, for Liudmila Ivanovna is old and ill and it's hardly likely that you'll have another chance to see her." Actually, Liudmila Shestakova outlived Tchaïkovsky by thirteen years!

The question of "Manfred" came up again before Tchaïkovsky left; Balakiref sent him a fresh key-scheme, disregarded like the former one, advice to include the organ at the end (which he did) and—a list of the compositions he was to take as his models in each movement! Tchaïkovsky was now more attracted by the subject. He bought a copy of the poem and set off for Davos with it in his luggage, the morning after the second performance of "Onegin". His object in visiting Switzerland was not, however, to get local colour for "Manfred"—although, as he said, his stay among the Alps "ought to have a very beneficial effect on the musical incarnation of Manfred"—but to visit Kotek, who lay dying of consumption at Davos. (He lived only a month or so longer.) At Davos Tchaïkovsky read "Manfred" and wrote to Balakiref promising that the Symphony should be written "not later than the summer". He also sent some of the church-music composed at the Tsar's wish, for Balakiref's use in the Imperial Chapel—and as in the old days received some very frank criticism.

From Davos Tchaïkovsky drifted on to Paris, more than ever dissatisfied with his homeless condition. The summer before he had told Nadejda von Meck that he wanted to take a small house of his own in the country. It must stand alone, have a nice garden—if possible with a stream, be near a forest, and not too far from a railway station so that he could get to Moscow without difficulty. He now wrote to Modest from Paris of his "homesickness, the desire for a place of my own. Life abroad has become loathsome . . . I must have a *home*, be it at Kamenka or in Moscow—at any rate I can't go on living like a wandering star". Soon after his return to Russia, his servant found him a rather large furnished house which answered most of his requirements, at

Maidanovo, not far from Klin, a town within easy reach of Moscow.

He settled at Maidanovo in February, 1885, under the happiest auspices. True, he was suffering from severe headaches, but he was no longer the neurotic weakling of the last few years. The Third Suite had just scored a tremendous triumph under Hans von Bülow in Petersburg, and one nearly as great under Erdsmanndörfer in Moscow a few days later. The Tsar had sent for him after another performance of " Onegin ", conversed with him for a long time in the most friendly way, enquiring about his life and work; the Tsaritsa, too, had been most kind. He had just been elected head of the Moscow branch of the R.M.S., while his enormous correspondence convinced him of his widespread popularity. And he was satisfied with the drastic revision of " Vakula the Smith ", at which he had been working since November, clarifying, cutting and adding new numbers. In its new form the work was rechristened, " The Little Shoes ", though the published edition bears the title " Oxana's Caprices ". He had just induced the dramatist Shpajinsky to prepare a libretto from his play, " The Sorceress ". But Shpajinsky delayed with his First Act, and in April Tchaïkovsky started instead to redeem his promise to Balakiref by beginning " Manfred ". (The work was dedicated to Balakiref and Tchaïkovsky seems to have gone out of his way, particularly in the scherzo, to write in a pseudo-Balakirefian vein.)

Tchaïkovsky once confided to his diary his conviction that " letters are not usually altogether sincere. At least, I judge by myself. To whomever I write, and whatever I write about, I always worry about the impression the letter will make, not only on my correspondent but on any chance reader. Consequently I pose. Sometimes I *strive* to make the tone of the letter simple and sincere, i.e. to make it *appear* so. But, except letters written in moments of *aberration*, I am never my true self in my correspondence. These letters are constant sources of remorse and regret, sometimes even very painful ones. When I read the letters of celebrated people, printed posthumously, I am always jarred by an indefinable feeling of falsity and mendacity ". The reader of Tchaïkovsky's own correspondence certainly receives a good many jars of that nature. The composer's habit of saying one thing to one person and another to someone else is very well illustrated by two letters written on the same day in June to Taneief, who was no friend of Balakiref's, and to Mme. von Meck. He tells Nadejda that he " has already taken such a fancy to this composition that the opera will probably have to wait for some time ", and that although he feels it would be a good thing " to write nothing, travel, rest ", he is quite unable to tear himself from his writing-table and piano. But he grumbles to Taneief about his " indiscreet promise " to Balakiref. " It's a thousand times pleasanter to write without a programme. In writing a programme symphony I feel as if I were a charlatan, cheating the the public by giving it worthless paper instead of good coin." Three or four months later Taneief rather maliciously told Balakiref about this, and Tchaïkovsky was at some pains to make peace: " S. I. Taneief's tittle-tattle is mere childishness. . . . This is the real truth: generally speaking I don't like *my own* programme-music, as I've already told you. I feel infinitely freer in the sphere of pure symphony, and it's a hundred times easier for me to write something in the way of a *suite* than a programme thing. Frankly, I began ' Manfred ' with reluctance and decided to write it *simply* because I'd *promised* you. . . . The letter I wrote to Taneief refers to the time when I *began*—unwillingly, with an effort, with no self-confidence. . . . Then very quickly I was awfully attracted by ' Manfred ' and I don't remember ever experiencing such pleasure in work; and so it went on till the end." Which, again, does not altogether agree with a remark to Mme. von Meck that " the work is so difficult and complicated that at times I myself become a Manfred . . . I'm straining all my powers to finish it as soon as possible: result—extreme exhaustion. That's the eternal '*cercle vicieux*' that I revolve in without finding a way out. If I have no work—I worry and get bored; when I have it, I work beyond my strength ". Surprisingly enough, he regarded " Manfred " for some time as the best of all his symphonic works, though he afterwards detested it, except the first movement.

" Manfred " was no sooner completed, early in September, than the composer began " The Sorceress ", finishing the First Act in three weeks. At about the same time he moved to another, smaller house on the Maidanovo estate. It was unfurnished and most of the furnishing and arrangement was left to the servant, Sofronof, who surrounded his master with an extraordinary collection of rubbish. " He himself ", says Modest, " assisted by buying utterly useless things—for instance, two horses which he had the greatest difficulty in selling again, and an old English clock that wouldn't go ". Sofronof's appalling taste did not worry him at all. " He was as pleased as a child and boasted of his ' own cook ', ' own washerwoman ', ' own silver ', ' own tablecloths ' and ' own dog '—all of which he considered extremely fine and praised to the skies." He always expressed his delight in the very plain food prepared by his " own cook ", delight not always shared by his guests. Casual visitors were most unwelcome, but he liked to entertain his brothers or intimate friends— Laroche, Kashkin, Jurgenson, Taneief—though only when he was not engaged in composition. Not only did he need absolute solitude while creating, but from this time onward he became extremely secretive about his new works, never playing them or showing them even to his most intimate friends. Jurgenson's engraver was the first man to see his later scores. At Maidanovo, too, he was able to adopt a

routine from which he hardly ever deviated by more than a
minute or so, and never abandoned when at home till the
end of his life. He rose between seven and eight, drank tea
and read the Bible, then studied English or read serious books
and took a short walk. He worked from half-past nine to one
o'clock, which was his dinner-hour. After dinner, no matter
what the weather, he took a solitary two-hour walk,
unaccompanied even by a dog, and it was during these afternoon walks that he did most of his creative work, jotting
down memoranda in innumerable little notebooks. These
notes were afterwards worked out at the piano into the
" sketch " or reduced score, and his full orchestra scores
seldom differed materially from the " sketch ". When he
was not composing on his walks, he would recite aloud—
usually in French. A four o'clock he had tea, worked from
five to seven; then took another walk, this time with company
if any were available, before supper at eight o'clock. After
supper he would read or play cards—patience, if alone—talk
or play the piano till eleven, when he retired.

In April, 1886, a week or so after the first performance of
" Manfred " (in Moscow under Erdmannsdörfer), Tchaïkovsky spent a month or so at Tiflis, where Anatol was
living, and where Ippolitof-Ivanof had produced
" Mazeppa " a few months before. The scenery of the
Caucasus delighted him and the weeks he spent at Tiflis were
among the happiest of his life. The Tiflis musicians organised
an orchestral concert entirely devoted to his works; the entire
audience rose and cheered as he entered the box at the
theatre; he was presented with wreaths and with an address
from the local Musical Society; and the concert was followed
by a supper in his honour. So far it was the greatest triumph
of his life and, though only in a distant provincial city, he
appreciated it to the full. Having business in Paris, he then
made the sea-trip from Batum to Marseilles, which he
thoroughly enjoyed, made himself much more agreeable to

his French colleagues than on previous visits to Paris, and returned to Maidanovo in June, much refreshed in mind and body. Within a couple of months the sketches for " The Sorceress " were finished and the orchestration begun. At about the same time, Vsevolojsky commissioned from him a ballet on his old favourite, Zhukovsky's " Undine ", though for some reason it was never written.

In December, after a terrible struggle with his nerves, he conducted not only the orchestral rehearsals of " The Little Shoes " (the revised version of " Vakula ") but the triumphant first performance itself on January 19th/31st, 1887. He had suffered " indescribable mental torture " all day and reached the theatre " half dead ", but pulled himself together and conducted successfully. This was a very different Tchaïkovsky from the man who had run away from the Petersburg *première* of " Mazeppa " only three years before. He followed up this conquest over his nerves by another, conducting a whole concert of his own works in Petersburg on March 5th/17th, and began to think of venturing on a concert tour abroad. " My nerves are astonishingly strengthened and things which were at one time out of the question are now quite possible." He also felt renewed confidence in his creative power, though he found that mere orchestration " gives me more trouble, the older I grow; I am more severely self-critical, more careful, more fastidious with regard to colours and nuances ". The score of " The Sorceress " was actually not finished till May, an exceptionally slow piece of work. As soon as this was out of the way, Tchaïkovsky set off on another Caucasian holiday, making the delightful steamer trip down the Volga from Nijni-Novgorod, and spent June with Anatol and his wife, and Modest, not in Tiflis but in the country at Borjom. He was delighted with the place; worked only for an hour a day at the orchestration of four pieces of Mozart's for the suite " Mozartiana ", the realisation of an idea that had been at the back of his mind for two or three years; and intended to spend the whole summer at Borjom.

But in July he was suddenly called by telegram from the borders of Asia to the other end of Europe, to Aix-la-Chapelle, where N. D. Kondratief was dying. It was a useless sacrifice on the altar of friendship, for Tchaïkovsky, sympathetic as he might be, was the most helpless of practical friends. He was conscious of the futility of his " good deed ", conscious that it was done under moral compulsion, not spontaneously from goodness of heart. He regretted Borjom, was bored at Aix—and all the time bitterly reproached himself for his selfishness. Both at Aix and at Maidanovo on his return, he brooded much over God, life, death and the ends of life. He felt that in the end he had clarified his religious outlook, but he was certainly unable to express it very clearly. " I should like to set down my *religion* in detail ", he wrote in his diary, " if only to make my faith clear to myself once and for all, to define the boundary between it and knowledge. But life keeps flying away "—a constant refrain of his—" and I don't know whether I shall manage to express that *symbol* of the faith which has recently developed in me. It has very definite forms, but I don't make use of it when I pray. I pray just as before, i.e. as I was taught ".

Tchaïkovsky was now called upon to sally out into the external world again as a conductor, and to a much greater extent than ever before. He conducted the first four Petersburg performances of " The Sorceress " (the *première* was on October 20th/November 1st), then in Moscow a whole programme devoted to his works, including the new " Mozartiana " (November 14th/26th). " Mozartiana " delighted his Moscow audience, but " The Sorceress " was a complete failure, a failure that " wounded him to the depth of his soul ". But these were only preliminary skirmishes. On December 15th/27th he set out on the main campaign, a campaign which had as its object nothing less than the conquest of Germany. In Berlin at the outset he met Desirée Artôt, for the first time since 1869; in Leipzig, where his concert-tour began, still more interesting characters—Brahms, Grieg and his wife, and Ethel Smyth—all at the house of his fellow-countryman Brodsky. Grieg charmed him. At first he and Brahms " didn't really like each other "; each felt instinctively that the other disliked his music, so that their relations remained only outwardly cordial. But " Brahms took great pains to be nice to me " and Tchaïkovsky soon found him " very pleasant ". He appears to have been a little puzzled by " Miss Smyth ", however. This memorable meeting occurred on New Year's Day (N.S.), 1888. The next day, Tchaïkovsky had to face the Gewandhaus Orchestra for the first rehearsal and on January 4th he conducted his First Suite, which was received very well by the public though rather critically by the press. Before going on to Hamburg, Tchaïkovsky rested for a few days at Lübeck where he learned that the Tsar had granted him a life-pension of three thousand rubles a year. In Hamburg he conducted a whole concert of his own works, with a Haydn symphony; he was fêted by the Philharmonic Society; and he was rather amusingly lectured by the eighty-year-old chairman of its committee, Theodor Avé-Lallement, who told the composer frankly that he didn't like his music—particularly the noisy orchestration—and that it was a pity his evident talents had been ruined by his education in such a backward country as Russia. " He implored me, with tears in his eyes, to settle in Germany." Tchaïkovsky took a charming revenge on the old man by dedicating his next Symphony (the Fifth) to him. After Hamburg, Berlin. Then Prague. Passing through Leipzig again on his way to the Bohemian capital, Tchaïkovsky was honoured by a serenade, or rather aubade, from a German military band which, in spite of the anti-Russian feeling just aroused by a speech of

Bismarck's, played under his hotel window early in the morning, awakening him with "God preserve the Tsar". In Prague, on the other hand, Tchaïkovsky's visit was made the excuse for Pan-Slav demonstrations; the ten days he spent there (February 12th to 22nd, N.S.) were one prolonged ovation, not so much to Tchaïkovsky's music, perhaps, as to a great Slav artist. His two concerts were mere episodes in a round of addresses, serenades and presentations. When he was shown the Town Hall, the city fathers, who were in session, rose as one man to greet him. In Paris also, where he went from Prague, conducting twice at the Châtelet, political considerations did much to increase the warmth of his reception. But in London, where he conducted his Serenade for strings and the Variations from his Third Suite at a Royal Philharmonic concert, his very considerable success must have been entirely musical. Francesco Berger, the Society's secretary, organised a dinner in his honour. Otherwise his four-day visit was completely ignored from a social point of view.

After all these excitements, Tchaïkovsky returned to Russia in March and, after a visit to Tiflis, settled in a new home at Frolovskoe between Klin and Moscow. The house was smaller than that at Maidanovo, but more secluded and amid infinitely more beautiful surroundings. He felt no inclination to work and again wondered if he had written himself out. "Still, I'm hoping gradually to collect material for a symphony." In the meantime he, literally, cultivated his garden. But he was "dreadfully anxious to prove both to others and to myself that I've not yet *sung myself out*". The new Symphony (No. 5 in E minor) was begun in June "with great difficulty", though "inspiration seemed to come" later, and finished by the middle of August, being immediately followed by the overture-fantasia, "Hamlet" (dedicated to Grieg). Tchaïkovsky conducted the Symphony in Petersburg on November 5th/17th and again a week later, with " Hamlet ", at an R.M.S. concert. Then after a flying visit to Prague for the production of " Onegin " and a performance of the Symphony, the Symphony was given again in Moscow. But the composer was profoundly dissatisfied with it. " There is something repellant about it; a patchiness and insincerity and ' manufacturedness ' which the public instinctively recognises. . . . Am I really done for already?"

It seemed not, for immediately after his return from Prague in December he took in hand a ballet, " The Sleeping Beauty ", commissioned by Vsevolojsky, the Director of the Imperial Theatres, who himself prepared a libretto from Perrault. Tchaïkovsky worked at it with pleasure; the work went easily; and the whole three-act ballet was sketched out by January 18th/30th, 1889. Six days later the composer set out on a second tour of the West, making his first appearance in Cologne, where he was already attacked by violent homesickness. After that, he appeared in Frankfurt, Dresden, Berlin, Leipzig, Geneva and Hamburg. At Hamburg he again met Brahms, who stayed an extra day specially to hear the Fifth Symphony—and found it not unpleasant with the exception of the finale. Tchaïkovsky himself began to like the work a little better, but poor old Avé-Lallement was too ill to come and hear it. Tchaïkovsky spent the greater part of March in Paris, though without making any public appearance. There were to be concerts of Russian music there in June in connection with the World Exhibition, but they were under Belaief's auspices, and Rimsky-Korsakof had been chosen as the conductor. Tchaïkovsky could hardly appear in rivalry and he was obliged to kill time before his London engagement on April 11th (N.S.), when he conducted his B flat minor Concerto (with Sapelnikof), and the First Suite. He left London for Marseilles early next morning, equally impressed by London's fog and London's orchestral players, and returned to Moscow by way of the Mediterranean, Batum and Tiflis.

Settling at Frolovskoe, Tchaïkovsky orchestrated " The Sleeping Beauty " during the summer and, curiously enough, although the actual composition had gone so quickly and smoothly, he again had trouble with the scoring. The new ballet, one of Tchaïkovsky's own favourite works, had its first public performance in Petersburg on January 3rd/15th, 1890, but the composer had already been deeply hurt by the Tsar's very restrained praise of his music after the gala rehearsal the evening before. A week or so later he left for Italy, which he had not seen for eight years.

Settled in Florence he at once began to work at a new opera, " The Queen of Spades ", commissioned by Vsevolojsky as what the magnates of the film-world call a " starring vehicle " for the tenor N. N. Figner and his wife Medea, then at the height of their popularity. As it happened, Modest Tchaïkovsky had written a libretto, an outrageously sentimental and melodramatic caricature of Pushkin's ironical story, some three years before for another composer, N. S. Klenovsky. Klenovsky had refused to have anything to do with it, but the librettist's brother liked it and set it *con amore*. The mood of life-weariness in which he had come to Italy, indifferent to her sunshine and blue skies, quickly passed. He began to " live in " the libretto so intensely that in writing the final scene he was " suddenly overcome by such pity " for the unheroic hero that he burst into tears. The whole sketch was finished by March 3rd/15th. " Speed in working is a most essential trait of my character! . . . I worked slowly at the ' The Sorceress ' and the Fifth Symphony and yet they turned out badly; on the other hand, I finished the ballet in three weeks, and ' Onegin ' was written in an incredibly short time. The chief thing is—to write with enthusiasm. ' The Queen of Spades ' has certainly been written in that way." " Modi ", he wrote to his brother, " unless I'm terribly mistaken ' The Queen of Spades ' is a masterpiece ". Next to

"Onegin", it is certainly his most successful composition for the stage.

After a week or so in Rome, Tchaïkovsky returned in May to Frolovskoe to find to his consternation that "*the whole, literally the whole of the forest has been cut down!*" He had lost his favourite walks. But his garden brought him compensation; his flowers had "never been so luxuriant". " I find more and more delight in the cultivation of flowers ", he told Nadejda von Meck, " and console myself with the idea of devoting myself to it entirely when my creative powers begin to show signs of old age. In the meantime, I can't complain. I had no sooner finished the opera, than I at once took up a new work, the sketch of which is already completed ". This " new work ", the String Sextet (" Souvenir de Florence "), sketched in little more than a fortnight, clearly reflects the tranquil happiness of the spring and summer, a happiness soon to be shattered for ever.

In September, during his now almost annual expedition to Tiflis, he sketched out a symphonic ballad, " The Voevoda ". (This had no connection with his early opera of the same name but was based on a poem by Pushkin.) Before leaving Tiflis, however, Tchaïkovsky received very unpleasant news from Nadejda von Meck. Only a couple of months before, she had sent him a considerable sum in addition to the annuity, but she now suddenly informed him that she was on the verge of bankruptcy and that consequently the annuity itself, which then amounted to about a third of his total income, would have to be discontinued. Don't forget; think of me sometimes ", she added at the end of her letter. Tchaïkovsky took this sentimental little gesture with more seriousness than it deserved. Reproaching her for suggesting that he might be ungrateful, he wrote: " I am glad you can no longer share your means with me, so that I may show my warm, unbounded and inexpressible gratitude." But despite these brave words, he was very worried at the prospect of having to " start quite another life, one on a more restricted scale ", as he told Jurgenson. " I shall probably be obliged to look for some sort of well-paid post in Petersburg. It's very, very bitter—yes, bitter! " But, as a matter of fact, his royalties from " The Queen of Spades " alone soon more than replaced the annuity. The real tragedy came later when he found that Nadejda's financial troubles were purely imaginary, the product of an imagination disordered by the nervous complaint of which she was slowly dying. But Tchaïkovsky now saw in the affair nothing but a pretext for stopping his annuity! " My relations with her were such that her generous gifts never oppressed me ", he told Jurgenson, " but now in retrospect they weigh on me. My pride is wounded; my faith in her unfailing readiness to help me materially, and to make any sacrifice for my sake, is betrayed ". Worst of all, when he tried to resume the old correspondence as if nothing had happened, she completely ignored his letters. It would be no exaggeration to say that the ending of this strange, precious friendship completely embittered the two or three remaining years of his life. For the manner of the ending changed and vulgarised for him the whole of the past. He saw himself as the mere plaything of a wealthy, eccentric woman. " I have never yet felt so lowered or my pride so deeply injured . . . I would sooner have believed that the ground would give way under me than that Nadejda Filaretovna would change her attitude to me. And yet the inconceivable has happened and all my conceptions of mankind, my faith in the best of it, have been overturned."

Fate compensated him a little by minor kindnesses. Both the *répétition générale* of " The Queen of Spades " on December 6th/18th, at which the Tsar and his family were present, and the public performance the following day were definite triumphs. The Theatre Directorate at once commissioned a one-act opera and a ballet for the following season and, in addition to these, he undertook to write incidental music for a benefit performance of " Hamlet ". (It must be confessed that he did this rather perfunctorily, cutting down and rescoring his overture-fantasia, drawing on " The Swan Lake " for one entr'acte, part of the second movement of his Third Symphony for another; though the funeral march was a new composition.) During these visits to Petersburg Tchaïkovsky had become more and more friendly with the Belaief circle of composers, largely, of course, through Rimsky-Korsakof. " He usually ended the night by sitting in a restaurant with Liadof, Glazunof and others till about three in the morning ", writes Korsakof. " Tchaïkovsky could drink a tremendous lot of wine without losing command of his faculties; very few could keep up with him in this respect." For the subject of his one-act opera Tchaïkovsky chose a play by the Danish poet Herz, " King René's Daughter ", from which Modest prepared a libretto, " Iolanta ". But the subject of the ballet, E. T. A. Hoffmann's story " Nutcracker and the Mouse King ", was forced on him and he disliked it. Nevertheless he began the composition of " Nutcracker " before he started on his Western tour in March. This time he was going much farther afield than before. " I have long dreamed of an American tour ", he told Jurgenson. Now the dream was to come true.

The beginning was more like a nightmare. Even before he reached Berlin he was suffering from homesickness, " the most agonising thing the world, for which the only remedy is—intoxication ". He was still homesick in Paris, where he conducted a whole programme of his works at a Colonne concert. And before sailing from Havre, he learned of the death of his dearly loved sister, Alexandra Davydova. His first impulse was to abandon the tour and return to Petersburg; but reflecting that that could do no good, he steeled himself and went on. He sailed on April 18th (N.S.)—

and the first day out one of the passengers committed suicide. His nostalgia became so acute that on the night of his arrival in New York he sat crying in his hotel bedroom. But he was much struck by the sincere kindness of the Americans and soon convinced that " I'm ten times more famous in America than in Europe ". He was annoyed that the critics thought it necessary to describe his personal appearance and his behaviour at the conductor's desk, but he got a remarkably good press, even for his conducting. He visited Niagara Falls and Washington, where he was a guest of honour at the Russian Embassy, gave concerts at Baltimore and Philadelphia—there were four in New York—and sailed on May 20th (N.S.), very weary, but very well satisfied with his expedition.

Hastening across Germany, he reached home early in June, returning to his old house at Maidanovo, for Frolovskoe had lost its charm since the woods had been cut down. At Maidanovo during the summer and autumn he orchestrated his " Voevoda " and worked at " Iolanta " and " Nutcracker ". While in Paris in March he had made the acquaintance of Mustel's new instrument, the celesta, and fallen in love with its " divinely beautiful tone ". He decided to use it in both " The Voevoda " and " Nutcracker ". Asking Jurgenson to have one sent from Paris secretly, he wrote that he was " afraid Rimsky-Korsakof and Glazunof may get hold of it and use the unusual effect before me. I expect this new instrument will produce a colossal sensation ". Writing to his favourite nephew, Vladimir Davydof, on June 25th/July 7th, to announce that he has finished the sketch of " Nutcracker ", he says: " No, the old chap is getting worn out . . ." (This was not, perhaps, mere playfulness; Tchaïkovsky aged at this period almost beyond recognition by those who had not seen him for some years; he was " old at fifty," says Anton Door.) " The ballet is infinitely poorer than ' The Sleeping Beauty '—no doubt about it. . . .

When I'm really convinced that I can set only *réchauffés* on my musical table, I shall leave off composing." His self-dissatisfaction was so extreme that after the first performance of "The Voevoda" in Moscow on November 6th/18th he destroyed the score in a rage. (It was posthumously reconstructed from the orchestral parts as Op. 78.)

The next month Tchaïkovsky set out on another concert tour, beginning at Kief. In Warsaw he was overwhelmed with nostalgia again; the production of "Eugene Onegin" at Hamburg, where Gustav Mahler was working miracles, cheered him; but in Paris he was so depressed and homesick that he abandoned the concerts he was to have given in Holland and fled back to Russia. The destroyed "Voevoda" was to have been played at an R.M.S. concert in Petersburg on March 7th/19th, 1892, and Tchaïkovsky, feeling under an obligation to give some new work of his own, filled the gap by hastily orchestrating a few of the best numbers from his new ballet and giving them as a concert suite. Thus the "Nutcracker" Suite was actually performed before the ballet. It won an immediate success, every movement but one being encored.

In May Tchaïkovsky made yet another move, his last, to a house near the town of Klin itself. (It is now preserved as a Tchaïkovsky Museum, the property of the Russian State.) In this new home he began a sixth Symphony in E flat. But the composition was interrupted by a three weeks' cure at Vichy and on his return to Russia his time was taken up by a mass of proof-correcting. However, by the autumn the Symphony was nearly finished. But it seemed to him " an empty pattern of sounds without genuine inspiration, written for the sake of writing ", and he destroyed it. Or rather, he diverted it to another purpose. The first movement was converted into a concert-piece for piano and orchestra, the so-called Concerto No. 3, Op. 75, while the *andante* and finale were also recast for piano and orchestra but never completed. In Taneief's orchestration, they were posthumously published as Op. 79.

The winter was one of triumphs. "The Queen of Spades" was given in Prague; the French Academy elected the composer a Corresponding Member; Cambridge offered him an honorary doctorate of music; the Sextet, now revised, won an immediate success and the composer was given the Petersburg Chamber Music Society's medal. The only reverse was on the occasion of the first performances of "Iolanta" and "Nutcracker" on December 5th/17th, for the success of the two new works was very moderate and Tchaïkovsky was proportionately downcast. "When one has been living for a long time in expectation of some important event, as soon as the event is over one feels a certain apathy, a dislike of any kind of work, and the emptiness and futility of all our efforts become all too obvious." It was in that mood of self-disillusionment that he abandoned the nearly finished E flat Symphony. A week after the unlucky double *première* he went abroad, first to Montbeillard to see his old governess, Fanny Dürbach, whom he had only recently discovered to be still alive. At Basel on the way he had "fits of crying", agonising homesickness which grew worse every time he left Russia for no matter how short a period. But the meeting with "Mlle. Fanny" cheered him; he gave a "brilliant concert" in Brussels; and on his return to Russia in January, 1893, he was fêted for more than a week at Odessa. (It was during this visit to Odessa that Kuznetsof painted the well-known portrait, of which Modest says: "There is no more living picture of my brother in existence.")

The "worn out", "done for" composer was already at work again directly after his return to Klin. "During the journey, I got hold of the idea for a new symphony", he writes on February 11th/23rd to Vladimir Davydof, to whom he dedicated the work. "This time a programme-symphony, but with a programme which shall remain an enigma for everyone—let them puzzle their heads over it. The symphony will be called simply 'Programme Symphony' (No. 6). This programme is subjective through and through, and during my journey, while composing it in my mind, I often wept bitterly. On my return I set to work at the sketches and worked with such fire and rapidity that the first movement was quite finished in less than four days, while the other movements are clearly defined in my thoughts . . . The finale will be a very long-drawn adagio. . . . You can't think what a delight it is to feel that my time is not yet over." He could even relax in a couple of dozen songs and piano pieces (Opp. 72 and 73) written for Jurgenson, and a military march for the 98th Infantry Regiment, commanded by his cousin, Andrei Tchaïkovsky. In March he was fêted at Kharkof, and in May came the still greater English triumph, though a triumph shot through with terrible nostalgia " not to be described in words (there is a passage in my new Symphony which, I feel, adequately expresses it) ". He arrived in London on May 29th (N.S.) and conducted his Fourth Symphony at a Royal Philharmonic Concert on June 1st ("a real triumph"). There was a concert at Cambridge on the 12th, and the next day he received the degree in company with Saint Saëns, Boïto, Grieg and Max Bruch.

At home once more, he resumed work on the Sixth Symphony. The orchestration again gave him much trouble, but it was finished on August 12th/24th, and after a short visit to Anatol he began the scoring of the new Piano Concerto, the original first movement of the discarded symphony. He was very pleased with the new Symphony, except the finale, which he thought he might ultimately replace by another. On October 10th/22nd he arrived in Petersburg in excellent spirits to rehearse the new Symphony for the first R.M.S. concert of the season, six days later. The success was moderate, no more. The morning after the concert Modest, with whom he was staying, found him puzzling over the question of a title. He had given up the idea of calling the work a " Programme Symphony "— " Why ' programme symphony ', when I'm not going to give the programme?"—and it had been played the night before simply as a " Symphony in B minor ", though it was generally rumoured that it " had a secret programme ". Modest first suggested that he should call it a " Tragic Symphony ", a title which his brother rejected. Then he thought of " Pathétique ". The composer accepted this at once, wrote it on the score and sent the manuscript immediately to Jurgenson. But the very next day he changed his mind and wrote asking that the Symphony should be published simply as " No. 6 ".

On the evening of October 20th/November 1st, Tchaïkovsky dined with his old friend, Vera Davydova, went to the theatre, and afterwards sat drinking in a restaurant till two in the morning with Modest, two of their nephews, Glazunof and one or two others. Next morning he complained of indigestion and insomnia, but went out for half-an-hour. At lunch he ate nothing but incautiously drank a glass of unboiled water, scoffing at his brother's fear of cholera. Though he felt worse later, he still declined to see a doctor. But in the evening Modest sent for the brothers Bertenson, two of the best physicians in Petersburg. Tchaïkovsky was now very ill and said more than once, " I believe it's death. Good-bye, Modi! " The Bertensons pronounced his illness to be cholera and only once did there seem to be hope of his recovery. After a day or two his mind began to wander. " He continually repeated the name of Nadejda Filaretovna von Meck indignantly and reproachfully ", says Modest. At three in the morning of October 25th/November 6th, after a momentary gleam of apparent consciousness, Tchaïkovsky died in the presence of two of his brothers, his favourite nephew and the doctors.

Twelve days later Napravnik conducted a performance of the Sixth Symphony which naturally, under the circumstances, made a profound impression and, no doubt, gave rise to the legend of the " prophetic " nature of the last movement and of Tchaïkovsky's " suicide ".

It is not without interest that Nadejda von Meck died less than three months after the man she had helped so generously and wounded so cruelly.

* * * * *

It is customary not to criticise Tchaïkovsky's music but to sniff at it. One either likes it or one doesn't and to confess a liking for it in these days is almost equivalent to an admission of bad taste. Yet an extraordinarily large proportion of his music—probably nearly two-thirds of it—is absolutely unknown in this country, even to intelligent musicians, while anything worth calling criticism of Tchaïkovsky is practically non-existent even in Russia.

The true nature of Tchaïkovsky's musical gifts is most easily studied from his earlier works. From these we see that he had a genuine lyrical talent, spontaneous, but easily lapsing into the commonplace and often *forced* into it by the pressure he put upon himself to keep on producing. His orchestration was always colourful in a crude, garish way, and it became a little more refined later. As a symphonic architect he was, from first to last, as inferior to Borodin as he was superior to Rimsky-Korsakof; in other words, he was able to develop organic sections but not organic wholes. Taneief summed up the nature of Tchaïkovsky's music in general with deadly accuracy when he spoke of the Fourth Symphony as " ballet music ".

All Tchaïkovsky's earlier works are as objective as those of most Russian composers; that is, they are either " abstract " music, or frankly pictorial or programmatic. And it was some time before his growing subjectivity—the inevitable consequence of unrelieved introspection—really began to show itself in his music. It conditioned his choice of subjects, limiting him in opera, for instance, to dramas in which he could identify himself with a principal character and contemplate the whole action from that limited point of view (above all, in " Eugene Onegin "). It suggested a " subjective " programme for the Fourth Symphony. But the programme remains external, like any literary programme; it does not affect the tissue of the musical thought. The " Fate " of the Fourth Symphony is a mere lay-figure compared with the " Fate " of the Fifth. But after " Onegin " and the Fourth Symphony—that is, after the fatal marriage with its consequent crisis—subjective emotion begins to force its way rather hysterically into the very stuff of the music. The essential material of Tchaïkovsky's musical mind remained the same, of course, but it was now brutally forced into a sort of expressiveness which it did not really possess. The quasi-ballet-tune no longer remained a pleasant, innocuous symbol of, say, " desire "; the composer now really used it as the—sadly imperfect—instrument of his self-expression; and so we get things like the slow movement of the Fifth Symphony and the second subject of the " Pathétique ". There is a curious contrast between the Fourth Symphony, professedly subjective but really very near absolute music, and the "Manfred" Symphony of a few years later, professedly based on an external programme but where (at any rate, in the first movement) the composer has identified himself with his hero and written music which, successful or not, is intensely subjective.

It is probable that much of this music written during the 'eighties served Tchaïkovsky as a cathartic. It is certainly this later, intensely emotional music of his, with its effective colours and pretty, obvious tunes, which has done most (more even than the comparatively early B flat minor Concerto) to endear him to the musical man-in-the-street—who seldom detects the essential falseness of the curious, self-deceiving, self-torturing personality behind it. But it would be no bad thing if musicians in general would take the trouble to discover the unknown Tchaïkovsky and so get him in more correct focus. Unfortunately, the composer himself has made this all the more difficult by his terrifying industry. He insisted on constantly manufacturing, even when he had no raw material of the least value to feed his machinery, and so turned out an astounding mass of shoddy. Yet in this mass there are things worth bringing to light. Not important things but separate movements, songs—things which exhale an atmosphere of their time and which, understandably, recall to Russian exiles the *byt* of the old Tsarist society as precisely as Mozart conjures up the culture which fell before the French Revolution. Tchaïkovsky's music will have a " period " value in the future, but it is possible that the Tchaïkovsky familiar to the concert-goer of a hundred years hence will differ materially from the neurotic Tchaïkovsky who swept Europe off its feet at the beginning of the present century.

G. A.

RIMSKY-KORSAKOF
by Repin

NICHOLAS RIMSKY-KORSAKOF

It was Rimsky-Korsakof's own opinion that he owed a great deal to his grandmothers. They were certainly intruders in such a distinguished family, though intruders of a kind not so very unusual in aristocratic Russian families in the good old days of feudalism and serfdom. It appears that Lieutenant-General Peter Voinovitch Rimsky-Korsakof, son of one of the Empress Elisabeth's pet admirals, adbucted a priest's daughter, who bore him five sons. Thanks to his influence, he was able to get them legitimised, and it was the third son, Andrei, Civil Governor of the Volynsky Government from 1831 to 1835 and for a time a leading Freemason, who was to become the father of the composer. He was a simple, kind-hearted man with no idea of how to look after money. Very devout in his later years, he voluntarily freed his serfs long before the ukase of 1861. Andrei's first wife, Princess Meshchersky, having borne him no children, he married in 1821 the illegitimate, but fairly well-educated daughter of a wealthy landowner, a girl of nineteen. Her mother, too, had been a peasant, indeed a serf, and it pleased the composer to fancy he derived his love of folk-song from the one grandmother, and his delight in religious rites and ceremonies from the other. At any rate the composer's mother, a beautiful, intelligent and devout woman, was thoroughly musical by nature; her son's collection of folk-songs contains four melodies which he learned from her lips.[1]

Andrei's married life with this girl eighteen years younger than himself was ideally happy. But for many years she bore

---

[1] Mussorgsky introduced one of them in the inn scene of " Boris " as the drunken Varlaam's second song.

him only one child. The elder son, Voin, who entered the navy and died a rear-admiral in 1871, was born in 1822, the year after their marriage. But Andrei had been living in retirement at Tikhvin in the Novgorod Government for nine years before his wife gave him a second child on March 6th/18th, 1844. So it came about that Nicholas Andreievitch Rimsky-Korsakof had a father of sixty, a mother of forty-two, and an only brother twenty-two years older than himself. The fifth member of the family at Tikhvin was Andrei's elder brother Peter, " Uncle Pipon ", an eccentric with the heart and mind of a child who, according to his grand-nephew, was " a sort of Dickensian original of the type of Mr. Dick ", his endless topic of conversation with himself being the arrival or non-arrival of the post. But Uncle Pipon had two other passions: he loved the songs of the peasants and he worshipped devoutly at the great Monastery of the Blessed Virgin which faced the Rimsky-Korsakofs' house across the river. He, too, was laid under contribution when his nephew was collecting the old songs and we are indebted to " Uncle Pipon " for some of the loveliest tunes in Russian music. His nephew's " Maid of Pskof " and " Tsar Saltan ", and Balakiref's C major Symphony all owe some of their material to poor cracked " Uncle Pipon ".

That Monastery, too, left indelible impressions on the small boy. He loved the singing of the monks, particularly when they sang the music of Bortniansky. Many years later he recorded the sound of the Monastery bells in his " Easter Overture ", while the cry of the herald in " Snow Maiden " is a recollection of the call of the mounted messenger sent from the Monastery each summer to summon the women of the place to help the monks with their haymaking: " Little aunts, little mothers, pretty maidens, please come and rake hay for the Mother of God." There was a good deal of music-making of a rather amateurish kind in the home, in addition to the folk-songs of the boy's mother and uncle; for the father, too, was musical in his way, playing things like the romance from Méhul's " Joseph ", " Di tanti palpiti " from " Tancredi ", the funeral march from " La Vestale ", and " Ein Mädchen oder Weibchen " from " The Magic Flute " by ear on their old piano. But the mother's influence seems to have been at least equally important, though she was no longer a pianist. (From her, incidentally, her son inherited a curious tendency to take all music far too slowly.) " The first signs of musical ability showed themselves in me very early ", Rimsky-Korsakof tells us in his memoirs. " Before I was two I could distinguish all the melodies my mother sang to me; at three or four I was an expert at beating time on a drum to my father's piano-playing.[1] Father often purposely changed the time and rhythm suddenly, and I always followed him. I soon began to sing very accurately everything he played, and often sang with him; then I began to pick out the pieces with the harmonies for myself on the piano; and, having learned the names of the notes, would stand in another room and call them out when they were struck." At six he had his first regular lessons from an old lady, a neighbour. But he was unable to remember afterwards whether or not she was a good teacher, only that he was a bad pupil. " I played inaccurately and was weak at counting." On the whole he was better at reading and arithmetic than music, for which his liking was still very lukewarm. After a year or two the old lady's place as music-teacher was taken by a young governess, and hers in turn by a neighbour's daughter. Through them he first made the acquaintance of Beethoven, but most of the pieces he learned were easy fantasias on opera-melodies, " Les Huguenots ", " Le Prophéte ", " Rigoletto ", " Zar und Zimmermann " and their kind. He also played duets with his teachers. But

[1] Judging from one of the boy's letters home when a thirteen-year-old cadet, one of his father's favourite melodies was a tune the title of which the son spells in Roman characters: " God saw Quine ". Perhaps the Crimean War had drawn attention to the enemy's national anthem.

there was no amateur violinist or 'cellist in Tikhvin; even the local dance-band consisted only of one violin and one tambourine; so concerted music of every non-pianistic kind remained quite unknown to the child. He always insisted that " generally speaking I was not an impressionable boy ". But it is not without significance that of all this music, other than that heard at the Monastery where the gorgeous ceremonial greatly deepened the impression, the pieces which gave him the greatest pleasure were Vania's song and the duet from " A Life for the Tsar ", of which he found a copy at home. The duet seems to have provoked him to try and write one of his own, while another of his first, quite secret, attempts at composition took the form of an " overture " for piano, a work of original design, beginning *adagio,* then quickening through an *andante,* a *moderato,* an *allegretto* and an *allegro* to a final *presto.*

He was twelve, and, except for a visit to his uncle, Admiral Nicholas Rimsky-Korsakof in Petersburg, he had left the town of Tikhvin only three times in his life on short visits to friends in the country. He was a normal, healthy boy, climbing trees and so on; though, as an only child, compelled to invent most of his own amusements, playing coach-and-horses with chairs and making up conversations with himself as if between the driver and his passengers. But all the time he was obsessed by one dominant idea—to be a sailor. From 1852 to 1857 his brother was cruising[1] in the Far East, and Voin's letters home excited " Niki's " imagination beyond measure. He devoured books about the sea, on which he had not yet set eyes, filled his head with nautical terms, and rigged up a model brig. Considering the number of sailors in the family it was natural enough that he, too, should enter the Imperial Navy. But the chief opposition came from Voin himself who, although he loved his profession, had a very

[1] Part of the voyage is described by the novelist Gontcharof in his travel-book, " The Frigate ' Pallada ' ".

poor opinion of his brother officers. " Of the five or six hundred officers of the Baltic Fleet barely ten or fifteen love the service for its own sake ", he wrote. " A young fellow entering the Navy with poetic dreams in his head and hopes in his heart is quickly and bitterly disenchanted." The general atmosphere of slackness was appalling. But " Niki " was not to be discouraged. Nor could his father afford to enter him in the more aristocratic Corps of Pages. So at the end of July, 1856, Nicholas left his mother for the first time in his life and was taken by his father to Petersburg to enter the Corps of Naval Cadets, donning a uniform strongly suggestive of that fabulous English force, the Horse Marines.

Nicholas seems to have made a good cadet and to have been popular with his comrades, though he evidently found the discipline irksome at first. Not that he complained. But his letters home reveal an unconfessed homesickness. For the rest they are very boyish letters full of enquiries about his canaries, little reminiscences of home-life, Papa's piano-playing and so on. Forty years later he clearly remembered the anguish of his return to Petersburg after the first summer holidays. There was a falling-off in his good behaviour, too. As for music, he had piano lessons for two years from one Ulich, a mediocre 'cellist and worse pianist, but took no interest in them. Nor was he taught the names of even the simplest chords and intervals. But he was allowed to spend each week-end with the Golovins, friends of his brother's, who were fond of Italian opera, particularly Rossini. Among other things they took him to hear " Lucia " " which made a great impression on me ". After that came " Freischütz " and other operatic classics, many of them now dead and buried (of which " Robert " particularly delighted him by the sense of mystery in its orchestral colouring) and then—
" A Life for the Tsar " which " completely enraptured " him. At the same time he found at the Golovins' some separate

numbers of " Ruslan ", the first music which awakened in him a sense of *harmonic* beauty. Besides, whereas genuine piano music was " so dry and boring ", " when you play an opera ", he wrote home, " you imagine you're sitting in the theatre, listening or even playing or singing yourself; you imagine the scenery. In fact, it's frightfully jolly ".[1] In the season of 1859-60 came a new revelation through the symphony concerts in the Grand Theatre. A couple of Beethoven symphonies and the " Midsummer Night's Dream " Overture aroused his enthusiasm, but Glinka's " Jota arragonesa " " simply dazzled me ". He also heard " Ruslan " at the Marinsky Theatre, and started buying the separate numbers with his pocket-money till Voin gave him the complete piano score, which had only just come out. " A Life for the Tsar " was also bought from his own limited funds. (According to his brother he had not the least sense of money—a trait inherited from his father.) Though his brother and the Golovins adopted a rather patronising attitude towards Glinka, the recently dead master became his idol. He began to make all sorts of arrangements of Glinka's music for piano duet, piano and violin, piano and 'cello (without the slightest knowledge of the instruments) and even tried to orchestrate the entr'actes in " A Life for the Tsar " from the piano score. " Naturally the devil knows how it turned out! Seeing that it wouldn't do at all, I went twice to the publisher's shop and asked to see the orchestral score. I only half understood it, but the Italian names of the instruments, the terms *col* and *come sopra,* the different clefs and the transpositions of the horns and other instruments— all this exercised on me a certain mysterious charm. In short, I was a sixteen-year-old *child,* passionately fond of music *and playing with it.*" But according to his brother, who took a keen interest in his musical education, as in everything else he

---

[1] A literal translation of his boyish slang, by the way; not a free, modernised equivalent.

did, and supervised his piano practice, he still played even his favourite compositions very carelessly.

On his return home in 1857, Voin Rimsky-Korsakof had been appointed to the command of the gunnery instruction ship " Prokhor " and for two summers " Niki " spent some time on board her with his brother. In June, 1858, he badly frightened Voin by falling out of the rigging into the sea, though without any serious consequences. The two brothers were devoted to each other, though, owing to the difference in their ages, Voin's relation to his younger brother was almost paternal. And fond of him as he was, he was too strict a disciplinarian to spoil him. Yet, in the summer and autumn of 1859, we find both of them, the boy of fifteen and the man of thirty-seven, in love with the same girl—a certain L. P. D—— —and it is delightful to read in the elder brother's reports to their parents of his wise and careful handling of Niki's calf-love, his amused delight in the boy's little gallantries, and his taking advantage of the affair to make Niki smarten himself and improve his French. In January, 1862, before Nicholas had left the Naval College, Voin was appointed its Director somewhat to the perturbation of their father, who feared, quite needlessly, that the situation might be bad for discipline. It was one of the old man's last thoughts, for he died the following month and his widow and Uncle Pipon moved to St. Petersburg to live with Voin.

In the meantime the dull and incompetent Ulich had been replaced in the autumn of 1859[1] by a much more capable teacher, F. A. Canille, the first really good pianist the boy ever heard. " I like Canille very much ", his pupil wrote home. " He makes the lesson interesting and not dry." Not only that but he discovered that Canille shared his admiration of Glinka, considering him " a great genius " and " Ruslan " " the best opera in the world ". In the spring of 1860, we find Niki writing that " I haven't been to the theatre as

[1] Not 1860, as Rimsky-Korsakof says in his memoirs.

they've been giving nothing but things like ' Il Trovatore ' and ' Traviata '—my musical ear doesn't care for that sort of trash; *we* love Glinka, Mendelssohn, Beethoven, Schumann, Chopin, Meyerbeer and, perhaps, Rossini. Oh! and I'm forgetting Fr. Schubert . . ." Canille took a keen interest in the sixteen-year-old cadet and not only introduced him to Bach's fugues, Balakiref's " King Lear " Overture, and other fresh music, but encouraged him to compose, making him ape early Beethoven in a sonata movement and Glinka in a set of variations. He also gave him chorale melodies to harmonise and explained some of the mysteries of an orchestral score to him, but all in a very confused and unsystematic way; so that the boy learned very little of even the most elementary things. After a year Voin decided that the lessons must end and Nicholas, bitterly disappointed, had to obey. But Canille invited the boy to visit him on Sundays, not for regular lessons, but to talk about music and play duets. Still knowing nothing, he says, of the most elementary laws of part-writing—in spite of his chorale exercises—or the names of chords, much less of counterpoint, he concocted with Canille's help two or three little piano pieces, " watery rehashes of Glinka, Beethoven and Schumann ". Among other musical activities at this time we find Rimsky-Korsakof organising a choir of eighteen fellow cadets and conducting them in choruses from " A Life for the Tsar " and other operas. But the authorities disapproved for some reason and the choir had to disband.

We now come to November 26th/December 8th, 1861, a most memorable date in Rimsky-Korsakof's life, even in the history of Russian music. " Last Sunday ", he wrote to his parents, " Canille introduced me to M. A. Balakiref, a well-known musician and composer, and also to Cui, who has written an opera. ' The Prisoner of the Caucasus ' ". And a month or two later: " Yesterday I was at Balakiref's as usual. I spend the time there so pleasantly that I simply don't know how to thank Canille for such a magnificent acquaintance." He had at once succumbed to the magnetism of Balakiref's personality. At the very first meeting Balakiref was shown the " watery " piano pieces and " a sort of beginning of a Symphony in E flat minor "—incredible key, almost worthy of a popular novelist. He approved of one of the pieces, a Scherzo in C minor, and insisted that the lad should go on with the Symphony! The twenty-two-year-old Mussorgsky was there, too, also struggling to write a symphony with very little better equipment. But even he was transfigured in Rimsky-Korsakof's eyes by the glamour of having had a couple of compositions performed in public. The seventeen-year-old cadet felt that he had fallen among real musicians at last. He was fascinated by their " shop-talk " and by Stassof's wide culture, and he paid the greatest respect to their likes and dislikes. In after years he contended that he had weakly echoed their opinions, but it is clear that in many respects their tastes harmonised with those he had already formed. They liked Glinka and Schumann above all, admired the " Midsummer Night's Dream " Overture, disliked what they knew of Liszt and Wagner. So did he. In other respects he may have taken the colour of his surroundings, but it was a little ungenerous of him in later years to blame the twenty-four-year-old Balakiref for his own rather narrow taste at this period. Actually, it was Balakiref who first opened his eyes to much in the world of culture outside music—to history, literature and criticism. The Naval College had not even taught him to spell properly, much less history or anything of literature off the high road of the Russian classics—Pushkin, Lermontof, Gogol.

If Rimsky-Korsakof was overpowered by Balakiref's personality, Balakiref in turn took the strongest fancy to his new friend. He needed a " pupil " of some sort. Gussakovsky, his chief hope, was abroad. He had a poor opinion of Mussorgsky's ability. But on Rimsky-Korsakof he built the most glowing expectations. " I put my trust in you ", he wrote a little later, " as an old aunt in a young lawyer nephew ". Absurd as it seems, he at once set him—this boy with his appalling ignorance, knowing nothing of such mysteries as " cadences "—to work at the already begun Symphony in E flat minor, and the first movement was finished within a month, during the Christmas holidays. With Balakiref's help Korsakof began to orchestrate it, and they all thought he showed a special aptitude for instrumentation. In the first few months of 1862, under Balakiref's close supervision, he wrote the scherzo (without a trio) and finale, composing the chief theme of the latter on the way back to Petersburg after his father's funeral, in March. But the Symphony, " the first symphony ever written by a Russian " as Cui pointed out, was destined to interruption. On April 8th/20th, 1862, the first of Russian symphonists left the Naval College as a *gardemarine* (neither cadet nor full-blown officer) and was appointed to the clipper, " Almaz ".

Now the " Almaz " was being fitted out for a two or three years' cruise in foreign waters, and Rimsky-Korsakof was in despair at the prospect of leaving his new circle of friends, for he had just discovered that he wanted to be a musician and not a sailor. And Balakiref was most anxious not to lose him. But Cui, himself a serving officer, thought the lad should stay in the service, and Voin's robust common sense decided the matter; he saw no evidence that his brother was anything more than an intelligent amateur; Nicholas had a career before him in another sphere and there must be no spoiling it for the sake of a whim. As Nicholas agreed later in life, " he was a thousand times right in considering me a dilettante, for that is all I was ". Even as a pianist, he was still very mediocre, a fair reader but with no technique.

In May, when Balakiref went to the Caucasus for the mineral waters and the other members of the circle and his relations also left Petersburg for the summer, Rimsky-

Korsakof was left kicking his heels about in Kronstadt, and the symphony (which he had been trying to orchestrate with one eye on Berlioz's " Traité de l'Instrumentation " and the other on Glinka's scores) came to a full stop. Even with Balakiref at his elbow, his attempts to write a slow movement had failed. Generally speaking, Balakiref disapproved of sustained, " singing " melody, considering it usually rather banal. And Rimsky-Korsakof found it was almost impossible to write slow music without lapsing into such *cantabile* melody. So during the summer he abandoned himself to the anything but intellectual society of his service-comrades. Three or four months passed in idleness, boredom and playing the fool generally. Balakiref came back and once more tried unsuccessfuly to stop his sailing. But one day in late autumn he, Cui and Canille had to wave good-bye to their young friend from the steamer-jetty at Petersburg as he left to join his ship at Kronstadt. Two days later, October 21st/November 2nd, she sailed.

The " Almaz " made first for England, spending nearly four months at Gravesend for re-rigging. With the three other *gardemarines*, Rimsky-Korsakof made two sight-seeing expeditions to London, visiting Westminster Abbey, the Tower, the Crystal Palace and the rest of the sights. He also went to the Royal Italian Opera at Covent Garden, but forgot in after years what he had heard there. Having few duties, the *gardemarines* spent their leisure in discussing politics. There was a good library on board and one of the *gardemarines* bought a lot of French and English books—Buckle, Macaulay and John Stuart Mill. And they read Herzen's famous Socialist weekly, " The Bell ", banned in Russia, which he was then publishing in London. In religion and politics Rimsky-Korsakof was a typical young Russian liberal rationalist of the 'sixties, the " age of reform ". Nor did he neglect music altogether, in spite of the obvious difficulties. He corresponded with Balakiref, who urged him to write the slow movement of his Symphony; and he obediently set to work, basing the movement on a folk-song given him by Balakiref, and posted the score home. (In accordance with some idea of Balakiref's, the *andante* was placed third, instead of second as in almost all classical symphonies.) " I wrote it without the help of a piano (we hadn't one on board) ", though they bought a harmonium in London, " but once or twice at a public-house on shore I managed to play through what I had written ". One wonders in which of Gravesend's hotels or public-houses the first performance of part of the first Russian symphony was given by its composer.

Leaving England, the " Almaz " was ordered back to the Baltic to stop gun-running for the Polish rebels, with whom Korsakof and some of his comrades secretly sympathised. In the summer she returned for a short time to Kronstadt and Rimsky-Korsakof was able to spend three or four days' leave in Petersburg, though his family and musical friends were all in the country. But war with England was believed to be imminent, owing to the Polish insurrection, and the " Almaz " was secretly dispatched to New York in readiness to act as a commerce-raider. Using her sails to save her coal and taking an unusual route to the north of Scotland, she took more than two months over the voyage. With the rest of the Russian squadron collected in American waters, the " Almaz " remained from October, 1863, to April, 1864, in the neighbourhood of New York, Baltimore and Annapolis, the officers and *gardemarines* making excursions to the Chesapeake Falls, to Washington and to Niagara, and spending a good deal of time on shore with drink and women. In New York Korsakof heard " Robert le Diable " and Gounod's " Faust " badly performed, but his own music-making was limited to vamping accompaniments on the cabin harmonium to American airs played on the fiddle by the pilot, Thompson. The correspondence with Balakiref nearly petered out.

Korsakof had gradually given up all thought of becoming a serious musician; his one ambition now was to see the world. Yet, quiet and timid by nature, he was by no means shaping into a good officer. As he admitted afterwards, he had " no presence of mind or administrative ability ". He was quite unable, he says, to shout and bully in the approved style. (His voice was nasal and rather shrill.) To see a sailor given two or three hundred stripes simply revolted him. He was certainly not going to be an ornament to the Imperial Navy.

The danger of war with England being over, the " Almaz " was ordered home by way of Cape Horn and the Pacific, to the joy of Gardemarine Rimsky-Korsakof and disgust of Captain Zeleny. While his junior was delighting in the marvellous tropical nights, watching the phosphorescent water and the stars—which had always held a special fascination for him—the good Captain seems to have been exercising his ingenuity to avoid the Pacific crossing. Having taken sixty-five days to reach Rio de Janeiro from New York under sail, he decided to continue under steam; broke down his engines; returned to Rio for repairs; sent home a highly-coloured report of the vessel's unseaworthiness; and stayed at Rio till October, waiting for instructions. He was rewarded by orders to return to Europe, and in December the " Almaz " rejoined Lesovsky's squadron in the Gulf of Villa Franca. Rimsky-Korsakof saw something of Nice, Toulon, Marseilles, Genoa and Spezzia, lost a few gold-pieces at Monte Carlo, and grew enthusiastic about " Faust ", the fashionable opera of the day. In April the Tsarevitch George died at Nice, and Lesovsky's squadron had the duty of taking the body back to Russia. Rimsky-Korsakof, now a midshipman, returned to Kronstadt early in the summer of 1865. " I had become an officer-dilettante, who sometimes enjoyed playing or listening to music; but all my dreams of artistic activity had completely flown away. Nor did I regret them." He caught a few fleeting glimpses of Balakiref and his own family. But they spent the summer in the country, he at Kronstadt while the " Almaz " was being dismantled. In September he was transferred to St. Petersburg, where he took a furnished room.

Visiting Balakiref, however, Rimsky-Korsakof—ever susceptible to environment—began to renew his serious interest in music. He found all sorts of changes in the musical life of Petersburg. Balakiref's Free School, founded a few months before he had sailed, was now well-established; the critic, Serof, had made a dramatic appearance as a composer with his " Judith "; the Balakiref circle had gained a new recruit in the chemistry professor of the Medical Academy, A. P. Borodin, who was already writing a symphony. As for Korsakof's own Symphony, Balakiref insisted on his finishing it by writing a trio to the scherzo (which he did in October) and reorchestrating the whole under his supervision. His naval duties consisted only of two or three hours' secretarial work each morning, so that he was able to devote plenty of time to music, spending much of his leisure at Balakiref's and sometimes even sleeping there. In November[1] he wrote his first song, a setting of Heine's " Lehn deine Wang' an meine Wang' ". Balakiref approved of the melody but not of the accompaniment, and provided the song with an accompaniment of his own—with which it was published.

The E flat minor Symphony—Rimsky-Korsakof's Op. 1 —being finished, Balakiref decided to play it at one of his Free School concerts; and, after the two rehearsals then customary in Russia, the Symphony was given its first performance (in the distinguished company of Mozart's " Requiem ") on December 19th/31st. It was well received,

---

[1] Not in December of the following year as he says in his memoirs. But the chronology of the memoirs is frequently incorrect, even the sequence of events being transposed.

and the audience were more than a little surprised when a young man in naval uniform appeared to take the applause. A second performance followed a month later at a Theatre Concert under Constantine Liadof. At about the same time (January or February, 1866) Balakiref introduced his young friend to Liudmila Shestakova, and from that time onward he was a frequent guest at her house. In her circle Rimsky-Korsakof made a number of fresh acquaintances, among others Dargomyjsky and a singer, S. I. Zotova, whose performance inspired him to further essays in song-composition. In February, March and April respectively, he wrote for her the well-known " The Rose enslaves the Nightingale ", a setting of the cradle-song from Mey's play " The Maid of Pskof " and one of Heine's " Aus meinen Tränen ", this time with his own accompaniments. With the earlier Heine song they were published by Bernard in the summer as Op. 2, though the composer did not receive a kopeck for them, and had to content himself with the satisfaction of appearing in print for the first time.

The summer brought forth not only a crop of eight more songs (Opp. 3 and 4) but a new orchestral piece, an " Overture on Three Russian Themes ". (It is numbered Op. 28, but Rimsky-Korsakof's opus-numbers are a quite unreliable guide to the chronological order of his compositions.) Balakiref's preoccupation with the harmonisation of his collection of folk-songs that spring had laid the foundation of Rimsky-Korsakof's serious interest in folk-music, while the melodies Balakiref had brought back from the Caucasus attracted him to oriental music. The immediate fruit of his new interest was the Overture, written during June and July. It was modelled on Balakiref's two folk-song overtures (the one in B minor and " Russia ") and two of the themes were borrowed from his new collection of " Forty Folk-Songs ", while the third is the well-known one used by Beethoven in the second " Razumovsky " Quartet and Mussorgsky in the coronation scene of "Boris". The Overture was performed at a Free School concert on December 11th/23rd, together with Liszt's "Mephisto Waltz", a work which particularly fascinated Rimsky-Korsakof.

At the same time Korsakof was struggling rather belatedly to improve his piano technique, practising scales in thirds and octaves, working industriously at Czerny's "Daily Exercises" and even struggling with Chopin's studies. But Balakiref's poor opinion of his pianistic ability frightened him from playing before his musical friends, though among his service comrades and in the family circle at Voin's he was considered a "beautiful pianist". At his brother's, too, he played for dancing on Sunday evenings—quadrilles of his own composition on themes from "Martha" and "La Belle Hélène"—dark secrets which he kept from Balakiref. But he seems to have found the company of the young people who gathered at Voin's—his sister-in-law's relations—more congenial than Liudmila Shestakova's card-parties, where Balakiref was in his element.

Both Cui and Balakiref agreed that Rimsky-Korsakof showed a decided talent for orchestration, and 1867 saw not only the beginning of a Second Symphony in B minor (which came to nothing, though the scherzo in 5/4 time was used in a later work) but the completion of two more orchestral pieces, a "Fantasia on Serbian Themes" written in a great hurry for Balakiref's Pan-Slavonic Concert on May 12th/24th—Balakiref's Pan-Slavonic enthusiasm then being at its height, just after his expedition to Prague—and the "musical picture" "Sadko", largely inspired by the Liszt "Mephisto Waltz". Rimsky-Korsakof began "Sadko" in June during a three-weeks' holiday at his brother's summer villa at Tervaïoki, near Vyborg, was obliged to interrupt it for a month's cruise in the Gulf of Finland, and finished it on September 30th/October 12th. Announcing this piece of news to Mussorgsky, the next youngest member of the circle, with whom he had lately been drawn into more intimate personal friendship, he says: " I don't mind telling you that I'm perfectly satisfied with it; it's decidedly the best thing I've done, considerably better even than that *andante* of the Symphony which took me such a devil of a time to write . . . . So ' Sadko ' is finished and I owe you my best thanks, Modest, for the idea—which you gave me, I remember, at Cui's the night before his wife went to Minsk.[1] Once more: thank you. Now I'm going to rest, for my noddle's a bit weary from the intense strain; I'm going to rest, be idle, write a few songs, and after that—I don't know myself, but I doubt if the B minor *allegro* " (of the projected Second Symphony) " will be resuscitated from the ashes—still, one never knows! Mily is quite satisfied with ' Sadko ' and didn't want to make any comments ". All these orchestral works were written for the old-fashioned " natural " horns and trumpets as described in Berlioz's " Traité ", the composer writing for horns in every possible crook and getting tied in all sorts of knots in trying to avoid " stopped " notes. As Korsakof said afterwards: " It would have been altogether beneath our dignity to have consulted some practical musician who would have put us right. We were the brothers-in-arms of Berlioz, not of some ungifted bandmaster. . . ."

That winter Berlioz, himself, came to Russia again, on Balakiref's invitation, to conduct six concerts for the Russian Music Society. But Rimsky-Korsakof had no chance of meeting the man whose chief rival in orchestral virtuosity he was destined to become. Berlioz was a sick man throughout the visit, spending most of his free time lying down—" ill with 18 horse-power, coughing like six donkeys with the glanders ", as he wrote to the Massarts—and had no relations with any Russian musicians except Balakiref, Cui, the Stassofs and the Directors of the R.M.S. He died a year later. But

---

[1] The idea of a musical treatment of the Sadko legend was originally suggested by Stassof to Balakiref in 1861.

Balakiref himself was the Society's conductor-in-chief that season; he gave the first performance of "Sadko" on December 9th/21st and also played the "Serbian Fantasia" again—both works winning the unstinted praise of the usually hostile Serof.

Rimsky-Korsakof was still living in a furnished room on Vassily Island, going to his brother's for meals and spending his evenings at Balakiref's, Borodin's or Lodyjensky's, or with Mussorgsky. Less often with Cui. And that spring, the spring of 1868, the whole circle found a new weekly rendezvous at Dargomyjsky's, where they heard and performed "The Stone Guest". In this house the twenty-four-year-old Rimsky-Korsakof made the acquaintance of the sisters Alexandra and Nadejda Purgold, aged respectively twenty-four and twenty. Alexandra was a singer, an excellent amateur, Nadejda a pianist, who had studied under Mussorgsky's old teacher Herke and at the St. Petersburg Conservatoire under Zaremba. Before very long the members of the Balakiref circle were visiting the Purgolds. (The family consisted of three sisters, their mother and uncle; while there were other married sisters and brothers.) These visits led to the most important consequences for Rimsky-Korsakof. But he never seems to have been much of a ladies' man; the great romance of his life, a most domestic, not to say bourgeois affair, was apparently not the result of love at first sight.

His head was full of plans. Within three months of the completion of "Sadko" he was thinking of a "symphony or four-movement symphonic poem" based on Senkovsky's oriental tale "Antar", and the first and fourth movements were written during January and February, 1868. He already had an idea for an opera on that play of Mey's, "The Maid of Pskof", from which he had taken the text of one of his first songs. But for the moment he concentrated on "Antar", his "Second Symphony" as he called it originally.

(In 1903, when he brought out a new edition, it was restyled " symphonic suite ".) As he said afterwards, " the term ' suite ' was at that time practically unknown to our circle. . . . Still I had no right to call ' Antar ' a symphony. My ' Antar ' was a poem, suite, legend, anything you like, but not a symphony ". It was during the composition of " Antar ", he tells us, that he first ventured to offer mild resistance to Balakiref's despotic interference in his work. He was at last beginning to feel able to stand on his own feet and assert his own artistic will. Another and more curious sign of ripening musical individuality was that sense of the colour associations of musical keys which began to awaken in him at this period and which afterwards exercised over him an influence amounting almost to tyranny.

The second movement of " Antar " was written in June. Most of Rimsky-Korsakof's friends and relations having left Petersburg for the country, he was left rather sadly with the not too congenial company of Dargomyjsky and Cui —who took the opportunity to get him to orchestrate the opening chorus of his opera, " William Ratcliffe ". As usual, during the summer months Nicholas occupied Voin's deserted quarters in the Naval College. One day he made an expedition with Dargomyjsky and the Cuis to the Purgolds' summer villa and, being rather bored and lonely, drifted back again and again—alone. (Of two songs written that summer, one was tactfully dedicated to Nadejda, the other to Alexandra.) Then one day, early in July, came an invitation to join the Borodins, who were staying on Lodyjensky's estate in the Tver Government. " I remember how, sitting alone in my brother's flat, I received Lodyjensky's invitation. I remember how the prospect of a journey into the solitudes of the very heart of Russia instantaneously evoked in me an overwhelming sensation of love for the life of the Russian people, for their history in general and for ' The Maid of Pskof ', in particular; and how, under the impression of that emotion, I went to the piano and immediately improvised the theme of the chorus with which the people greet Tsar Ivan." After three weeks in the country, riding and walking with his hosts and the Borodins—and " eating an awful lot of berries and cream ", as he wrote to Mussorgsky—and another week at Tervaïoki with his family, he returned to Petersburg in August, and wrote the third movement of " Antar " and several numbers of the First Act of " The Maid of Pskof ". Both " Antar " and the " Greeting Chorus " from " The Maid " were given that winter at R.M.S. concerts, under Balakiref. (It was the last season he conducted for the Society.) Rimsky-Korsakof himself had been invited to conduct his compositions and had applied to his commanding-officer for permission to do so. But Krabbe, the Minister of Marine, solemnly decreed that " It is not agreeable to His Imperial Majesty that his officers should appear publicly as performers at concerts, any more than in theatrical representations ". So Rimsky-Korsakof had to content himself with appearing on the platform to take the applause.

The production of Cui's " William Ratcliffe " in February, 1869, was the occasion of Rimsky-Korsakof's only two excursions into the field of musical journalism. Cui, being busy with rehearsals, induced Borodin and Rimsky-Korsakof to devil for him as critic of the " St. Petersburg Gazette ", and it fell to the latter's lot to criticise not only " Ratcliffe " itself, but a new opera by Napravnik, who had just succeeded Constantine Liadof as chief conductor at the Marinsky Theatre. Full of the prevalent ideas of operatic realism, Rimsky-Korsakof ridiculed the conventionalism of Napravnik's work and amused himself (if not his readers) by pointing out the unfortunate wealth of reminiscence in the music. To the end of his life he blamed this youthful indiscretion for spoiling his relations with a fine artist, who for many years was to be one of the outstanding figures in Russian musical life, particularly in the sphere of opera. (Indeed, almost immediately after this, Napravnik succeeded Balakiref as conductor of the Russian Music Society.)

In 1869, in accordance with the dead composer's wish, Rimsky-Korsakof began the scoring of Dargomyjsky's " Stone Guest ". His own " Maid " progressed—rather slowly. And he revised the orchestration of " Sadko ", the first sign of that profound self-dissatisfaction, revealed in the constant working over of old material, which flowed in such a strong undercurrent throughout the remainder of his career. Given in this new version at a Free School concert, " Sadko " was even more successful than before. " The public was entraptured ", Borodin wrote to his wife. " Korsinka was called out three times." Even Serof wrote that " Mr. Rimsky-Korsakof, alone of all his party, gifted with enormous talent . . .glitters amid his unfortunate entourage like a diamond among cobble-stones ". But trouble with his eyes condemned Rimsky-Korsakof to a long stretch of inactivity at this period. An expedition to Moscow with Balakiref in January, 1870, and a two months' holiday at Tervaïoki with his mother in the following summer—the Purgold girls being on holiday in the West—were the only breaks in an uneventful routine of service duties. The orchestration of " The Stone Guest " was finished at Tervaïoki; some more songs appeared—those published as Op. 8; and by February, 1871, " The Maid of Pskof " was sketched out and the orchestration begun. Then, after three months of unexplained idleness, the scoring was resumed in June and the first two acts, with the first scene of Act III, completed by September.

Contrary to his usual custom, Mussorgsky spent the summer of 1871 in St. Petersburg, and, delighted to have his company, Rimsky-Korsakof frequently took him to Voin's. And they often went together to visit Stassof and the Purgold girls, motherless since the previous December, who had summer villas at Pargolovo. This was the period of their closest friendship. And fate was to bring them even closer for a while. Voin Rimsky-Korsakof's health, long bad, took a turn for the worse that autumn and his doctor ordered him abroad. Shutting up his flat, he set out with his wife and children for Italy; his mother went to Moscow to live; and Nicholas decided to join forces with Mussorgsky. How the two youngest members of the "handful" lived together that winter in a single room, Mussorgsky revising and adding to "Boris", Rimsky-Korsakof scoring the Fourth Act and Overture of "The Maid of Pskof", and working together during February and March, 1872, at the Second and Third Acts of the Gedeonof "Mlada"—all this has already been told elsewhere. Yet already in the summer of 1871 Rimsky-Korsakof had taken a step which was the direct cause of Mussorgsky's gradual estrangement from him a year or so later, a step which was to lead to a complete change of direction in his musical development.

The history of this almost incredible business is best told in Rimsky-Korsakof's own words. "One fine day, I received a visit from Azantchevsky, newly appointed to the Directorship of the St. Petersburg Conservatoire in succession to Zaremba. To my surprise he invited me to accept the Professorship of Practical Composition and Instrumentation and the direction of the orchestral class, with a salary of one thousand rubles" (roughly, £100 a year). During the four years, 1867-71, that Rubinstein's successor Zaremba had reigned over the Conservatoire, these branches of study had got into a bad state and Azantchevsky seems to have had the bright idea of enlivening them by introducing young blood in the person of this twenty-seven-year-old naval officer, who had attracted such favourable notice by his "ultra-modern" orchestral pieces. He knew Rimsky-Korsakof to be an amateur, but he cannot have had an inkling of the incredible truth. "It was not merely that I couldn't at that time have harmonised a chorale properly, had never written a single contrapuntal exercise in my life, and had only the haziest understanding of strict fugue; but I didn't even know the names of the augmented and diminished intervals or of the chords, other than the tonic triad and the dominant and diminished sevenths; though I could sing anything at sight and *distinguish* every conceivable chord, the terms ' chord of the sixth ' and ' six-four chords ' were unknown to me. In my compositions I strove after correct part-writing and achieved it by instinct and by ear. My grasp of the musical forms (particularly of the rondo) was equally hazy. Although I scored my own compositions colourfully enough, I had no real knowledge of the technique of the strings, or of the practical possibilities of horns, trumpets and trombones. As for conducting, I had never conducted an orchestra in my life . . . ." To do him justice, Rimsky-Korsakof did hesitate at first. But " my friends advised me to accept. Even Balakiref, who alone really knew how unprepared I was, took the same view—being chiefly influenced by the wish to *get a footing* in the hostile Conservatoire ". Morevover, Korsakof himself was " young and self-confident " and ignorant of his own ignorance. " I agreed. In the autumn I was to become a professor at the Conservatoire without taking off my naval uniform." In a letter to his mother (July 15th/27th) he reckons up the advantages the position will bring him: " First, pecuniary; second, I shall be occupied with matters which give me pleasure and for which I am most adapted; third, it will be good practice for me, particularly as regards the conducting; and finally, here is a chance of definitely launching myself on a musical career and leaving the service, to continue in which for long I do not consider altogether fair and honest. Taking all this into consideration, I have agreed to go to the Conservatoire." (It appears not to have occurred to him that it was not " altogether fair and honest " to accept this new post!) And so the appointment was made. Nor was it the first instance of an utter incompetent being given such a post in Russia, for in 1834 Gogol had been appointed Professor of History in Petersburg University with no more knowledge of history than Rimsky-Korsakof had of musical theory. But whereas Gogol failed miserably and was obliged to resign, Rimsky-Korsakof bluffed his way through with astounding success. As he said, none of his pupils could have suspected his ignorance at first; he put them off with commonplaces, eked out by his personal tastes and his practical experience; and by the time they had begun to find him out, he had already learned something. Later he did teach himself to some purpose. " And so, undeservedly given a professorship in the Conservatoire, I soon became one of its best pupils—perhaps the best of all—as regards the quantity and quality of the knowledge I acquired there." And few will dispute the fact that this most incompetent of professors made himself a very great teacher, the greatest composition teacher (except perhaps Taneief) Russia has so far managed to produce.[1] But that was not yet. The Rimsky-Korsakof who shared a room with Mussorgsky, finished " The Maid of Pskof " and collaborated with Cui, Borodin and Mussorgsky in " Mlada " was a young man whose self-confidence had far outrun his ability, and who was now rather frightened at the extent of his own ignorance and perhaps already secretly a little ashamed of the course of humbug in which his temerity had involved him.

That winter the pattern of Rimsky-Korsakof's life was shot through with other, most varied colours in generous compensation for the drab monotony of the last two or three years. First a streak of black. On November 4th/16th, 1871, Voin Rimsky-Korsakof died at Pisa; Nicholas had lost his second

[1] Rimsky-Korsakof seems to have been adored by all his later pupils. Sokolof, who entered his class at the Conservatoire in 1878, was " at once charmed by his simple, utterly un-' professorial ' manner, his childlike capacity for rejoicing over a good piece of work and being very deeply distressed by our failures. I am not ashamed to confess that Rimsky-Korsakof's outward appearance—his ill-cut, shabby clothes and his old boots—complied with the unconscious demands of my democratic leanings ". (" Reminiscences of Rimsky-Korsakof. ")

father. He was at once dispatched to Italy by the Ministry of Marine to bring home the Admiral's embalmed body. (It is characteristic of Rimsky-Korsakof's cool, phlegmatic temperament that in the middle of this sad duty he found time to call on Anton Rubinstein in Vienna and hear him play through Liszt's " Christus ".) But Voin's death had one most unexpected consequence, for Nicholas suddenly found himself the favourite of Krabbe, the Minister of Marine. Krabbe, a good courtier and bad sailor, great lover of music and the theatre—and still greater lover of pretty actresses, had been Voin's determined and lifelong antagonist. But no sooner was Voin dead than he good-naturedly took the warmest interest in his family, saw that his mother, widow and children were well provided for, and, sending for Nicholas, assured him of his friendship and help in case of difficulty. Before long Nicholas was glad to avail himself of Krabbe's help, though in a matter quite unconnected with the service.

On the day after his arrival in Pisa, Rimsky-Korsakof had written to Nadejda Purgold: " Coming home from your house that last evening, I was so upset that I forgot myself and wrote to you almost in a state of fever, and now this letter presents itself to my mind in a sort of fog, but I will only say that I don't withdraw a single word of that letter. The next day I left Petersburg with an extremely painful feeling; though naturally fatigue and travel impressions blurred it. I thought about you a great deal on the way . . . and when I happened to see something nice, I always wanted you to look at it with me." It needs no great skill to read between such lines as those, and one is not surprised to learn that they were betrothed the next month.

From this point—if not, of course, before—the influence of Nadejda (a far better trained musician than himself, we must remember) began to play a very important part in Rimsky-Korsakof's musical development. He said little about it himself, but his friends recognised it. Next to Balakiref, who at this very period was just on the eve of his breakdown, Nadejda was the chief formative influence in his life. She was a quiet woman but one with very decided artistic views; she did not hesitate to alter Tchaïkovsky's "Romeo and Juliet" when transcribing it for piano! Nor were her own musical activities limited to piano-playing and the wholesale transcription of contemporary Russian orchestral works. She was a composer herself until the growth of her family obliged her to lay musical work aside. Only a week or two before her marriage she completed a "musical picture", "The Enchanted Spot", based on one of Gogol's "Evenings on a Farm near Dikanka", which she orchestrated the following year. And her enthusiasm for Gogol's "Evenings" is reflected in the subjects of her husband's works and those of his friends. On the day of their betrothal Nadejda and Nicholas read "May Night" together and she was very anxious that he should write an opera on it. And a week or two later she wrote to him: "I've been reading yet another of Gogol's stories to-day, 'The Fair of Sorotchintsi'. This is good, too, and would even be suitable for an opera, but not for *you*; in any case, it's not like 'May Night'. As for *that*, it's so stuck in my head that nothing will drive it out." She, or her sister, at once suggested "The Fair" to Mussorgsky, who turned it down at the time but returned to it a couple of years later.

In the meantime Rimsky-Korsakof was busy with other operatic matters. In February, 1872, "The Stone Guest" was produced and he eagerly attended the rehearsals to study the effect of his orchestration. Then, perhaps in consequence of Gedeonof's contact with the young nationalist composers in the course of the "Stone Guest" rehearsals, the "Mlada" commission came along. And, more important still, there was the fate of "The Maid of Pskof" (completed in

January) still undecided. The libretto had been sent to the dramatic censor, who was making all sorts of difficulties. For one thing, the picture of the semi-independent, republican constitution of the city of Pskof in the year 1570 was considered highly objectionable. Instead of a free city defending its rights, Pskof had to be shown as a rebellious city. Again, Ivan the Terrible was one of the principal characters, and according to an edict of Nicholas I in 1837, members of the House of Romanof might be represented on the stage in drama or tragedy *but not in opera*, since it would never do for a tsar to be shown doing anything so undignified as singing. (Boris Godunof, being a usurper, escaped this prohibition and presumably might have been shown dancing the *can-can*.) From this impasse Rimsky-Korsakof escaped by a typically Russian avenue. He turned to his new friend, the Minister of Marine. Krabbe was as good as his word; the machinery of court favouritism began to work, and the interest of the Grand Duke Constantine Nikolaevitch, the Tsar's brother, was enlisted on behalf of the new opera. It is true Rimsky-Korsakof had to give way in the matter of the republican popular assembly, but all other difficulties vanished. The Directorate of the Imperial Theatres accepted the work at once, in spite of the fact (according to Solovief and other unfriendly newspaper critics) that, like " Boris ", it had been rejected by the selection committee. In the meantime, " The Maid ", like most of the other new Russian operas of the period, was tried out privately in the composer's own circle, both at Krabbe's and at the Purgolds', Mussorgsky, Korsakof and the sisters all taking part.

Early in the summer of 1872 Rimsky-Korsakof left the apartment he had been sharing with Mussorgsky and took a room at Pargolovo, so as to be near his fiancée. On June 30th/July 12th they were married, Mussorgsky acting as best man, and went abroad for their honeymoon. They spent

July in Switzerland and among the Italian lakes, then in Milan and Venice, returning to Russia by way of Vienna and Warsaw in the middle of August. After a round of visits to relations they settled down in their house in Petersburg early in the autumn. Nicholas was twenty-eight, Nadejda four years younger.

Owing to their absence abroad the proof-reading of the vocal score of " The Maid ", made by Nadejda, had been left to Cui, who had done it very carelessly. Consequently the very rare first edition (published by Bessel) has a fine crop of misprints in both words and music, misprints which were the joy of unfriendly critics. N. F. Solovief, for instance, pouncing on an incorrectly printed tremolo, acidly remarked that " such ignorance of an elementary rule is rather surprising in the publication of a production by a professor of the Conservatoire ". Rehearsals began in the autumn, not too happily. Napravnik, thorough and conscientious as ever, was not quite successful in concealing his dislike of the work, which, like " Boris ", was a compromise between melodic, folk-songish opera of the Glinka type and realistic " truth " in the manner of " The Stone Guest ". (Moreover, the original " Maid of Pskof " was a very much cruder affair than the version which, as " Ivan the Terrible ", has reached Western Europe.) Petrof, who sang Ivan, was also dissatisfied with his part. But the first performance on January 1st/13th, 1873, at the Marinsky Theatre (for the benefit of Platonova, who sang the heroine) was entirely successful. The composer was called out " ten or fifteen times ", according to Solovief, and in spite of a bad press the opera was given nine times more before the season came to an end six weeks later. The revolutionary element in it, as in " Boris ", captured the young people and Borodin's students sang the rebel chorus from the Second Act about the corridors of the Army Medical Academy.

That might easily have had unpleasant consequences for the composer. But at this period Rimsky-Korsakof could hardly do anything wrong in the eyes of the authorities. Krabbe even created a new post with a handsome salary specially for him, that of Inspector of Naval Bands, and so put an end to the anomaly of a serving naval lieutenant who was also a professor at a musical conservatoire. Accordingly, in May, Rimsky-Korsakof took off his uniform and became a civil official with the rank of " collegiate assessor ". He was delighted with his new duties and entered upon them with a certain excess of zeal, bewildering the good bandmasters with his ridicule of the pearls of their repertoire, and hunting down bad instruments and wrong notes in the band-parts (" of which there were a great many ", he remarks) with the exuberance of a witch-doctor smelling out evil spirits. " The bands treated me as ' authority '—standing to attention " he recollected with naïve pleasure. In short, he made himself the terror of every naval band in Petersburg and Kronstadt. The fact that he knew very little about the technique of the band instruments was not the sort of thing to discourage a man like Rimsky-Korsakof, but it is characteristic that he at once set to work to study the instruments for himself. When he and Nadejda went to Pargolovo for the summer, he took with him a trombone, flute, clarinet and one or two other instruments, with a collection of diagrams and tutors, and " regardless of the neighbours " as he said, learned, if not to play them, at least *how* they were played. It is equally characteristic that, with this very elementary knowledge, he at once began to plan a colossal treatise on instrumentation, a book that was to contain a lengthy monograph on each instrument with innumerable sketches and tables and diagrams explaining the mechanism which he hardly understood himself. From Tyndall and Helmholtz he cooked up an introduction dealing with the acoustic laws underlying the construction of the instruments, and worked at this *magnum opus* off and on for two years before he finally abandoned it. Yet this was not wasted labour. He learned from it and from his intercourse with the naval bands " what " (as he said) " every German military bandmaster knows but what, unfortunately, artist-composers don't know ": " the difference between virtuoso-difficulties and impracticabilities " on each instrument. His natural sense of orchestral colour was gradually being reinforced by practical knowledge—a formidable combination, as he was to prove later.

Then, again, he was teaching himself harmony and counterpoint, studying the former from Tchaïkovsky's text-book, the latter from Cherubini's " Cours " and G. H. Bellermann's treatise. The Conservatoire Professor of Composition, composer of a successful opera and several successful orchestral works, conscientiously worked innumerable figured basses and *canti fermi* and harmonised countless simple melodies like any beginner, gradually educating himself during the next year or two, till by 1875 he could write a fugue as well as any fairly advanced counterpoint student at a German conservatoire. But in the meantime he was unable to resist the temptation to embody his dangerous " little learning " in practical composition. Just as he had embarked on his great treatise when he had only just begun to understand the mechanism of the instruments, he now—with only the most elementary knowledge of counterpoint—began nothing less than a symphony full of contrapuntal tricks, theme-combinations and so on. For the scherzo he used the old scherzo in 5/4 time, composed for the projected B minor Symphony of 1867 (and now provided with a trio composed during a steamer trip on one of the Italian lakes during his honeymoon). He worked at this so-called " Third " Symphony in C major during that summer of 1873 at Pargolovo in the intervals of his tours of band-inspection and his very immature flutings and trombonings. In August the imminence of a happy event sent the Rimsky-Korsakofs back to Petersburg, no doubt to the great joy of everyone within earshot, and on the 20th (September 1st) Nadejda presented her husband with their first child, Michael (" Misha ").[1]

Rimsky-Korsakof had for some time been conducting the orchestral class at the Conservatoire, but so far he had never made a public appearance as a conductor. However, he was asked that winter to conduct a choral and orchestral concert in aid of the Samara famine sufferers. He agreed and, after worrying himself nearly to death for a month beforehand, made a fairly successful debut (February 18th/March 2nd, 1874), satisfying almost everyone but the soloists he had to accompany. His programme was an all-Russian one with two novelties, his own new Symphony and the new version of Mussorgsky's " Destruction of Sennacherib ". Cui hailed the Symphony as " the best of all Mr. Korsakof's productions —the fruit of ripe thought, happy inspiration and strong talent combined with deep and solid technical knowledge ". But the rest of his friends disagreed. They simply thought it dull—and posterity has agreed with them. Even Borodin, more sympathetic than most, said it was very evidently the work of a professor who had put on his spectacles to write " *Eine grosse Symphonie in C* ".

Just before this concert Rimsky-Korsakof received from Balakiref, in his retirement, a very warm and affectionate letter wishing him success. But Balakiref, though he had completely disappeared from the musical world, had not resigned the Directorship of the Free School of Music, and that unfortunate institution, deprived of its founder and chief, was nearly bankrupt and slowly dying. Possibly as a consequence of Rimsky-Korsakof's appearance as a conductor, some of the members of the committee saw an opportunity of saving

---

[1] " Misha " became a Professor of Zoology. There were six other children : Sonia (b. 1875), Andrei (b. 1878), the famous musicologist, head of the Leningrad Public Library, Vladimir (" Volodia ") (b. 1882), Nadia (b. 1884), now the wife of the composer Steinberg, Masha (b. 1888) who died at the age of five, and Slavtchik (b. 1889) who died when only twelve months old.

the wreck, induced Balakiref to resign, and offered the Directorship to Rimsky-Korsakof, who accepted it in May, though he was unable to devote much time to the work till the following autumn and winter.

It was at this period that Mussorgsky began to regard Rimsky-Korsakof as a " traitor " to his old ideals. Their intimacy was beginning to be spoiled and Korsakof drew correspondingly nearer to Borodin, enlisting him as a fellow-student of instrumental technique. He seldom appeared at Borodin's for the evening without some wind instrument which they " studied together and amused themselves with ". Rimsky-Korsakof also set about enriching the repertoire of the brass and wood-wind naval bands and transcribed a number of works by Glinka, Meyerbeer, and others—the " Lohengrin " Prelude among the rest! In the summer he went with his wife and baby to Nikolaef on the Black Sea to reorganise the band of the naval garrison there. (Russia had recently denounced the Treaty of Paris which forbade her to maintain a Black Sea Fleet.) From Nikolaef they crossed by steamer to Sevastopol and visited the south of the Crimea. In Bakhtchisaraï, where there was then no hotel and they had to stay with some *mullah* opposite the famous Fountain of Tears which inspired Pushkin's " Fountain of Bakhtchisaraï ", Rimsky-Korsakof heard genuine eastern music for the first time. He was deeply impressed by it and by what he calls the " gypsy-musicians " who played in the streets from morning to night. When he returned to Bakhtchisaraï seven years later, he was disgusted to find that the unimaginative authorities had suppressed these picturesque minstrels as public nuisances.

Returning to St. Petersburg Rimsky-Korsakof organised and conducted in October a concert by the massed naval bands of the Petersburg and Kronstadt commands and took in hand the revitalisation of the Free School. He got a choir together and in March, 1875, gave a concert—the first Free

School concert since Balakiref's disappearance in 1872. But the programme was very different from the old "ultra-modern" Free School programmes. Rimsky-Korsakof, in the course of his contrapuntal studies, had discovered Bach and Palestrina, and the one-time progressivist staggered Petersburg with a programme in which the most modern composer was Haydn. The rest was all Palestrina and Allegri, excerpts from "Israel in Egypt" and three arias and the final chorus from Bach's "Matthew Passion" (two of them heard for the first time in Russia.) Korsakof pursued his own contrapuntal studies with exceptional industry that spring and summer, working his exercises even on the Petersburg-Kronstadt steamer as he went on his visits of inspection. That summer the exercises flowered—if that is the right word—into six fugues for piano, published as Op. 17, which he humbly submitted to his colleague, the theorist, Johannsen, for approval, and two three-part female choruses, Op. 13. They had already produced more monstrous fruit in a String Quartet in F, Op. 12, a first essay in chamber music which was performed by the Auer Quartet the following November. Anton Rubinstein thought it "showed promise" and Tchaïkovsky expressed inordinate admiration for the first movement, but the composer himself knew better. He was frankly ashamed of his "incessant fugato"—" I felt involuntarily that in this Quartet I was really not myself . . . Technique had not yet entered into my flesh and blood "—and he stayed away from the concert.

1875 was indeed a critical year for Rimsky-Korsakof. Others besides Mussorgsky considered him a "traitor" to the cause of progress. In fact all his old friends except Borodin regarded him as a lost soul. Balakiref was moved by the Free School concert programme to write him bitter reproaches for his "spiritual flabbiness", while Stassof wrote to Golenishchef-Kutuzof (September, 1875): "The Roman has not been sitting with folded hands; he has written sixty-one fugues (!!!) and a dozen or so canons.[1] I won't comment. *De mortuis* . . . ." Only Borodin, who had himself just horrified Stassof and Mussorgsky by beginning a string quartet—chamber music being frowned on in those quarters—took a different view. " Korsinka is fussing about with the Free School ", he wrote to Liubov Karmalina (April 15th/27th, 1875), " writing all sorts of counterpoints, learning and teaching all sorts of musical tricks. He's writing a course of instrumentation—phenomenal, there's never been anything like it; but he has no time at present and has laid it aside till he has some leisure . . . . For the present he is not writing any music . . . A lot of people are up in arms because Korsakof has turned back and taken to the study of musical antiquity. But that doesn't worry me. It's quite understandable: Korsakof developed in just the opposite way from me. He began with Glinka, Liszt and Berlioz—well, being surfeited with them, it's only natural that he should turn to a field which is unknown to him and which still has the interest of novelty." As for Tchaïkovsky, he considered " these innumerable contrapuntal exercises, these sixty fugues[2] and the host of other musical tricks—such a feat for the man who had written ' Sadko ' eight years before ", such " heroic exploits ", that he wanted " to proclaim it to the whole world ", to " bow down before " the other's " artistic modesty and strength of character ". (Though it is true Tchaïkovsky anticipated correctly, if he did not already know, that Rimsky-Korsakof would be one of the judges in the opera competition for which he had just submitted his " Vakula the Smith "!) But there was a real danger that in " making technique part of his flesh and blood ", Korsakof would entirely kill his own spontaneous creative talent. With

[1] According to Borodin, in a letter of only a week earlier, it was " 36 fugues and 16 canons ".

[2] How the number varies! Rimsky-Korsakof himself said later that the rumour that he had written *fifty* fugues was " a little exaggerated ", though he had forgotten the exact number.

his wife seriously ill from the birth of their second child, Sonia, he buried himself in his exercise-books and went on manufacturing dry little piano pieces (Op. 15) and *a capella* choruses (Op. 16). He even tortured a Russian folk-song into " Four Variations and a Fughetta " for four-part female choir, inflicting all these ingenuities on the Free School choral class.

He blushed for the " harmonic impurities " of his " Antar ", cleaned them up, entirely reorchestrated the work and, in this new form, conducted it at an R.M.S. concert in January, 1876. This was the first time the Society had played one of his compositions since Balakiref's departure, and even now Napravnik had declined to conduct " Antar " himself. Of the Free School concerts that season, the first (in February) was nearly all Bach and Handel,[1] while the second was entirely devoted to Russian music—which rehabilitated him in the eyes of his friends but wiped out the financial profit on the first concert. At the rehearsals, as he faithfully confesses in his memoirs, he occasionally lost his temper and spoke in a " too commanding tone ", a slip which he attributes to his naval habits. But the truth is that he was exceptionally mild and easy-going as a conductor and, on his own showing, a far from reliable one, losing his place in Beethoven's Fifth Symphony, bungling starts, and performing other feats of the same nature.

Rimsky-Korsakof's rescue from bone-dry academicism was effected by two main agencies, his study of folk-song and the editing of Glinka's opera scores. Already in 1875 he had been thinking of making a collection of folk-songs; now through Balakiref, who was beginning to reappear rather furtively in musical circles, he was approached by the latter's friend, T. I. Filippof, later Mussorgsky's official chief, to

---

[1] The " Kyrie ", " Qui sedes ", " Crucifixus " and " Dona nobis " from the B minor Mass; and " Then round about the starry throne ", " My faith and truth ", " Hear, Jacob's God ", " Great Dagon ", " Weep, Israel, weep ", " Glorious hero " and " Let their celestial concerts " from " Samson ".

collaborate in such a collection. Filippof was a keen amateur of folk-songs and Korsakof noted down forty of them from his singing and provided them with piano-accompaniments, work which had to be done all over again since the first version was " not simple and Russian enough " to satisfy him.[1] But the songs Filippof knew were mostly lyrical and comparatively modern, while Rimsky-Korsakof was much more interested in the ritual songs and singing games originally connected with ancient pagan customs, principally with the old Slavonic sun-worship. So, having dealt with Filippof's collection, he pressed ahead with his own monumental " Collection of One Hundred Russian Folk-Songs ", most of the work being done in 1876, though not actually completed till November, 1877. He took and reharmonised a number of the songs from older collections like that of Ivan Pratch, while the rest came from his mother, friends and acquaintances, and his recollections of his Uncle Peter. One of the most valuable collaborators—and almost the only genuine peasant contributor—was the Borodins' maid, Duniasha, the " A. E. Vinogradova " whose help is acknowledged. On one occasion Korsakof sat late into the night trying to get the right rhythmic notation for one of her songs (No. 72). The harmonisation also gave him a great deal of trouble. Melgunof did not startle Russian musicians with his revolutionary, but perfectly correct, theory of the polyphonic nature of Russian folk-music till three or four years later, and Rimsky-Korsakof had no idea that his own " truly Russian " harmonisations were on the wrong track. (In any case, when Melgunof's collection did appear, Rimsky-Korsakof thought it " barbarous ".) But it has long been recognised that his famous collection, valuable as it is artistically, is far from authentic as a scientific record of Russian folk-music. Nevertheless his study of the old customs in which so many of the songs had originated was to have an extraordinarily fertilising effect

[1] For some reason the collection was not published till 1882.

on his own creative imagination. " Pictures of the old pagan days and their spirit arose before my mind's eye with great clearness, and attracted me irresistibly."

But for the time being he remained entangled in terribly contrapuntal chamber music, the String Sextet in A and the Quintet in B flat for piano and wind. Both were submitted for a competition promoted by the R.M.S.—and both were unsuccessful. That summer, too, he wrote the first chapter of his fascinating, if not in every respect completely reliable, " Record of my Musical Life ", though, having made this beginning, he laid the manuscript aside for eleven or twelve years. He also wrote two mixed choruses (Op. 18) and some unaccompanied male choruses (Op. 23) that summer, and planned a sort of Handelian cantata, " Alexander Nevsky ", to words by Mey. A little later came some even more wonderful compositions: a Trombone Concerto, " Variations on a Theme of Glinka's " for oboe, and a " Concerstück " for clarinet, all with wind-band accompaniment, written, of course, for the naval bands.

It was at this period, the autumn of 1876, that Balakiref once more began to play an active part in Rimsky-Korsakof's life. Balakiref sent him private pupils in elementary theory, mostly dabbling young ladies who benefited Korsakof's pocket more than their own musical culture,[1] and invited him and his young pupil, Anatol Liadof, to collaborate with him in the magnificent edition of Glinka's operas which he was preparing on the commission of Liudmila Shestakova. The work occupied them, off and on, for four years; and, though the result was not a model piece of editing, the intensive study of Glinka's beautifully transparent scoring and simple, natural part-writing reawakened and even deepened Rimsky-Korsakof's old passion for the composer of " Ruslan " and led him back from the early eighteenth century to the nineteenth.

[1] Among them a certain Mme. Glazunova, who in December, 1879, also sent along her fourteen-year-old son, Alexander.

Balakiref may have been an " altogether changed man " in some respects, but his character was in no way changed. He at once adopted his old attitude of mentor to Rimsky-Korsakof, and at first the other meekly gave way " from old habit and from my submissive nature ". Balakiref censured Korsakof for entering the chamber music competition, began to meddle in the affairs of the Free School and the constitution of its concert programmes, and interfered in Rimsky-Korsakof's revision of his " Maid of Pskof ". Before long their relations became badly strained.

The colossal task of rewriting his opera, which occupied Rimsky-Korsakof from the autumn of 1876 until January, 1878, originated with the idea of adding a prologue based on the First Act of Mey's play (which had been cut out of the first version), and in the composer's dissatisfaction with the " harmonic exaggerations ", the " absence of a contrapuntal element " and the orchestration of the opera in its original form. Now Balakiref demanded the insertion in Act IV of a chorus of begging pilgrims, based on the song of " Alexeï the Man of God " (from the Filippof collection of folk-songs), not because begging pilgrims had anything to do with the action, but simply because he liked the tune; Korsakof himself thought it would be nice to introduce a " Royal hunt and storm " like Berlioz's in " Les Troyens "; and in this absurdly childish spirit he proceeded to recast the work, entirely ruining it by the forcible introduction of quite uncalled for " contrapuntal interest ", though, curiously enough, he still avoided the use of valve-horns and trumpets in the reorchestration. On the whole the new version pleased no one, neither his friends nor his wife nor himself. He had got rid of the amateurish crudities and turned " The Maid " into a respectable, professorial opera but—" I felt myself that it was long, dry and heavy ". He made a half-hearted attempt to get the new version produced and was annoyed, rather than discouraged, by its failure. " I felt it was all for the best" and that, at any rate, " my course of education was finished ", though he still wrote a few more rather academic piano pieces, Opp. 10 and 11. The " chorus of begging pilgrims " was almost immediately published separately as Op. 20, while the composer made an orchestral suite of " Music to Mey's Drama, ' The Maid of Pskof ' " from the new miniature overture to the Prologue and four of the entr'actes.

Even while still engaged on this unlucky second version of " The Maid ", during the summer of 1877, Rimsky-Korsakof's thoughts had been turning more and more often to his wife's cherished idea of an opera based on Gogol's " May Night ", and he actually began it in February, 1878—with the Third Act. He wrote the full score at once, sometimes working far into the night. The composition went so quickly and easily that by the end of April not only the bulk of the Third Act but two numbers of the First were finished and could be played to Mussorgsky, Cui, Stassof and the young Liadof. They must have felt that Korsakof was himself again, for everything in " May Night " is lyrical or humorous and delicately coloured, shot through with folk-song and with scoring frankly modelled on Glinka's (even with natural brass still). Of counterpoint for counterpoint's sake there is hardly a trace. However, Rimsky-Korsakof had an opportunity to gratify his love of " musical tricks " that spring and summer in the famous " Paraphrases " in which he collaborated with Borodin, Cui and Liadof. Indeed, he was so much more industrious than the rest that some of his pieces—a sonatina, a chorale (" Eine feste Burg "), a " recitative *alla Bach* " and others—had to be omitted from the printed edition.

The R.M.S. had organised several concerts of Russian music in Paris in connection with the World Exhibition during the summer of 1878, and it was proposed to send Rimsky-Korsakof, incompetent conductor as he was, to direct them.

He regarded the matter as quite settled when, fortunately for the credit of Russian music, it was decided to send Nicholas Rubinstein instead. There was a storm, and for a time Rimsky-Korsakof avoided Rubinstein during the latter's visits to Petersburg. The composition of " May Night " proceeded smoothly at the summer-villa at Ligovo, being interrupted only by a few duty visits to Kronstadt and by the birth of a second son, Andrei. The full score was finished, all but the Overture, in October. (It seems that, in spite of Rimsky-Korsakof's statement in his memoirs, the Overture was not written till the following summer.) The vocal score was finished that winter; the work was at once accepted by the Theatre Directorate; and the choral rehearsals began in the spring of 1879. Even before this, three choruses from the new opera had been performed at the Free School concerts.

From lack of money the School had given no public concerts the previous season, but in January and February of 1879 Rimsky-Korsakof conducted four. They are important landmarks in the history of Russian music, for in addition to the " May Night " pieces, they included first performances of Borodin's Polovtsian Dances and two other numbers from " Prince Igor " (hurriedly orchestrated specially for these concerts) and of the " Pimen's cell " scene from " Boris ". At the fourth concert there was a disaster in a Liszt concerto, caused by a nervous pianist. " I literally wept for shame ", Korsakof confessed, " when I reached home after the concert ". Nevertheless we find him, undismayed, conducting a couple of concerts in Moscow for the pianist Shostakovsky a month or two later.

That summer, again spent at Ligovo, the composer wrote a string quartet entirely based on Russian folk-tunes, the movements being entitled respectively " In the Fields ", " In the Maidens' Room ", " Khorovod " and " At the Monastery ". It was tried through by the 'cellist K. Y.

Davidof, who had succeeded Azantchevsky as Director of the Conservatoire in 1876, and his quartet. But the work displeased the composer and it was never publicly performed though, as we shall see, none of the material was wasted. He also took with him to Ligovo another scene from " Igor ", intending to " revise ", complete, and score it in postal consultation with Borodin. But Borodin, who had accepted his friend's pressing offer of assistance only with reluctance, made it clear that he did not care for the idea, and nothing came of it. Before returning to Petersburg Korsakof began " an orchestral piece of fantastic character on Pushkin's Prologue to ' Ruslan and Liudmila ' ". The Prologue enumerates all the characteristic figures of Russian folk-lore and it appears from a letter to his friend the Moscow critic, S. N. Kruglikof, that the composer intended to name it after one of the most striking of these figures: " I've done nothing during the summer." (Evidently the quartet counted as " nothing ".) " Only begun a musical picture ' Baba Yaga ', but it's not going very well and I don't know whether I shall go on with it yet for a while." Balakiref also disapproving of the fragment, Korsakof laid it aside and instead set about the revision and reorchestration of his early " Overture on Three Russian Themes ", which occupied his spare time throughout the winter.

Of " spare " time he really had very little, for in addition to his official duties there were four Free School concerts to prepare—with Balakiref butting in at rehearsals and, much to his annoyance, publicly teaching him how to conduct; he had to orchestrate Mussorgsky's " Persian Dances " from " Khovanshchina " so that they should be ready in time for the concert (and he characteristically took the opportunity " to correct a great deal of the harmony and part-writing "); there were the administrative affairs of the Free School to attend to; and the rehearsals of " May Night " having begun in October, he had to be present to accompany the soloists. Orchestral rehearsals of his opera began in the middle of December (just a week before the fourteen-year-old Glazunof came for his first lesson) and the first performance took place, after several postponements, on January 9th/21st, 1880. Napravnik conducted, Kommissarjevsky sang Levko, and another father of a famous son, F. I. Stravinsky, took the part of the Headman. It was a success but by no means a triumph. Two numbers were encored and the opera was repeated seven times more before the end of the season, but after a year or so it was withdrawn from the current repertoire.[1]

But Rimsky-Korsakof was already pressing ahead with a third opera. As early as 1874 he had read Ostrovsky's charming play, " The Snow Maiden ", for which Tchaïkovsky had supplied the incidental music, but had not been impressed by it. It had struck him as too fantastic. " Why? Were the ideas of the 'sixties still alive in me, or was I in the grip of the fashion of the 'seventies for ' subjects taken from *life* '? Or was I caught in the stream of Mussorgsky's naturalism? Probably all three." But now, reading it again in February, 1880, his eyes were opened to its " marvellous poetic beauty ". " I at once wanted to write an opera on this subject, and the more I thought about it the deeper I fell in love with Ostrovsky's legend. My mild interest in the ancient Russian customs and heathen pantheism flamed up. There seemed no better subject in the whole world than this, no more poetic figures than Snow Maiden, Lel or the Spring Fairy, no better realm than the kingdom of the Berendeys with their marvellous Tsar, no better religion and philosophy of life than the worship of the

---

[1] From this period (January, 1880) dates Korsakof's contribution to the series of " living pictures " projected by Tatishchef and Korvin-Krukovsky, a piece " Slava " for chorus and orchestra, Op. 21, furbished up from an old fugal exercise of 1876 on the well-known folk-song used in the coronation scene of " Boris " and in Korsakof's own " Overture on Three Russian Themes ".

Sun God, Yarilo." He at once sketched out the final sun-worshipping chorus. " My head was immediately thronged with motives, themes and chord-progressions, and the moods and colours of the different moments of the action presented themselves to my imagination, first elusively, then more and more clearly." All these fragments were noted down in " a fat book of music-paper ". Visiting Moscow in April to conduct a concert, the composer took the opportunity to call on Ostrovsky himself and get his permission to adapt his play. The dramatist willingly granted it, gave him a copy of the play and later expressed not only his delight in Korsakof's wonderful music " but his approval of Korsakof's libretto. " I have found very few verses which, in my opinion, need revision ", he wrote to the composer in November.

That summer the Rimsky-Korsakofs found a new summer residence on the Stelëvo estate, twenty miles from Luga. " The house, though old, was comfortable; it had a lovely great shady garden with fruit-trees." They arrived on May 18th/30th. " For the first time in my life I spent the summer in the heart of the Russian countryside. Everything delighted me. The beautiful position, the delightful woods, the great forest of Volchinets, the fields of rye, buckwheat, oats, flax, and millet, the host of scattered trees, the little stream where we bathed, the nearness of the great Lake Vrevo, the isolated villages with their ancient Russian names—all this enchanted me. The lovely garden with its multitude of cherry- and apple-trees, currant-bushes, strawberries, gooseberries, with its flowering lilacs, its host of wild-flowers and the ceaseless singing of the birds—all this peculiarly harmonised with my pantheistic feeling at the time and with my delight in the subject of ' The Snow Maiden '. Some thick and twisted bough or tree-stump, overgrown with moss, would seem to me the Wood Spirit or his dwelling; the forest of Voltchinets, the forbidden forest of the tale; the summit of Mount Kopytetsky, Yarilo's mountain; the threefold echo which we heard from our balcony—the voices of the wood spirits." And years afterwards Rimsky-Korsakof confessed to Yastrebtsef that at that period he actually " began to *pray to nature*—to a crooked old tree-stump, to some willow or century-old oak, to the forest stream, to the lake, even to a great head of cabbage, to a black ram or at the cockcrow scattering the sorcery of the night. In all these things I saw something peculiar and supernatural. It sometimes seemed to me that animals, birds, and even trees and flowers, know more of the magic and fantastic than human beings do; that they understand the language of nature far better! You will say that all this was fearfully exaggerated and illogical, and yet it seemed to me that it was all really so! I warmly believed in it all, as a child would, like a dreamer surrendering himself to his fancies, and yet, strangely enough, in those minutes the world seemed to me nearer, more understandable, and I was somehow merged with it! And even now "—that was in 1894—" when the period of the summer solstice has lost some of its old significance for me, I still can't altogether renounce every kind of pantheistic idea ". We must remember that pantheism was very much in the air in Russia at that period. Tchekhof was a pantheist and, according to Merejkovsky, the great majority of cultured Russians were toying with some variety or other of pantheism.

In that extraordinary state of mind Rimsky-Korsakof " composed all day and every day " all through the hot and thundery summer, though he found time to help his wife make jam and find mushrooms. With nothing but a cracked old piano, a whole tone flat (so that he called it his " piano in B flat "), to try over what he had composed, he began writing directly in the full score as he had done with " May Night ". But his thoughts ran far ahead of his fingers and he was obliged to content himself with making an ordinary vocal score. The whole opera, one of his most delightful works, was finished in this form on August 12th/24th! Nor was it his only work that summer, as appears from a letter to Kruglikof (July 21st/August 2nd); " I've sketched out the whole of my ' Legend ' in score; it only remains to put the finishing touches, i.e. to add a bit here and there in the *tuttis*. Have also roughed out the instrumentation of my Russian quartet, turning it into a sinfonietta." The " Legend " in question was the orchestral piece, Op. 29, begun the summer before and originally called " Baba Yaga ", while the " Russian quartet " was, of course, the one based on folk-tunes. Korsakof completed the " Legend " before returning to Petersburg in September, but the Sinfonietta, Op. 31, consisting of the first three movements of the quartet, drastically revised as well as orchestrated, was laid aside and not completed till the summer of 1884. (The material of the fourth movement of the quartet was used years afterwards in the opera " Sadko ".) Rimsky-Korsakof at once set to work at the orchestration of " The Snow Maiden ", this time with chromatic brass, beginning it on September 7th/19th and finishing the six-hundred-page score on March 26th/April 7th, 1881. Having completed it, he felt himself " a mature musician, standing firmly on my feet as an opera composer ". To Kruglikof he expressed his view of his own position in relation to his friends with characteristic candour: " Owing to deficient technique Balakiref writes little, Borodin slowly, Cui perfunctorily, Mussorgsky untidily and often nonsensically. Don't imagine that I've altered my opinion of their compositions. If only these people had good, sound technique, what mightn't they do! Although I'm perfectly sincere in saying that I consider them far more talented than myself, I don't envy them a straw."

In January, Rimsky-Korsakof conducted his new " Legend " at an R.M.S. concert; in February, the first Free School concert of the season. Three others had been advertised, but the assassination of Alexander II, at the beginning of March, put an end to all concert-giving. Mussorgsky, who had appeared to take the applause for his " Destruction of Sennacherib " at the Free School concert, was taken ill shortly afterwards and died a fortnight after the Tsar, and Rimsky-Korsakof undertook the colossal task of preparing his dead friend's works for publication. The labour was an unselfish one and occupied nearly two years of valuable time, no mean sacrifice, and it is infinitely regrettable that, owing to the pedantic spirit in which he carried it out it has earned him more abuse than gratitude. Perhaps his own excuse is the best: " If Mussorgsky's compositions are fated to last unfaded for fifty years after his death, then an archæologically exact edition can be issued " (which is exactly what has happened). " In the meantime what was needed was an edition for performance, for practical artistic purposes, for the making known of his great talent, not for the study of his personality and artistic transgressions."

In June Korsakof went to Nikolaef again to inspect the bands of the Black Sea Fleet, and conduct them in an open-air concert. " I've been doling out thanks and praise ", he wrote to Nadejda, " and generally playing the Khlestakof " —the comic hero of Gogol's " Revizor "—" a stupid rôle that doesn't suit me a bit. I never know how to carry it out with the proper solemnity and importance ". His duty finished he was joined by Nadejda for a holiday trip in the Crimea. At the hotel at Yalta, run by Stassof's son-in-law, they met a number of old acquaintances, including Korsakof's old commander, Zeleny of the " Almaz ", and made a new one, the young Felix Blumenfeld. From Yalta they went on to Sevastopol and thence to Constantinople for three days, returning home by way of Odessa and Kief, and spending the rest of the summer with the children at Taitsa.

For at least a year Rimsky-Korsakof had been anxious to wash his hands of the Free School, which was constantly in financial difficulties and which occupied a great deal of time to little purpose. The choir had too many bad voices; the women were all too old; there were very few good men; the tenors were woolly. And so on, and so on. In short, the Free School choir was like almost every other amateur choir that has ever existed in any country. All that induced him to persevere was the opportunity it gave him of performing whatever he liked—and the fact that he saw no alternative to himself, except Liadof, who was not energetic enough, and not yet well enough known. It now seemed to him that as Balakiref was once more taking an active interest in the School the original Director might as well resume his post. Accordingly, he resigned in September and Balakiref, after a show of hesitation, accepted the committee's invitation and again took over the direction. In his memoirs, which are marked throughout by an unpleasant tone of hostility towards Balakiref, Rimsky-Korsakof gives a rather different account of this episode. He says that " Balakiref's constant interference in the affairs of the School became intolerable for me ". But his correspondence shows that that was quite a secondary reason. He frankly told Kruglikof at the time that Balakiref was " a thousand times more suited to the position than I."

Rimsky-Korsakof's immediate task was the editing and scoring of Mussorgsky's " Khovanshchina "; the last act, with which he began, was completed and orchestrated by December. And in the meantime, rehearsals of his own " Snow Maiden " were going ahead. Nadejda, although pregnant, insisted on being present at them, and actually gave birth to a son (Volodia) just after attending one of the last. In consequence, she was unable to attend the first performance on January 29th/February 10th, 1882, and her husband, much distraught and (it appears) slightly intoxicated, hung about behind the scenes in a state of profound gloom, hearing practically nothing of his music. Like " May Night ", the new opera had reasonable success and a bad press, even from Cui.

The Third Act of "Khovanshchina" was finished in May, the First and Second at Stelëvo during the summer, the Fourth after Korsakof's return to St. Petersburg. The "Night on the Bare Mountain" at first defeated his efforts to make a "practical edition" of it, but Mussorgsky's other smaller works were soon polished up and at once published by Bessel. A reorchestration, with chromatic brass, of his own suite from the second version of "The Maid of Pskof" also dates from this period.

The stay at Stelëvo was interrupted in August by a fortnight's visit to Moscow for the All-Russian Art and Industrial Exhibition, a visit which had unexpectedly important consequences. Korsakof, who had been invited to conduct a couple of concerts, had included in one of his programmes the sixteen-year-old Sasha Glazunof's First Symphony. "Before the first rehearsal of the Symphony, a tall, handsome man came up to me.... introduced himself as Mitrofan Petrovitch Belaief and asked permission to attend all the rehearsals. Belaief, a passionate lover of music, had been so completely enraptured by Glazunof's Symphony at its first performance at the Free School" (in March, under Balakiref) "that he had come to Moscow specially to hear it again". The meeting of Rimsky-Korsakof and Belaief is a milestone in the history of Russian music.

The orchestration of "Khovanshchina" being practically completed,[1] Rimsky-Korsakof again found time for original composition. His Piano Concerto, based on a Russian theme, but frankly Lisztian in design, was finished on January 3rd/15th, 1883. But he was on the eve of a fresh appointment, which, at first, allowed him little time for creative work.

[1] The opera was rejected by a majority vote of the opera committee in April, and more than a quarter of a century was to pass before Mussorgsky's second opera was given on the Imperial stage!

Among the wholesale changes consequent on the accession of Alexander III, the long reign of the seventy-six-year-old Bakhmetef as Intendant of the Imperial Chapel at last came to an end. (He had been Intendant since 1861.) But his successor, Count Sheremetef, was not even an amateur musician, and it became necessary to revive the post of Musical Director, as had been done in the days of Glinka and the younger Lvof. Thanks to the wire-pulling of Filippof, who had great influence both in Government circles and with the Holy Synod, Balakiref was, in February, 1883, appointed to the Directorship, with Rimsky-Korsakof as his assistant. In May the entire Chapel were obliged to spend three weeks in Moscow for the coronation ceremonies and, although his family moved to Taitsa for the summer, the journeys to the Chapel at Old Peterhof twice a week left Korsakof little time for the composition of anything but a little church music. In November he writes: " I'm very busy with the Chapel and not writing anything. Nor do I want to. It seems to me that I've written a full stop after ' Snow Maiden ', and that the songs, Concerto and religious music are only in the nature of reminiscences of days long past. My head at the moment is simply a Torricellian vacuum." Rimsky-Korsakof was at first genuinely interested in his new work and, in view of his expanding family, was no doubt glad of the additional salary (2,300 rubles a year); at any rate he had moved into a bigger town house in the autumn. (In September, 1889, he was given quarters in the new official buildings of the Chapel.) On the other hand, he lost his other official post in March, 1884. Krabbe had been supplanted by a new Minister of Marine who, in the interests of economy, abolished the Inspectorship of Naval Bands. And already in January, in less than a year, Korsakof began to find his new duties " boring and dry ". " I'm writing nothing ", he tells Kruglikof again.

In every way Rimsky-Korsakof's life was changing. The

old circle of friends was loosening. Mussorgsky was dead; he saw little of Cui; Balakiref now moved mostly in a new circle of his own, a coterie pious rather than musical. Of the old band, only Borodin and Stassof were still frequent visitors at the Rimsky-Korsakofs'. Instead there were new faces, mostly ex-pupils who were now on the footing of friends— Liadof, Glazunof, Blumenfeld, Ippolitof-Ivanof and Arensky —trained musicians very different in outlook from the hot-headed young amateurs who had banded together in the early 'sixties. And now this circle found a new focus in the house of the Mæcenas, M. P. Belaief, a curious character—hater of women, masterful, hospitable, good-hearted, brutally frank. Belaief, himself an amateur viola-player, was passionately fond of chamber-music, and every Friday the circle gathered at his house to play and hear string quartets. At 1 a.m. they would adjourn to supper; after that Glazunof or one of the other young men would play through some new composition. They seldom broke up till three in the morning, and even then Belaief would carry off some of the livelier members to continue the festivity at a restaurant—a practice of which the temperate and strictly moral Rimsky-Korsakof strongly disapproved. In this atmosphere the younger composers were naturally encouraged to write, bring and try out chamber-music—especially as Belaief made it a practice to " christen " every new work generously with champagne. The immediate result was an extraordinary crop of Russian quartet music, mostly of a rather light kind, which Belaief himself launched into publicity.

Having had Glazunof's First Symphony printed at his own expense, in score, parts and piano-duet arrangement, by the Leipzig firm of Röder, he began to issue the works of his other new friends in the same manner, and so found himself embarked on a career as a music-publisher. In the same lavish way, in March, 1884, he hired a hall and the Opera orchestra for a private rehearsal of some of Glazunof's works; in

November, 1885, financed a public concert of Russian orchestral music; and in 1886 founded a regular series of concerts, the "Russian Symphony Concerts". Rimsky-Korsakof was, naturally, at Belaief's elbow as his adviser in all these matters, and a large batch of his works, early and later, was at once published by the new firm, with opus-numbers in very misleading sequence. Cui, it may be mentioned, had very little connection with the Belaief circle; Balakiref, none at all.

All this time Rimsky-Korsakof remained quite unproductive, though busily engaged in wiping out the sins of his musical past. In March, 1884, a day or two after the above-mentioned private performance of Glazunof's First Symphony, he took out the score of his own "naïve and youthful" First Symphony. It seemed to him that, brushed up, it might be of use to amateur orchestras, and he spent the early part of the summer in revising and reorchestrating it. Among other changes he transposed it up a semitone to E minor and altered the sequence of movements, putting the *andante* before the scherzo. In this form it at last got into print, being published by Bessel. For the rest he finished the orchestration of the Sinfonietta and in August began the scherzo of a Fourth Symphony. But this came to nothing after only four days' work, and the composer devoted the rest of the summer and autumn to the writing of a harmony text-book, primarily for the use of his young students, the lads of the Imperial Chapel, whose musical education was in his hands. At this period he was completely in the rut of administrative routine, and he declined even to change one rut for another when Tchaïkovsky, in April, 1885, sounded him as to his willingness to accept the Directorship of the Moscow Conservatoire.

The summer of 1885 passed just as unproductively at Taitsa and in visits to the Chapel at Peterhof. Still living in his musical past, he now began to brood over his unlucky

Third Symphony, and revised and rescored the first movement. A melancholy change from the white-hot inspiration of the summer of 1880 at Stelëvo! Nor did a two months' holiday in the Caucasus with Nadejda in the summer of 1886 reawaken his creative impulse. The lovely scenery around the Caucasian spas inspired him to nothing but the rewriting of the third movement of the Third Symphony. Piatigorsk, Tiflis, the steamer trip to Batum, Yalta and Simferopol in the Crimea, all gave him delightful memories, but nothing more. He went back to Taitsa with no other idea than the futile attempt to breathe life into the dry bones of the Symphony, a labour accomplished without much success soon after his return to Petersburg in September. He did break his long silence that winter with the first movement of the " B-la-F " Quartet, in which he collaborated with Borodin, Liadof and Glazunof in celebrating Belaief's name-day in November. But the movement is hardly one of his most masterly compositions. Nor did the " Fantasia on Russian Themes " for violin and orchestra, written for Krasnokutsky, the violin teacher of the Imperial Chapel, suggest that the composer was on the eve of a fresh burst of creative activity. Though the themes are attractive, their treatment is of slight interest, the orchestral part being very evidently written for the pupils' orchestra of the Chapel. And yet the piece was to have a most brilliant sequel.

In February, 1887, almost the last link between Rimsky-Korsakof's past and his present was broken by the death of Borodin. It is recorded that he spent a sleepless night when he heard the news. Only four months before (October 15th/27th) at the very first of the new " Russian Symphony Concerts " financed by Belaief, Rimsky-Korsakof had conducted his version of Mussorgsky's " Night on the Bare Mountain " and so closed his account, as he thought, with one dead friend. Now it fell to him to carry out the same duty for another. Above all, there was " Prince Igor " to be finished and orchestrated. " Well, now there will be an end to ' Igor ' ", someone had said when Borodin died. And Rimsky-Korsakof, hearing the remark, determined to make it true in a sense not thought of by the speaker. With Glazunof he set about the work in the spring, and it went ahead by leaps and bounds during the summer, uninterrupted even by the duty visits to the Chapel at Peterhof—for Glazunof happened to be spending the summer there, and they had plenty of opportunities for consultation. Instead of Taitsa, the Rimsky-Korsakofs had taken a new villa at Nikolskoe, on Lake Nelaï, and the air must have worked beneficially on the composer's dormant faculties for he took up the sketches for a violin fantasia on Spanish themes, which he had thought of writing as a companion-piece to his Russian fantasia, and used them instead for a purely orchestral work, the famous " Spanish Capriccio ", a piece of virtuoso orchestral writing which seems to glitter with all the power and brilliance accumulated during the six years of almost complete silence since " The Snow Maiden ". That the orchestral effect of the " Capriccio " is the " very essence of the composition, not its mere dressing-up ", the composer was careful to insist himself. The " Capriccio " completed on July 23rd/August 4th, Rimsky-Korsakof returned to the orchestration of " Igor " and, incidentally, wrote another chapter of the memoirs tentatively begun eleven years before.

That year only three composers collaborated in the quartet for Belaief's name-day (" Jour de Fête "), Korsakof contributing the finale. But the dead comrade was commemorated in the first Russian Symphony Concert of the season, which was entirely devoted to Borodin's compositions. At the fifth concert, December 5th/17th, Rimsky-Korsakof conducted the first performance of the " Spanish Capriccio " which was received with such enthusiasm that it had to be repeated. The first rehearsal had been interrupted again and again by the applause of the orchestra, and the composer gracefully returned thanks by dedicating the work to them. The " Capriccio " was immediately followed by two other orchestral works of the same exceptionally brilliant type—the " Easter Overture " and " Sheherazade ", both sketched in Petersburg in the early months of 1888 and, as usual, completed in the country (this year at Nejgovitsky, some twelve miles from Luga). " Sheherazade " was finished on July 26th/August 7th, almost exactly a year after the completion of the " Capriccio ". These three compositoins, Korsakof considered, " close a period of my work, at the end of which my orchestration had attained a considerable degree of virtuosity and warm sonority without Wagnerian influence, limiting myself to the normally constituted orchestra used by Glinka ".

But Rimsky-Korsakof was no longer to live in virginal innocence and almost complete ignorance of the mature Wagner. That very winter Neumann's Travelling Opera Company visited Petersburg and gave the whole of the " Ring " for the first time in Russia, at the Marinsky Theatre, Karl Muck conducting. Korsakof and Glazunof attended every rehearsal, following from the score. " Wagner's handling of the orchestra astonished both of us ", says Rimsky-Korsakof, " and from this time onward Wagner's methods gradually permeated our orchestral writing ". It is strange that a composer of forty-four who had just written three such masterpieces of orchestration as the " Capriccio ", the " Easter Overture " and " Sheherazade " should have been so ready to pick up someone else's tricks. Actually, the first fruit of Wagner's influence on Korsakof was his orchestration of the polonaise from " Boris ", which he considered Mussorgsky had scored very ineffectively. The conducting of all six of the Russian Symphony Concerts that winter, " Sheherazade " and the " Easter Overture " both being given for the first time on December 3rd/15th, left Rimsky-Korsakof little leisure for original composition, but he reorchestrated his early " Serbian Fantasia " and in January actually began to tinker again at his " Maid of Pskof ". But a trifling incident sent his thoughts off at a fresh angle.

On the second anniversary of Borodin's death (that is, on February 15th/27th, 1889) a party of friends—Stassof, Glazunof, Liadof, Belaief and the Rimsky-Korsakofs—gathered at his old house " to spend the evening together in memory of the dear fellow ". Among other of his manuscripts which they played over and discussed was that of the finale of his Fourth Act of " Mlada ", which Korsakof made up his mind to orchestrate. " In the middle of our conversation and our reminiscences of Borodin, Liadof all of a sudden remarked that ' Mlada ' would make a suitable subject for me. Without hesitation, I replied, ' Very well, I'll get on with it at once.' " To Stassof's great delight, the subject completely captured his fancy. He determined to rewrite the original unsatisfactory libretto himself and to lay the music out on the most generous scale, with full Wagnerian orchestra. The revision of " The Maid of Pskof " was postponed indefinitely; ideas for " Mlada " began to accumulate.

The composition of the new opera was interrupted in the summer by a visit to Paris for the World Exhibition. Belaief was financing two symphony concerts of Russian music by the Colonne Orchestra in the Palais du Trocadéro and Rimsky-Korsakof was to conduct both. Sending the children with his mother to Nejgovitsky, he and Nadejda set out with Belaief, Glazunof and the pianist Lavrof. The concerts were successful from an artistic point of view, but as Belaief with truly Russian philosophy, had done very little to advertise them, on the ground that those who were really interested were bound to find out about them in any case, the audiences were very poor. Rimsky-Korsakof was no lover of the Parisians, and he has left us some caustic impressions of an official dinner " after which a repulsively fat old operetta singer sang " and of some of the musicians with whom he came in contact. "Delibes gave me the impression of a simple, amiable man, Massenet—that of an artful fox; Augusta Holmes was a very *décolletée* person; Messager struck me as rather colourless...." and so on. From the playing of panpipes in a Hungarian band and the music accompanying the Algerian dancing girls at the Exhibition, he took one or two hints for "Mlada". But when the concerts were over the Rimsky-Korsakofs left their companions as soon as possible and made an excursion to Switzerland and the Salzkammergut, returning by way of Vienna. In July they rejoined the children at Nejgovitsky, where the composition of "Mlada" proceeded at such a rate that on August 31st/September 12th, Rimsky-Korsakof could report to Kruglikof: "Liadof gave me the idea of writing 'Mlada' on February 15th and on August 15th I wrote the last note of the draft; in other words, all this has taken just six months, to say nothing of a month and a half spent over the examinations, a month of travelling abroad and two weeks spent in making the duet arrangement of 'Sheherazade'." (He notes in his memoirs that "the Wagnerian system of *leitmotifs* considerably hastened the process of composition".) On the other hand the scoring for an exceptionally large orchestra was to take unusually long and was moreover subjected to all sorts of interruptions.

In April, 1890, Rimsky-Korsakof was invited to go to Brussels to conduct a concert of Russian music in the Théâtre de la Monnaie. Belgium was just then at the height of her enthusiasm for Russian music, excited by the visits of Borodin and Cui, and Rimsky-Korsakof was fêted and made much of by the leading Belgian musicians, who appear to have impressed him much more favourably than the Parisian ones. But he returned from Brussels to find Nadejda dangerously ill with diphtheria; and Andrei soon caught the infection. "Everything in the flat is turned upside-down", he writes in May. " The children have been sent away to different houses; I've had to arrange for them to be sent into the country as soon as possible...The present year has been very unlucky for me; I've had nothing but dangers and commotion, and all this has descended on my unfortunate ' Mlada ', which will probably be my last composition.... (at any rate, the last important one)." In the summer they all, with his eighty-seven-year-old mother, moved as usual to Nejgovitsky, where he found time to orchestrate Borodin's " Mlada " finale, besides working at his own opera. But in August, his mother fell ill and had to be taken to Petersburg, where she died on the 31st/September 12th. However, three days later the composer was able to inform Kruglikof that " I finished the orchestral score of ' Mlada ' some days ago ". But the same ill-fortune pursued him till the end of the year. The first performance of " Igor " in October brought him much satisfaction. But the festivities, including a concert, with which his friends and pupils celebrated the twenty-fifth anniversary of his career as a composer in December (reckoning from the performance of his First Symphony) were streaked with unpleasantness owing to a squabble with Balakiref, who curtly refused to attend the official lunch. The same month the Rimsky-Korsakofs lost their baby Slavtchik, and the second youngest child, the two-year-old Masha, fell ill directly afterwards.

In February, 1891, the Third Act of " Mlada " was given a concert performance at one of Belaief's concerts and the work was accepted by the Theatre Directorate. That disposed of, Korsakof again returned to the revision of " The Maid of Pskof ", discarding the second version as a whole and basing this third and final version mainly on the first. He also entirely rescored it, the bulk of the work being done between April, 1891 and April, 1892. With yet another revision made in 1891, a fresh orchestration of " Sadko ", " I closed my account with my past. Not one of my major works *of the period before 'May Night'* remained in its original form ". But nothing new came from him. The outburst which had produced the three big orchestral works and " Mlada " seemed to have exhausted itself. It really looked as if " Mlada " were going to be his " last important work ", though it is true he was thinking of an opera on the " Sadko " subject or perhaps one on a play of Mey's—" Servilia " or " The Tsar's Bride ". He actually began some sketches for a " Zoriushka ", at which Liadof also was to try his hand a little later, but they came to nothing.

The Rimsky-Korsakofs spent the summer in Switzerland, vainly hoping the change would do little Masha good. Nicholas was too disturbed to work; even a little scoring which he began turned out badly. Two letters written that August bear witness to his profound pessimism and sense of disillusionment at this period. " While I was abroad, it seemed to me that music didn't grip and satisfy me; and now, it appears, I have no use for it at all." A week later he found the new compositions of his nearest and dearest young friends " boring... paltry and worthless.... dry and lifeless ". " In short, pretty harmonies and the interweaving of melodious phrases don't affect me at all; it all seems to me cold and dry. ' Mlada ' is as cold as ice. Now a Beethoven quartet or symphony is another matter. Technique and working out are there only the outward form, and everything is filled with life and soul. . . . I fancy that a great part of the Russian school is not music, but cold, brain-spun stuff. . . Having such thoughts, I ought to leave off composing. . . Don't regret that I've torn up the book I was writing, in a fit of stupid bitterness, and that I can't remember what I'd written. None of it was worth a farthing." (What this " book " was remains unknown.) Autumn, spring and winter passed in the same way. The second version of " The Maid " progressed slowly; Korsakof amused himself in the winter by orchestrating the coronation scene from " Boris " according to his own ideas; relations with Balakiref became more and more strained. There are some curious and contradictory phrases in a letter of April, 1892: " I teach and learn, teach and learn, am vexed by many things and cultivate an objective outlook. I nurse within myself a feeling of extreme repugnance towards Balakiref—(and with success)."

The summer at Nejgovitsky was one of real crisis, a crisis of a nature partly physical, partly intellectual, curiously similar to those which have overcome so many Russian artists in mid-career, in which they lose themselves and change the course of their lives. (For instance, Gogol, Tolstoy and Balakiref.[1]) At first Korsakof worked for three or four weeks at the new version of the Overture to " The Maid of Pskof ", but " with extraordinary reluctance, feeling a sort of weariness and disgust ". That finished, he thought of writing an essay or even a book on Russian music, particularly his own compositions, Borodin's and Mussorgsky's. There was to be an introduction dealing with æsthetics in general, which would lead to musical æsthetics in particular and this in turn to the Russian school. It was quickly written—and as quickly destroyed as hopelessly inadequate, like the book begun the previous summer. Rimsky-Korsakof began to read books on musical æsthetics—Ambros and Hanslick—and La Mara's biographies of the great composers. Hanslick annoyed him but sent him back with fresh energy to his own book. But the more he wrote, the bigger grew his plan and the more conscious he became of his ignorance of æsthetics and philosophy in general. He broke off his work to study G. H. Lewes's " Biographical History of Philosophy ", but in the intervals of reading wrote short studies of " Mozart and Glinka "[2] and similar subjects, only to condemn them as

[1] See an article by the present writer in " The Contemporary Review " for November, 1933.

[2] These fragments were published posthumously with his other prose-writings. They are of very moderate interest.

"unripe". Lewes filled his head only with a mass of disconnected thoughts, and he sat "for whole days" while they turned over and over in his mind. "Then one fine morning at the end of August or beginning of September, I felt extreme weariness, accompanied by a rush of blood to the head and complete confusion of my thoughts. I was seriously alarmed and on the very first day completely lost my appetite. When I told my wife about this she naturally persuaded me to stop all work, which I did until we returned to Petersburg, read nothing, walked all day, endeavouring not to be left alone. When I was left alone certain unpleasant fixed ideas thrust themselves importunately into my head. I thought about religion and a humble reconciliation with Balakiref. However, the walks and rest helped, and by the time I returned to Petersburg I had got myself completely under control. But to music I was completely indifferent, and the thought of pursuing my philosophical studies constantly haunted me. In spite of the doctor's advice, I began to read a lot—a textbook on logic, the philosophies of Herbert Spencer and Spinoza, the æsthetic writings of Guyav, various histories of philosophy, etc. Almost every day I bought new books and read them, skipping from one to another, scribbling marginal notes, thinking and thinking and making notes. I wanted to write a great work on the æsthetics of musical art. For the time being I put the Russian School on one side. But instead of æsthetics I got involved in metaphysics in general, fearing to begin in too shallow a way. And then the very unpleasant phenomena began to reappear more and more frequently in my head; not so much rushes of blood to the head or from it, or dizziness, but rather a sensation of weight and pressure. These sensations, which were accompanied by various obsessing ideas, weighed very heavily on me and alarmed me."

The rehearsals of "Mlada" brought a certain amount of distraction, but after a brilliantly-successful *première* (October 20th/November 1st, 1892) the opera gradually fell into neglect, the public—including the Imperial family—preferring " Cavalleria Rusticana " and Tchaïkovsky's " Iolanta ". Among his friends, Rimsky-Korsakof himself made no secret of the fact that he considered the new work, elaborate as it was, " far inferior to ' Snow Maiden ' ". His brain was playing him such tricks that on one occasion he could not remember the name of the latter opera. " No, what-d'you-call-it ", he said to his young friend and Eckermann, Yastrebtsef, " why, you know. . . Not ' Mlada ', no— the other one; I don't mean ' May Night '. . ." But his interest in music was not reawakened by either the production of " Mlada " or the exceptionally fine performances of " Snow Maiden " in Moscow in January, 1893, which drew him to the old capital—though the latter production left him with " the conviction that ' Snow Maiden ' is not only my best opera but, on the whole, perhaps the best of all contemporary operas ". He simply went on with his study of philosophy until the renewal of the " fatigue and unpleasant sensations in the head " became so serious that he was compelled to stop altogether. His doctor, diagnosing *Neurasthenia cerebrospinalis*, ordered complete mental rest and plenty of outdoor exercise. " Not feeling the slightest inclination for manual work, I took long walks. . . From time to time I read a little, but this brought on the old sensations and I was obliged, despondently to leave off." He handed over the conductorship of the Russian Symphony Concerts, which had begun to bore him the season before, to Glazunof and Liadof, and he seldom appeared at Belaief's " Fridays ". They, too, had " fallen off in interest ". His brain was in such a curious state that the morning after the second concert of the season he asked Yastrebtsef why the latter had not attended the concert the night before, although Yastrebtsef had actually talked to him in the artists' room! The brief visit to Moscow in January brought welcome relief; for a week or two

Rimsky-Korsakof even contemplated leaving indifferent Petersburg for the city " where life seemed somehow younger and fresher ". But he soon thought better of it. " I must make an end of old-womanishness, illness and getting vexed with Balakiref, and get on with my work—that's all."

Yet he was so disgusted not only with Balakiref's dictatorial methods, but the entire atmosphere of the Imperial Chapel " so saturated with spying, scandal-mongering and toadyism " that he began to talk of resigning. Balakiref, being informed of his intention to leave " for reasons of health ", showed him every kindness and promised to see him liberally pensioned. But for one reason and another the resignation was postponed for nearly a year—till January, 1894.

Meanwhile little Masha's health grew steadily worse; she had already been ill for two and a half years. In the spring of 1893, her mother took her with Nadia, to Yalta in the Crimea, hoping the climate of the Russian Riviera would save her. In May, as soon as the Conservatoire and Chapel examinations were over, their father hastened to join them, having been granted three months' leave from the Chapel. This summer at Yalta was the most wretched in Rimsky-Korsakof's life. He read, bathed and took long walks; but with his sick brain and his little daughter dying under his eyes, all life had lost its savour. He tried to work at the orchestration and piano-score of " The Maid of Pskof "—he had hardly touched a piano for a whole year, he says—then turned restlessly to his writing and began some little text-books " which grew into philosophical treatises " and were afterwards burned. Finally he turned to the reminiscences begun years before, and spent much of the sad, weary summer writing a great part of that " Record " with its sharp self-criticism and its harsh judgments of old friends, particularly of Balakiref. But he wrote it all " dully and lifelessly ". " I have never experienced such lack of energy ", he writes to his eldest son, Misha, in these months of July and August. " But how can you be energetic when a weight is hanging over you? . . . . We have sunk into a sort of mental torpor here; we live from day to day and try not to speak of the future. . . I can do absolutely nothing in these days; the greater part of the time I pace from one corner of the room to another, or sit and smoke endlessly." His leave having expired, he left for Petersburg on August 20th/ September 1st, only to be overtaken at Kharkof by a telegram announcing Masha's death. The official quarters in the Chapel buildings had now acquired so many sad memories that in view of his imminent resignation, they moved at once to a new house.

Curiously enough, it was another death, that of Tchaïkovsky in October, which rescued Rimsky-Korsakof from his gloomy apathy. He considered it a moral duty to dedicate the first Russian Symphony Concert of the season to Tchaïkovsky's memory; he was anxious to conduct it;[1] and so, to Belaief's joy, he resumed the direction of the series. Not only that but in January, a week after his resignation from the Imperial Chapel had taken effect, he went with Nadejda to Odessa to conduct yet another Tchaïkovsky memorial concert, and returned to Petersburg feeling refreshed by the change. Walking on the sea-shore at Odessa he had even experienced a desire to compose again—on a Homeric subject, the Nausicaa episode from the " Odyssey ". But this plan was soon thrust aside by another. And here, again, Tchaïkovsky's death was a determining factor. Tchaïkovsky had written an opera, " Vakula the Smith ", based on Gogol's " Christmas Eve ", and although Rimsky-Korsakof had long coveted the subject for himself he had feared to hurt the other's feelings by appearing to enter into rivalry with him. Now that obstacle was removed and a private performance of his own " May Night ", a sort of

---

[1] The following winter he had the less congenial duty of opening the season with an Anton Rubinstein memorial concert.

companion-piece, at his sister-in-law's in April, decided him. He laid aside Polonsky's libretto (written for Serof and used by Tchaïkovsky), prepared one of his own, and began to sketch out the music. Within a fortnight he had not only written, but scored the introduction, and played it to his friends, asking them to guess what it represented. For at first he made a great mystery of his new opera, telling no one what the subject was. " Even if you guess right, I shan't admit it ", he told Yastrebtsef.

The summer of 1894 passed very differently from that of the previous year. The Rimsky-Korsakofs found a new country house at Vetchasha in the Luga district, with surroundings very like those which had so happily inspired the composer at Stelëvo. " Vetchasha is a charming spot ", he wrote, " thanks to the wonderful great Lake Pesno and a huge old garden with century-old elms and lindens. . . The bathing is lovely. At night the moon and stars are marvellously reflected in the lake. There are a host of birds ". In these surroundings " Christmas Eve " progressed rapidly. Not only that but another long-meditated plan suddenly ripened and thrust itself importunately on the composer: an opera on the subject of " Sadko ". Even as he worked at " Christmas Eve " the scenario of " Sadko " began to take shape, with Stassof's assistance by correspondence. Korsakof decided to draw on the themes of his early orchestral piece as *leitmotifs* while other musical ideas began to throng his head, " for instance, the melody of Sadko's aria, the theme of Nejata's tale and part of the finale of the opera. I remember that the place where most of these ideas came to me was the long bathing-stage built out into the lake from the bank. It went out through the reeds; on one side you saw the great slanting willows in the garden, on the other spread Lake Pesno. All this put me in the mood for 'Sadko'. But the actual composition of 'Sadko' was laid aside till 'Christmas Eve' was finished ".

But if " Sadko " was, evidently, inspired and spontaneous, a good deal of " Christmas Eve " was manufactured—and the composer knew it. Even before going to Vetchasha he had talked of abandoning it altogether. " You know ", he had said suddenly to Yastrebtsef, after playing over part of the new music, " *only lyrical music is good*, the rest is all *bad*. It won't do for me to write the new opera—not a bit. For there's nothing lyrical in me. And, generally speaking, I'm no longer good for anything. If I ever had any creative power it's left me—and for ever. And what a weak subject this is, which I was so tremendously anxious to compose only a little while ago!" And at Vetchasha, where Yastrebtsef visited them, there was a similar scene one afternoon. Korsakof began to play over what he had just composed but suddenly broke off. " ' No ', he cried in a voice full of sadness, even despair, ' I can't play any more—it won't do. . . . ' He began to walk nervously up and down the room, looking at nobody. . . .he was obviously seriously agitated. After dinner Korsakof had a short nap, while the rest of us went into the field of rye to pick cornflowers for Nadia. When we came back, Nicholas Andreievitch, having mastered himself and his nerves, played his new scene to the end. Nadejda Nikolaevna remained silent as before. Then Korsakof got up, closed the music and this time, not without humour, remarked: ' Well, if my future biographer wishes to describe the present evening, he will be obliged to cry triumphantly: The celebrated composer's second scene was performed by the author himself amid the deathly silence of the listeners!' This idea evidently tickled him and he even began to cheer up!" Nevertheless, he pressed on with the work and before his return to Petersburg at the beginning of September he had not only sketched out the whole opera but orchestrated well over a hundred pages of the score. " How curious! I evidently prefer to orchestrate rather than to compose ", he writes to Yastrebtsef.

The orchestration of "Christmas Eve" was finished that winter, but in the meantime the libretto was wrinkling brows in the censorship office owing to the appearance in Scene Seven of a "Tsaritsa", anonymous, it is true, but obviously identifiable through Gogol's story as Catherine the Great. But fate was (temporarily) kind to Rimsky-Korsakof. Balakiref having just resigned the Directorship of the Imperial Chapel, the Court Minister, Count Vorontsof-Dashkof, called on Rimsky-Korsakof and offered him the vacant post. But the Chapel had become hateful; pensioned freedom was pleasant; and so he declined. Finding the Minister amiably disposed, however, Korsakof seized the opportunity to get him to arrange a special dispensation for the "Empress" in "Christmas Eve". Choral rehearsals began forthwith, and the composer was able to go back to Vetchasha happily conscious of one new opera in course of production and another partly composed.

The greater part of "Sadko" was finished in reduced score during the summer of 1895. The work went easily and Korsakof never had to rest more than a day or two at a time. But in the middle of things he made an important addition to his plan. The previous winter he had met in St. Petersburg a shy, clever man, V. I. Bielsky, lawyer, mathematician, amateur archæologist and warm admirer of Rimsky-Korsakof's music. Bielsky spent the summer on an estate only five or six miles from Vetchasha and was naturally a frequent visitor there. On his advice Korsakof (reverting to a suggestion made by Vladimir Stassof the year before) decided to introduce Sadko's wife into the action; this necessitated one entirely fresh scene, for which Bielsky wrote the libretto, and additions to two other scenes. In the meantime the composer pressed on with the orchestration of the rest of the opera, working very hard till toward the end of the winter he was suddenly overpowered by "dreadful weariness, loss of interest and almost dislike for work. This was the first time I had felt anything of the kind, but it reappeared afterwards towards the end of all my major works. It always came on suddenly; the composition would be going ahead splendidly, I would be keenly interested, and then all of a sudden I would be overcome by weariness and indifference. After a time this unpleasant mood would vanish and I would return to the work with all my former enthusiasm. This condition had nothing in common with that which had troubled me in 1891-93. I was troubled by no fearful fermentation of thoughts about philosophy and æsthetics ".

" Christmas Eve " was produced at the Marinsky Theatre on November 21st/December 3rd, 1895, in a somewhat thunder-laden atmosphere. Chaliapin, then twenty-two and as yet unknown, who had only a minor part, has given us a graphic impression in his memoirs[1] of the composer as he saw him for the first time at the rehearsals: " The magical composer impressed me by his extreme shyness and modesty. He was very unfashionably dressed; his black beard, that grew unchecked, flowed over a narrow, carelessly-knotted black stock, he wore a black frock-coat that was hopelessly out of date, and his trouser-pockets were inset horizontally in the manner of bygone days. He had two pairs of spectacles on his nose, one in front of the other. A deep crease between his brows gave him a melancholy look. He was profoundly silent . . . . At practically every rehearsal, Napravnik, the conductor, would make some remark to the composer. For instance, he would say: ' In my opinion, Nicholas Andreievitch, this act drags—I suggest that you cut it.' Rimsky-Korsakof would get up, looking disturbed, lean over the conductor's stand, and say in a somewhat tremulous and deprecatory voice: ' Frankly, I can't see that the act drags . . . .' Then, hesitatingly, he would explain: ' The construction of my work necessitates in this act

[1] Published in English as " Man and Mask " (Victor Gollancz).

a musical interpretation of the theme which is the foundation on which the rest of the opera rests.' Whereupon the cold, methodical voice of Napravnik would reply, in a Czech accent and with pedantic emphasis: ' You may be right, but you are influenced by love of your own work. You must consider your public . . . Years of experience have convinced me that when a composer rigidly refuses to alter a note of his music, the result is often very long drawn out and wearisome to an audience. I am saying all this because I really feel for you. You'll have to condense it.' " But everything had gone reasonably well up to the *répétition générale*, which was unfortunately attended by the Grand Dukes Vladimir Alexandrovitch[1] and Michael Nikolaevitch. The two princes were outraged almost beyond words at finding their illustrious ancestress portrayed upon the stage. The Grand Duke Michael particularly objected to the Petropavlovsk Fortress being painted as part of the scenery, on the ground that his ancestors were buried in it! While the Grand Duke Vladimir's finer feelings were so pained by the outrage on the Empress Catherine that at the interval he hastened behind the scenes and, sarcastically addressing the singer who had taken the part, said, " You are now my great-grandmother, I perceive ". " Which ", says the composer, " upset her not a little ". The Tsar forthwith withdrew his permission for the production in that form and Vsevolojsky, the Director, in despair, saved the situation by " translating " the mezzo-soprano " Tsaritsa " (like Bottom) into a baritone " Serene Highness ", thereby reducing the central incident of the plot to absurdity and, if he had but seen it, making the Imperial family appear more ridiculous still. The Tsar was mollified but the Imperial family showed their displeasure by staying

---

[1] The Grand Duke Vladimir Alexandrovitch almost deserves a chapter to himself in the history of Russian music. He afterwards became Diaghilef's patron, but the refinement of his musical taste may be judged by his request to Tchaïkovsky that the poor composer would arrange the " Dance of the Blue Bird " from " The Sleeping Beauty " *for two cornets with military band accompaniment.*

away from the *première*, and the composer demonstrated *his* disapproval of the outrage on Gogol and himself by staying away too. But his children went, and the faithful Yastrebtsef brought home a wreath for him.

It is amusing to observe that the very month after this mutilation of his own work, Rimsky-Korsakof began that " revision " and reorchestration of Mussorgsky's " Boris " which has brought such wrath on his well-meaning, pedantic head. The impertinence of " correcting " and " improving " his dead friend's completed work seemed to him, of course, merely a pendant to his earlier task of completing and issuing Mussorgsky's unfinished works; it was carried out in the same spirit. There is delightful irony in these " improvements " being made by one who was so quick to resent Balakiref's corrections of *his* work, these slashing cuts by a composer whose supreme grievance was that almost every one of his own operas had been cut by Napravnik.

This " repainting " of " Boris " having been completed in May, 1896, Rimsky-Korsakof returned to " Sadko ", taking it with him to a new summer residence at Shmerdovitsy and finishing it in September. Nadia and Volodia were down with the measles, but otherwise he had no troubles but his own fits of fatigue, of which he relates a curious instance (hardly confirmed, however, by the dates on the autograph score). Having just completed the last scene but one, Korsakof says he was overcome by one of these " fits of disgust " at having yet another to do. It was only in turning over his pile of manuscript that he discovered the score of this last scene already completed! Yet he found time that summer also to make notes for another book on instrumentation. And this time they were not destroyed.

With " Sadko " Rimsky-Korsakof reached the highest peak of his creative activity since " Snow Maiden ". It is, as he was fully conscious, one of his finest works, the consummation of an epic-fantastic operatic genre, peculiarly his own. Perhaps it was this feeling that " Sadko " was unsurpassable in its kind which sent him during the next few years on a curious career of operatic exploration, beginning the year after " Sadko " with a complete reversion to Dargomyjskian " dramatic truth " in his setting of Pushkin's " little tragedy " " Mozart and Salieri ". But the immediate sequel to " Sadko " was a tremendous spate of songs (with a few vocal duets), the opus-numbers running from 39 to 56 almost without a break. " I had written no songs for a long time ", he says. " Turning to Alexei Tolstoy's poems, I set four of them "—Op. 39— " and felt that I was now composing in a different way. The melodies, following the text, turned out purely vocally, with no more than hints of harmony and modulation. I worked out the accompaniments after the melodies were finished, whereas before, with few exceptions, the melodies had been conceived more or less instrumentally—i.e. agreeing only with the general feeling of the text, even derived from the harmonic basis of the song ".

Feeling that his new way of composing had produced " genuine vocal music ", he embarked on it with reckless industry. By the spring of 1897 he had not only begun to sketch " Mozart and Salieri " and made yet another revision and reorchestration of " Antar ", but had written a score of songs. As for the summer, a letter to Kruglikof, written at the end of September after his return from the country, speaks for itself: " The news that I've composed thirty-nine songs and the opera ' Mozart and Salieri ' is really false, for I've written forty songs, two duets, ' Mozart and Salieri ', a cantata ' Svitezianka ' for soprano, tenor, chorus and orchestra, and besides that a trio for piano, violin and 'cello, but only in sketches, which will now be worked up; all the rest, i.e. 'Mozart and Salieri' and 'Svitezianka' are completely scored. Having returned to Petersburg in September, I wrote something else—will tell you about it later. Perhaps you're surprised. But there's nothing surprising in all this; it's how things ought to be. Thirty years have passed since the days when Stassof used to write that in 186-, such-and-such-a-year, the Russian school had been extremely active: Lodyjensky had written one song, Borodin was planning something, Balakiref intended to alter something else, etc. It's time I left that sort of thing behind and took a normal artistic path."[1] (Nor does he add that he had also written a number of fugal exercises that summer.) The " something else " was a String Quartet in G which, like the trio, remained unpublished, " since both these productions convinced me that chamber-music is not my sphere ". Instead he resumed his book on orchestration.

In the autumn " Sadko " was submitted to the Theatre Directorate. But after " Christmas Eve " Rimsky-Korsakof was regarded as a scapegrace. The trial run-through at the piano turned out badly and was broken off " owing to the lateness of the hour ". Without definitely refusing the work, Vsevolojsky hummed and hawed and Rimsky-Korsakof decided in a huff that he " would never trouble the Directorate with his operas again ". As a matter of fact he was already secure in the knowledge that another means of production was open to him. Even in the summer S. I. Mamontof, the railway magnate, who ran an excellent opera company of his own in Moscow, had been enquiring about " Sadko ". Now Korsakof sent him the score, and the first performance of the opera was accordingly given under Esposito in the Solodovnikovsky Theatre in Moscow on December 26th (January 7th, 1898). It was a bad, under-rehearsed performance, but a few weeks later the Mamontof

---

[1] Compare this with Tchaïkovsky's remark in a letter to Nadejda von Meck : " One must always *work*, and a self-respecting artist must not fold his hands on the pretext that he isn't in the mood. If one waited for the *mood* without going half way to meet it, one would very easily become *lazy* and *apathetic*. . . I have learned to master myself and am glad I've not followed in the footsteps of those of my Russian colleagues who have no self-confidence and no patience, and who throw up the sponge at the slightest difficulty. That is why, in spite of their great gifts, they produce so little and in such a desultory way. "

company visited Petersburg and opened its season in the Conservatoire Theatre with a very fine production of " Sadko ", conducted by the composer himself.

Rimsky-Korsakof's industry at this period was so unflagging that the story of his life becomes little more than a record of work done. In the spring of 1898 he reconstructed the Prologue to " The Maid of Pskof " (omitted from the final version) as a separate one-act opera " Boyarina Vera Sheloga ", and began a full-length opera on a long-cherished subject, Mey's melodramatic play, " The Tsar's Bride ". In accordance with the general trend of his ideas he was determined to make the work " above all, singable ". And he wrote the part of the heroine specially for the voice of Nadejda Zabela, one of the ladies of Mamontof's company, who had sung the part of the Sea Princess in " Sadko " and who, perhaps, aroused in him something more than a purely artistic interest. At any rate he corresponded with her frequently, though only fragments from the letters have as yet been published. Zabela's voice certainly inspired one extraordinarily lovely song, and there are other fine pages in " The Tsar's Bride ", but the work—more than a little suggestive of Bizet-with-a-Russian accent—is a mournful decline from " Sadko ". The actual composition and the orchestration of nearly two acts were done very quickly during the summer (again spent at Vetchasha which they had deserted for the last two years). The score was finished in November and produced by Mamontof in October, 1899. In the meantime Mamontof in the last months of 1898 brought out " Mozart and Salieri ", " Vera Sheloga ", and the new version of " The Maid " (Chaliapin scoring a tremendous success as Ivan the Terrible) in Moscow, repeating them in Petersburg in the new year, while officialdom in the person of Vsevolojsky made a gesture of reconciliation by reviving " Snow Maiden " with new costumes and scenery—magnificent but all wrong, in the composer's view. " Father Frost ", for instance, " looked more like Father Neptune ". Korsakof's operas also began to cross the frontier. Prague accepted them warmly, but " May Night " suffered a fiasco at Frankfurt-am-Main in May, 1900.

Nor was Rimsky-Korsakof in the mood to rest on his laurels. With Bielsky he discussed various possible opera subjects that winter: Pushkin's " Tale of Tsar Saltan ", a work in which the legend of the Invisible City of Kitej could be linked with that of St. Fevronia of Murom, Byron's " Heaven and Earth ", " Odysseus at the Court of Alkinous ". But the choice fell on " Tsar Saltan "; Bielsky himself undertook to prepare a libretto from Pushkin's text; and the summer at Vetchasha again brought forth a nearly complete opera, one infinitely more delightful and characteristic than its predecessor. Also from the summer of 1899 dates a piece of " relaxation ", as the composer called it, a cantata " The Song of Oleg the Wise ". The score of " Saltan " was completed on January 19th/31st, 1900, but owing to a passing unpleasantness with Belaief these new works, including the concert suite of " musical pictures " from " Tsar Saltan ", were published by Bessel. New figures were appearing in the Belaief circle, not only Rimsky-Korsakof's own young men, but less congenial strangers from Moscow—notably Scriabin. " Signs of decadence from the West began to appear." The ardent young modernist of the 'sixties, the leader and teacher of the 'eighties, was in danger of surviving in the new century only as a back-number. Certainly the work which he began immediately after " Saltan " must have confirmed any detached observer in that view.

Rimsky-Korsakof's lifelong attachment to such a fourth-rate dramatist as Mey is incomprehensible, for in each case, except " The Maid of Pskof ", Mey inspired his weakest operas. " Oh, how I want to write an opera! " the composer wrote to Zabela in April, 1900. But he wanted it above all things to be non-Russian; he wanted " freedom of style ", escape from the nationalism he had practised so successfully and which had so long seemed to him the very mainspring of artistic creation. Accordingly, he took the Way of the Cross, finding in Mey's "Servilia", a melodrama of ancient Rome complete with senators, centurions and persecuted Christian maidens, the necessary pretext for writing colourless music. It must be admitted that he took the fullest advantage of it. Returning from a brief visit to Brussels in March—he had refused more than one such invitation to Paris—he began "Servilia" at once. But it was finished abroad. Andrei Rimsky-Korsakof was studying at Strasbourg University and in order to be near him, his parents spent the summer partly in Strasbourg, partly in the Black Forest, where he was able to visit them at week-ends. At the beginning of the vacation, they all moved to Switzerland. The greater part of "Servilia" was composed by the time the composer and his wife returned to Petersburg in September, and the orchestration was done, as usual, during the winter and spring.

Korsakof found that a new reign had begun in the Imperial Theatres. Tchaïkovsky's friend, the lazy and reactionary Vsevolojsky, had been superseded by Prince Volkonsky, according to Theodore Kommissarjevsky[1] "a man with exquisite artistic taste", who "lost his appointment after eighteen months because he had been too straightforward and not sufficiently hypocritical". Volkonsky at once approached Korsakof with a request for a "fantastic ballet", which was never written, however; and in February, 1901, "Sadko" was at last produced on the Imperial stage. The performance was very fine, though still not without cuts grievous to the composer's heart. The previous October "Saltan" had had its *première* in Moscow. (Mamontof himself, a financier to the core, had retired to Paris after a term in jail in consequence of certain transactions connected with the

[1] "Myself and the Theatre."

Archangel Railway; but his opera company had taken its affairs into its own hands and was carrying on with Ippolitof-Ivanof as conductor.) In fact, Rimsky-Korsakof at fifty-six found himself by no means without honour in his own country; in December, 1900, the thirty-fifth anniversary of his first public appearance as a composer was celebrated by special concerts organised by various societies (though *not* by the Imperial Theatres), dinners, addresses and presentations. " I was very grateful for all this but it was intolerably boring and upsetting .... Really, to hear every day: ' Deeply respected Nicholas Andreievitch, during thirty-five years ...' or ' Thirty-five years have now passed since . . . .', etc. is intolerable. And what is more I don't believe in the perfect sincerity of all this. I can't help feeling that my jubilee was used in some cases as a pretext for other people to advertise and draw attention to themselves."

Rimsky-Korsakof was at this time wavering between no fewer than four opera subjects. With Bielsky he constantly discussed " Kitej " and " Nausicaa ", and Bielsky even began the libretto of the latter. But the composer also wanted to write a Polish opera, partly as a tribute to Chopin, whom he had long worshipped, partly because he wanted to introduce in it some melodies his mother had heard in the days when his father had held a Polish governorship and which she had sung to him as a baby. He commissioned a librettist to prepare an original " book ", " Pan Voevoda ", on lines laid down by himself: plenty of drama, no politics, a slight fantastic element and plenty of dancing. The libretto was written and, poor as it was, he seems to have liked it. At the same time someone else offered him the libretto of a short fantastic opera on a subject from Russian folk-lore, " Kashchei the Immortal ". He liked the subject but was not entirely satisfied with the libretto. It was a curious dilemma. But having put the finishing touches to the orchestration of " Servilia " in May, 1901, he began a sort of prelude-cantata for female voices and orchestra which was to form the introduction to " Nausicaa ". However, he soon laid it aside and took up the " Kashchei " libretto which, with the help of his daughter Sonia, he altered to his liking. He determined to issue his " prelude-cantata " as an independent work, " From Homer ", Op. 60, and in the meantime went ahead with the surprisingly modern (if not particularly Russian) music of " Kashchei ", finishing the first two scenes by the beginning of September. Having completed and scored the whole work in the course of the winter, Rimsky-Korsakof turned industriously to " Pan Voevoda " and not only completed that very dull work during the summer and autumn of 1902 (all but the orchestration), but actually rescored Dargomyjsky's " Stone Guest " during the same period. He had long been dissatisfied with his own youthful orchestration; no one blames him for that, of course. But he characteristically took the opportunity to " soften some of the extreme harshness and the harmonic crudities of the original ", a labour rather less praiseworthy.

The bulk of this work, " Pan Voevoda " and the new edition of " The Stone Guest " was done during July and August at Heidelberg, where Andrei was now studying and where he introduced to his father a fellow-student named Igor Stravinsky. They again spent the vacation in Switzerland and returned leisurely by way of Munich, Dresden and Berlin in time to hear the *première* of " Servilia " under Felix Blumenfeld at the Marinsky Theatre on October 1st/14th, while " Kashchei " was brought out in Moscow by the ex-Mamontof company just two months later (December 12th/25th).

Even before the scoring of the Polish opera was finished, in the spring of 1903, Rimsky-Korsakof began the sketches of " Kitej ". The bulk of the composition was roughed out by the autumn, the rest, with most of the scoring, being completed during the summer of 1904 at Vetchasha. The

Christian ideology of "Kitej" not unnaturally suggests that Rimsky-Korsakof had abandoned his lifelong rationalism for a faith definitely Christian, if by no means Orthodox, particularly when we find in it such a strong element of that imaginative pantheism with which his rationalism had always been so strongly tempered. It is possible, but improbable. In considering the relation between Korsakof's life and his work it is of the highest importance to recall a saying recorded by Yastrebtsef, even though the saying dates from December, 1893, the period of crisis and depression: " I doubt if you would find anyone in the whole world more incredulous of everything supernatural, fantastic, phantasmal or lying beyond the grave, and yet as an artist it is just *these* things that I love above all. And *ceremonial*—what could be more intolerable than ceremonial? .... Yet with what delight I have depicted ' ceremonial ' in music! No—I'm definitely of the opinion that art is essentially the most enchanting and intoxicating of lies!" That view would, of course, explain the fundamental weakness of so much of his music. On the other hand, in May, 1907, a little more than a year before his death, he wrote to Glazunof that " generally speaking ' there is no truth on earth '—although that is itself untrue, for truth does exist on earth, but only in science and art ".

In the last days of December, 1903, M. P. Belaief died, leaving a triumvirate of Rimsky-Korsakof, Glazunof and Liadof to administer the vast fortune he had bequeathed to Russian music—the continuance of the publishing house, the Russian Symphony Concerts, the Glinka Prizes for orchestral works, the chamber music competition schemes, and the fund for the assistance of needy musicians. Rimsky-Korsakof at once wrote a memorial piece, a short orchestral prelude, " On the Tomb ", which opened the first Russian Symphony Concert of the season (February 19th/March 3rd), conducting it himself. But for the most part he now left the conducting of these concerts to the younger men.

Summer—the summer that Tchekhof died in Germany, while thousands of Russians were dying round Port Arthur—passed peacefully with the work on "Kitej" and more plans for the book on orchestration. The disasters of the Japanese War wounded Rimsky-Korsakof's patriotic pride, but he could have had no suspicion that the repercussions of the War were to affect his own fate. But when in November the Imperial Theatres at last produced his version of "Boris", with Chaliapin as the hero, the authorities soon thought it advisable to cut out the insurrection scene "near Kromy". Everywhere in Russia the revolutionary elements had been encouraged by the reverses of the War; in January, 1905, Petersburg was practically in a state of revolution. The student class as usual were foremost in the disturbances, those of the Conservatoire among the rest. They held illegal meetings and the "cowardly and tactless" Director, Bernhard (backed by the heads of the Russian Music Society, the body which had founded the Conservatoire and which still exercised a certain control over it), began to devise repressive measures—the expulsion of the ringleaders, the bringing of police into the building, even the closing of the Conservatoire. Rimsky-Korsakof stood up for the rights of the students and was in consequence regarded by the conservative members of the staff "almost as the leader of the revolutionary movement among the students". Bernhard continued to "behave tactlessly" and Korsakof brought things to a head by publishing in the paper "Russ" (in amplification of a briefly reported speech) a letter advocating the emancipation of the Conservatoire from the control of the R.M.S. Bernhard took exception to the letter at a sitting of the Council of the Conservatoire; words ran high; and Bernhard cut short the meeting. On March 16th/29th, the Conservatoire building being surrounded by mounted and foot police, Rimsky-Korsakof with a number of the other professors sent the Director a written demand for his resignation and within three days the higher authorities settled the matter "impartially" by the dismissal of both Bernhard and Rimsky-Korsakof, the expulsion of more than a hundred students, and the temporary closing of the Conservatoire. Rimsky-Korsakof having retorted by sending another letter to the press and by resigning his honorary membership of the Russian Music Society, he at once found himself the martyr-hero of liberal and intellectual Russia. From every part of the country came a flood of letters and addresses of sympathy both from institutions and individuals. Deputations from various societies visited him and the press was full of the affair. The Directorate were abused high and low and some of its members resigned, while Glazunof, Liadof, Felix Blumenfeld and one or two other members of the Conservatoire staff also resigned in sympathy with Rimsky-Korsakof. Rimsky-Korsakof and Glazunof each orchestrated one of the popular revolutionary songs of the day—Korsakof "Dubinushka"; Glazunof, the all too celebrated "Volga Boat Song".

Matters reached a climax on March 27th/April 9th, when the students gave a concert, conducted by Glazunof, in the Kommissarjevsky Theatre. The first part was to consist of "Kashchei", the second of a miscellaneous programme. But after "Kashchei" the affair became a political demonstration, almost a revolutionary meeting. "They called me on the platform and began to read me addresses from different societies and associations and to make inflammatory speeches. They say that somebody yelled 'Down with the autocracy!' The uproar after each address and speech was indescribable." Finally the police intervened, lowered the iron saftey curtain, and cleared the hall. Fearing a repetition of this demonstration the Petersburg police suppressed the next Russian Symphony Concert, announced for four days later, and forbade the performance of any of Rimsky-Korsakof's compositions! Their example was followed in certain provincial centres, with the natural result that when the ban was lifted after a couple of months or so his music enjoyed far more popularity than ever before.

All this might have intoxicated a man of more flamboyant temperament, but Rimsky-Korsakof, shy and scholarly if obstinate and a little hot-tempered when roused, longed for peace. He withdrew to Vetchasha, badly ruffled, depressed and in no mood for composition, resumed the " Record of my Musical Life " after a break of twelve years (though again, as it happened, in a melancholy mood), and began a very interesting thematic analysis of his " Snow Maiden ". Writing at the beginning of July to Nadejda, who had gone to Bad Nauheim with Andrei, he said: " I feel it's time I began to occupy myself with musico-literary work instead of composition; I'm very much afraid of doing something weak and letting myself down. In any case, after ten years of intense creative activity it will be a good thing to stop or wait a bit. In former years I used to allow myself a break here, but I haven't done so for ten years. Besides, music is now beginning to enter on a sort of new and incomprehensible phase of development (Strauss, d'Indy, Debussy, etc.). But I and many of us—well, we belong to a different, earlier period." After a week or so he broke off his analysis of " Snow Maiden " and began to work more steadily at his book on the orchestra, continuing this after his return to Petersburg.

The Conservatoire remained closed, though pupils came privately to Rimsky-Korsakof's house, and the political air was still thunder-laden. The production of " Pan Voevoda " in Moscow in September, under Rachmaninof, could not be advertised owing to a strike of printers. In October there was an all-Russian general strike, suppressed only with bloodshed. The R.M.S. was sadly discredited in consequence of the events of the beginning of the year, and even the Russian Symphony Concerts were in financial difficulty.

All Rimsky-Korsakof's public actions savoured of defiance; his " Dubinushka " was played at a Ziloti concert in November and a little later he organised a concert in aid of the families of destitute workers. The Director of the Imperial Theatres was obliged to *ask permission* to produce " Kitej ", since the composer flatly refused to submit it in the usual way. Even the reopening of the Conservatoire, with a fresh and slightly freer constitution, brought more unpleasantness. Rimsky-Korsakof and the professors who had resigned were invited to return, the expelled pupils were allowed to come back, and the Council of Professors was requested to elect a new Director. But although Glazunof was unanimously chosen, he soon came into conflict with the conservative members of the Council. There were more stormy scenes and on January 26th/February 8th, 1906, Korsakof lost his temper and walked out, saying that he would have nothing more to do with the Conservatoire; he was fetched back and pacified; but it was some time before he could be persuaded to give up the idea of resignation. His nerves were far too upset to compose, though he brooded over various opera-subjects—Byron's " Heaven and Earth ", for which he made notes once more, and " Stenka Razin ". Instead, he turned again to Mussorgsky's works, restoring the cuts he had made in " Boris "—though not the original harmonies and so on—and having persuaded Stassof (who died a few months later) to let him have the score of the " Marriage " fragment for publication, began to orchestrate it.

In June with his son and daughter, Volodia and Nadia, he travelled south by way of Vienna to Riva on Lake Garda, where they were joined by his wife and Andrei and where he orchestrated a few songs, his own and Mussorgsky's, and touched up " Dubinushka " and " Kashchei ". And, after an expedition through the North Italian cities—Milan, Genoa, Florence and Venice—he completed at Riva the " Record of my Musical Life ", dating it " August 22nd, old style ", the eve of their return to Russia. " It is rather muddled, not equally detailed throughout, and written in a bad literary style, often very drily; but there is *nothing in it but the truth* . . ." (Which is unfortunately *not* quite true, for it contains numerous unintentional inaccuracies.) And the last paragraphs are overcast with autumnal melancholy. " The thought that it is time to end my career as a composer, which has pursued me ever since I finished ' Kitej ', has not left me here . . . I don't want to find myself in the ridiculous position of ' a singer who has lost his voice '. We shall see what time will bring . . ." He had not long to wait. Within six weeks of his return to Petersburg his notebooks contained the cockcrow theme of " The Golden Cockerel ".

Bielsky had undertaken the construction of a libretto from Pushkin's fairy-tale satire on stupid autocracy. By the middle of November the new work was well under way and Yastrebtsef was able to note in his diary that " N.A. is obviously awfully glad to be composing again ". Before the end of the year the First Act was finished as far as the entrance of the Astrologer, the full score being made first this time and the piano reduction afterwards. At about the same time Rimsky-Korsakof acquired a fresh private pupil, Igor Stravinsky, who with his brother Gury had for some time been a member of the circle which attended the Rimsky-Korsakofs' Wednesday evening music-makings. By a curious chance the appearance of this new pupil exactly coincided with the celebration of the twenty-fifth anniversary of the debut of an old one, Glazunof. Korsakof naturally took a leading part in the commemorations.

Rehearsals of " Kitej ", one of the finest of all Rimsky-Korsakof's works, had been going on at the Marinsky Theatre throughout the winter, and Felix Blumenfeld conducted the first performance on February 7th/20th. The ovations began at the end of the First Act and the triumph was complete. " The ' Cockerel ' doesn't get on very well, what with all these concerts and jubilees and rehearsals ", the composer complained to Yastrebtsef. And Diaghilef was urging him to go to Paris in May for the festival of five Russian orchestral concerts he had organised. For a while Rimsky-Korsakof held out, then consented in the words of a humorous catch-phrase: " Here goes—as the parrot said when the cat hauled him out of the cage." Ten days before he set out—with his wife, Nadia, Andrei and Volodia—Maximilian Steinberg had played through the manuscript First Act of the " Cockerel " to a small audience which included Bielsky, Yastrebtsef and Igor Stravinsky. This Act was already orchestrated and the Second well under way.

Diaghilef's Paris programmes included the orchestral suites from " Christmas Eve " and " Tsar Saltan " and excerpts from " Mlada ", " Sadko " and " Snow Maiden ". Korsakof himself conducted two or three numbers, Nikisch the others. He did not wish to direct a whole programme and declined all invitations to conduct after his return to Russia. During this visit to Paris he had one more brush with the " new and incomprehensible " music and its composers, not only the " Poème de l'Extase " of Scriabin, who was in Paris with a host of other Russian composers and whom Korsakof had always disliked—the man as much as his music, but Strauss and Debussy. He heard Strauss conduct " Salome " at the Châtelet and was introduced to Strauss by Colonne. Glazunof has told us that Rimsky-Korsakof heard " Pelléas et Mélisande " at the Opéra-Comique and said, " I will have nothing more to do with this music, lest I should unhappily develop a liking for it ". With two members of the Imperial family who happened to be in Paris Rimsky-Korsakof would have nothing to do; in spite of kind invitations, he would neither attend the Grand Duke Paul Alexandrovitch's party nor join the Grand Duchess Maria Pavlovna in her box at the Opéra. He was much more interested in getting " Sadko " produced at the Grand Opéra and when Diaghilef's lieutenant, Calvocoressi, pointed out that without cuts (to which the composer would agree only as a last resource) it was very long, he replied with the amazing suggestion: " If it is found too long for one evening, why not give it in two halves?"

Returning to Russia in June, Rimsky-Korsakof settled for the summer on the beautiful estate of Liubensk which he thought of buying—it was quite near Vetchasha, on high ground overlooking his beloved Lake Pesno—and there resumed work on " The Golden Cockerel ", completing the full score of Act II and the sketches of Act III by the end of August. Glazunof wrote to him from Folkestone sounding him as to his willingness to accept an honorary doctorate from Oxford or Cambridge, adding his personal assurance that " the ceremony is by no means tiring and there's no need to make a speech ". But Korsakof replied (June 20th/July 3rd): " I most decidedly don't want to be made a doctor of Oxford or Cambridge University: first, because I don't consider such honorary degrees appropriate to composers in general and to myself in particular (perhaps that's only a whim of mine, but there it is); secondly, because I don't intend to go to England. Of course, you must only mention the second reason . . . and give my thanks to those who commissioned you to approach me for the—in their opinion—flattering and complimentary intention." But in November, whether he liked it or not, he was elected a corresponding member of the " Académie des Beaux Arts ", in the place of Grieg who had just died. The political alliance between France and Russia was arousing in France an ever keener interest in Russian art, and (conversely) important people in Russia were backing Diaghilef with the idea of fostering sympathy between the two countries—of all of which Rimsky-Korsakof was quite aware and slightly contemptuous. Nevertheless, while Diaghilef was meditating the production of

" Sadko " at the Grand Opéra, Albert Carré was also actively preparing " Snow Maiden " at the Opéra-Comique and N. N. Tcherepnin went to Paris to supervise it for the composer. It is fortunate that Korsakof could not foresee the fell use to which Diaghilef was to put " Sheherazade ", for in January, 1908, he wrote of Isadora Duncan: " I haven't seen her once. I dare say she is very graceful, a beautiful mime, and so on; but what I dislike about her is that she connects her art with musical compositions dear to me . . . How vexed I should be if I learned that Miss Duncan danced and mimed to my ' Sheherazade ', ' Antar ' or ' Easter Overture '."

On February 16th/29th, 1908, the day after the first Moscow performance of " Kitej ", Felix Blumenfeld conducted the " Introduction and Wedding Procession " from " The Golden Cockerel " at a Russian Symphony Concert. Nine days later the dramatic censor refused to sanction the libretto without cuts—forty-five lines in all. " So the ' Cockerel ' won't come out in Russia ", Rimsky-Korsakof wrote defiantly to the publisher Jurgenson. " For I don't intend to change anything. Perhaps it will do in Paris." A French translation had already been prepared. " Both Bielsky and I are very pleased with it ", he wrote. " Calvocoressi has got on the right track." But a day or two later he seemed more willing to compromise. Bielsky and Teliakovsky, the Director of the Theatres, who was a genuine artist and an admirer of Korsakof's work,[1] soon induced him to agree to a few alterations. Jurgenson, who was going ahead with the printing, received a letter asking his " much respected proof-reader not to smother the sheets with question-marks; where there are obvious mistakes let him correct them. I'm not a Richard Strauss and I don't write false harmonies on purpose . . . ."

[1] The " diminutive ex-colonel of Horse Guards " described in Theodore Kommissarjevsky's " Myself and the Theatre ". He managed the Imperial Theatres brilliantly from 1901 till the Revolution and " died in misery a few years later, forgotten by nearly everyone.".

Rimsky-Korsakof, it may be mentioned, always gave the proofs of his full scores to pupils whom he knew could not afford to pay one hundred and fifty rubles for a score.

Already on his birthday Rimsky-Korsakof had complained of his heart, difficulty of breathing and so on; and on April 10th/23rd, after sitting up late into the night, discussing his book on instrumentation with Steinberg (who was now betrothed to Nadia), he had a severe attack of *angina pectoris*. Accustomed to activity, he could not be induced to rest and a second attack followed five days later. He had to be given oxygen and morphia, and the doctor ordered complete rest, the giving-up of smoking, a strict diet—no coffee or meat— and no visitors. For a week the composer stayed obediently in his bedroom, then, assisted by Steinberg, began to occupy himself with the proofs of the "Cockerel" and work at his book on the orchestra. He was allowed one visitor a day. Glazunof was the first, and then came Liadof, Cui, Bielsky, Yastrebtsef and others. From Paris came telegrams announcing the success of the interpolations he had made in "Boris" at Diaghilef's request and of "Snow Maiden" at the Opéra-Comique. He seemed much better and went to Liubensk on May 21st/June 3rd. Two days before, he had gathered from a telephone conversation with Teliakovsky that the "Cockerel" might be given in Petersburg that season, but not in Moscow. Still, Zimin's private company were willing to give it at once in Moscow. But a few days later came a blow. The Governor of Moscow had forbidden the production there and Teliakovsky had fears of a similar veto in Petersburg. The authorities were willing enough to use Korsakof to dress their political shop-window in Paris. But the satirical "Cockerel" at home—that was a different matter.

The first night at Liubensk Rimsky-Korsakof had a fresh attack from which he quickly recovered. He worked at his book and was able to walk " slowly and not very much " in his garden, delighting in the lilacs, the acacias and the apple-trees in bloom. On Wednesday, June 4th/17th Nadia was married quite simply in the village church to Maximilian Steinberg, but her father was not present at the ceremony and the next day he had a particularly bad attack. On the Friday he wrote to Jurgenson expressing his indignation at Teliakovsky's news and at Teliakovsky's " being frightened by the Moscow scarecrow "; on the Saturday he wrote a few more pages of his book. In the early hours of Sunday the 8th/21st, after a short but severe thunderstorm, he had another attack and died.

Two days later, after a service in the chapel of the St. Petersburg Conservatoire, he was buried in the cemetery of the Novodevitchy Monastery in St. Petersburg.

* * * * *

Looking back on Rimsky-Korsakof's work as a whole, one sees at once that the Korsakof who matters is Korsakof the opera-composer. True, his first three operas were squeezed out at rather long intervals and he was forty-five before he definitely devoted himself to the stage. But, broadly speaking, his non-operatic music, other than the charming early orchestral works and the later trio of masterpieces, is negligible. Even the best of his concert-works for orchestra are hardly " symphonic " in the true sense; their delightful material and magical scoring have deservedly won them a unique place in the repertoire, but they reveal the composer's lack of skill as a musical architect all too clearly. In the field of opera, however, lack of symphonic mastery is of no consequence to a composer who has no wish to emulate Wagner by writing symphonic music for the stage. It is true that Rimsky-Korsakof constantly reiterated in the prefaces to his later operas that he " regarded an opera as first and foremost a *musical* work ". But the course of the story provided him with a ready-made shape, a skeleton to be covered with the flesh of his music. And he usually managed to do the covering very delightfully.

" Opera ", Rimsky-Korsakof once remarked to Yastrebtsef, " is essentially a false artistic genre, but alluring in its spaciousness and its endless variety of forms ". He certainly made the most of that " endless variety " and one might almost claim that his work summarises the whole of Russian opera. " The Maid of Pskof " is a less virile, less realistic counterpart of " Boris ", " Mozart and Salieri " obviously a companion-piece to " The Stone Guest ". " Sadko " and " Kitej " belong, each in its way, to the world of " Prince Igor ". " May Night " and " Snow Maiden " are purely lyrical in Glinka's vein. And though he never wrote anything quite as fine as " Boris " or " Igor ", Korsakof must be granted the quite peculiar power of evoking a fantastic world entirely his own, half-real, half-supernatural, a world as limited, as distinctive and as delightful as the world of the Grimms' fairy-tales or as Alice's Wonderland. It is a world in which the commonplace and matter-of-fact are inextricably confused with the fantastic, naïveté with sophistication, the romantic with the humorous, and beauty with absurdity. He was not its inventor, of course; he owed it in the first place to Pùshkin and Gogol. But he gave it a queer touch of his own, linking it with Slavonic antiquity and hinting at pantheistic symbolism, which makes it peculiarly his. And musically, of course, he reigns in it undisputed. He invented the perfect music for such a fantastic world: music insubstantial when it was matched with unreal things, deliciously lyrical when it touched reality, in both cases coloured from the most superb palette musician has ever held.

That he achieved anything higher or deeper than this, Rimsky-Korsakof himself would have been the first to deny. (Though he must have taken himself more seriously than we can as a genuinely *dramatic* composer.) Fully conscious of his own ability, Rimsky-Korsakof—with characteristically cool candour—never made any secret of the fact that he knew his limitations. He was seriously annoyed when people spoke of him as " a genius ". He knew that he had marvellous talents, but he knew that " genius " was another matter altogether. " Don't you think that you value me far too high?" he once said to Yastrebtsef. " Study Liszt and Balakiref more closely and you'll see that a great deal in me is—*not* me." Again, later in the course of the same conversation: " I repeat—by no means from modesty—you over-value me." But he was dealing with a hero-worshipper. There is little fear of his being over-valued by people who know him only by a handful of orchestral pieces—and perhaps the " Hindu Song " from " Sadko ".

G. A.

ANATOLE LIADOF

LIADOF is a composer whom everybody knows by name, and of whom everybody knows a piece or two. There, as a rule, the matter ends. He occupies no very prominent place in books on Russian music; and people are accustomed to think of him—when they think of him at all—only as a minor member of the so-called " nationalist " group.

Lazare Saminsky, in *Music of our day*, reminds us that he played an important, although unobtrusive, part in his time; that he was " the link between Rimsky-Korsakof and the new Russians ", a splendid teacher who influenced Stravinsky, Prokofief and many others, and also a composer whom his peers and the critics held in high esteem. Why then, has his output attracted so little notice? The reasons are various, and most of them can be traced back to idiosyncrasies of his own nature—to the fact that he had no ambition, no desire to assert himself or to stand in the limelight, and suffered from an unconquerable indolence and taste for self-effacement. He loved comfort and inactivity, disliked change and excitement; he was quiet and methodical—set, indeed—in his habits, very fond of solitude and addicted to cutting himself away from all people on the slightest of excuses. Above all things, he hated worries and obligations of any kind: " I am ", he wrote to a friend, " a bird of the air. The word ' duty ' has no meaning for me. My fancy is my only law ". In other words, he was a Bohemian at heart, only without any of the usual implications of the term applying to him.

It is very strange that this gentle, cheerful, easy-going man, who, as will presently be told, was born and lived in utterly favourable circumstances, enabling him to carry on without a

LIADOF

Reproduced by kind permission of J. & W. Chester Ltd., London, W

care in the world, should have spent his life feeling and proclaiming that " the world was tedious, disappointing, trying, purposeless, terrible ", and that art (especially, it would appear, the contemplative moods which it induced) was an escape and a refuge—the kingdom of unreality and pure fancy. " Give me ", he once wrote " fairies and dragons and mermaids and goblins, and I am thoroughly happy. Art feeds me on roast birds of paradise. It is another planet—nothing to do with our earth ". Stranger still, maybe, that feeling so deeply about that wonderful world of fancy and gifted as he was, he should have opened so few avenues into it to his fellow-men. His scepticism and his fondness for withdrawing into his ivory tower were stronger than his creative impulses. And so his output remained far more slender than might have been.

He was born (on April 29th/May 11th, 1855), endowed with all the gifts which a musician might wish for; and all, at first, seemed to be in his favour. He belonged to a family of professional musicians. His father, Constantine, was the conductor of the Petersburg Marinsky Theatre from 1850 to 1868, and a composer in a small way. One of his uncles, too, was a conductor, another a singer, a third a 'cellist. Thus, he had every opportunity not only of growing familiar with the current repertory, but also of practising music. When the time came for him to begin his training, professional education for composers was organized on a sound basis, so that he had not to contend with the difficulties which his elders had encountered in their quest for technical advice (the Petersburg and Moscow Conservatoires were founded in 1862 and 1866 respectively). But, as pointed out by the Russian critic Karatyghin in an essay published on the occasion of Liadof's fiftieth birthday (June, 1905) this was not all to the good. His education was carried out on lines rather too methodical and too monotonous to suit him. His inborn facility enabled him to yield to his inborn indolence. So much so that at one time he was dismissed from Rimsky-Korsakof's harmony class at the Petersburg Conservatoire for slackness. He completed his curriculum at that institution in 1877, with high honours. A letter from Mussorgsky to Stassof, written in the summer of 1873, may be selected among many testimonies of the excellent impression he produced in the musical circles to which he was introduced during his student days: it contains a remarkable thumb-nail sketch of him.

> A new talent has appeared in our midst, a genuine, thoroughly original, thoroughly Russian talent: Constantine Liadof's young son. He is bright and unaffected, he has boldness and power. Cui, Borodin, and my humble self are delighted with him. Let me describe him: fair-haired, thick-lipped, the forehead not very high but full of character, especially in conjunction with the high cheek-bones. Irregular little wrinkles run round his nose and mouth. He is extraordinarily nervous and highly-strung, and even more extraordinarily taciturn. He will sit listening, uttering no single word: but suddenly the crinkles around his nostrils begin to work and quiver, and that means praise! As to his own scribblings, well, you will judge for yourself. Korsakof has been holding forth on them quite a lot.

He made a brilliant debut in 1877 with a cantata " The Bride of Messina ", performed at the Petersburg Conservatoire (not his first composition—the opus number is 28—but the first to be performed publicly). In 1878 he was appointed a professor there, and in 1885 a professor at the Imperial Chapel. Later the Imperial Geographical Society invited him to join the commission for collecting and publishing the folk-music of Russia. This is practically the whole story of his public life.

In proportion as he acquired experience, his shyness seems to have increased rather than diminished. Often he expressed

—in terms delicately tinged with criticism, in the subtleties of which *"sans avoir l'air d'y toucher"* he was past master—his admiration for the speed with which other composers turned out work after work:

> How fortunate is Glazunof, he once wrote. He starts, speeds straight along as if on rails, and there he is. And Tchaïkovsky! He follows every dictate of his fancy, never pausing to consider what effect the outcome will have on other people, never fearing disapproval, never shunning commonplaces! How fortunate to be thus!

This seems to show that over-scrupulousness and an excessive inclination for self-criticism may have been responsible, as much as indolence and lack of will-power, for the slowness of his work. Karatyghin has remarked:

> His nature is strange and contradictory indeed. He has every conceivable gift: a marvellous technique, originality, a genuine poetic fancy, an abundance of rare humour (his Children's pieces rank with Schumann's and with Mussorgsky's " Nursery ") unerring taste, great intelligence: and all he gives us, year in year out, is about ten pages of music, or even less. This is a mortal sin against Apollo who endowed him so lavishly. He himself realises this, I think. For just now (1905) he seems to devote more energy to composing. He is writing a big ballet on a subject by Remizof. May his artistic conscience continue to stimulate and sustain him!

Unfortunately, the ballet in question was never finished. A plan for an opera fared no better. In 1895 Rimsky-Korsakof wrote to him:

> Dear friend, do write an opera—and a really Russian opera. You are splendidly equipped for the venture, and

nobody else could do it as you will. A legendary opera, for sure: and above all things, one free from DRRRAMA!

Liadof had been toying with the idea for many years. As early as 1879 he had thought of asking the poet Golenishchef-Kutuzof to provide him with a libretto based on a play by Dahl entitled " Night at the Crossroads ", but the plan was given up after one scene of this libretto had been written. Later, upon Stassof's suggestion, Liadof made the same request to another poet, Polonsky, who agreed, wrote several scenes, and then—for reasons not quite clear—also gave up the job. Liadof then turned to Stassof's daughter, Varvara Komarova. She, too, was unable to carry the task to completion. Under her *nom de plume*, Vladimir Karenin, she gave in the special Liadof number of the Petrograd " Musical Contemporary " (1916) the following reason:

> In order to satisfy the requirements of his poetic taste and critical sense, it would have been needful for me to grow wings. He ought to have selected a real poet such as Gorodetsky or Remizof, whom he met later only. Then maybe, " Zoriushka " (this was the title selected for the opera) would have been composed.

Portions of the music outlined for " Zoriushka " were used by Liadof in his tone-poems " Kikimora " and " The Enchanted Lake ".

Among the principal works he planned or began but did not finish should be mentioned a string quartet at which he worked in 1877. Rimsky-Korsakof, in his " Memoirs ", describes the portions which he showed to his friends as admirable. The first movement was actually written down, and the manuscript is preserved in the library of the Leningrad Conservatoire. Towards the end of his life, he thought of writing a pendant to his tone-poem (Op. 66) on the Book of Revelation—seeking inspiration, this time, on the fourth chapter. He also thought of writing incidental music for one of Maeterlinck's plays. Diaghilef, who admired him greatly, did his utmost to persuade him to finish his ballet. And at the time of his death (1914) he was hoping to write an orchestral work founded on a Russian legend.

Such is the sad tale of what Liadof might have done but lacked the perseverance to do. Even without inclining to praise him as hyperbolically as Karatyghin did (saying, for instance, that " as regards imaginativeness in the matter of harmony, he equalled the most significant of revolutionary innovators ") one may justifiably aver that he never gave his true measure, and regret that the catalogue of his output should not be richer in works of a lofty and sustained order such as his admirable " From the Book of Revelation ". This, by virtue of its earnestness and breadth, of the austere vigour of its eloquence, and its truly dramatic quality, stands unique among his compositions, except maybe for the grave meditative " Nénie " or dirge for orchestra (Op. 67). Elsewhere, he usually appears genial, cheerful, slightly detached at times, although always sincere and never purposeless. His other orchestral works—the tone-poems " Baba Yaga ", " Kikimora " and " The Enchanted Lake ", and the eight orchestral pieces on Russian folk-songs (Op. 58) among others —are attractive enough fully to deserve a place in the sun. A few of his songs—especially the lovely children's songs Op. 14 and 18—could hold their own on the concert platform. And pianists might profitably explore the fairly long catalogue of his music for their instrument.

Another reason (not a very good one) for the small place given by historians and critics to consideration of his output is, maybe, that his music induces delight rather than excitement and affords little food for thought or discussion. It is music of the kind that everybody can take in his stride, and that will never surprise or bewilder. Its merits are charm, grace, polish, alertness, and moderation. He has neither the power and glow of Borodin and Balakiref, nor the exuberant fancy of Rimsky-Korsakof at his best, nor the energy and abundance of Glazunof; but of the minor poets of music—not only Russian—he remains one of the most lovable.

M. D. C.

GLAZUNOF
by Repin

GLAZUNOF

IN Glazunof we have the unusual case of a composer who, owing to his remarkable gifts and capacity for work, acquired at an early age a big reputation which endured for a fairly long period, but afterwards declined instead of rising, until a time came when not only his new works, but also those which had contributed most to his fame, were relegated more or less to the background: a strange fate, the reasons for which (obvious enough but not entirely satisfactory, nor, maybe, final) will presently appear.

He is of purely Russian descent. In 1782 his great-granduncle Matthew Glazunof, founded at Moscow a publishing firm. A branch was opened at Petersburg two years later, and Ivan Glazunof, Matthew's brother, settled in that city, where Alexander, his great-grandson, was born on July 29th/August 10th, 1865.

Alexander, during his early childhood, showed no special inclination for music; but from the time when he was given his first piano lessons, he began to make speedy headway. His father, Constantine, was a violinist, and his mother an excellent pianist, who, we are told, but for her extreme shyness, might have made a name for herself. She was the pupil of a teacher of repute, Elenkofsky, whom, in 1877, she decided to entrust with the musical education of her son. Elenkofsky, from the outset, strove to develop the boy's musical gifts, to educate his taste, and to teach him theory. Alexander responded readily, and soon began to display, besides an extraordinary memory (of which he was to give signal examples later), a fine sense of part-writing and harmonic combinations. He also proclaimed that he wished to become a composer " not of piano music but of orchestral "—a declaration which accurately foretokened the course of his career: most of his output consists of orchestral and chamber music.

In 1878, Elenkofsky left Petrograd, and Mrs. Glazunova went to Balakiref for further lessons. She introduced her son to him, and he urged her to give the boy a thorough theoretical education, recommending Rimsky-Korsakof as a teacher. Alexander became Rimsky-Korsakof's pupil in 1880. Balakiref, who was so struck with the youth's gifts that he nicknamed him " the little Glinka ", watched his progress closely and gave him useful advice—especially for the composition of his first symphony and of a piano suite on the theme S-A-S-C-H-A (S as in Schumann's " Lettres Dansants " is E flat; and H, German for B—" Sascha " is the Russian diminutive of " Alexander "). The symphony was outlined in 1881, finished in the course of the winter, and performed in March, 1882, at a concert of the Free School of Music, Balakiref conducting, with triumphant success. During the rehearsals, he was presented with a laurel wreath bearing the inscription " To our Hermann and Cazeneuve " (Hermann and Cazeneuve were two conjurors whose skill, just then, amazed Petersburg). On the day of the performance, he took the call in his schoolboy uniform, and again was presented with a wreath. Cui and Stassof spoke of his work in high terms. Stassof's admiration for the young composer's vitality and energy was aptly expressed in the habit he had of referring to him as " our young Samson ". Other critics, after emphasising the many evidences of technical maturity in the work, spread the rumour that the symphony had been written, for a consideration, by " a well-known composer ".

This anonymous provider, had he existed, would have been kept busy during the following period. For a string quartet by Glazunof was performed in the autumn; and before having completed his twentieth year, he had turned out, besides another quartet, half a dozen other orchestral works, including the two fine overtures on Greek folk-tunes and the tone-poem " Stenka Razin ". He had also outlined other important works, which he completed soon afterwards, and submitted his first symphony to several revisions, eventually giving it the final form in which it appeared in 1886.

In 1884, he made a long journey abroad, beginning with Weimar, where he paid a visit to Liszt, whose music he admired greatly and to whose memory he was to inscribe his second symphony and an Elegy for 'cello and piano. He went to Spain and to Africa, and on his way back, to Bayreuth, where he heard " Parsifal " but was not much impressed by it (later, he developed a great admiration for Wagner, whose influence on his technique was to be almost as great as Liszt's). Among the works that immediately followed his second and third symphonies, the " Oriental Rhapsody " and the tone-poem " The Forest " deserve special mention, and should be better known than they are. He soon began to enjoy an international reputation. His first symphony was performed at Weimar in 1884; the second, and also " Stenka Razin " created a great impression when performed at the concerts of the Paris Universal Exhibition, 1889. In 1895, he was commissioned to write a Triumphal March for the Chicago Exhibition. He visited England in 1896, 1902 and 1907 (when he was made a Doctor of Cambridge University). As early as 1899, he was appointed professor of instrumentation at the Petersburg Conservatoire; and in 1909, its principal.

Apart from the continuous progress of his career, his life was uneventful until the War. He remained a quiet, unassuming worker, loving his work for its own sake, and concerned neither with theories nor with any form of self-assertion—he is one of the few composers of today who have never written a line on musical topics, at least for publication. The catalogue of his output grew steadily. It consists mainly of symphonic and other instrumental music, including three ballets, eight symphonies, the last of which was finished in 1904. Since then, although his interest in abstract music continued to grow—as shown by his fine string quartets and other works for small combinations—some of his principal orchestral compositions have been of the " poetic " order: not tone-poems, similar to those that occupy so big a place in his earlier output, but Fantasias on Finnish themes, preludes in memory of Rimsky-Korsakof and Stassof, and so on.

The first twelve years that followed the War he remained in Russia, devoting, as before, much of his time to the Conservatoire, where he organised a students' orchestra and an opera studio. Then he settled in Paris, where he now lives.

His career as a composer began at a turning-point in the history of Russian music, at the time when the national movement started under the influence of Glinka not only was being challenged more vigorously than ever by the conservative circles, but had nearly spent itself and was tending to run in a groove—when " national " commonplaces were tending to become as current as scholastic commonplaces. Yet, the early works he wrote in a style that owed much to that of Balakiref, Borodin, and Rimsky-Korsakof, lack neither freshness nor vigour; they betoken spontaneity of conception and execution, and are worthy of ranking as original and not derivative achievements. They helped, in their time, to popularise Russian music abroad. On the other hand, he was more interested than any of his elders in problems of pure form and scholastic methods of working-out and architecture. German influences eventually changed his style and the character of his music. His late works, indeed, are so dissimilar in spirit from those of his youth and early maturity, that they won him an altogether different category of admirers.

His Russian biographer, Ossovsky, has said:

> He effected the reconciliation between the Russian music of his time and Western music. In this respect his part

was even more decisive than that of Tchaïkovsky, who was in the thick of the struggle between Eastern and Western tendencies—wherefore it was impossible for him to fulfil the part of an actual peacemaker.

But other, less favourable opinions have also been expressed. It was felt—as bluntly stated, for instance, in Stravinsky's recently-published " Memoirs "—that he was becoming more and more academic, and following a path alien to both his own nature and that of Russian music. His early works are neglected, and the late ones, sharing the fate of those of the other typical conservative Russian composers, such as Taneief and Metner, have not found great favour. This, no doubt, is a temporary state of affairs; an adjustment is bound to take place, and to give his best works the place they unquestionably deserve.

M. D. C.

SERGEÏ LIAPUNOF

SERGEÏ Liapunof, a quiet, earnest figure, an industrious and sincere musician, a composer whose lyrical inspiration has distinctive and attractive qualities quite of his own, and the last representative, after Liadof, of the nineteenth-century " national " Russian school, never came very much into the limelight, but his work won warm appreciation from the many who knew it.

Born on November 30th/December 12th, 1859, at Yaroslavl, he first studied music at Nijni-Novgorod, and showed himself gifted enough to attract the attention of Nicholas Rubinstein, who advised him to complete his professional education at Moscow. At the Moscow Conservatoire he became Nicholas Rubinstein's pupil, studied both the piano and composition, and finished his curriculum brilliantly in 1883. Then he went to Petersburg, and forthwith became Balakiref's friend and disciple, remaining in close association with him until the end (Balakiref died in 1910) and following a similar path both in his compositions and in his artistic creeds.

To describe him as a mirrored counterpart, or even an understudy, of Balakiref would be inaccurate. His reason for moving from Moscow to Petersburg certainly was that he wished to join the " national " circle of which Balakiref was the leader, rather than remain in the more eclectic and conservative atmosphere of Moscow, when Tchaïkovsky stood supreme. And he was attracted at the very outset by Balakiref's magnetic personality—at a time, let it be remembered, when Balakiref's influence on the original members of the circle was already very much on the wane. As has been

LIAPUNOF

said in a previous chapter, the coming of Liapunof at that time was a piece of good fortune for the lonely and disenchanted Balakiref; and the seventeen years of friendship that were to follow meant as much to the master as to the disciple. But, despite all the spiritual affinities between the two, Liapunof, as a composer, remained very different from Balakiref. His music is more purely lyrical, less vehement, fundamentally contemplative. He was endowed with a keen sense of colour and poetry, but not with the burning energy (and attendant restlessness of imagination) that characterises Balakiref.

So his music, let it be repeated, has an identity of its own, well marked although not exactly striking. Its merits were acknowledged from the first, when Rimsky-Korsakof, in 1884, conducted the first performance of an overture of his (in C sharp minor). From that moment on, his career was, in a small way, a successful one. In 1894, he was appointed assistant director of the Imperial Chapel, in 1910 he was given charge of a piano class at the Petersburg Conservatoire, and a little later was appointed professor of theory and composition there. During the War and after, he composed little. In 1923, he came to live in Paris. There, he was invited to organise and direct the Russian Conservatoire, founded by the Russian exiles; and he devoted his activities to this task unsparingly until death struck him suddenly on November 9th, 1924. During the last years of his life he displayed great activity in composition, turning out, among other things, a suite, a Psalm and a poem for baritone and orchestra.

His output comprises two symphonies, several tone-poems and other orchestral works, two piano concertos and a " Ukrainian Fantasy " for piano and orchestra, a piano sextet, a great amount of piano music and many songs.

Generally speaking, it shows the influence of Glinka and Liszt as well as that of Balakiref. Yet his treatment of the piano—an art in which he was past master—while prolonging, so to speak, the practice of Liszt and Balakiref, does not echo it any more than his lyricism and nationalism are mere echoes of Balakiref—even when he, in turn, finds inspiration in the scenery, atmosphere, and folk-music of the Caucasus ("Terek" and "Lesghinka" in his "Études d'execution transcendante"), or the epic and religious tunes of old Russia "Carillon" and "Chant Epique" in the same set.) And he is equally genuine when, without any preoccupation of nationalism, he gives us, in "Nuit d'Été" and "Idylle" (also in the same set) lovely, tender, glowing music which might serve as a worthy setting of the night of Lorenzo and Jessica in the "Merchant of Venice".

After the "Études" and certain other piano pieces, among which his "Third Impromptu" may be mentioned, it is probably his songs that will keep his memory alive. There are very fine things in his symphonies and concertos; but he lacked the architectural vision failing which no composer can deal in big forms unless he is endowed, as Balakiref was, with an almost uncanny instinct for achieving formal unity in defiance of every known principle. All the other gifts of the born composer were his: the sense of melody and harmony, of writing for the voice and for instruments, the capacity for heroic eloquence and delicate colour play. He remains, with Liadof, the most attractive of the minor poets of Russian music.

M. D. C.

TANEIEF

Reproduced by permission of Kegan Paul, Trench, Trubner & Co., Ltd

SERGEÏ TANEIEF

THE roll of Russian composers bears the names of two Taneiefs. The elder by six years, Alexander Sergeïevitch, a man with three symphonies, an opera and several smaller orchestral works to his credit, was one of the minor nationalists. He was an amateur, a Government official by profession. On the other hand, his namesake Sergeï Ivanovitch disliked the " mighty handful " and most of its works, and was perhaps the most remarkable purely academic musician Russia has ever produced. It is of him that one thinks when one speaks of " Taneief " without qualification or initials.

Taneief was born on November 13th/25th, 1856, in the Vladimir Government where his father held an official post. The father, Ivan Ilitch Taneief, was not only a keen amateur musician but a man of exceptional all-round intelligence; his family was aristocratic, his brother being Marshal of the Imperial Court, while one of the latter's daughters became a lady-in-waiting. Ivan Taneief had graduated in three subjects at Moscow University—literature, medicine and mathematics—and this breadth of interest was inherited by his son. The boy had his first piano lessons at five, and in September, 1866, before he was ten, was sent to the newly-opened Conservatoire of Music in Moscow, studying the piano and elementary theory with E. L. Langer. At eleven he went to the ordinary high school and his musical education suffered for a couple of years. But Nicholas Rubinstein then persuaded Ivan Taneief that his son was born to be a musician, and in September, 1869, the boy entered the harmony class of Professor Tchaïkovsky—and at once became his favourite pupil. Two years later he entered Nicholas Rubinstein's piano class and in

January, 1875, made his debut at an R.M.S. concert, playing Brahms's D minor Concerto. To play *that* in particular was, to some extent, a portent, though the choice was Rubinstein's, not his own. In the following May he left the Conservatoire, carrying off the Grand Gold Medal, awarded only for a double first, which no one had won before. He had already composed a Symphony in E minor, an Overture in D minor, and begun a string quartet. But these were only school works, never published or even performed. Although Taneief wrote a great deal, it was long before anyone but Tchaïkovsky saw his compositions.

For the time being, Taneief was first and foremost a pianist. Eight days after his nineteenth birthday he played Tchaïkovsky's B flat minor Concerto for the first time in Moscow. It had already been given in Petersburg, but all the rest of Tchaïkovsky's works for piano and orchestra were introduced to the public by Taneief. After a concert-tour of the Russian provinces with Leopold Auer, Taneief went abroad in November, 1876, and spent a year in Paris, perfecting his piano technique and meeting Turgenef and Saltykof-Shchedrin among his compatriots and Franck, Gounod, Saint-Saëns, d'Indy and Fauré among French musicians. Before leaving Russia Taneief had begun a piano concerto, never finished, but his first composition in Paris was of a very different nature, a March for two pianos, harmonium, three trombones, 'cello, oboe and glockenspiel, written for performance at Duparc's on the *Mardigras*. That was symptomatic. Taneief had a dual nature rather like Lewis Carroll's, half mathematician, half humourist. Practically all his published works and a great many unpublished ones are as severely intellectual as anything a musician has put on staved paper. The rest, which one fears will never be published, consist of " Quartets of Government Officials ", humorous choruses, comic fugues and variations, toy symphonies, a mock ballet for Tchaïkovsky's birthday with an absurd scenario and music which is an ingenious contrapuntal pot-pourri of themes from Tchaïkovsky's works, and other *jeux d'esprit* of the same nature. In the middle of the 'nineties Taneief became interested in Esperanto and wrote several songs to Esperanto texts. His pupil and fellow-Esperantist, L. L. Sabaneief, once received from him a " letter " consisting of three four-part canons, each canon being a setting of a sentence in Esperanto: " I have received your letter ", " Your counterpoints are very good ", " I thank you ".

Artistically, Paris seems to have made little impression on Taneief. He returned to Moscow and began a Second Symphony in B flat minor, but this was interrupted and never finished. The interruption was flattering enough. Tchaïkovsky was accustomed to pay every attention to his young ex-pupil's criticisms of his compositions, candid as they often were, and in September, 1878, when he left the Conservatoire, both he and Nicholas Rubinstein pressed Taneief, not yet twenty-two, to take his place. At first Taneief agreed, after some hesitation, to take only the harmony and instrumentation classes. Not feeling himself a sufficiently good contrapuntist to teach counterpoint he now began to study it—with the most remarkable results. He had already been attracted by the writings of Laroche to the music of Bach and still more to that of the older Netherland masters of strict counterpoint, Okeghem, Josquin des Prés, and Lassus. He now studied them to such purpose that he became one of the greatest theoretical contrapuntists of all time, though even his driest studies betray the humorous side of his nature, his delight in the incongruous. In the winter of 1879-80 we find him writing a " Fugue in the Strict Style " on one Russian folk-song from Balakiref's Collection and a twelve-part " Netherlandish Fantasia " on another! On June 6th/18th, 1880, he made his debut as a composer with a Cantata for the unveiling of the Pushkin Memorial in Moscow. Two years later he wrote for the All-Russian Exhibition of Art and Industry an " Overture on a Russian Theme ", " full of contrapuntal ingenuities " according to Rimsky-Korsakof, which was played under Taneief himself at the Exhibition on June 13th/25th, 1882, and repeated at R.M.S. concerts in both capitals the same year. But it was long after this before it was generally known that he took himself seriously as a composer.

Taneief now became more and more deeply involved in the affairs of the Moscow Conservatoire. Klindworth left and Rubinstein died a few months later (March, 1881) and Taneief was put in charge of the piano classes. Then in 1883 N. A. Hubert left and he found himself teaching the composition class. Finally in 1885, before he was twenty-nine, Tchaïkovsky got him made Director of the Conservatoire, very much against his will. Taneief came back from a summer holiday in the Caucasus, where he often returned in later years, his notebooks full of folk-songs, and took charge of his *alma mater*. The institution had been in a bad way since Rubinstein's death, but Taneief not only reformed the teaching system but, by careful administration, put the Conservatoire on a sound financial footing, while with the help of F. P. Kommissarjevsky, the student opera-productions begun by Rubinstein were continued on the most ambitious scale. On becoming Director, Taneief handed over his theory and piano classes respectively to Arensky and Safonof, who had both just left the Petersburg Conservatoire.

All this time—indeed, until he was nearly forty—Taneief lived with his elder brother, Vladimir, one of the most prominent lawyers in Moscow and the centre of an intellectual circle which included the famous satirist Saltykof-Shchedrin and most of the professors of the Moscow University. In this circle, and with his friends the Maslofs (likewise intellectuals), with whom he spent almost every summer at Selishche in the Orlof Government, Taneief's non-musical interests were fostered and deepened. He studied natural science, history, mathematics and social questions, Plato and Spinoza, not in the usual Russian way as an idle diversion, but as seriously as he studied the scores of the old contrapuntists. Naturally, with his Conservatoire duties and his work as a concert-pianist, he had little time left for composition, and most of his creative work was done during the summers at Selishche. Still, he managed to compose a cantata " John of Damascus " (a curious hybrid, by Tchaïkovsky out of Bach), dedicated to the memory of Nicholas Rubinstein, in 1884; a Third Symphony in D minor, dedicated to Arensky, which was played under his own direction in Moscow in January, 1885 —and then forgotten for thirty years;[1] and two or three string quartets, to say nothing of numerous smaller works, all unknown. The cantata was published as Op. 1, but for the most part Taneief was completely indifferent to the publication of his works, if not actually opposed to it! At the same time, he was anxious to give more time to composition and, strangely enough for a man of his temperament, was ambitious to write an opera. Even at fifteen he had wanted to compose an opera on a French Revolutionary subject; then in 1877, while in Paris, he had asked Tchaïkovsky about Constantine Shilovsky's " Ephraim " libretto; in 1884 he thought of adapting Lope de Vega's " Fuente Ovejune "; but finally in 1887 he decided on the " Orestes " of Æschylus, of which the Overture, an independent composition, was conducted by Tchaïkovsky in Moscow in the autumn of 1889. The composition of this, his only stage-work, occupied Taneief for seven years—partly owing to his peculiar method of composing. Before he began the actual construction of a big work he would collect all his thematic material and write all sorts of preparatory contrapuntal exercises on it, fugues and canons and what not. Only when he had completely mastered

---

[1] Tchaïkovsky criticised it rather severely as " not orchestral music but an orchestral arrangement of abstract music ". But nearly everything Taneief wrote seems to have been conceived as " abstract music " for no special medium.

his material in this way—pressed and rolled and kneaded it, as it were—and discovered all its latent possibilities, would he begin the actual composition.

The more Taneief was attracted to composition, the more irksome became his administrative work at the Conservatoire; in 1889 he resigned the Directorship in favour of the brilliant piano professor, V. I. Safonof (who was later to win fame as a conductor), though he continued to take the counterpoint classes. In the same year he definitely began his monumental book on " Invertible Counterpoint " which had already been in his mind for some time and which occupied him for nearly twenty years, a masterly and exhaustive examination of the laws of counterpoint treated as a branch of mathematics.

" Orestes " being finished by the summer of 1894, Taneef turned to chamber-music, writing a whole series of quartets which for years were neither published nor performed. But now at last, approaching forty, he was to appear a little more openly as a composer. The change was largely due to Rimsky-Korsakof, whom he had got to know through Tchaïkovsky. In the 'eighties Taneief had held the most contemptuous view of the " handful "—as of Wagner.[1] He had no use for the early works of Glazunof; according to Korsakof, " he considered Borodin a merely capable dilettante and laughed at Mussorgsky. Probably he had no higher opinion of Cui and me ". As for Balakiref, he disliked him both as composer and conductor. " Honourable, blunt and straightforward ", says Rimsky-Korsakof, " Taneief always spoke his mind with perfect candour ". And at the Glinka Memorial concert at Smolensk in May, 1885, Taneief called out publicly to Balakiref, " Mily Alexeievitch, we're not satisfied with you!" But even Balakiref did not dislike Taneief. " Greet

---

[1] " How right Peter Ilitch " (Tchaïkovsky) " was when he said all this was ' nasty chromaticism ' ", Taneief grumbled at the Prelude and " Liebestod " from " Tristan ".

Taneief warmly from me ", he writes to Tchaïkovsky—it is true, before the incident at Smolensk. " I find his nobility of character very sympathetic; he always expresses himself with complete frankness and without beating about the bush. An honourable and good-natured enemy is far better than a Jesuitical friend." But being satisfied by Tchaïkovsky that Rimsky-Korsakof had really made himself quite a respectable contrapuntist, Taneief began to visit him when he was in Petersburg and a friendship sprang up which was severed only by Rimsky-Korsakof's death. Taneief also changed his opinion of Borodin and Glazunof, and, in the train of his former pupil Scriabin, joined the fringe of the Belaief circle, though he cannot have taken part in their all-night restaurant sittings, for he was a teetotaller. Playing them his newly-completed " Orestes ", he " struck us all " (says Korsakof) " with its pages of unusual beauty and expressiveness ". Later, after hearing one of Taneief's quintets, Rimsky-Korsakof said to Kashkin: " You know, before such mastery one feels a mere pupil."

" Orestes " was given at the Marinsky Theatre on October 17th/29th, 1895, and met with more success than might have been expected for an opera written by a man of Taneief's frame of mind (in spite of the queer streak of Tchaïkovskian lyricism which shows so strangely through the rocky strata of counterpoint). But Napravnik wanted to cut it. (Was there ever a Russian opera on which Napravnik did not wish to perform these surgical operations?) Taneief refused his consent. And so " Orestes " disappeared from the stage till after the composer's death twenty years later. But Belaief forthwith astonished Taneief with an offer to publish the opera. And not only the opera but some of his chamber music as well. After some hesitation Taneief revised the score, consulting Glazunof about the orchestration of certain unsatisfactory passages, and finally agreed. There is a legend that Taneief refused for some time to accept any payment from

Belaief, on the ground that his music was not really worth the money. And, considering Taneief's character and his comfortable financial position, one hesitates to deny the truth of the legend categorically.

In January, 1898, Taneief finished his Fourth Symphony in C minor, dedicated to Glazunof. It waited four years before it was played (in Moscow, under Ziloti), and was published misleadingly as " Symphony No. 1 ", Op. 12.

At about the time of the production of " Orestes " Taneief made the acquaintance of Leo Tolstoy and thenceforward became a frequent visitor at Yasnaia Poliana, though his music was of the kind Tolstoy most detested Nor did he ever become a whole-hogging Tolstoyan. But both were men of very wide interests, and Taneief certainly sympathised with many of Tolstoy's ideas. Besides, Tolstoy loved music in a narrow, rather naïve way, and Taneief was always welcome as pianist if not as composer. Yet his visits to Yasnaia Poliana produced a complication which would have been specially embarrassing to a man so chaste and honourable as he, had he been aware of it. For the Countess Tolstoy, a woman twelve or thirteen years older than himself, fell in love with him—he was a very handsome man—and for eight or ten years was tormented with a passion which frequently aroused Tolstoy's jealousy. Her diary is full of entries about Taneief. " Nearly all my photos came out well ", she writes in July, 1897.[1] " I took several of Taneief, and this time Leo Nikolaevitch did not mind. He ... has not been angry with me at all. As if there were any reason why he should! What evil can there be in my friendly attachment to such a kind, pure, talented man? What a pity Leo Nikolaevitch's jealousy should have marred our friendship." And ten days later: " I have been thinking a lot of Taneief. ... There is something in him that everybody loves. I think of him

---

[1] " The Countess Tolstoy's Later Diary (1891–1897) ", translated by Alexander Werth (Gollancz).

serenely—it is always like this after seeing him. But I always miss him, especially during the summer months." Nor did her feeling grow more Platonic as the years passed. " I want to cry ", she wrote in 1903, when she was nearly sixty, " I long to see the man who is the focus of my shameful insanity. But let no one raise his hand against me, for I have suffered horribly ".[1] To the end Taneief seems to have been happily unaware of the emotional storm which centred about him, though the Countess's infatuation was well known to most of their friends.

In 1905, however, he became involved in a storm of a different nature. Like Rimsky-Korsakof, Taneief sympathised with liberal tendencies in politics, in strange contrast with his extreme conservatism in music. His relations with Safonof, the reactionary and bureaucratic, though musically progressive, Director of the Moscow Conservatoire, had been strained for some time, and when in 1905 at the crisis of the revolutionary movement Safonof, apparently anxious to demonstrate that he was a true son of a Cossack general, took severe repressive measures against the students, Taneief resigned from the staff of the institution with which he had been connected for almost the whole of his life, while Safonof himself shook the dust of Russia from his feet altogether and crossed the Atlantic to take charge of the New York Philharmonic Orchestra.

Thus set completely free, Taneief resumed his career as a pianist, touring Russia as a soloist and also appearing in Berlin, Vienna and Prague in chamber music with the Bohemian Quartet. He was able to devote more time to composition, producing a whole series of trios, quartets, and quintets—those from Op. 16 onwards—with a few choruses and songs. In 1909 at last appeared his *magnum opus*, the treatise on " Invertible Counterpoint ", with its motto from Leonardo da Vinci: " Nissuna humana investigatione si po

[1] This last part of the Countess's diary has not yet (1935) appeared in English.

dimandare vera scientia, s'essa non passa per le mattematiche dimostrationi." (Freely: "No branch of study can claim to be considered a true science unless it is capable of being demonstrated mathematically.") That completed, Taneief at once began another study of " Canon ", which remained unfinished. In addition, he found time to institute a musical library in Moscow, to take an active part in the musical activities of the Ethnographical Society, to edit Laroche's critical writings, and to plan a new opera, " Hero and Leander ". In 1910 he even began to study Wagner, whom he had hitherto disliked so, and found some good things in " Parsifal ".

Taneief had long wanted to set Khomiakof's poem, " On the Reading of a Psalm ", but had been unable to spare time from his teaching. But a generous advance royalty paid by Kussevitsky's Russian Music Publishing Company enabled him to devote himself entirely to the work; he completed the cantata, his last and best work, Op. 36, on December 31st, 1914/January 13th, 1915. It was performed twice in each capital in the following March under Kussevitsky, and universally hailed as a masterpiece. The following month Taneief caught a cold at Scriabin's funeral in Moscow and died from an affection of the heart on June 6th/19th, 1915.

With his resemblance to Brahms, not only physical but mental, and with not dissimilar tastes and ideals, it is all the more strange that Taneief disliked Brahms's music. But he lived entirely in the past and was far more interested in Josquin des Prés than in Chopin. Except Tchaïkovsky, for whom his affection must have been entirely sentimental, Mozart was the most modern composer for whom he felt whole-hearted admiration. His gods were Lassus and Palestrina, Bach and Handel. As for Strauss, Debussy and Scriabin, they were anathema—like the telegraph, telephone and electric light. After the separation from his brother, caused by family differences, he lived in a tiny house without even running water, just outside Moscow. There, looked after by his old nurse, he was visited by a host of friends, pupils, and ex-pupils, loved even by the modernists whose compositions he bludgeoned with ponderous wit and boisterous laughter—the Dr. Johnson of Russian music.

G. A.

ALEXANDER SCRIABIN

EARLY in the year 1871, a twenty-one-year-old law student of Moscow University named Nicholas Alexandrovitch Scriabin took unto himself a wife just a year younger than himself, Liubov Petrovna Shchetinina. Nicholas Alexandrovitch himself, one of the eight children of an artillery colonel, was fond of music though not specially gifted, but his sister—likewise named Liubov—was a Beethoven-loving amateur pianist, while his bride had been one of Leschetizky's best pupils at the Petersburg Conservatoire and a special pet of the Rubinstein brothers. (She called Anton " papa " and Nicholas " uncle ".) Liubov Petrovna had just started on a career as a concert pianist when she met the young law-student. Just what happened it is difficult to say, but Nicholas suddenly left the University without a degree and apparently tried to practise in some way in Saratof for a few months. Things evidently went badly with the young couple, however; Liubov was expecting a child; they gave up the struggle for independence, threw themselves on Colonel Alexander Scriabin's mercy and hurried to his house in Moscow—only just in time. At two o'clock on the very day they arrived, Christmas Day, 1871/January 6th, 1872, Liubov gave birth to a son. In later years Alexander Nikolaevitch was to attach a special mystic significance to the fact that he was born on Christ's birthday.

The young father went back to his classes, while Liubov, in spite of continued bad health, began to think of returning to the concert platform. But she grew worse instead of better. In September, 1872, she was ordered to the Southern Tyrol, and there in the following April, she died of gallop-

SCRIABIN
by L. O. Pasternak

Reproduced by kind permission of J. & W. Chester Ltd., London, W

ing consumption, at Arco, on the shores of Lake Garda, where she was buried. After her death Nicholas studied at the School of Oriental Languages at Petersburg; then, leaving his baby in the care of his parents, entered the consular service, and after holding various posts in Turkey and Crete became Consul-General at Erzerum. About 1880 he married again, this time an Italian girl, who bore him three sons (one of whom was killed in the Great War) and a daughter, none of them in the least interested in music. Every three years he received four months' leave, which he spent with his family in Russia or Switzerland, and which enabled him to see his eldest son. But the child's upbringing was left entirely in the hands of his grandparents. Or rather, since the grandfather died in 1879, in the hands of his grandmother, an exceedingly strong-minded lady who actually outlived her famous grandchild by several months, and of his aunt Liubov Alexandrovna. It was this aunt, a girl of twenty-one at the time of his birth, who really took the place of his mother and superintended his education as long as she was able.

There can be no doubt that this upbringing in an almost entirely feminine atmosphere had a predominating influence in moulding the boy's naturally gentle character to definite effeminacy. His aunt and grandmother worshipped him and spoiled him. He had no playmates of his own age, nor did he care for other children. All he wanted to do was to sit quietly in the room with his elders. He could not bear to be left alone and the custom of never leaving him ingrained in him such a dislike of solitude that as a young man he preferred not to be alone even when composing. He was quite fourteen before his aunt allowed him to go about the streets by himself, and at the time of his first lessons with Taneief, the latter often had to escort the boy home. This " cotton-wool " upbringing left numerous other traces in after life—a fear of draughts, even in summer; a fear of germs and infection which led him invariably to wear gloves in the street and to put them on before handling money. Like Glinka he was always over-concerned about his health and pathetically anxious to drink medicine, often in larger doses than had been prescribed.

The boy was five before his aunt taught him his alphabet; under her leisurely instruction, he did not learn to read and write till he was nearly seven. At five his aunt began to take him to the opera—the Scriabins had a box at the Grand Theatre—and from that time onward one of his favourite pastimes was the production, with a toy theatre, of things he had seen or even made up for himself. From adapting Gogol's " Nose ", which his aunt had read to him, he progressed at seven or eight to the writing of tragedies of his own, partly in prose, partly in verse, " getting awfully excited, jumping up, beginning to declaim, gesticulating, then sitting down again and going on with his writing ". Like Wagner in *his* youthful " Shakespearian tragedy ", Sasha Scriabin's dramas were so crowded with murder and suicide that on more than one occasion the entire *dramatis personæ* were annihilated half-way through the proceedings. These childish tragedies, long preserved by his aunt, with all the letters he wrote as a child, were unfortunately destroyed at the time of the great Moscow flood.

Even at four the child's ear and musical memory were exceptionally good. In 1877, at the outbreak of the Russo-Turkish War, having been taken to say good-bye to one of his uncles, a Guards officer, he went home and reproduced on the piano a popular dance-tune he had heard played by a military band at the railway station. Although he also tried to play the fiddle and guitar, it was the piano that specially fascinated him. Not only its music, but the instrument itself and " the works ". He loved to lie at full-length under the piano, looking up while his aunt played. And he tried to make toy pianos of wood. His aunt's piano was to him not a mere instrument, but a living thing; when it had to be moved he was indescribably agitated; sometimes before going to bed he would kiss it as if it had been an ikon. He loved to improvise, especially if other people would listen to him, and at eight varied his series of tragedies with an " opera " which he named after a little girl who had made a deep impression on his youthful heart—" Liza ". (Scriabin's eroticism showed itself early; he told Sabaneief that at nine he was " in love in the full sense of the word ".) But with all this he had not learned to read music, and when his aunt tried to teach him his notes he was not in the least interested. As a matter of fact, Scriabin never did become a good reader. Long after he had become famous as a pianist, he confided to G. E. Konius: " If I had to be examined in sight-reading, I should come a cropper over a Kuhlau sonatina!" As a child he was bored by the effort—and Liubov Alexandrovna was no disciplinarian. And at seven, when he was exhibited to Anton Rubinstein, the great man advised: " Don't worry the child. Let him develop in freedom. Everything will come right in time."

Scriabin's serious education, both musical and general, did not begin till he was ten, when in the autumn of 1882 he entered the Second Moscow Cadet Corps. But it is a tribute to his aunt's training that in the entrance examination he headed the list of seventy candidates. It was his own wish that he should go into the army, just as Rimsky-Korsakof had been determined to become a sailor; and his misdirected childish ambition was due to the same sort of influence. Sasha's uncles were all in the army—the youngest, Dmitri, only six years older than himself, was still a cadet; he was continually hearing army talk, talk of life in the Cadet Corps; and, although his father wished him to enter a civil school, Sasha was allowed to have his own way as usual, a way made all the easier by the fact that another uncle was on the tutorial staff. Indeed, military training became a sort of primrose path for him. Instead of sharing quarters with the other cadets, Scriabin lived at his uncle's official residence; he quickly became the special pet of the Director's daughter, who played duets with him; and he was excused target-practice and part of his drill! One can imagine what a life such a favourite would have been led by English school-fellows. But they do these things differently in Russia. (At least, they used to.) Scriabin was by no means unpopular with his comrades; they were interested in his poetry and his piano improvisations; the quiet little weakling was spared even the normal amount of teasing and bullying. As for his studies, he seems to have been a good all-round pupil. In spite of a serious illness at twelve, an illness that nearly proved fatal, he was at the head of his class the following year (1885), getting hundred per cent. markings for French and natural history, and high marks for religious knowledge, German, geometry and history.

During his very first year in the Cadet Corps, we hear of the boy playing a Bach gavotte semi-publicly at a musical evening at the Director's, though it is doubtful whether he played exceptionally well, for he had still had no proper lessons. But his musical sense was such that, having lost himself near the end, he was able to improvise a conclusion of his own. His repertoire also included one of Mendelssohn's " Songs without Words ", the " Gondellied " in Book I. But it was not till the following summer (1883) that his aunt took him to G. E. Konius for his first serious music-lessons. Konius, who was then only twenty, still one of Pabst's students at the Moscow Conservatoire, says of his pupil: " He was a puny looking little chap—pale, short, looking younger than he really was. He knew not only his notes, but about scales and keys, and with weak fingers, hardly squeezing out the sounds, played me something—I forget what—fairly cleanly and fluently. The extent of his previous study may be gauged by the fact that one of the first pieces we worked at was Weber's ' Perpetuum mobile ', Op. 24.

He learned things quickly but, probably owing to his weak physique, his performance was always ethereal and monotonous." Konius fed him with the easier of Cramer's studies, Mendelssohn's " Songs without Words " and easy Chopin, but the lessons came to an end in the spring of 1884, at the time of the illness already mentioned. From this period dates the composition of a little Canon in D minor for piano, published in 1929, which already shows (in the use of the augmented triad) a feeling for the " pathetic " qualities of harmony. And there is a Chopinesque Nocturne in A flat, probably written at the same time as the Canon, though Sabaneief dates it 1881-2, i.e. when the child was only nine or ten!

It was apparently at this time that the boy decided he wanted to be a musician and not, after all, a soldier. There could be no question of his leaving the Cadet School prematurely, however, and he remained there till about 1889.[1] But he now wanted to enter the Moscow Conservatoire and, by way of preparation, was placed under N. S. Zveref, a piano pupil of Henselt and Dubuque. Zveref was not only a fine musician but a remarkable character of a type to be found, perhaps, only in the Russia of the old days. An aristocrat of the old school, he had squandered his fortune and been obliged to fall back on music to earn a living. A despot of the type of Balakiref and Nicholas Rubinstein, he was at once kind-hearted and irritable to the point of ferocity.[2] From 1870 till his death in 1893, he was a professor at the Moscow Conservatoire, but he was also the most fashionable private teacher in Moscow, mixing in the highest society and nearly always accompanied by two or three star pupils who lived with him and whom he boarded, clothed and

[1] It is difficult to determine the exact date. 1889 is probably correct, though Sabaneief in his " Reminiscences " says Scriabin was still wearing the cadet uniform when he first saw him in 1891.

[2] A lengthy and graphic account of him will be found in " Rachmaninof's Recollections " (Allen & Unwin).

taught for absolutely nothing. Ziloti had been one of his earlier pupils; and at the time Scriabin began to take lessons from him, his three boarders were S. V. Rachmaninof, M. L. Pressmann, afterwards Director of the Conservatoire at Rostof-on-Don, and L. A. Maximof, a brilliant young pianist who died of typhoid in 1904, when barely twenty. Being in the Cadet Corps, it was impossible for Scriabin to share with them Zveref's treats and his more than military discipline. But every Sunday night it was Zveref's custom to entertain a score or so of the leading Moscow intellectuals—his table was as renowned as his pupils—and his boys played to the guests. The fourteen-year-old " Scriabushka ", as Zveref called him, soon became a favourite pupil; we hear of his playing " magnificently " at these Sunday evenings, not only music of the difficulty of Schumann's " Paganini Studies " but compositions of his own.

One of these compositions, a Valse in D flat dated four days after his fifteenth birthday, has been preserved and published posthumously. Like the Nocturne in A flat it is true piano music and completely Chopinesque. At this period, and for years afterwards, Chopin was his idol. He is said to have slept with certain favourite pieces of Chopin's under his pillow. By this time he had already begun to take private lessons in elementary theory from S. I. Taneief, though just when these lessons began it is impossible to say. Taneief himself remembered only that it was " one spring ". It is just possible that it was the spring of 1884, more probably that of 1886. In 1887 Taneief, being pressed for time, handed him over to his first piano teacher, Konius, for a course of more advanced harmony in preparation for his Conservatoire studies, and in January, 1888, at sixteen, Scriabin entered the Moscow Conservatoire itself.

At the Conservatoire Scriabin took two studies, piano and composition. His piano professor, V. I. Safonof, who succeeded Taneief as Director the following year, was delighted with him, above all with his pedalling. " He made the instrument *breathe*." " Sasha-like pedalling " was the highest praise Safonof could give. " Don't look at his hands; look at his feet ", he told the class once when Scriabin was playing particularly well. Spoiled in his home, spoiled at the Cadet School, Scriabin was again the spoiled darling of the Conservatoire. Which was unfortunate, for Scriabin very definitely liked to be first in all things. Indeed, his envy of Joseph Lhévinne, whose technique was more brilliant, if less subtle than his own, nearly brought about a disaster. Through over-practice of Balakiref's " Islamey " and Liszt's " Don Juan " Fantasia, he temporarily lost the use of his right hand. He regained it after a time, but it was during this period of single-handedness that he wrote the well-known " Prelude and Nocturne for the left hand only ", as well as a left-handed concert-paraphrase of a Strauss waltz, which has never been published. (Long after he had tired of Beethoven, Schubert and Tchaïkovsky, Scriabin still loved the waltzes of Johann Strauss.) Even at his leaving examination he could use his right hand only with difficulty, but this was taken into account by the examiners and he was granted a gold medal.

Simultaneously with his piano studies, Scriabin (again with Rachmaninof as a classmate) studied first counterpoint with that formidable theorist Taneief, then fugue and free composition with Arensky. Scriabin and Rachmaninof both scamped their work with Taneief, who was too kindly to be a good disciplinarian, and both got on badly in Arensky's fugue class. Scriabin in particular incurred the displeasure of Arensky who, not without reason, considered him arrogant and self-opinionated. He failed in the examination of the spring of 1891, which Rachmaninof passed brilliantly, and had to do a special holiday task before he was allowed to enter the free composition class. There the relations between him and Arensky became even worse. " Scatterbrain! " Arensky is reported to have said. " You set him one thing, and he brings you something altogether different." It appears that instead of an orchestral scherzo he was supposed to have written, Scriabin submitted the introduction to a Lithuanian opera, " Keïstut and Peïruta ", of which he composed one or two other numbers. Finally, annoyed that a favour granted to Rachmaninof was not also extended to himself, Scriabin left the composition class without passing the final examination.

Yet when Scriabin left the Conservatoire—"already at twenty firmly convinced that I should do something big ", as he said in later years—he had already produced better evidence of his skill as a composer than any conservatoire diploma. Besides the F minor Valse, Op. 1, and Three Pieces, Op. 2, remarkably good work for a boy of fourteen, he had already written an unpublished Fantasia for piano and orchestra, a Piano Sonata in E flat, two (Nos. 4 and 6) of the well-known set of Preludes, Op. 11[1] and the Mazurkas, Nocturnes and Impromptus, Opp. 3, 5 and 7. The next year, (1893) Jurgenson printed Opp. 1 and 2 at the composer's expense and Opp. 3, 5 and 7 at his own, though without paying Scriabin a kopeck in royalties. Through these early compositions, however, Scriabin was to find a more generous publisher and benefactor. But at first he was generally regarded solely as a brilliant young pianist. His compositions were ignored—which must have been more than a little galling to a young man who was already well-known to conceal a quite unbounded conceit of himself beneath his delicate, shy, sensitive exterior and his perfect manners. " If he noticed in others a doubt of his own powers ", says the critic Y. D. Engel, " he never hesitated to consider the other man wrong—and ceased to attach any value to his judgment. That was what happened with Arensky, and it was to happen many times more in the course of Scriabin's life ".

Poised rather uneasily on the brink of a career as a pianist,

---

[1] No. 4 was originally intended to form part of a Ballade.

Scriabin still lived with his grandmother and aunt; indeed, went on living with them till the time of his marriage. His closest musical friend was still the fifteen-months-younger Rachmaninof, already far better known as a composer than he was. As for his life in general, it is significant that, according to Sabaneief, he was hardly ever mentioned in the circle which centred about " the ascetic and rather puritanical Taneief ". He was " at this time going through the *Sturm und Drang* period of his youth ". At the outset of his pianistic career, his right hand still gave him trouble. " In 1893 he wore on both arms red woollen oversleeves, obviously home-made and very conspicuous ", Engel tells us. " When playing in public, before he began, he would point to his right hand as if asking for indulgence. He was thin, pale and sickly looking." In the spring of 1894 Scriabin gave his first recital in Petersburg, playing among other things some of his Etudes, Op. 8, at that time still in manuscript. The recital was more that a debut. It marked a turning point in his life.

M. P. Belaief had already seen those first few piano pieces issued by Jurgenson and been very much taken by them. And one of his musical advisers, Liadof, himself a Chopin-worshipper, confirmed his judgment. (On the other hand, Rimsky-Korsakof seems to have been unimpressed, and quickly took a personal dislike to the " conceited " young man.) Belaief attended Scriabin's Petersburg recital and was enraptured. Although he had never before had dealings with any composers outside the Petersburg circle—Taneief came along a little later—he at once made Scriabin's acquaintance and offered to publish his music on his usual generous terms. To clinch the matter Belaief forthwith went to Moscow and interviewed the young man's grandmother and aunt, and the latter became a sort of business agent for her nephew, or at least an intermediary between him and Belaief. For Sasha was no man of affairs—absent-minded, careless about proof-reading, a hater of letter-writing—and Belaief expected his *protégés* to be at least as businesslike as himself. Belaief at once published the " Allegro appassionato ", Op. 4 (a revised version of the first movement of the E flat Sonata written six or seven years before), the so-called First Sonata, Op. 6, the Etudes, Op. 8, and the " Prelude and Nocturne for the left hand "; and from that time till 1908 all Scriabin's compositions were issued by Belaief's firm. Belaief paid generously—for instance, two hundred rubles down for the F minor Sonata—but Scriabin was in no urgent need of money, for his grandmother kept him, and his father made him an allowance. He was able to treat his royalties as pocket-money. Nor was the relation between him and Belaief purely a business one. When in Petersburg he always stayed with Belaief, who treated him in the most fatherly way; and he usually made an annual visit to Petersburg for Belaief's name-day in November.

Sabaneief gives a vivid pen-picture of Scriabin at this period, in the course of his amusing description of an evening at Taneief's in 1894, when " Tristan " was played through to Scriabin, Rachmaninof, Catoire and others—Rachmaninof sitting in a corner with the score and grumbling " 1,500 pages more!" " It was then that I first asked Scriabin his opinion of Wagner. Scriabin was at that time a callow young man with a long face and decidedly turned-up nose." (Of which he was very conscious. One of his most characteristic mannerisms was a stroking of his nose, as if to persuade it to turn downward—and this actually seems to have had some effect!) " He had an absent-minded air and a very strongly marked cleft in his chin—for as yet he had no beard. This deep cavity in his chin somehow set me against him . . . and besides, I disliked his haughty, supercilious air, so definitely manifesting an infernal conceit. I noticed no particular marks of intelligence in his face and inwardly decided that he was simply a ' Conservatoire young man ' . . . . All the same I was interested to know what this ' Conservatoire young man ' thought of Wagner. I can't say that the result impressed me very much . . . Scriabin replied rather shortly and reluctantly "—his questioner was a boy of only thirteen—" that ' Wagner is amorphous, so he doesn't attract me ' ". However, Scriabin, like Rachmaninof, was to change his opinion of Wagner later and to come strongly under his influence. Indeed, although he valued Wagner as an all-round artist and thinker rather than as a musician pure and simple, Wagner's music (e.g. the *Feuerzauber* from " Die Walküre") was among the little, other than his own, that he never lost delight in to the very end.

Belaief did not content himself with publishing Scriabin's music. Just as he had founded the Russian Symphony Concerts to perform the orchestral works of Glazunof and the rest, he now took it upon himself to supervise Scriabin's career as a pianist. He arranged Scriabin's first concert tour of Europe in 1895-6 and, enjoying the novelty of having a pianist under his wing, accompanied him throughout, not even leaving him on the platform—to the intense amusement of the audiences. Indeed, the contrast between Belaief's massive figure and Scriabin's small and fragile one might well have made them think of a little performing animal with its burly keeper. The pair first visited Heidelberg, Dresden and Berlin. In June, 1895, they stayed for a time at Vitznau, near Lucerne, where we hear of a love-affair with the wife of a German sculptor and where four of the Op. 11 Preludes were written. (Nearly all the pieces of this set were composed during this tour.) Thence they made for Italy and the Mediterranean, and the following year Scriabin played in Paris, Berlin, Amsterdam and Brussels. After his two Paris recitals (January 15th and 18th, N.S.) one critic wrote of him as " une nature d'élite, aussi eminent compositeur, que pianiste; aussi intellectuel, que philosophe; tout nerf et sainte flamme ". While another, who considered him " lacking in character and personality . . . an echo of Chopin ", nevertheless, ended by advising his readers " not to forget the name of this interesting artist, who will assuredly not allow himself to be forgotten ". From that time onward, Scriabin showed a particular affection for the French capital.

The " *Sturm und Drang* period of Scriabin's youth " was now coming to an end. Fond of women as he was, Scriabin was no Don Juan. He needed a permanent mate. It was simply that he had hitherto been rather unfortunate in his more serious love-affairs. He had proposed to and been rejected by one of the daughters of Monighetti, the medical officer at the Cadet School. In 1894-5 he was very seriously in love with a beautiful young girl, also half-Italian, N. V. S———na, who inspired him to write the words and music of a " very weak, ' officer-like ' " song (according to E. K. Rozenof) which has never been published. But the lady's mother considered him no match for her daughter, and he went abroad with Belaief, with a more or less broken heart, consoling himself, as we have seen, with the German lady at Vitznau. In Paris in 1896 he even became engaged to " a very interesting and cultured girl, a Russian ", whose name has likewise not been disclosed. But that also came to nothing. Yet soon after his return to Russia, in October, he was betrothed to the brilliant young pianist, Vera Ivanovna Isaakovitch, still a student at the Moscow Conservatoire in the class of Paul Schlözer. Belaief, a confirmed misogynist, disapproved; but, as we shall see, took a magnificent " revenge ".

Vera Ivanovna had entered the Conservatoire a few months after Scriabin had left it. He made her acquaintance in December, 1893, at a students' evening in memory of Nicholas Rubinstein. " When you played ", he told her, " I thought to myself: now here at last is a woman pianist to whom I can listen with pleasure ". All the time she was at the Conservatoire, Vera lived with the family of her professor, Schlözer; it was there that Scriabin frequently met her; and—it will be seen later that there was an extraordinary irony in all this—it was Schlözer's sister who was the real match-maker. Scriabin, unlike most composers, always loved to show people his compositions in every stage of their development, even the first sketches. He found Vera an attentive and sympathetic listener, and by all accounts told her not only of his ambitions as a composer but, with his customary childlike candour, of his various love-affairs. Now he proposed to marry the gentle consoler. In the spring of 1897 she left the Conservatoire, a gold medallist like himself, and they were married at Nijni-Novgorod, spending their honeymoon in the Crimea.

During the Crimean honeymoon Scriabin completed the two-movement Second Sonata (in G sharp minor, Op. 19) which he had begun at Genoa in 1895, and during the same summer wrote his only Piano Concerto, Op. 20. When the first two movements of the Concerto were finished he took them to Taneief, who criticised them gently from a technical point of view, but carefully refrained from speaking of the real substance of the work. " He's very, very talented ", Taneief sighed when Scriabin had gone. But his tone implied that it was a talent sadly misused. Scriabin himself gave the first performance of the Concerto at an R.M.S. concert at Odessa on October 11th/23rd, 1897, Safonof conducting. Safonof's view of Scriabin was already diametrically opposed to Taneief's. " Scriabin is not a Chopin ", he said. " *He is cleverer than Chopin.*" And already other pianists, notably Josef Hoffmann, were beginning to play Scriabin's music.

Immediately after the concert at Odessa, the young couple went to Paris, staying there for about six months. A few weeks after their arrival they received a very pleasant surprise in the form of a letter from Vladimir Stassof (November 27th/December 9th). " I have some very important news for you ", he wrote. " You have been awarded a prize of a thousand rubles for various compositions of yours, though by *whom* I don't know. It is some mysterious admirer of the Russian school, who wishes to remain unknown, but who has been acting through me since 1884 and who every year gives certain sums *to Russian composers* whom he nominates. This happens every November 27th, i.e. Glinka's day, as both ' Life for the Tsar ' and ' Ruslan and Liudmila ' were given for the first time on November 27th. My only link with the unknown is through the Petersburg *Poste-restante*. Now in carrying out this year's award I must ask you: *are you willing to accept this prize or not?* Throughout these thirteen years none of our composers has refused, except *Shcherbatchef* once and *Balakiref* on one occasion. *Tchaïkovsky* once thought of refusing, on the ground that he was making enough from his operas. But I wrote to him (in Paris) that it would be a great pity if he refused, as it would be a sort of *slight* on those who loved, respected and highly valued him, and at the same time *an insult* to his other comrades who had accepted the prizes. So Tchaïkovsky agreed and I sent the money to him in Paris. Permit me to hope for a favourable reply from you. . ." Scriabin did send a favourable reply and in the course of the next few years received further sums from the same mysterious benefactor, five hundred rubles in 1899 and 1900, a thousand in 1901 and 1902, fifteen hundred in 1903. Then death revealed the secret. The unknown benefactor was none other than Belaief, who all the time had been making Scriabin generous presents in his own name—now a grand piano, now a magnificent set of Chopin, on another occasion a travelling trunk, and so on. How much truth there was in Stassof's letter and how much playful fiction, it is difficult to say. But after Belaief's death annual Glinka Prizes were awarded openly by a committee—though only once to Scriabin.

On January 31st, 1898, Scriabin and his wife gave a joint recital of his compositions in the Salle Erard. But on the whole their stay in Paris was not particularly pleasant.

Scriabin was very run down physically, suffering from neurasthenia and pains in the head. Returning to Russia, they spent the summer at Maidanovo, near Klin, Tchaïkovsky's old home, where they were joined by the composer's father and stepmother. Both Alexander and his wife were productive that summer, for he wrote his Third Sonata[1] Op. 23, at Maidanovo, while she bore him a daughter, Rimma. The composer's stepmother is said to have often sung the newly born baby to sleep to the melody of the second subject of the finale of the Sonata. At the end of the summer, the elder couple returned to Turkey, while the younger pair at last settled down in Moscow. The means which had been ample for Scriabin as a bachelor were naturally hardly adequate now that he had a wife and baby to support. For a month or two they had to live in a " very nasty little flat " behind the Ekaterininsky Institute. He was therefore only too glad to accept Safonof's offer of the piano professorship at the Conservatoire, made vacant by the death of Vera's old master, P. Y. Schlözer. He entered on his new duties in October, 1898.

Scriabin had already taken a few private pupils, not for the sake of the fees, which he had not needed, but principally at the pressing request of intimate friends. His teaching had all been of the *dilettante* nature of Glinka's and Dargomyjsky's. It was, as he soon found, a very different matter to teach in a Conservatoire. He had no system, no real experience of teaching, and no aptitude for it. Above all he grudged every moment of the time that he was prevented from giving to composition. (During the first year of his professorship he wrote nothing but the Mazurkas, Op. 25.) He usually sat with an undisguised expression of painful boredom on his face throughout his lessons, and some of his pupils

[1] At least his third published Sonata. In 1895 Rozenof heard him play an almost completed Sonata in G sharp minor, which he styled " The Gothic " and which he said had been inspired by the sight of some ruined castle. It has completely disappeared.

left his class altogether. But he would occasionally take an interest in some particularly promising player. The bulk of his teaching material was drawn from Chopin and Liszt, less often from Schumann, Bach, Beethoven, Grieg and Tchaïkovsky. He hardly ever used his own compositions, and then only on special request. He demanded above all " soul, nervous excitement ". All his interpretations were intensely subjective, completely changing from day to day, his pupils tell us. Everything had to take the stamp of his own personality. A Beethoven sonata became merely a pretext for the expression of *his* individuality. " No passages! *Everything* must live!" he would cry. " Even though a passage is smudged, if it ends brilliantly, you still get an impression of cleanness and brilliance!" " Art must reorganise life!" " Intoxication —above all!" " *Il faut se griser!*" " Fight the platitudes of life!" " The atmosphere of art—above all!" Unfortunately one cannot teach the piano by shouting war-cries and letting off aphorisms, though he did manage to infect a few young chosen spirits with his own enthusiasm.

At home, Vera, who bore him two more daughters and a son, arranged everything for his convenience. He was given a quiet room away from the children, and she almost entirely gave up her own playing so as not to disturb him. But he generally worked late at night, especially as he often suffered from insomnia, preferring to spend his evenings in lively company, behind a glass of wine. " He was very expansive ", says M. K. Morozova, one of his pupils. " He was ready to give his art to all and played willingly whenever he was asked... His nervous excitement was combined with naïveté, kindliness, and charming manifestations of a sort of childishness. It was impossible to be angry with him. His was a fluttering spirit . . . taking life as a game full of enjoyment. A winged soul! His moods of dreaminess and contemplation were combined with eroticism—but it was a pure kind of eroticism. There was nothing of the titan about him; he gave one rather the impression of a simple, good-tempered Russian nature. But he loved the *illusion* of the titanic."

Apart from an unperformed " Poème symphonique " in D minor, written at about the period of his first European tour with Belaief, and the Piano Concerto, Scriabin had so far composed no orchestral music. But on March 12th/24th, 1899, Safonof conducted a little orchestral " Rêverie " of his (Op. 24) at an R.M.S. concert with such success that it had to be repeated. In the summer of 1900, during his holiday in the country, Scriabin wrote his First Symphony in E minor, Op. 26, with its choral finale, a setting of a poem by Scriabin himself, glorifying art as a form of religion. Safonof, who was enraptured with this rather dull work, conducted it on March 16th/29th, 1901; and rumour, probably lying, relates that after one of the rehearsals, Rachmaninof said: " I thought Scriabin was simply a swine, but it seems he is a composer after all." The success of the Symphony was very moderate, the press being respectful, but by no means flattering, and the composer was deeply annoyed. " Striking himself on his breast ", Engel says, " he cried in a strained voice: ' Well! If my health will let me, I'll show them what I can do! I still have something to say!' He felt himself called to achieve something great in art and so could not bear it when his importance was belittled by comparison with other composers. He attacked these ' others ' when they attacked him and defended them when they did him justice ". The Symphony was played again just a year later (March 5th/18th, 1902), again under Safonof, at a special Scriabin concert in the Great Hall of the Nobles' Assembly in Moscow, a concert organised and financially backed by Scriabin's old friends, the Monighettis. Besides the Symphony, the programme on this occasion included the " Rêverie ", the Third Sonata and a number of shorter piano pieces.

The " art-religion " adumbrated in the finale of the Symphony is symptomatic of the line Scriabin's thoughts were taking—towards a " fusion of music with philosophy ". Like most educated Russians, Scriabin had from his youth been fond of airing philosophical notions. But those who knew him tell us that his learning was very superficial. " Even in maturity Scriabin never cared to *study* a book thoroughly. All he wanted was an impulse—a remark from someone he was talking to or a peep into the pages of a book—and he would get hold of the essence of an idea (details didn't interest him) and then develop it along his own lines. . . . Working on a strange idea, he would either completely assimilate it or discard it altogether; the process of thought, for its own sake, hardly interested him at all."[1] From about 1900 Scriabin was strongly influenced by the mystic philosopher, Prince S. N. Trubetskoy, an exponent of the not altogether original idea that " God is love ", and a warm admirer of Scriabin's music. Scriabin was very fond of him and his family—" the best family in the world ", as he called it—and Trubetskoy induced the composer for a time to attend the sessions of the Philosophical Society. Scriabin " assimilated " Trubetskoy's religious philosophy in his usual manner, read Goethe's " Faust ", and at last began to interest himself in Wagner's music and Wagner's ideas.

He still loved Chopin and Liszt, indeed his enthusiasm for Liszt, " the ideal type of artist ", was at its height, but of Beethoven he could no longer tolerate anything but the Fifth Symphony. Later, not even that. As for Richard Strauss, who was just beginning to be known in Moscow, Scriabin only " found his orchestration interesting in places ". But Wagner led him to Nietzsche, if not to Strauss; he found Nietzsche's egotistic philosophy, with its glorification of the artist type, peculiarly congenial; and from 1901 to 1903 he was completely under the spell of the conception of the *Übermensch*.

[1] Y. D. Engel.

No doubt he saw himself as one of those " higher men " who, according to Nietzsche, are steps toward the Superman. Trubetskoy's intellectual influence correspondingly weakened, though the personal friendship continued for a while. The phrase, " Thus spake Zarathustra ", was constantly on Scriabin's lips at this period; he even began an opera with a Nietzschean hero, an artist who was to triumph over the world. But the plan was constantly being changed and enlarged, and so remained for ever unwritten. " In January, 1902 ", says Rozenof, " Scriabin read me the libretto, written by himself, of this 'philosophical opera', as he called it. I don't remember the details, but I recollect that in the First Act the hero-poet sat in his study while before him passed a series of visions, expressing the ideals of the Scriabinesque-Nietzschean *Weltanschauung*. Then came the persecutions of fate, life's banality, the verge of imprisonment... It was all very high-flown and pathetic, but there was a complete absence of action and dramatic plot. The characters were not living people but philosophical abstractions. I told Scriabin so, and from that time his attitude toward me cooled off perceptibly ". At this period the composer was also working at his Second Symphony in C, Op. 29.

Rumour in Moscow already said that Scriabin was " half-mad ". It also said more scandalous things, for his life was by no means ascetic.[1] According to Sabaneief, " he was a great dandy at this period: little, restless, insignificant in appearance and unnoticeable in a big crowd, he was always exquisitely dressed, and my attention was always caught by his feet in their polished, elastic-sided boots, with toes turned out like a ballerina's. This all struck me as coxcombery and desire for originality. ' So that's the philosopher who's going to combine music with philosophy ', I thought to myself. ' How is

---

[1] He once held forth at Safonof's on the theme that " since it is far more difficult to do all one wants to, than *not* to do what one wants, it is nobler to do what one likes."

he going to reconcile his polished boots and his fancy waistcoats with philosophy?' " And, except the intimate circle about Safonof and some of the Belaief group, the Russian musical world in general thought the same. But it was Safonof more than anyone who believed in him. " Sasha Scriabin is a great, great composer ", he said. " A great pianist and a great composer." It was he, again, who conducted the first performance of the Second Symphony on March 21st/April 3rd, 1903, at a Moscow R.M.S. concert. The composer was called out twice and, although a little hissing was mingled with the applause, there is no truth whatever in Gunst's highly-coloured account of " the performance proceeding amid the deafening whistles, hisses and cat-calls of many of the audience!"

In November, 1902, Scriabin formed a new friendship which was destined to change the whole course of his life. Already in 1898 he had made the acquaintance of Paul Schlözer's nephew, Boris, and the latter's mother, who had been a fellow-pupil of his own mother under Leschetizky. Now, four years later, Boris introduced him to his sister, Tatiana Fedorovna Schlözer, a girl of nineteen. The year before at Piatigorsk in the Caucasus, Tatiana had heard Scriabin's Third Sonata played by a visiting recitalist. " It was "—in her own words—" the strongest impression of my life. After that I wanted to play nothing but Scriabin. I dreamed of seeing the composer ". Boris took her to Moscow and invited Scriabin to visit them one evening. He came late and before he had played to them very long, they were interrupted; the Schlözers were living in a furnished flat and no one was allowed to play after eleven. " To my brother and me it seemed like sacrilege to forbid Scriabin to play. But he only laughed and suggested that if we wanted to hear more, we had better go to his house. So we did. And he played to us till two in the morning. And that was the first day of our acquaintanceship! My aim in coming to Moscow was to study composition under some competent teacher. I had not dreamed of Alexander Nikolaevitch in this connection. So much the greater then was my delight when he himself, after seeing my compositions and improvisations, offered to teach me. . . . Alexander Nikolaevitch evidently taught me on the same lines as he had been taught himself, made me construct two-bar and four-bar phrases, etc., forbade consecutive fifths and so on. When things went wrong, he was distressed—and I cried. . . Under the fascination of his creative personality I soon gave up all thoughts of composition. I still went on working with Alexander Nikolaevitch, but my aim was no longer to find a means of self-expression but to understand *his* compositions better."

At this period Scriabin had just finished the Second Symphony and already begun the Third, " The Divine Poem ", Op. 43. But he was still full of his Nietzschean opera. (" How I want to write the opera!" he told Boris Schlözer again in September, 1903.) " In my opinion, this ' opera ' was the seed from which sprang the later ' mystery ' ", writes Schlözer. " It was actually to bring about that unity in the world, of which he dreamed. The idea of unity—social, religious, philosophic—already occupied the centre of his thoughts . . . . though as yet he understood this unity only in a somewhat external form, a unity of society and the annihilation of opposition and difference, not in a mystical sense."

In the spring of 1903, soon after the first performance of the Second Symphony, Scriabin resigned his professorship at the Conservatoire (refusing an invitation to go to the Vienna Conservatoire in the same capacity) and the musical inspectorship of the Ekaterininsky Institute, which he had held for three or four years, in order to devote himself entirely to composition. He wanted to live in Switzerland, but it was first necessary to earn a little extra money by composing. Settling in the country, some sixty or seventy miles from

Moscow, he worked with feverish industry that summer, producing all the works numbered Op. 30 to Op. 42, the Fourth Sonata in F sharp and thirty-five shorter piano-pieces. " I'm literally wallowing in work ", he wrote to Schlözer towards the end of July. " I am scoring the Symphony ", i.e. the " Divine Poem ", " and composing piano things, so that the libretto makes slow progress and I have little time for philosophy... I must finish thirty compositions during August or my journey to Switzerland won't come off—and that's all I'm thinking about ".

But in spite of this industry and in spite of a specially generous gift from the " unknown benefactor " that year, it would have been no easy matter to support a wife and four children in the comparative luxury indispensable to Scriabin. Recital-giving had also temporarily become distasteful to him. And at the end of the year Belaief died. But at this point his friend and former pupil, M. K. Morozova, came to the rescue with an offer of an annuity of two thousand four hundred rubles " until better days came ". Scriabin gratefully accepted it and, with his family, left Russia on February 29th/March 13th, 1904. They settled in Switzerland at Vésenaz on the shores of Lake Geneva, and Tatiana Schlözer followed soon after " for reasons of health ". She stayed at Belle-Rive, barely twenty minutes' walk from Vésenaz.

Scriabin liked Switzerland for two reasons. For one thing, it was " a free country ", which made it " easier to produce new ideas in it ". For another, he was captivated by its scenery and " unable to understand why anyone should live in Russia when there was such a marvellous place as Switzerland ". Meeting Y. D. Engel, by chance, in Geneva that summer, he poured out to him on the lake steamer a multitude of ideas and information about the " Divine Poem "— " there has never yet been such music "—about the nature of art, about Socialism and about religion. " There will have to be a fusion of all the arts ", he told Engel, " but not a theatrical one like Wagner's. Art must unite with philosophy and religion in an indivisible whole to form a new gospel, which will replace the old Gospel we have outlived. I cherish the dream of creating such a ' mystery '. For it, it would be necessary to build a special temple—perhaps here, perhaps far away in India. But mankind is not yet ready for it. It must be preached to; it must be led along new paths. And I do preach. Once I even preached from a boat, like Christ. I have a little circle of people who understand me perfectly and follow me. Particularly one—a fisherman. He is simple, but a splendid fellow ".

Engel did not meet this fisherman, " Otto ", but he learned from the composer's wife that he was " really a nice little chap " and that he and Scriabin called each other by their Christian names. " Once ", said Vera Ivanovna, " Alexander was away from home all day... In the evening I went along the tramway which leads from Geneva, thinking he might have been there and that I should meet him. I was just passing a café when suddenly I heard his voice. I went up to the door. There were a lot of people in the café, quite simple folk; and Otto was there, too. They were listening to Alexander Nikolaevitch. He was excited, preaching passionately ". It appears that Otto and his friends were Socialists, who listened with pleasure to Scriabin's denunciation of the existing order of things and to his doctrine: " There must be no more money, no more poor... Everyone should do whatever he wants to do." As for the " new art " and the " new Gospel " which he also told them about, no doubt they accepted both on trust. Years later, when Scriabin returned to Geneva on a short visit, he visited Otto and his family and was joyfully greeted with a cry of " *Voilà Alexandre!* "

During this same visit to Vésenaz, Engel was introduced to Tatiana Schlözer. " She was present all the time while he played me his compositions, every note of which she obviously knew and loved. It was she, not Alexander Nikolaevitch, who drew attention to this or the other detail; it was she who, in reply to some remark of mine, broke in confidently, wittily parrying my open or indirect criticisms and joyfully joining in my delight. She seemed to have taken his cause to her heart, as if it had been her own and his compositions hers. And this impression was correct, as was proved by the near future."

Hitherto Scriabin's wife had avoided playing in his presence, and he had preferred it so. But that summer at Vésenaz he worked through the whole of his compositions, up to Op. 42, with her, telling her frankly that he was soon going to leave her as he " was obliged to make a sacrifice to Art ". To that end he was preparing her for an independent existence. She also copied out the whole score of the " Divine Poem " for him.[1] Directly that was finished, in November, her husband betook himself to Paris, where he was immediately followed by Tatiana Schlözer.[2] But for a time he continued to correspond with Vera, and when Nikisch gave the first performance of the " Divine Poem " at the Châtelet on May 29th, 1905, his wife appeared in Paris and they met as friends.

This performance was entirely due to M. K. Morozova, who secretly paid Nikisch three thousand rubles to play the work, as if on his own initiative, at one of his concerts. A few whistles were heard at the end but they were drowned in the applause. Tatiana tells how, late that night, after the supper which followed the concert, Scriabin having insisted on going to a restaurant and ordering champagne, confided to the startled waiter with typical naïveté, " I've written a symphony! But I dream of a much greater one—when all the peoples of the earth will unite in a great festival ", and

---

[1] After the " Poem " had been printed, the composer rewrote the harp part, as the result of hearing one of Glazunof's symphonies.

[2] The five pieces, Op. 44 and Op. 45, were written at Vésenaz during the summer, those of Op. 46 to Op. 49 during the winter in Paris. For some reason there is no Op. 50 or Op. 55.

so on in the same strain. ("*Bon bourgeois!*" said the waiter approvingly.) The "Poem" attracted general attention, perhaps almost as much on account of the "programme" written by Tatiana as of the music itself. This programme is worth giving in full, since it indicates the nature of Scriabin's attempt to "unite music with philosophy": —

"The Divine Poem" represents the evolution of the human spirit which, torn from an entire past of beliefs and mysteries which it surmounts and overturns, passes through Pantheism and attains to a joyous and intoxicated affirmation of its liberty and its unity with the universe (the divine "Ego").

Struggles. The conflict between the man who is the slave of a personal god, supreme master of the world, and the free, powerful man—the man-god. The latter appears to triumph, but it is only the intellect which affirms the divine "Ego", while the individual will, still too weak, is tempted to sink into Pantheism.

Delights. The man allows himself to be captured by the delights of the sensual world. He is intoxicated and soothed by the voluptuous pleasures into which he plunges. His personality loses itself in nature. It is then that the sense of the sublime arises from the depths of his being and assists him to conquer the passive state of his human "Ego".

Divine Play. The spirit finally freed from all the bonds which fastened it to its past of submission to a superior power, the spirit producing the universe by the sole power of its own creative will, conscious of being at one with this Universe, abandons itself to the sublime joy of free activity—the "Divine Play".

During that winter in Paris, Scriabin had made the acquaintance of theosophical teaching. Having heard theosophy mentioned in conversation and finding that it had something in common with his own trend of thought, he bought some theosophical literature and " studied " it in his customary superficial way. But the theosophical element in Scriabin's so-called thought has been greatly exaggerated; it went no deeper than his former Nietzscheanism, little deeper than his short-lived Socialism of a few month later. As usual, he took from theosophy just what appealed to him, remoulded it to suit himself—and passed on. Even Boris Schlözer, who considers theosophy the only really strong outside influence Scriabin ever experienced, says that this influence was " short-lived . . . Scriabin very soon entirely twisted the theosophical doctrines about and cut completely adrift from theosophical orthodoxy ". At the same period Scriabin read a number of books on India and even played with a Sanskrit grammar.

After the performance of the " Divine Poem ", Scriabin and Tatiana left for Italy. He saw Vera only once more, a month or two later, when their eldest daughter, the seven-year-old Rimma, died. She had been his favourite, and he hurried to Switzerland and " sobbed bitterly over her grave ". But there was no sentimental reconciliation with Rimma's mother. Vera returned to Russia and in the autumn, thanks to the efforts of Safonof and her husband, obtained a post at the Moscow Conservatoire. She continued to correspond with Alexander till January, 1906. Two months after this final break she gave her first recital of Scriabin's music in Moscow, the prelude to a whole series of such recitals not only in Moscow, Petersburg and the Russian provinces, but in Berlin, Leipzig, Dresden, Brussels, Vienna and other Western cities. In the meantime the composer had settled with Tatiana at Bogliasco, near Genoa, where she bore him a daughter and where they stayed for ten months, till February, 1906.

Seeing that he had abandoned Vera " for the sake of Art ", it appears rather curious that the first two years of his life with Tatiana were so little productive. It is true he had begun another big orchestral work, " Le Poème de l'Extase ", Op. 54, but other than that the sole fruit of about twenty months was Op. 51, four very short piano pieces. At Bogliasco they had a charming little garden with oranges, pines and cacti, overlooking the sea; and there, according to Tatiana, the composer would sit sunning himself through even the hottest hours of the day, occasionally working but more often surrendering himself to blissful indolence. " He was never afraid of even the strongest heat; sunshine was his favourite element." Sometimes he read—or at any rate glanced at the pages of—a massive volume, perhaps the last book one would have expected to find in Scriabin's hands. It is pleasant to think of the little mystic-artistic dandy, the Nietzschean of two or three years before, taking his ease in his Mediterranean garden, his mistress at his side, and idly turning the pages of—Marx's " Das Kapital ". But Russia was in turmoil that year, dangerously near revolution— Rimsky-Korsakof was fuming at Vetchasha after his battles with the Conservatoire authorities—and Scriabin had as his neighbours several Russian Socialist-*emigrés*, among them G. A. Plekhanof, who particularly impressed Scriabin by his wide culture. The Socialist was willing to recognise a " spiritual aristocracy ", while Scriabin had some vague idea that Socialism might serve as " a step to a higher metaphysical-mystical plane of existence "; and so the extremes were reconciled. Scriabin " studied " Karl Marx and flirted with Socialism. But Plekhanof had no hesitation in making fun of his claim that " the artist creates a world ". " So we're indebted to you, Alexander Nikolaevitch, for such a blue sky and such warm sunshine to-day?" he would say. " Thank you! Thank you!" Incidentally, Scriabin's piano at Bogliasco, the piano he had to use for his initial work on the " Poem of Ecstasy ", was an out-of-tune upright taken from a café.

When Scriabin and Tatiana, with their baby, left Italy for Geneva in February, 1906, he found himself in an unexpectedly difficult position. Since Belaief's death, his publishing business had been directed by an administrative board, of which only one member, Liadof, admired Scriabin's work. Scriabin was now informed that in future he would have to accept royalties at half the former rate, and in a fit of annoyance he decided to find another publisher. But that was easier said than done, for his compositions were not commercial propositions. In spite of the reputation, vividly streaked with notoriety, which he had acquired, Jurgenson would have nothing to do with his music. He then negotiated with a German publisher, Zimmermann, who had published a number of works by Balakiref and Liapunof, submitting the manuscript (of four unspecified preludes, possibly Op. 48) which Jurgenson had rejected. But Zimmermann's reader, said to have been a well-known Leipzig professor, also turned them down, though Zimmermann expressed his willingness to pay the composer fifty marks apiece for melodious salon waltzes if he cared to write them! Finally, Scriabin found himself without a publisher at all.

He gave a recital in Geneva early in the summer, playing his Third Sonata among other things; worked at the " Poem of Ecstasy "; and produced the four pieces, Op. 51. Nothing else. It must have been one of the blackest periods of his life. He had alienated many of his old Moscow friends, including Safonof, by his treatment of his wife; and to the end bitter warfare was waged between the partisans of Vera Ivanovna and those of Tatiana Fedorovna. And he was probably aware that the wildest rumours were circulating about him in Russia, though it is true some of them were hardly wilder than the actual facts. It was generally known that he proposed to build a temple in India, globe-shaped and situated on a lake. He was said to be " plotting the end of the world ", a consummation in which his music was to play an important part. But Moscow was disposed to believe absolutely anything about him. One musician seriously assured Sabaneief that Tatiana, like Tsar Saltan's bride, had given birth in Paris to something " not a mouse and not a frog, but a quite unheard of monster " and that the monstrosity in question had been preserved in spirits and placed in a museum! " He considered ", says Sabaneef, " that this was clear and convincing proof that Scriabin was a ' degenerate ' ".

It was at this critical juncture that Scriabin learned from Russian newspapers that Modest Altschuler in New York was inviting Russian composers to send him their orchestral scores for performance at his " Russian Symphony Society " concerts. Altschuler, a Russian Jew who had studied the 'cello at the Moscow Conservatoire, had settled in America some years before, formed an orchestra of his own, largely composed of emigrants like himself, and in spite of very limited financial resources was carrying on a plucky and by no means unsuccessful campaign of propaganda for Russian music.[1] Scriabin wrote to Altschuler, who at once suggested that he should not only send his scores but make a personal visit to America, appearing as soloist in his own Concerto. Altschuler could offer only poor terms but there was no reason why Scriabin should not arrange a recital tour of his own. The composer agreed. After giving a couple of recitals in Brussels on November 8th and 21st,[2] he sailed from Rotterdam, leaving Tatiana and the child in Amsterdam in the care of two of her aunts.

At two concerts in the Carnegie Hall, New York, on

---

[1] Altschuler was no purist and he annoyed some of the composers, with whose works he took liberties. For instance, he performed Glazunof's Third Symphony with cuts and played the finale of his " Middle Ages " Suite *first*, with the first movement last.

[2] Among other things he played his Third Sonata, now for the first time provided with a programme by Tatiana, " Etats d'âme ", couched in similar terms to that of the " Divine Poem ".

December 1st and 20th, Altschuler gave successful performances of the First Symphony, minus the choral finale, and the " Divine Poem ". Scriabin himself gave recitals in New York, Chicago and Detroit. His old friend and champion, Safonof, had just settled in New York, having left Moscow in consequence of political unpleasantnesses at the Conservatoire, and was in charge of the New York Philharmonic Orchestra. But Safonof disapproved both of his more recent compositions and of his union with Tatiana Schlözer; there could be no question of Scriabin's music being included in the New York Philharmonic programmes. Still, Safonof was at first outwardly friendly and even offered to conduct the Piano Concerto at one of Altschuler's " Russian concerts ". But Scriabin had sent for Tatiana and her arrival in January ruined everything. Safonof would have nothing more to do with him. Not only that but the secret of Scriabin's " immorality " leaked out and, like Maxim Gorky's, gave serious offence to what Y. D. Engel calls " the social hypocrisy of the Americans ". One night in March, warned by Altschuler, the Scriabins had to fly at a bare five hours' notice to escape " serious unpleasantness ". They arrived in Paris with just thirty francs in their pockets. Fortunately they had good friends.

It was 1907, the year of Diaghilef's first Paris festival of " Cinq concerts historiques russes ", and two of Scriabin's works were included in the scheme. Josef Hoffmann was to play the Concerto at the third concert on May 23rd (N.S.), while Nikisch was to conduct the Second Symphony at the last concert (May 30th). The concerts naturally filled Paris with Russian musicians. To a company consisting of Rimsky-Korsakof, his wife and two of his sons, Rachmaninof, Glazunof, Felix Blumenfeld, Josef Hoffmann, M. K. Morozova and others, Scriabin gave a sort of demonstration of his " Poème de l'Extase ", first reading his poetic programme, then playing his music at the piano, helped out in the more complicated passages by Tatiana. Then, at the request of Hoffmann who admired Scriabin and was at that time also admired by him, the composer played some of his piano pieces. These pleased his audience, the " Poem " quite definitely did not. According to Andrei Rimsky-Korsakof, the music of " l'Extase " and Scriabin's dreamed of " Mystery " gave his father " an impression of unhealthy eroticism ". " He's half out of his mind already ", said Korsakof. Yet these two, the tall pillar of moral and musical respectability and common sense and the amoral little mystic, meeting in the Café de la Paix after a rehearsal, found themselves in agreement on one point, the definite association of musical keys with certain colours—though their scales of colour-values by no means agreed. However, this personal contact with Korsakof, Glazunof, and the other members of the board of trustees of the Belaief firm, led to a reconciliation; misunderstandings were cleared up; and in spite of their dislike of the work, the board agreed to publish the " Poem of Ecstasy " as soon as the full score was completed. (They even awarded it the second " Glinka Prize " the following year, the first going to Rachmaninof for his E minor Symphony.) Although Scriabin saw Kussevitsky in Paris he did not make his acquaintance.

From Paris—where Scriabin had caused a mild sensation by going about without a hat " for hygienic reasons ",[1] then an innovation as daring as the " Promethen chord " itself and one which led to his being followed about by a crowd of urchins chanting " le Monsieur sans chapeau "—Alexander and Tatiana went to Switzerland, spending the summer at Beattenberg on the shores of Lake Thun, then moving in the autumn to Lausanne, where they stayed till the end of July, 1908. Scriabin's father had retired and settled at Lausanne, while Tatiana's brother Boris, and his wife, also spent some

[1] Scriabin was always afraid of losing his hair; his domestic shampooing was " an elaborate ceremony ".

time with them there. The score of the " Poème de l'Extase " made slow progress, though Scriabin promised Altschuler, who visited them at Beattenberg, that he should have it for performance that season. It was finished at Lausanne in a desperate hurry, neither Scriabin nor Tatiana taking more than about four hours' sleep a day for three weeks—he writing, she revising and copying. Even so they were too late for Altschuler, but the score was published in January, 1908, a week or two before the birth of Tatiana's second child, Julian, and within a few days of Kussevitsky's Berlin debut as a conductor. It was given its first performance in Petersburg later in the year, under Hugo Warlich. As a sort of by-product of the " Poem ", the Fifth Sonata, Op. 53, was written in a few days. But the only other products of the Lausanne period were the six pieces, Op. 56 and Op. 57. (The autograph scores of both the " Poem " and the Fifth Sonata were given to the Canadian pianist La Liberté, whom the composer had met in New York and who came to Lausanne to study with the " maître ".)

Scriabin gave three recitals in Lausanne (in November, 1907, and April and July, 1908), playing the favourite Third Sonata on each occasion and reprinting Tatiana's Brussels programme. From the directorate of the Moscow branch of the Russian Music Society, recently joined by M. K. Morozova, came an invitation to appear as soloist at their concerts. But for the time being he hesitated, principally because he did not wish to be separated from Tatiana and was doubtful of the reception she would get in Moscow.

It was at Lausanne that Scriabin had the crazy idea of publishing his own works. At least, his piano compositions; for the Belaief firm was welcome to his expensive orchestral scores. With no idea of the complicated business of placing printed music on the market, for which the private individual has no resources, he imagined that by acting as his own publisher he would be able to pocket the publisher's profits. He actually had the Fifth Sonata and the " Trois Morceaux ", Op. 52, printed in this way at his own expense, and induced the Paris firm of Enoch to act as distributing agents for the " Edition des œuvres de A. Scriabine ". But Enochs took no interest in this very peculiar music and neglected to advertise it. At the end of two years Scriabin received in all only a few francs—of which, however, he is said to have been exceptionally proud! But fate was usually very kind to Scriabin. At this very point, in the spring of 1908, Serge Kussevitsky, fresh from his Berlin debut as a conductor, came to Lausanne to make his acquaintance. Backed by his wife's millions, Kussevitsky was on fire with a twofold ambition, to run symphony concerts of his own in Russia and to found a publishing company like Belaief's, one that would disregard ordinary commercial considerations. Kussevitsky needed a good horse to back, Scriabin needed a backer. It was an ideal conjunction, and the two men at once took to each other personally. " Scriabin told me ", says Kussevitsky, " that he had long been thinking of a grandiose composition, a ' Mystery ', which he had already begun, but that circumstances gave him no chance to concentrate on a big work, compelling him instead to write trifles ". (A typically Russian excuse for typically Russian inactivity; Scriabin had been dallying over the completion of the " Poème de l'Extase " in exactly the same way, and had written hardly any " trifles " at all.) " If he could be guaranteed a few years of quiet work, he would finish the ' Mystery '—in five years at the outside. He wanted a guarantee of five thousand rubles. For this he would give the firm some small pieces, and when the ' Mystery ' was ready, that also should be handed over to the Russian Music Publishing Company " (the name Kussevitsky proposed to give his business). " To all this I agreed at once." For the next year or two Scriabin's affairs were managed by Kussevitsky just as they had been managed in his early days by Belaief. Scriabin also became a member of the advisory board of the new Company, with Rachmaninof, Medtner and others.

Scriabin and Tatiana visited the Kussevitskys at Biarritz in August, then joined Tatiana's mother and their children in Brussels, where they remained for three or four months. In Brussels Scriabin renewed contact with theosophist circles. Among his Belgian friends were the artist Jean Delville, a leading theosophist, who afterwards designed the cover for "Prometheus", and Emile Cygogne, a professor of elocution. Cygogne was a man of all-round culture, but Scriabin took a particular pleasure in discussing languages with him. For his "Mystery" he thought of devising a new language, "not so much a word-language (with Sanskrit roots)", says Engel, "as a language of cries, sighs and interjections". Scriabin needed such sympathetic souls as Cygogne and Delville. An "aureole of sympathy" was always necessary to him, and he found this in Brussels perhaps more perfectly than at any other period of his life. But Kussevitsky was calling him to action. Leaving the children in Brussels, Scriabin and Tatiana joined the conductor in Berlin and towards the end of January, 1909, set foot in Moscow for the first time for nearly five years.

On February 21st/March 6th, 1909, the Moscow branch of the R.M.S. devoted an entire concert to Scriabin's works, including the "Divine Poem" and the "Poem of Ecstasy", the cost of the extra rehearsals (six in all) being defrayed by M. K. Morozova. Emil Cooper conducted and the composer played his Fifth Sonata. He heard the "Poem of Ecstasy" for the first time at Cooper's rehearsals (and expressed delight at the effectiveness of his own scoring) but, before the actual concert in Moscow, he was able to hear it also in Petersburg under Felix Blumenfeld (January 31st/February 13th) at a Russian Symphony Concert. The preparations for these performances aroused a tremendous amount of interest, particularly in Moscow. "Practically every musician in

Moscow was present at these rehearsals ", says Engel, " many with Scriabin's scores . . . . It is difficult to describe the excitement which reigned. Perfect strangers who happened to get into conversation quarrelled warmly or shook each other's hands in delight; sometimes there were even more unrestrained scenes of agitation and enthusiasm ". It was the real beginning of " Scriabinism " in Russia. That austere old humourist Taneief was there, too, irritated like many others by Boris Schlözer's windy programme-notes. " Look, six notes and—' *the essence of the creative spirit is revealed to us* ' ", he growled. " What a pitiful conception of the essence of the creative soul one must have to be able to put it into six notes." On Sabaneief, the composer now made a rather more favourable impression: " He had an insignificant little beard and a fluffy, surprisingly *dashing* moustache, a sort of survival of his ' officerism ' . . . His physiognomy was nervous, livid; he gazed absent-mindedly upward; he had brown eyes, small but with wide open lids, with a sort of intoxication in his glance. There was something of a wild animal in his eyes, not of a beast of prey, but of some little creature such as a marmot. It was not till afterwards that I read something else in those eyes. The former superciliousness seemed to have vanished; on the contrary, this little man who was near to the very ' spirit of the universe ' and who was engaged in organising the end of the world, had a modest, apologetic air. He was affable and exquisitely polite—but in this politeness there was an awful *distance* from all these people who surrounded him with friendly effusiveness "— Nietzsche's " aristocratic distance "! " Later I always noticed in Scriabin this strange politeness, which had the effect of at once placing a gap of some millions of kilometres between himself and those he was talking to; with this politeness and ' gentlemanliness ' he protected himself from intrusion upon his psychology . . . And there was Tatiana Fedorovna Schlözer, a pale little brunette, with her tight lips and her rare glances at the face of the person she was speaking to. She carried herself with exaggerated rigidity. 'Like a princess of the blood', I thought to myself. There, too, was the aunt who had brought him up—quiet, exultant, utterly devoted to her 'Sasha'. A grey-haired general—his uncle . . . During the performance Scriabin was nervous; sometimes he would suddenly raise himself a little, make an involuntary movement of joy, then sit down again. His face was very young considering his real age . . . but he was as mercurial as a boy and there was something childlike in the expression of his moustached physiognomy. I noticed that while listening to his music, he sometimes lowered his face rather strangely, his eyes closed and his appearance expressed an almost physiological enjoyment; then he would open his eyes and look upwards as if wishing to fly; but in tense moments of the music he breathed violently and nervously, sometimes gripping his chair with both hands. I have seldom seen a composer's face and figure so mobile while listening to his own music; it was as if he could not constrain himself to conceal the profound experiences he derived from it." After the rehearsal Scriabin went up to Taneief and asked smilingly, " Well, what was your impression, Sergeï Ivanovitch?" " My impression?" spluttered Taneief (" red as a lobster ", according to Sabaneief, " and seemingly on the point of bursting with inward tension "). " As if I'd been beaten unmercifully with sticks—that's my impression." That would have earned anyone else Scriabin's undying hatred, but Taneief was a privileged person, so fatherly and loveable that he could say the most outrageous things without arousing resentment. And worse was to come. " You know ", he said to Scriabin, " you're the first composer who instead of indicating the *tempi* writes *praise of his own compositions* . . . . There, you see: ' *Divin, grandiose* '. And ' *Sublime, divin* ' . . ."—roaring with laughter at his own joke. But even Taneief, probably more good-naturedly than sincerely, confessed to having been " enormously impressed " by the " Divine Poem ". And the actual concert was such a success, in spite of one or two very hostile criticisms, that the entire programme was repeated a week later in aid of a fund for the widows and orphans of musicians. Scriabin also made two or three other appearances as a recitalist and, after a couple of months in Moscow, he and Tatiana returned to Brussels very well satisfied with their expedition and assured that, in spite of Vera Ivanovna's partisans, it would be quite " safe " for them to settle in Russia.

Scriabin spent the greater part of 1909 in Brussels, where he began a new big orchestral work " Prometheus: a Poem of Fire ", Op. 60. " Prometheus " was a sort of preliminary study for the long contemplated " Mystery ", for not only was a wordless chorus introduced but there was a part for a *clavier à lumières,* a " light keyboard " to control the play of visual colour on a screen during the performance. In January, 1910, Scriabin with his entire *ménage* returned to Russia for good. Settling in Moscow they not only drew about them old friends like the Monighettis, but new ones— the Kussevitskys, Medtner, the pianist A. B. Goldenweiser, the writer Oskar von Riesemann, and, last but far from least, that same Leonid Leonidovitch Sabaneief who, as a boy, had been so repelled by Scriabin. Sabaneief, then rapidly winning a reputation as a critic, became not only Scriabin's intimate friend but, thus belatedly, his most skilful propagandist.

Shortly after Scriabin's arrival in Moscow, he received a tremendous ovation after a performance of the " Divine Poem " under Oskar Fried, at a Kussevitsky concert. The programme announced that a special concert of Scriabin's works would be conducted by Kussevitsky himself three weeks later, including first performances of " Prometheus " and some " Symphonic Dances ". But the score of " Prometheus " was not finished for some months after this, while the

"Symphonic Dances" were never finished at all! Indeed, never even begun; though the composer is said to have played bits of them to his friends. (Balakiref, if he heard about this —he still had a few months to live—must have been satisfied that in at least one respect his spirit would still live on in Russia.) But in spite of their disappointment—they were given the "Poem of Ecstasy" instead—the audience greeted the composer with tremendous enthusiasm. In May, Scriabin and Tatiana accompanied Kussevitsky on the first of his famous Volga tours, with full symphony orchestra travelling on a specially chartered steamer. They gave nineteen concerts at eleven different towns and in each town Scriabin appeared as soloist in his Concerto, playing on a Bechstein which travelled on the steamer, and giving his own early and middle period pieces as encores.

Scriabin spent the rest of the summer in the country on the Marck estate, where he finished "Prometheus", and shortly after their return to Moscow Tatiana gave birth to their third and last child, Marina. In November and December, Scriabin appeared as recitalist in both Petersburg and Moscow, and in February, 1911, in Leipzig and Berlin, his programmes including compositions up to Op. 52. On November 27th/December 10th his "Divine Poem" had been one of the works selected for the Jubilee Concert of the Moscow section of the R.M.S. (As the others were Taneief's "John of Damascus" and Rachmaninof's Third Concerto, no one could have complained of narrowness of taste or dull uniformity.) And at last, on March 2nd/15th, 1911, more than a year after it had been originally promised, Kussevitsky was able to give the first performance of "Prometheus", though it was found after all that, owing to practical difficulties, the "play of lights" could not be managed satisfactorily and this feature had to be cut out. (Altschuler in New York was the first conductor who managed to give "Prometheus" with colour accompaniment.) Kussevitsky gave the work nine rehearsals; the orchestra seems to have played magnificently; Scriabin himself played the piano part; but " Prometheus " was received very differently from the " Divine Poem " and the " Poem of Ecstasy ". Hisses mingled with the applause and, apart from the avowed Scriabinists among the critics, " Prometheus " had a bad press. Shortly afterwards, Scriabin broke with Kussevitsky.

Rather frequent disagreements had recently begun to mar their previous close friendship, and though the immediate cause of the break was a quarrel over Scriabin's proposed appearance in a series of Kussevitsky's concerts, it had been evident for some time that they were heading for a rupture. Two such decided individualists could hardly have managed to work very long in close partnership. Nevertheless, Kussevitsky continued to play Scriabin's music, though less frequently than before. And the Russian Music Publishing Company, which was only just beginning to function, issued not only " Prometheus " and the earlier pieces it had acquired (including the Fifth Sonata), but a number of new works written at this period: the Sixth and Seventh Sonatas (Opp. 62 and 64) and the " Poèmes ", Op. 61 and Op. 63. All these compositions were written in the summer in the country on the estate of Obraztsovo.

Scriabin always went into the country intending to rest, but always after a week or two became absorbed in work again. The fact is that Scriabin made a very queer country-dweller. As Engel says, " he wanted to enjoy everything from morning to night, sunshine and starlight. He wanted nature—like life—to provide him with one continual feast. But at the same time, face to face with nature, he often felt by no means at home with it. For instance, he would never sit or lie directly on the grass—he always wanted a ground-sheet or something of the sort; he never wanted to go for a walk if there was any prospect of a storm. He was terrified of grass-snakes etc.; he was a 'dilettante nature-lover', says one of his closest friends, who adds that Scriabin produced a curious effect in the country among the peasants, with his English clothes, his white trousers, and his French speech ".

From October, 1911, to March, 1912, in addition to giving concerts in Petersburg and Moscow, Scriabin was obliged, for financial reasons to embark on an extensive recital tour of the provinces, Odessa, Vilna, Minsk, Taganrog, Rostof-on-Don, Kazan and other towns, sometimes appearing under the auspices of local branches of the R.M.S., sometimes independently. His programmes consisted almost solely of his early and middle period works, the centre-point of his programmes generally being the Second Sonata. Tatiana almost invariably accompanied him. And all this concert-giving, though it completely interrupted his creative work, was by no means irksome to Scriabin. He enjoyed being the focus of attention, enjoyed the ovations and the general " holiday " feeling of the tour. He was always nervous before a concert, always as " surprised " as any popular actress at the " love " shown him by the audience. After one of these provincial recitals he liked to sit in a restaurant, drinking wine or tea, and chatting with newly-made acquaintances.

It was during this winter, at the very height of the thoroughly Russian press-warfare waged in Moscow between the conservative Rachmaninofists and the progressive Scriabinists, that the two old friends appeared together at a Philharmonic Concert, Rachmaninof conducting Scriabin's First Symphony and Piano Concerto, with the composer as soloist. There was also a *rapprochement* with Ziloti, who helped Scriabin out of his rather awkward relationship with Kussevitsky's Russian Music Publishing Company by putting him in touch with the firm of Jurgenson. The founder of the firm, P. I. Jurgenson, was now dead and his sons were not only willing to publish Scriabin's music but offered him very generous terms. And so it came about that Scriabin's first publishers were also his last, though on very different conditions.

The Scriabins spent the summer of 1912 again in Switzerland, at Beattenberg. Then, after six weeks near Brussels, came three concerts in Holland (Amsterdam, the Hague, and Haarlem) and one at Frankfurt-am-Main, with Mengelberg. (Berlin had heard " Prometheus " in March—and it had made the acquaintance of the " Poem of Ecstasy " as early as December, 1909, under Khessin; the following year Kussevitsky had conducted " Ecstasy " in both Berlin and London.) These Mengelberg concerts, arranged largely through Ziloti's good offices, were entirely devoted to Scriabin's works, including the First Symphony, " Prometheus " and the Concerto—with the composer as soloist. Returning to Moscow in November, the Scriabins settled with Tatiana's mother, taking a house in the Arbat suburb which remained their home for the rest of the composer's life and which in 1922 was converted into a Scriabin Museum.

In these last years the forty-year-old Scriabin became quite a domestic character, preferring to entertain his friends at home instead of meeting them in restaurants as in the old days. He took to chess and, like Tchaïkovsky, to patience. A certain reserve began to show itself in his intercourse with friends, and he was no longer so extraordinarily willing to confide his plans and play his music to everyone he met. His self-adoration, great as it always had been, became even more pronounced—though not in his dealings with others. Like Nietzsche he treated his " inferiors " with the utmost courtesy, but that " distance " between him and them was now immeasurable. So was the " distance " between himself and other composers, though he could still be delighted by Wagner. He placed Mussorgsky above all other Russian musicians, but though he spoke of Mussorgsky as a " genius ", Mussorgsky's music actually left him cold. He also " valued " in the same way Borodin and Rimsky-Korsakof—

at any rate much more than Rimsky-Korsakof had ever admired *him*. But Tchaïkovsky was, in his view, "too Philistine a nature", too pessimistic, too " coarse " technically. Scriabin loved a strong element of aristocracy in music, as in everything else. As for his Western contemporaries, he disliked Strauss and detested Schönberg. Nor was he now very deeply interested in his own earlier works, though of course he still had to go on playing them in public. He refused to make piano transcriptions of his orchestral works, nor was he interested in those made by Sabaneief and Leo Konius. Living in the excessively rarefied harmonic atmosphere of Opp. 66 to 70, including the Eighth, Ninth and Tenth Sonatas, he breathed ordinary fresh air with difficulty.

The Scriabins spent the summer of 1913 as usual in the country at Oka, on the Bera estate. The next winter was a busy one, with numerous concerts and recitals in both capitals as well as in various provincial cities, and to crown all this activity came a five weeks' visit to England in February and March. On this occasion, no doubt remembering his American experience, Scriabin left Tatiana at home. Instead he was accompanied by an old acquaintance (though hardly an intimate friend) A. N. Briantchaninof, who happened to have business in London and who was familiar with English ways and the English language. (Scriabin had tried to learn English, but without much success.) Early in the previous year (February 1st) Henry Wood had introduced " Prometheus " to a London audience by the drastic process of playing it twice at one concert. Now, on March 14th, 1914, Wood again conducted " Prometheus " (though still without the very necessary chorus and, of course, without colours) and the Piano Concerto, the composer playing the piano part in each work. Scriabin also gave recitals at the Bechstein Hall on March 20th and 26th, and at all three appearances was so well received that he looked forward with pleasure to a second visit to England, a visit prevented by the outbreak of the Great War. Indeed, he took a great fancy to England, and on his return to Russia was kind enough to inform all and sundry that we were in the very forefront of mankind! Human relationships were more reliable; people were more conscientious, knew how to value their leaders, were more receptive to new ideas than elsewhere. (After all, the poor little man had known us for only five weeks.) Cambridge, which he visited on the invitation of Professor Myers, who like himself was interested in the colour scale, pleased him even more than London. He returned to Russia a complete Anglophile—with a sun-helmet in his luggage.

The purchase of the sun-helmet and other necessities of life in the East was the first definite step toward the practical realisation of the long contemplated " Mystery ". Moreover Scriabin had applied to a London travel agency for particulars of routes to India and the cost of tickets. And during the summer, spent in the country not far from Moscow, he wrote the text of the " Preliminary Action " which was to be a sort of grand rehearsal for the " Mystery " itself. And what was this supreme " Mystery ", after all? It was perhaps the most extraordinary conception with which the mind of a famous artist has ever become pregnant. For the " malignant rumours " that Scriabin considered himself the new Messiah and that he was " planning a work which was to bring about the end of the world " were, after all, nothing but the simple truth divested of the occult verbiage beloved of mystics of his cast of mind. For the " Mystery ", to the composition of which he considered himself " consecrated ", *was* to be an apocalyptic affair, the occasion of a " world cataclysm ". Our race, he believed, is doomed to perish, to be replaced by another, higher and nobler. And the performance of his " Mystery " was to be the final manifestation of the human soul as it exists at present, the point of transition from the old to the new plane of existence. In his hemispherical temple in India (mirrored in the waters of a lake to form a sphere, the most perfect of all shapes) every means known to art—dancing, music, poetry, colours and even scents—were to unite to produce in the worshippers a " supreme, final ecstasy ". (One says " worshippers " advisedly, for everyone was to take part in this " liturgy in the form of art ".) And, according to Sabaneief, " this liturgical act was to be only the Prologue to the ' Mystery ' itself, which was to begin afterwards in forms of which it is impossible to speak. Then would come the moment of collective creative ecstasy, and in the consciousness of the moment of harmony ", harmony between the Spirit and the World, " the physical plane of our consciousness would disappear and a world cataclysm would begin ". As for the composer himself, even in 1904 he had been quite happy about his own fate. " I shall not die ", he said. " I shall suffocate in ecstasy after the Mystery." It was his favourite topic of conversation in after years, though only with the elect—not, as in the earlier days when he had first conceived the " Mystery ", with anyone who cared to listen—to review the history of mankind, through all its stages of development, from the creation of the world up to himself and the projected final cataclysm. And in this limited circle of the chosen he made no secret of the fact that he considered himself the true Messiah. Christ was " not the central Messiah ". " The central Messiah is he who will sound the final chord of our race, reuniting it with the Spirit." The only point which worried this spiritual-artistic Guy Fawkes was the condition of mankind, which he considered unfit to " accept " his " Mystery ". But he was fairly confident that that would all come right in a few years and when the Great War broke out he was delighted at the prospect of its " purifying " the world in preparation for his grand finale. He had for some time been composing the music—which, as we have seen, was to be published by the Russian Music Publishing Company, presumably well in advance of the catastrophe. " All his best ideas were intended for the ' Mystery ' ", says Sabaneief, " but as new, even more perfect forms appeared, he gradually used the old material of the ' Mystery ' for other productions ". Not only the last piano pieces, Op. 71 to Op. 74, written in 1914, but a great deal of his earlier work actually originated as music for the " Mystery ". As for the " Mystery " itself, it always remained one. He kept on putting it off to the future. Not the distant future, but a quite equally hazy " four or five years' time ". Since neither he nor the world was quite ready for the " Mystery " itself, he went ahead with the " Preliminary Action " by way of experiment and rehearsal.

The " Preliminary Action " was itself to be a combination of all the arts; and, as in the grand final " Mystery ", there were to be no spectators or audience but only performers. He reckoned that about two thousand of these would be needed and, having a practical mind—as the purchase of the sun-helmet had rather surprisingly demonstrated—he was more than a little worried about his soloists. He carefully considered the desirability of entrusting the chief part to Chaliapin and the leading of the dances to Karsavina, but finally rejected them as unsuitable. He wanted artists equally gifted, but " consecrated "—and he did realise that they would not be easy to find. As for the rank and file of the performers, he came to the conclusion that he would have to give them courses of instruction and wondered whether it would not be advisable to advertise such courses in the newspapers. He " would have to get hold of some people with practical energy ", he said. The locale of the " Preliminary Action " troubled him less. Since his visit to London, he had come to the flattering conclusion that, next to Russia, the most suitable place was—England. (Someone must have taken him to the Albert Hall.) By the end of 1914, the text of the " Action " was finished, some of it being borrowed from the libretto of the Nietzschean opera of nine years before. This rhythmical, alliterative flood of mystical nonsense was written in a tremendous state of excitement—and approved by two genuine poets, his friends the well-known symbolist Viatcheslaf Ivanof and Y. K. Baltrushaïtis. The music was not begun, though the composer had it " all ready in his head and could finish it in eight months ", he told B. P. Jurgenson, who was to publish it.

During the winter of 1914-15 Scriabin gave a number of concerts in both capitals for Serbia, for war-sufferers, and similar patriotic and charitable causes.[1] The two Petrograd recitals in February were so successful that Scriabin arranged yet a third, in the small hall of the Conservatoire, on April 2nd/15th. This was his last public appearance. He returned to Moscow two days later. On the 6th/19th he felt unwell and the following day took to his bed with a boil on his upper lip. He had suffered from a painful boil in the same place the year before, but it had disappeared while he was in London. But this time the " boil " turned out to be a carbuncle, and his temperature rose alarmingly. The doctors operated three times in three days, but in vain. On the 13th/26th the blood-poisoning developed into pleurisy and the doctors gave up hope. In the evening the patient began to lose consciousness, a release from terrible suffering, and was given the Holy Sacrament at three in the morning. A few hours later, at five minutes past eight on April 14th/27th, 1915, Scriabin died, just four months after his father.

His funeral was attended by the whole of musical Moscow, friend and foe alike, and he was laid to rest in the cemetery of the Novodevitchy Monastery—in the courtyard of which is laid the opening scene of " Boris Godunof ".

* * * * *

The history of Scriabin's creative career is the history of

[1] On December 20th/January 2nd his father died at Lausanne.

the decline and fall of a remarkable creative talent through unlimited egotism. Few composers have begun more brilliantly. No one but a Cui would think of reproaching him for his devotion to Chopin; a young composer who was not derivative would be a freak—and a highly suspicious freak. Granted the early Chopinism and the later influences of Liszt and Wagner, Scriabin's own personality begins to emerge quite as soon as we have any right to expect. Nothing could be more individual than the two beautifully serene Preludes, Op. 11, No. 15 and Op. 15, No. 4, both of which date from 1895. And, incidentally, the temperament revealed by these two pieces, if not very strongly masculine, is by no means sickly. The salon element in so much of Scriabin's earlier music is unpleasant, but he atones for it by the perfection of his craftmanship. As a miniaturist. Scriabin was the equal of any. And he had what most musical miniaturists have lacked—a sense of the epigrammatic. Given a normal maturing of his powers and deepening of experience, Scriabin might have become a real master.

But obsessed with ideas which were not merely egocentric but gradually excluded everything outside himself, he followed a certain narrow line of harmonic development to its remote conclusion with such disregard of intelligibility that none but his devotees could follow him there. If he had continued to produce from a genuine, spontaneous impulse, all might still have been well. The circle of initiates would gradually have widened and Scriabinism would have established itself as Wagnerism had done half a century earlier. But it soon appeared that Scriabin's genuine creative impulse, after all, was weak and soon exhausted. (It may be that his physical life exhausted it.) When he had sloughed off the skins of Chopinism and Wagnerism, he could do nothing but manufacture music, hypnotising himself and the little circle about him (and, to a lesser extent, the vast crowd of the gullible everywhere) into the belief that these esoteric harmonies were spontaneously generated by his insane mystic-erotic dreams. Nothing could be more curious than the success with which Scriabin deluded himself and, for a time, a large part of the musical world that his elaborately calculated structures—" paper " music, rigidly symmetrical in outline and based on harmonic schemes worked out beforehand, bar by bar—were genuine expressions of ecstasy, of supreme mystical aspiration, and of erotic desire. The naked harmonic schemes which Scriabin so naïvely showed to his intimates, and which they have so naïvely told us about, are concealed by such cunning craftsmanship—the craftsmanship of that consummate miniaturist now being applied to every bar of large-scale compositions—and dressed up in such super-Meyerbeerian orchestration that it is hardly surprising that even now people find it difficult to believe in the coldly intellectual basis of it all.

Scriabin (and Tatiana) gave the final touch to self-hypnotism by the lavish markings sprinkled on every page of the music. When he (or she) had written " *voluptueux* " or " *avec émotion et ravissement* " against a theme, that settled it—for them. It *was* voluptuous or emotional and rapturous to their imaginations, though as a matter of fact most of these ecstatic ejaculations are as meaningless as the titles Erik Satie gave his pieces: " Embryons desséchés ", " Morceaux en forme de poire ", and so on. But, after all, these were only among the least of the New Messiah's flights of imagination!

G. A.

CHRONOLOGY

1804. Glinka born.
1813. Dargomyjsky born.
1820. Serof born.
1833. Borodin born.
1835. Cui born.
1836. Production of *A Life for the Tsar*.
1837. Balakiref born.
1839. Mussorgsky born; Dargomyjsky's *Esmeralda* finished.
1840. Tchaïkovsky born.
1842. Production of *Ruslan and Liudmila*.
1844. Rimsky-Korsakof born; Glinka in Spain.
1855. Balakiref's debut in St. Petersburg; Anatol Liadof born.
1856. Dargomyjsky's *Russalka* produced; Taneief born; Rimsky-Korsakof a Naval Cadet.
1857. Mussorgsky meets Balakiref; death of Glinka.
1858. Cui begins *Captive in the Caucasus*; Balakiref's first songs.
1859. Serof meets Wagner; Cui's *Mandarin's Son*; Tchaïkovsky enters Civil Service; Liapunof born.
1862. Borodin becomes Balakiref's pupil and begins First Symphony; Balakiref founds Free School of Music; Tchaïkovsky enters Petersburg Conservatoire (just founded); Rimsky-Korsakof in England.
1863. Serof's *Judith* performed; Mussorgsky begins *Salammbo*; Mussorgsky enters Civil Service, Tchaïkovsky leaves it.
1865. Serof's *Rogneda* produced; Rimsky-Korsakof's First Symphony performed; Glazunof born.
1866. Dargomyjsky begins *The Stone Guest*; Tchaïkovsky becomes Professor at new Moscow Conservatoire and writes First Symphony.
1868. First Russian performance of *Lohengrin*; Serof begins *Hostile Power*, Mussorgsky *The Marriage* and *Boris*, and Rimsky-Korsakof *The Maid of Pskof*; Cui finishes *William Ratcliffe*.
1869. Borodin's First Symphony performed and *Igor* begun; Mussorgsky finishes first version of *Boris*; Balakiref's *Islamey*; Tchaïkovsky's *Voevoda* performed and *Romeo and Juliet* written; death of Dargomyjsky.
1871. Borodin's Second Symphony begun; Rimsky-Korsakof becomes Professor at Petersburg Conservatoire; Scriabin born.
1872. Cui, Borodin, Mussorgsky and Rimsky-Korsakof write *Mlada*; Balakiref withdraws temporarily from active musical life; second version of *Boris* completed.
1873. Mussorgsky begins *Khovanshchina*; Tchaïkovsky's Second Symphony performed.
1874. *Boris* performed; Mussorgsky begins *Fair of Sorotchintsi*; Tchaïkovsky's *Vakula the Smith* and Concerto in B flat minor.

1877. Borodin's Second Symphony performed and First String Quartet finished; Tchaïkovsky's Fourth Symphony and *Eugene Onegin*; Tchaïkovsky marries.
1878. Korsakof's *May Night*; Liadof and Taneief become Professors at the Petersburg and Moscow Conservatoires respectively.
1879. Mussorgsky's concert tour.
1880. Korsakof's *Snow Maiden*; Glazunof becomes pupil of Korsakof.
1881. Death of Mussorgsky and Nicholas Rubinstein; Balakiref's *Tamara* completed.
1882. Glazunof's First Symphony; Scriabin enters Cadet Corps; Stravinsky born.
1883. Balakiref head of Imperial Chapel, with Korsakof as assistant.
1885. Tchaïkovsky's *Manfred*; Taneief Director of Moscow Conservatoire.
1887. Death of Borodin; Rimsky-Korsakof's *Spanish Capriccio*; Taneief begins *Orestes*.
1888. Tchaïkovsky's Fifth Symphony; Korsakof's *Sheherazade*; Scriabin enters Moscow Conservatoire.
1890. Tchaïkovsky's *Queen of Spades*; Rimsky-Korsakof's *Mlada*.
1891. Tchaïkovsky in America; *Nutcracker* ballet; Prokofief born.
1892. Korsakof's neurasthenic crisis.
1893. Tchaïkovsky writes *Pathétique* Symphony and dies; Scriabin's first compositions published.
1894. Korsakof's *Christmas Eve*; Liapunof Assistant Director of Imperial Chapel in succession to Korsakof.
1895. Korsakof writes *Sadko* and revises *Boris*; Taneief's *Orestes* produced; Scriabin's concert tour in West.
1898. *The Tsar's Bride*; Taneief's C minor Symphony; Scriabin Professor at Moscow Conservatoire; Balakiref's First Symphony finished.
1899. *Tsar Saltan*.
1900. Korsakof's *Servilia*; Scriabin's First Symphony.
1902. Korsakof's *Pan Voevoda*; Scriabin's Second Symphony.
1904. Korsakof's *Kitej*; Scriabin's *Divine Poem* and separation from wife.
1905. Korsakof dismissed from Petersburg Conservatoire; Taneief leaves Moscow Conservatoire; Scriabin begins *Poem of Ecstasy*.
1906. Death of Vladimir Stassof; Scriabin in America; Korsakof begins *The Golden Cockerel*.
1907. Diaghilef's Festival of Russian Music in Paris.
1908. Death of Rimsky-Korsakof; *Boris* performed in Paris.
1910. Stravinsky's *Fire Bird*; death of Balakiref.
1911. Scriabin's *Prometheus* performed.
1912. Stravinsky's *Rite of Spring*.
1914. Scriabin in England; Taneief's *On the Reading of a Psalm*; death of Liadof.
1915. Death of Scriabin and Taneief.
1918. Death of Cui.
1924. Death of Liapunof.
1926. Glazunof settles in Paris.

BIBLIOGRAPHY
A. Russian Periodicals

Isvestiya S. Peterburgskovo Obshchestva Muzykalnykh Sobranii (Petersburg, 1901 seq.).
K Novym Beregam (Moscow, 1923 seq.).
Muzyka (Moscow, 1910 seq.).
Muzyka i Revolutsiya (Moscow, 1926 seq.).
Muzykalnaya Lietopis (Leningrad, 1922 seq.).
Muzykalnaya Starina (Petersburg, 1906 seq.).
Muzykalnoe Nasliedstvo, Vol. I (Moscow, 1935).
Muzykalny Sovremmenik (Petrograd, 1915–1917).
Russkaya Muzykalnaya Gazeta (Petersburg, 1894 seq.).
Sovietskaya Muzyka (Moscow, 1932–1935).

B. Russian Books

General

Arnold, Youri : Recollections (three vols., Moscow, 1891–93).
Cui, César : Musical Critical Articles (Vol. I, Moscow, 1913).
Cui, César : The Russian Song (Petersburg, 1896).
Karenin, V. : Vladimir Stassof (two vols., Leningrad, 1926).
Kashkin, N. D. : A History of Russian Music (Moscow, 1908).
Kuznetsof, N. : A History of Russian Music (Vol. I, Moscow, 1924).
Laroche, Hermann : Collected Articles (Petersburg, 1894).
Rimsky-Korsakof, N. A. : Memoirs of my Musical Life (Fourth Edition, edited by A. N. Rimsky-Korsakof, Moscow, 1932; Sixth Edition, *ibid*, 1935).
Rimsky-Korsakof, N. A. : Correspondence with M. Balakiref (published only in part in " Muzykalny Sovremennik ").
Rimsky-Korsakof, N. A. : Correspondence with V. Stassof (" Russkaya Mysl ", 1910).
Serof, A. : Collected Articles, etc. (four vols., Petersburg, 1892–95).
Stassof, V. V. : Collected Writings (three vols., Moscow, 1926).

Glinka

Findeisen, N. F. : Catalogue of the Glinka Museum of the St. Petersburg Conservatoire (Petersburg, 1902).
Findeisen, N. F. : Glinka's Life and Works (two vols., Petersburg, 1896).
Glinka, M. I. : Collected Letters (edited by Findeisen) (two vols., Petersburg, 1908).
Glinka, M. I. : Memoirs (edited by A. N. Rimsky-Korsakof) (Moscow, 1930).

Dargomyjsky

Dargomyjsky, A. : Autobiography, Letters, and Recollections of Contemporaries (edited by Findeisen) (Leningrad, 1922).
Findeisen, N. F. : Dargomyjsky (Moscow, 1904).

Serof

Baskin : Serof (Moscow, 1904).
Lobanof, D. : Serof and his Contemporaries (Petersburg, 1889).
Molchanof, A. : Serof (Petersburg, 1888).
Serof, A. : Letters to his Sister (Petersburg, 1898).

Balakiref

Balakiref, M. : Correspondence with Stassof (edited by V. Karenin) (Vol. I, Petrograd, 1917).
Balakiref, M. : Correspondence with Tchaïkovsky (edited by Liapunof) (Petersburg, 1912).
Grodzky, B. : M. I. Balakiref (Petersburg, 1910).
Timofeief, G. : Balakiref (" Russkaya Mysl ", Petersburg, June–July, 1912).
Yakovlef, V. : Balakiref (" Muzyka i Revolutsiya ", 1926) (contains a comprehensive bibliography).

Borodin
Borodin, A. P. : Letters (edited by S. Dianin) (Vol. I, Moscow, 1928).
Braudo, E. : Borodin (Petrograd, 1922).
Khubof, G. : Borodin (Moscow, 1933).
Stassof, V. V. : Borodin, his Life, Correspondence, and Musical Articles (Petersburg, 1889).

Mussorgsky
Mussorgsky, M. P. : Articles and Materials (edited by Y. Keldysh and V. Yakovlef) (Moscow, 1932) (contains a full bibliography up to 1928).
Mussorgsky, M. P. : Letters and Documents (edited by A. N. Rimsky-Korsakof) (Moscow, 1932).
Sletof, P. and V. : Mussorgsky (Moscow, 1934).
Various authors : " Boris Godunof " (Moscow, 1930).

Tchaïkovsky
Kashkin, N. D. : Reminiscences of Tchaïkovsky (Moscow, 1896).
Tchaïkovsky, M. I. : Life of P. I. Tchaïkovsky (three vols., Moscow, 1903).
Tchaïkovsky, P. I. : Correspondence with N. F. von Meck (edited by V. A. Zhdanof and N. T. Zhegin) (Moscow : Vol. I, 1934 ; Vol. II, 1935).
Tchaïkovsky, P. I. : Diary (edited by I. I. Tchaïkovsky and N. T. Zhegin) (Moscow, 1923).
Tchaïkovsky, P. I. : Documents and Materials (Vol. I of " Proshloe Russkoy Muzyki ", Petrograd, 1920).
(A bibliography of literature on Tchaïkovsky published between 1917 and 1934 appeared in " Muzykalnoe Nasliedstvo ", Vol. I, Moscow, 1935.)

Rimsky-Korsakof
Rimsky-Korsakof, A. N. : N. A. Rimsky-Korsakof, his Life and Works (Moscow : Vol. I, 1933 ; Vol. II, 1935).
Yastrebtsef, V. V. : My Recollections of Rimsky-Korsakof (two vols., Moscow, 1917).

Glazunof
Belaief, V. : Glazunof (Vol. I, Petrograd, 1922).
Ossovsky, A. : Glazunof (Petersburg, 1907).

Taneief
Various authors (edited Kuznetsof) : S. Taneief (Moscow, 1925).

Scriabin
Sabaneief, L. L. : Reminiscences of Scriabin (Moscow, 1925).
Sabaneief, L. L. : Scriabin (second edition, Moscow, 1923).

C. Foreign Books

Abraham, Gerald : Studies in Russian Music (London, 1935).
Belaief, Victor : Mussorgsky's " Boris Godunof " and its New Version (translated by S. W. Pring) (London, 1928).
Blom, Eric : Tchaïkovsky's Orchestral Works (London, 1927).
Calvocoressi, M. D. : Glinka (Paris, 1911).
Evans, Edwin : Tchaikovsky (revised edition, London, 1935).
Fedorof, Vladimir : Moussorgsky (Paris, 1935).
van der Pals, N. van Gilse : N. A. Rimsky-Korssakow : Opernschaffen (Leipzig, 1929).
von Riesemann, Oskar : Monographien zur Russischen Musik : Vol. I (Glinka, Serof and Dargomyjsky) (Munich, 1923).
Swan, Alfred J. : Scriabin (London, 1923).
Tchaïkovsky, Modest : Das Leben P. I. Tschaikowskys (Übersetzt von Paul Juon) (two vols., Leipzig, 1903).

INDEX

A

Abraham, Gerald, 165
Adamof, V. S., 253, 255
Æschylus, 443
Aïvazovsky, 36
Alabief, 13, 60
Albrecht, K. F., 46
Aldridge, 109
Alexander II (Tsarevitch Alexander), 27, 51, 54, 59, 91, 93, 108, 170, 245, 304, 361, 379–80
Alexander III (Tsarevitch Alexander), 119, 264, 305, 309–14, 320, 323, 325, 383
Allegri, 367
Altschuler, 479–80, 484, 488
Ambros, 393
Apukhtin, 253, 255
Arensky, 384, 442–3, 457–8
Arnold, Youri, 40, 47, 69
Artôt, Desirée, 268–70, 320
Auber, 56, 70, 153, 269
Auer, Leopold, 305, 367, 440
Aumann, 15
Avé-Lallement, 320, 322
Azantchevsky, 356, 375

B

Bach, 59–60, 114–5, 190, 242, 342, 367, 369, 373, 441, 443, 448, 454, 466
Bakhmetef, 383
Bakhturin, 38–9, 45
Bakunin, 80
Balakiref, 9, 43, 56, 60, 62, 71, 73, 86, 89, 93, 97–148, 150, 152–3, 160–4, 168, 170, 181–93, 195–7, 199, 205–7, 212, 214–5, 231, 235–8, 240, 243, 252, 255, 257–8, 261, 264, 267, 270–3, 275–8, 281, 297–8, 308–9, 312–5, 336, 342–6, 348–55, 357, 360, 365–7, 369, 371–2, 375, 379, 381–5, 391, 393–4, 396, 400, 403, 405, 423, 430, 432, 436–8, 441, 444, 455, 457, 464, 478, 488
 Chopin Suite : 145
 Fantasy on " A Life for the Tsar " : 103–4, 107

Balakiref—continued
 Fire Bird : 121
 Forty Russian Folk Songs : 120, 272, 349
 Glinka Memorial Cantata : 109
 In Bohemia : 121
 Islamey : 100, 120, 125, 133, 146, 457
 King Lear : 109–10, 120, 130, 342
 Overture on a Spanish Theme : 104, 109
 Overture on Czech Themes (see *In Bohemia*)
 Overture on Three Russian Themes : 109, 120, 349
 Piano Concerto No. 1 : 104, 107
 Piano Concerto No. 2 , 120, 127, 145
 Piano Sonata : 146
 Russia : 120, 137, 140, 146, 349
 Sérénade espagnole : 104
 Song of Georgia : 120
 Song of the Golden Fish : 120
 Symphony No. 1 : 142, 146, 336
 Symphony No. 2 : 143, 145, 146
 Tamara : 100, 120, 127, 132–3, 135, 137, 146

Baltrushaïtis, 496
Basili, Francesco, 22–3
Beethoven, 17, 29, 37, 40, 56, 62, 68, 77–8, 81, 85, 94, 101, 108, 114, 117–8, 124, 142, 151, 156, 168, 179, 181, 184, 191, 198, 242, 254, 257, 260, 274, 337, 340, 342, 349, 369, 392, 450, 457, 466, 468
Begitchef, 268, 271
Bekker, 253
Belaief, M. P., 11, 139–40, 142, 322, 326, 382, 384–7, 389, 391, 395, 397, 407, 411, 445–6, 459–62, 464, 470, 472, 478, 481–3
Bellermann, 364
Bellini, 23–4, 77, 250

Belloli, 18
Berger, Francesco, 321
Bergmann, Valentina (see Serova, Valentina)
de Bériot, 147
Berlioz, 17, 48–9, 84–5, 115, 120, 124, 132–3, 136, 141–4, 151–2, 242, 244, 265, 309, 345, 351, 372
Bernard (composer), 68
Bernard, M. I., 180, 241, 349
Bernhard, A. R., 412–3
Bertenson (brothers), 331
Bertin, Louise, 68
Bessel, 219, 221–2, 275, 280, 362, 382, 385, 407
Betz, 210
Bianchi, Eliodoro, 22
Bianchi, Valentina, 60, 88
Bielsky, 400, 407, 409, 416–7, 419–20
Bismarck, 321
Bizet, 284, 297, 406
Blumenfeld, Felix, 238, 380, 384, 410, 413, 416, 419, 480, 484
Boccaccio, 57
Böhm, 15
Boieldieu, 15
Boïto, 330
Borodin, 63, 97, 105–6, 111–2, 117, 124–5, 128–9, 132, 145–6, 148, 150, 152, 155–77, 180, 186, 191, 204–7, 212–4, 217, 228, 231, 238, 243, 258, 270, 276, 332, 348, 352–5, 362, 365–8, 370, 373–5, 379, 384, 386–7, 389–91, 393, 405, 426, 430, 434, 444–5, 491
 B-la-F Quartet : 386
 Bogatyrs : 163, 171
 Dissonance : 165
 Enchanted Garden : 173
 In the Steppes of Central Asia : 170–1, 173, 176, 243
 Mlada : 165, 358, 389, 391
 My song is fierce and bitter : 165
 Paraphrases : 170
 Petite Suite : 173

503

INDEX

Borodin—continued
 Prince Igor : 63, 106, 164–5, 167, 169–75, 217, 374– , 386–7, 391, 422
 Queen of the Sea : 164
 Scherzo in A flat : 173
 Sea : 164
 Serenade of Four Swains : 171
 Sleeping Princess : 164
 Song of the Dark Forest : 164
 String Quartet No. 1 : 166, 169, 172, 177, 368
 String Quartet No. 2 : 172, 175
 Symphony No. 1 : 160–3, 168, 172–3, 176, 205, 348
 Symphony No. 2 : 117, 164–5, 168, 172, 176, 276
 Symphony No. 3 : 174–5
 To the Shores of my Distant Fatherland : 175
 Tsar's Bride : 164
Borozdin, Nikolai, 115
Borrow, George, 50
Bortniansky, 180, 305, 336
Boswell, 88
Bourgault-Ducoudray, 143
Brahms, 297, 320, 322, 440, 448
Braudo, 158, 175
Breughel, Pieter, 246
Briantchaninof, A. N., 492
Brodsky, 305, 307, 320
Bruch, Max, 330
Büchner, 163
Buckle, 345
Buffon, 76
Bulakhova, 71
Bull, Ole, 71
von Bülow, Cosima, 93
von Bülow, Hans, 93, 283, 314
Burenin, 307
Byron, 110, 192, 197, 308, 407, 415

C

Calvocoressi, M. D., 122, 235, 418–9
Canille, 341–3, 345
Carré, Albert, 419
Carroll, Lewis, 440
Catherine the Great, 65, 400, 402
Catoire, 460
Cavos, 31
Chaliapin, 401, 406, 412, 495
Cherubini, 15, 17, 364
Chopin, 43, 101, 114–6, 133, 136, 141, 145, 147–8, 159, 186, 238, 250, 342, 350,

Chopin—continued
 409, 448, 455–6, 459, 461, 463–4, 466, 468, 497
Cibber, 246
Clementi, 52
Colonne, 300, 326, 389
Constantine Constantinovitch (Grand Duke), 302, 304
Constantine Nikolaevitch (Grand Duke), 282, 302, 361
Cooper, Emil, 484
Cornelius, Peter, 25
Cramer, 455
Crusell, Bernhard, 14
Cui, 71–3, 75, 89–90, 93, 97, 105–6, 110, 112–3, 115, 120, 124, 129, 147–54, 165, 170, 173, 181, 184, 189, 197–8, 201, 203, 205–7, 209, 214, 224–5, 230–1, 238, 244, 249, 261, 266, 278, 283, 285–6, 305, 342, 344–5, 350–4, 358, 362, 365, 373, 379, 381, 384–5, 390, 420, 426, 432, 444, 497
 Angelo : 150, 230
 Captain's Daughter : 151
 Captive in the Caucasus : 120, 148–9, 173, 342
 Feast in Time of Plague : 150
 Le Flibustier : 150
 Mademoiselle Fifi : 150
 Mandarin's Son : 149
 Mlada : 150
 Paraphrases : 170
 Saracen : 150
 Scherzo : 149
 William Ratcliffe : 120, 149–50, 205, 353–4
Cygogne, Emile, 484
Czerny, 350

D

Dahl, 428
Danilevsky, 66
Dargomyjsky, 9, 27, 58, 63, 65–75, 80, 90, 92–3, 103–4, 117, 120, 130, 139, 148–9, 152, 181, 184–5, 189, 201–2, 204–5, 207, 227, 238, 247, 268, 290, 349, 352–3, 355, 404, 410, 465
 Baba Yaga : 72
 Esmeralda : 67–8, 70, 72
 Finnish Fantasy, 72
 Kosachok : 72
 Lucréce Borgia : 67–8
 Paladin : 75
 Rogdana : 72
 Russalka : 58, 65, 69–73, 75, 103, 181
 Stone Guest : 65, 72–5, 149, 152, 201–2, 204, 207, 352, 355, 360, 362, 410, 422

Dargomyjsky—continued
 Tarantelle Slave : 73
 Titular Councillor : 75
 Triumph of Bacchus : 70, 72
 Worm : 75
Darwin, 216
Davidof, K. Y., 307, 375
Davydof, L. V., 254, 259, 283
Davydof, Vladimir, 296, 327, 329
Davydova, Alexandra (née Tchaïkovskaya), 249, 254, 256–7, 262, 265, 277, 286, 288, 305, 326
Davydova, Vera, 258, 264, 331
Debussy, 63, 141–3, 154, 306, 414, 417, 448
Dehn, Siegfried, 25, 48, 55, 57, 60–1, 67
Delibes, 297, 390
Delvig, 21
Delville, Jean, 484
Diaghilef, 91, 402, 417–20, 429, 480
Dianin, Alexander, 155, 175
Dianin, Sergei, 9, 155, 175
Dickens, 310, 336
Dist, 147–8
Donizetti, 23–4, 77, 250
Door, Anton, 327
Dostoevsky, 52, 54, 94, 233, 242, 244
Dryden, 246
Dubuque, 100, 264, 455
Dukas, 143
Dumas, 150
Duncan, Isadora, 419
Duparc, 440
Dürbach, Fanny, 249–51, 329

E

Eckermann, 395
von Eckstedt, 103
Eiserich, 100–1
Elenkofsky, 431–2
Elisabeth (Empress), 335
Engel, Y. D., 458–9, 467–8, 472–5, 480, 484–5, 489
Engelhardt, V. P., 16, 56, 58–9, 61
Enoch, 483
Erdsmanndörfer, 310–1, 314, 317
Esposito, 405

F

Famyntsin, 125, 200, 207
Fauré, 440
Ferrero, 210, 223
Fétis 70
Field, John, 15, 100, 179
Figner, Medea, 323
Figner, N. N., 323

# INDEX

Filippof, T. I., 127, 138, 235–7, 240–1, 243, 369–70, 372, 383
Findeisen, 67, 70, 97, 144–5, 156, 158, 246
Flaubert, 193
Fodor-Mainvielle, Mme., 24
Fomin, 13
Ford, Richard, 50
Franck, 440
Freyer, August, 54
Fried, Oskar, 487
Fuchs, J. L., 16

G

Galli-Marié, Célestine, 284
Gavrushkevich, 158, 160, 176
Gebel, F. X., 160
Gedeonof, A. M., 30–1, 36–7, 46–7, 209
Gedeonof, M. A., 45, 209
Gedeonof, S. A., 165, 209, 213, 223, 271, 356, 360
Gerwinus, 242
Gevaert, 259
Ghedeanof (Prince), 155
Giacometti, 87
Gibbon, 44
Girard, 56
Giustiniani, 87
Glazunof, 11, 97, 139–40, 175, 326–7, 331, 371, 376, 382, 384–9, 395, 411, 413, 415–8, 420, 427, 430–5, 444–6, 461, 474, 479–81
  B-la-F Quartet : 386
  Elegy : 433
  Fantasia on Finnish Themes : 434
  Forest : 433
  Jour de Fête Quartet : 387
  Middle Ages : 479
  Oriental Rhapsody : 433
  Overtures on Greek Themes : 433
  Piano Suite S-A-S-C-H-A : 432
  Stenka Razin : 433
  String Quartets : 432–4
  Symphony No. 1 : 382, 384–5, 432–3
  Symphony No. 2 : 433
  Symphony No. 3 : 433, 479
  Symphony No. 8 : 434
  Triumphal March : 433
  Volga Boat Song : 413
Gliebof, 163, 175
Glinka, 13–65, 67–71, 79, 81, 84–5, 92, 97, 100–1, 103–5, 108–9, 114–5, 117, 119–20, 122, 130, 133, 135, 137, 139–41, 144–6, 156, 158–60, 164, 175, 181, 194–5, 205, 209, 217, 227, 236, 238, 254, 256–7, 261, 263, 312,

Glinka—continued
  340–3, 345, 362, 366, 368–9, 371, 373, 383, 388, 393, 411, 422, 434, 444, 452, 464–5, 481
  Bigamist : 59
  Capriccio on the Jota Arragonesa : 50, 64, 340
  Capriccio on Russian Themes : 25
  Farewell to Petersburg : 43
  Festival Polonaise : 59
  Ivan Susanin (see *Life for the Tsar*)
  Kamarinskaya : 43, 53, 55, 62, 64
  Lark : 43
  Life for the Tsar : 21, 25–6, 28–32, 34, 36, 46–7, 49, 51, 58–60, 63, 70, 79, 91, 101, 103, 109, 122–3, 185, 227, 251, 253, 290, 309, 338–40, 342, 464
  Midnight Review : 33
  Night in Madrid : 50, 53, 55, 64
  Oak-trees Murmur : 25
  Prayer : 52, 194
  Prince Kholmsky : 26, 44, 58, 63
  Quartet in D : 18
  Quartet in F : 22
  Ruslan and Liudmila : 21, 34, 36–9, 42–9, 53, 55, 57, 59, 61, 63–4, 81, 85–6, 90, 103, 105, 107, 122–3, 133, 135, 137, 141, 164, 169, 175, 182, 209, 217, 263, 340–1, 371, 464
  Spanish Overtures (see *Capriccio on the Jota Arragonesa* and *Night in Madrid*)
  Symphony in D minor : 25
  Tarantella : 44
  Ukrainian Symphony : 56
  Valse-Fantaisie : 42, 49, 59
  Viola Sonata : 18, 20
Gluck, 53, 57, 184, 242
Godunof, Boris, 185, 361 (see also Mussorgsky : *Boris Godunof*)
Goethe, 77–8, 80, 239, 468
Gogol, 27, 31, 37, 52, 56, 82, 91, 184, 202, 209, 227–8, 279, 281, 343, 358, 360, 373, 380, 393, 397, 400, 403, 422, 452
Goldenweiser, A. B., 62, 487
Golenishcheff - K u t u z o f (Count), 220–1, 226–9, 232–4, 367, 428

Golitsyn (Prince), 21, 49, 84
Gorky, 480
Gorodetsky, 428
Gounod, 238, 346, 440
Gretchaninof, 153
Griboedof, 21
Grieg, 320–1, 330, 418, 466
Grimm (brothers), 422
Gunst, 470
Gurskalin, 38, 43
Gussakovsky, 111, 141, 343
Guyau, M. J., 394

H

Habeneck, 56
Hadow, 176
Halévy, 70
Handel, 369, 371, 448
Hanslick, 257, 305, 393
Hartmann, Victor, 210, 215, 221, 226
Haydn, 17, 114, 119, 156, 320, 367
Heine, 149, 193, 348–9
Helena Pavlovna (Grand Duchess), 95, 124–5, 128, 207, 271, 281
Helmholtz, 363
Henselt, 77, 101, 141, 179, 455
Herke, Anton, 179–80, 195, 257, 352
Herz, 179
Herzen, Alexander, 186, 345
Hirschfeld, Magnus, 295
Hoffmann, E. T. A., 77, 326
Hoffmann, Josef, 463, 480–1
Holmes, Augusta, 390
Homer, 56–7, 397, 410
Hubert, N. A., 276, 442
Hugo, Victor, 67–8, 150, 180
Hummel, 15, 59, 66, 77, 101
Hunke, Josef, 80

I

Ilissa, 75
d'Indy, 117, 142, 414, 440
Ippolitof-Ivanof, 317, 384, 409
Isabella II (of Spain), 51
Ivanof, N. K., 21–4
Ivanof, Viatcheslaf, 496

J

Jadoul, 173
Jahn, Otto, 101
Johannsen, 367
Johansen, 200
Johnson, Samuel, 88, 449
Josquin des Prés, 441, 448
Jurgenson, B. P., 419, 421, 490, 496

INDEX

Jurgenson, P. I., 102, 254, 259–60, 272, 294, 300, 304–6, 310, 316, 325–7, 330–1, 458–9, 478, 490

K

Karatyghin, 246, 425, 427, 429
Karenin, Vladimir, 9, 115, 428
Karmalina, Liubov, 72, 132, 169, 227–8, 368
Karsavina, 495
Kashkin, 124, 131, 135, 261, 263, 265, 270, 273, 276, 286, 292–4, 296, 316, 445
Keldysh, 9
Kern, Anna, 21, 39, 42, 44
Kern, Ekaterina, 39–45, 48
Khessin, 491
Khomiakof, 448
Khubof, 175–6
Klamroth, 104, 210
Klenovsky, N. S., 323
Klimenko, 304
de Kock, Paul, 57–8
Koltsof, 194
Komarova, Varvara (see Karenin, Vladimir)
Komissarjevskaya, Vera, 214
Komissarjevsky, F. F. (producer), 214, 408, 419
Komissarjevsky, F. P., 75, 214, 218, 376, 442
Kondratief, G. P., 214, 218, 280, 282
Kondratief, N. D., 275, 280, 319
Konius, G. E., 453–6
Konius, Leo, 492
Kontsky, 102, 115
Korvin-Krukovsky, 376
Kotek, 288, 305, 313
Kovalevskaya, Anna, 108
Krabbe, 354, 359, 361, 363, 383
Krasnokutsky, 386
Kreutzer, 14
Kruglikof, 173, 375, 379, 381, 383, 390–1, 404
Krupsky (Father), 180
Krylof, Victor, 149, 163
Küchelbecker, 19
Kuhlau, 453
Kukolnik, Nestor, 27, 35–40, 42–5, 49, 56, 58–9
Kukolnik, Platon, 35, 38
Kullak, 25
Kündinger, Rudolf, 253
Kussevitsky, 448, 481–4, 487–91
Kuznetsof, 329

L

Lajetchnikof, 273
La Liberté, 482
La Mara, 393
Lamm, Paul, 163, 246
Langer, 439
Lanner, 25
Laroche, 94, 224, 257–9, 261, 265–6, 270, 276, 283, 285, 316, 441, 448
Laskovsky, 102, 104, 141
Lassus, 441, 448
Latysheva, 185
Laub, 284
Lavater, 183
Lavrof, N. S., 235, 389
Lavrovskaya, 290
von Lenz, 83, 85
Leonardo da Vinci, 447
Leonova, Daria, 52, 59–60, 71, 90, 149, 185, 236–43
Leibrock, 254
Lermontof, 52, 194, 220, 227, 343
Leschetizky, 450, 470
Lesovsky, 347
Lewes, G. H., 393–4
Lhévinne, Joseph, 457
Liadof, A. K., 9, 97, 122, 139, 153, 167, 170, 184, 326, 371, 373, 381, 384, 386, 389–90, 392, 395, 411, 413, 420, 424–30, 436, 438, 459, 478
  Baba Yaga : 429
  B-la-F Quartet : 386
  Bride of Messina : 426
  Children's Songs : 429
  Eight Russian Folk-Songs: 429
  Enchanted Lake : 428–9
  From the Book of Revelation : 429
  Jour de Fête Quartet : 387
  Kikimora : 428–9
  Nénie : 429
  Zoriushka : 392, 428
Liadof, K. A., 93, 184, 189, 349, 354, 425–6
Liapunof, 97, 121, 126, 138–9, 143, 145, 235, 436–8, 478
  Overture in C sharp minor : 437
  Piano Concertos : 437
  Piano Pieces : 437–8
  Symphonies : 143, 437
  Ukrainian Fantasy : 437
Liszt, 23, 47, 57, 79, 85, 87, 89, 114–5, 117, 120, 124, 136, 138, 141–2, 151, 168, 170–1, 179, 195, 199, 222, 238, 242, 258, 285, 300, 343, 350, 359, 368, 374, 382, 423, 433, 437–8, 457, 466, 468, 497
Litolff, Henri, 258
Lodi, 36, 40
Lodyjensky, 352–3, 405
Lomakin, 119–20, 123, 252
Lope de Vega, 443
Lucca, Pauline, 94
Ludwig II (of Bavaria), 89

Lukashevitch, 214, 223
Lvof, A. F., 16, 19, 33, 58, 68, 81, 105, 107–8, 141, 383
Lvof, F. P., 16, 33

M

Macaulay, 345
Maeterlinck, 429
Mahler, 328
Maikof, 87, 193
Malherbe, Charles, 143–4
Mamontof, S. I., 405–6, 408
Maria Nikolaevna (Grand Duchess), 32, 42
Maria Pavlovna (Grand Duchess), 417
Mario, 94
Markevitch, 37, 45
Marx, Karl, 477
Maslof, 442
Massenet, 390
Maupassant, 150
Maurer, 210
Maximof, L. A., 456
Mayer, Charles, 15, 17, 30, 32
von Meck, Nadejda, 62, 94, 136–7, 287–9, 291, 294, 296–9, 301, 304, 306, 311, 313, 315–6, 324–5, 331–2, 405
Medtner, 435, 484, 487
Méhul, 14, 15, 17, 56, 119, 337
Melgunof, 370
Melnikof, 75, 149
Mendelssohn, 23, 68, 86, 101, 119, 156, 159, 186, 257, 342, 454–5
Mengden, 188, 195
Mengelberg, 491
de Mercy-Argenteau (Countess), 172–3
Merejkovsky, 378
Merelli, 268
Merten, 163
Meshchersky (Princess), 335
Messager, 390
Metastasio, 80
Mey, Leo, 164, 220, 253, 349, 352, 371–3, 392, 406–8
Meyerbeer, 55, 57, 60–1, 70, 77–8, 84–5, 88, 157, 163, 238, 342, 366, 498
Michael Nikolaevitch (Grand Duke), 402
Michael Pavlovitch (Grand Duke), 47
Mickiewicz, 21
Miliukova, Antonina (Mme. Tchaïkovskaya), 291–5
Mill, J. S., 345
Monighetti, 462, 467, 487
Moniuszko, 110, 147–8
Morozova, M. K., 466, 472, 474, 480, 482, 484
Mozart, 16–7, 23, 48, 62, 83, 101, 114, 119, 168, 184, 252, 257, 318, 348, 393, 448

INDEX 507

Muck Karl, 388
Mürger, 174
Mussorgsky, Filaret, 178–9, 189–90, 194–5, 202–3
Mussorgsky, Modest, 9, 11, 65, 71–4, 93, 97, 105–7, 110–2, 118, 120, 124, 129, 141, 145, 148, 150–2, 154, 160, 164–5, 168–70, 174–248, 255, 257, 268, 272, 278, 280, 290, 335, 343, 349–50, 352, 354–6, 358, 361, 365–9, 373, 375–6, 379–82, 384, 386, 388, 393, 403, 415, 426–7, 444, 491
 Alla marcia notturna : 189
 Allegro in C : 188–9
 An die Türen : 192, 196
 Boris Godunof : 11, 106, 111, 129, 149, 152, 194, 201, 204–6, 209–20, 222–7, 230, 233, 236, 238, 246–7, 274, 278, 280, 335, 350, 356, 361–2, 374, 376, 388, 392, 403, 412, 415, 420, 422, 496
 Capriccio : 239
 Carousal : 200
 Child and Nurse : 201, 203, 210
 Classicist : 200, 208
 Cockchafer : 210
 Cradle Song : 194
 Cradle Song (Songs and Dances of Death) : 228
 Darling Savishna : 196, 198, 200, 203, 233, 248
 Destruction of Sennacherib : 120, 197, 243, 365, 380
 Evil Death : 226
 Fair of Sorotchintsi : 151, 154, 227–8, 232–4, 238, 241, 360
 Field-Marshal : 234
 Forgotten : 227, 238
 From Memories of my Childhood : 194
 Gathering Mushrooms : 200
 Going to Sleep : 210
 Gurzuf : 239
 Hebrew Song : 198
 He-Goat : 200, 208
 Hopak (piano) : 241
 Hopak (song) : 196, 201, 237–8
 Impromptu passioné : 186
 Intermezzo in modo classico : 191–2, 196, 198
 In the Corner : 210
 Jesus Navinus : 234
 Kallistratushka : 194, 196

Mussorgsky—continued
 Khovanshchina: 106, 164, 209, 214–7, 219–22, 227–33, 238, 240–1, 247–8, 311, 375, 381–2
 Kinderscherz : 188
 King Saul : 192
 Magpie : 198, 248
 March (with trio " alla turca " (see *Taking of Kars*)
 Marriage : 202 4, 230, 233, 247, 415
 Meines Herzens Sehnsucht : 184
 Mlada : 213–4, 228, 235, 243, 358
 Night : 194
 Night on the Bare Mountain : 188, 195, 198–200, 213, 228, 235, 238, 382, 386
 Nursery : 210, 216–7, 222, 248, 278, 427
 Œdipus : 182, 184, 188–9, 204, 213
 On the Don : 200
 Orphan : 200, 203, 238
 Outcast : 196
 Peepshow : 124, 207–8, 248
 Pictures from an Exhibition : 226, 247–8
 Porte-Enseigne Polka : 179
 St. John's Night (see *Night on the Bare Mountain*)
 Salammbô : 193–5, 204, 213, 234
 Scherzo in B flat : 182, 184, 187
 Scherzo in C sharp minor : 182, 184
 Seminarist : 196, 207
 Serenade (Songs and Dances of Death) : 228
 Shamil's March : 186
 Sonata in E flat : 182–3
 Sonata in F sharp minor : 183
 Song of the Flea : 239
 Songs and Dances of Death : 228, 234, 248
 Souvenir d'enfance : 182
 Street Arab : 200, 208
 Sunless : 226–7, 248
 Symphony in D : 189–91, 343
 Taking of Kars : 243
 Trepak : 228
 Where art thou, little star? : 182
 Winds Blow : 194
 With the Doll : 210
 Yarema's Song : 196

Mussorgsky—continued
 Yeromushka's Cradle-Song : 201, 203
Mustel, 327
Myers (Professor), 493

N

Napravnik, 128, 165, 210, 213, 218, 223–4, 243, 280, 282, 294, 304, 310, 332, 354–5, 362, 369, 376, 401–3, 445
Naumann, Emil, 95
Naumof, P. A., 229, 238
Nekrassof, 194, 220
Neumann, 388
Newmarch, Rosa, 143, 148
Nicholas, I., 19, 26, 31–4, 54–5, 59, 77, 179, 245, 361
Nicholas II, 402
Nietzsche, 94, 468–9, 471, 476–7, 485, 491, 496
Nikisch, 417, 474, 480
Nikolsky, 198, 203, 205, 207, 209, 213
Nozzari, 23

O

Odoievsky (Prince), 27–8, 30, 53, 105
Offenbach, 163
Okeghem, 441
Olkhovsky, 252
Opotchinin, Alexander, 203, 207, 212
Opotchinina, Nadejda, 185–6, 203, 207, 212, 226–7
Ossovsky, 434
Ostrovsky, 92, 94, 194, 209, 258, 264, 279, 376–7

P

Pabst, 454
Padilla-y-Ramos, 270
Palestrina, 242, 367, 448
Papkof, 210
Pasdeloup, 286
Paskevitch (composer), 13
Paskevitch (Prince), 53, 55
Pasta, 23
Patti, Adelina, 94
Pergolesi, 119
Perrault, 322
Peter the Great, 57, 214
Petrof, 30, 32, 36, 40, 47, 71, 75, 90, 214, 218, 227–8, 232, 234, 238, 362
Petrova-Vorobieva, 30, 32, 38, 46–7, 60
Piccioli, 253
Pisemsky, 242
Plato, 443
Platonova, 73, 75, 149, 201, 214, 218, 222–3, 280, 362
Plekhanof, G. A., 477

INDEX

Pollini, 23
Polonsky, 95, 281, 398, 428
Pomazansky, 223
Popof, S., 163, 270
Porman, 156
Pratch, 370
Pressmann, M. L., 456
Prévost, 14
Prokofief, 424
Purgold, Alexandra (by marriage, Alexandra Molas), 74, 207, 211-4, 352-3, 355, 361
Purgold, Nadejda (see Mme. Rimskaya-Korsakova)
Purgold, Vladimir, 207, 211-4
Pushkin, 19, 21, 27, 29, 33-7, 39-42, 45, 52, 70, 73, 150-1, 194, 201, 205, 213, 220, 227, 234, 254, 258-9, 290-1, 293, 307, 323-4, 343, 366, 375, 404, 407, 416, 422, 441

R

Rachmaninof, 414, 455-61, 467, 480-1, 484, 488, 490
Ravel, 141, 143
Remizof, 427-8
Repin, 94, 215, 221, 225, 241, 244
Richepin, Jean, 150
Richter, 93, 286
Ricordi, 24
Riemann, Hugo, 178, 242
von Riesemann, Oskar, 487
Rimskaya-Korsakova, Mme. (Nadejda Purgold), 73-4, 207, 211-4, 234, 278, 352-3, 355, 359-66, 380-1, 386, 389-90, 397, 399, 414-5, 417, 480
Rimsky-Korsakof, Alexander, 19
Rimsky-Korsakof, Andrei, 9, 118, 134, 365, 374, 390, 408, 410, 414-5, 417, 481
Rimsky-Korsakof, N. A., 9, 17, 61, 64, 75-6, 90-1, 93, 97-8, 105-6, 111, 113, 115-6, 118, 120-4, 127, 129-30, 132, 134-40, 142, 146, 148, 152-3, 155, 161-2, 164-6, 170, 172-5, 181, 190-1, 198, 200-1, 203-7, 210-5, 217-8, 224-6, 230-2, 234-6, 238-40, 243-4, 246, 255, 257, 260-1, 266-8, 270, 272-3, 276, 278, 281-3, 297-9, 302, 306, 311, 322, 326-7, 332, 334-424, 426-8, 430, 432, 434, 442, 444-5, 447, 453, 459, 477, 480-1, 491-2
    Alexei, the Man of God : 372-3
    Antar : 206, 270, 352-4, 369, 404, 419

Rimsky-Korsakof— continued
    Aus meinen Tränen : 349
    B-la-F Quartet : 386
    Boyarina Vera Sheloga : 406
    Choruses : 367, 369, 371
    Christmas Eve : 397-402, 405, 417
    Dubinushka : 413, 415
    Easter Overture : 336, 388, 419
    Fantasia on Russian Themes : 386-7
    Fantasia on Serbian Themes : 121, 267, 350, 352, 389
    Forty Russian Folk-Songs : 370, 372
    From Homer : 410
    Fugues, Op. 17 : 367
    Golden Cockerel : 416-20
    Hundred Russian Folk-Songs, Op. 24 : 231, 370
    Ivan the Terrible (see Maid of Pskof)
    Jour de Fête Quartet : 387
    Kashchei the Immortal : 409-10, 413, 415
    Kitej : 407, 409-12, 415-6, 419, 422
    Legend (Baba Yaga), Op. 29 : 375, 379
    Lehn deine Wang' : 348
    Maid of Pskof : 129, 149, 152, 212, 218, 234, 336, 349, 352-6, 358, 360-2, 372-3, 382, 389, 391-3, 396, 406-7, 422
    May Night : 234, 360, 373-6, 378, 381, 392, 395, 397, 407, 422
    Mlada (1872) : 356, 358, 360
    Mlada (1891) : 389-92, 394-5, 417
    Mozart and Salieri : 404, 406, 422
    Nausicaa : 397, 409-10
    On the Tomb : 411
    Overture on Russian Themes : 120, 349-50, 375-6
    Pan Voevoda : 409-10, 414
    Paraphrases : 170, 373
    Piano Concerto : 382-3
    Piano Pieces, Opp. 10 and 11 : 373
    Piano Pieces, Op. 15 : 369
    Quintet for Piano and Wind : 371
    Rose Enslaves the Nightingale : 349
    Sadko (musical picture), Op. 5 : 106, 198, 350-2, 355, 368, 391

Rimsky-Korsakof —continued
    Sadko (opera) : 106, 379, 392, 398-400, 403-6, 408, 417-8, 422-3
    Servilia : 392, 408-10
    Sheherazade : 388, 390, 419
    Sinfonietta : 379, 385
    Slava, Op. 21 : 376
    Snow Maiden : 306, 336, 376-9, 381, 383, 387, 395, 403, 406, 414, 417, 419-20, 422
    Song of Oleg the Wise : 407
    Songs, Opp. 2, 3, and 4 : 349
    Songs, Op. 8 : 355
    Songs and Duets, Op. 39 to Op. 56 : 404
    Spanish Capriccio : 387-8
    String Quartet in F, Op. 12 : 297, 367
    String Quartet in G : 405
    String Quartet on Russian Themes : 374-5, 379
    String Sextet : 371
    Svitezianka : 404
    Symphony in B minor : 350-1, 364
    Symphony No. 1 : 116, 120, 191, 260-1, 267, 343-6, 348, 385, 391
    Symphony No. 2 (see Antar)
    Symphony No. 3 : 364-5, 386
    Trombone Concerto : 371
    Tsar Saltan : 336, 407-8, 417
    Tsar's Bride : 392, 406
Rimsky-Korsakof, N. P. (Admiral), 46-7, 338
Röder, 384
Rosen (Baron), 28-9
Rossini, 16, 163, 252, 339, 342
Rousseau, 300
Rozenof, E. K., 462, 465, 469
Rubens, 246
Rubini, 23
Rubinstein, Anton, 25, 61-2, 86, 88, 90, 94, 103, 115, 118, 123, 140, 152, 187, 189, 195, 225, 256-64, 281, 301, 356, 359, 367, 397, 450, 453
Rubinstein, Nicholas, 92-3, 103, 125, 131, 135, 259, 261-3, 265, 267, 269-72, 274-5, 277, 280, 282-3, 285, 287, 294-5, 299, 304-6, 374, 436, 439-43, 450, 455, 462

S

Sabaneief, L. L., 441, 453, 455, 459-60, 469, 479, 485, 487, 492, 494-5

INDEX

Safonof, 442, 444, 447, 456–7, 463, 465, 467, 469–70, 476, 478, 480
Saint-Saëns, 300, 330, 440
Saltykof-Shchedrin, 440, 442
Saminsky, Lazare, 424
Sand, George, 94
Sapelnikof, 322
Sariotti, 88
Satie, 498
Schiller, 25, 260, 299
Schlözer, Boris, 470–2, 476, 481, 485
Schlözer, P. Y., 462–3, 465, 470
Schlözer, Tatiana, 470, 472–82, 484–8, 490–2, 498
Schoberlechner, 66
Schönberg, 117, 492
Schubert, Franz, 181, 238, 342, 457
Schubert, Karl, 77, 104, 157
Schumann, 108, 112, 114, 120, 124, 141, 151, 153, 159, 181, 186, 238, 342–3, 427, 456, 466
Scriabin, 9, 407, 417, 445, 448, 450–98
  Allegro appassionato, Op. 4 (see *Sonata in E flat*)
  Canon in D minor : 455
  Divine Poem : 471–2, 474–6, 479–80, 484, 487–9
  Etudes, Op. 8 : 459–60
  Fantasia for Piano and Orchestra : 458
  Keīstut and Peīruta : 458
  Mazurkas, Op. 25 : 465
  Mystery : 471, 473, 481, 483–4, 487, 493–5
  Nocturne in A flat : 455–6
  Piano Concerto : 463, 467, 479–80, 488, 490–2
  Piano Pieces, Opp. 1, 2, 3, 5 and 7 : 458
  Piano Pieces, Op. 30 to Op. 42 : 472, 474
  Piano Pieces, Op. 44 to Op. 49 : 474
  Piano Pieces, Op. 51 : 477–8
  Piano Pieces, Op. 52 : 483
  Piano Pieces, Opp. 56 and 57 : 482
  Piano Pieces, Op. 71 to Op. 74 : 495
  Poem of Ecstasy : 417, 477–8, 480–6, 488–9, 491
  Poème symphonique in D minor : 467
  Poèmes, Op. 61 and Op. 63 : 489

Scriabin—continued
  Preliminary Action : 493, 495
  Prelude and Nocturne for left hand : 457, 460
  Preludes, Op. 11 : 458, 461, 497
  Preludes, Op. 15 : 497
  Preludes, Op. 48 : 478
  Prometheus : 484, 487–9, 491–2
  Rêverie : 467
  Sonata in E flat (unpublished) : 458, 460
  Sonata in G sharp minor (Gothic) (unpublished) : 465
  Sonata No. 1 : 460
  Sonata No. 2 : 463, 490
  Sonata No. 3 : 465, 467, 470, 478–9, 482
  Sonata No. 4 : 472
  Sonata No. 5 : 482–4, 489
  Sonatas Nos. 6 and 7 : 489
  Sonatas Nos. 8, 9, and 10 : 492
  Symphonic Dances: 487–8
  Symphony No. 1 : 467–8, 480, 490–1
  Symphony No. 2 : 469–71, 480
  Symphony No. 3 (see *Divine Poem*)
  Valse in D flat : 456
Scriabina, Vera (née Isaakovitch), 462–6, 473–4, 476, 478
Senkovsky, 352
Serof, Alexander, 18, 58, 76–96, 104, 109, 125, 163, 192, 207, 238, 251, 257, 261, 266, 272, 281–2, 348, 352, 355, 398
  Christmas Eve : 91, 95, 281
  Christmas Hymn : 86
  Hostile Power : 92, 94–5
  Judith : 87–90, 92, 94, 163, 192, 257, 348
  Rogneda : 90
  Stabat Mater : 94
Serof, Valentine, 91
Serova, Valentina, 89, 92, 95
Shakespeare, 109, 246, 248, 279, 452
Shcherbatchef, 464
Shchiglef, Michael, 156–7
Sheremetief, D. N. (Count), 119
Sheremetief, S. D. (Count), 383
Shestakof, 184
Shestakova, Liudmila, 20, 52, 55, 58–9, 61, 100, 104, 112, 122, 127–8, 132, 178, 185,

Shestakova, Liudmila—con.
  191, 195, 202, 205, 207, 215, 222, 228, 231–2, 234–5, 237–9, 243, 312–3, 349–50, 371
Shevtchenko, 196, 242
Shiff, Seymour, 102
Shilovskaya, Maria, 184–5, 188, 268, 290
Shilovsky, Constantine, 268, 284, 290, 293, 443
Shilovsky, S. S., 184, 188
Shilovsky, Vladimir, 268, 274–5, 277, 279, 284, 296
Shirkof, 38–9, 43, 45
Shleiko, 157
Shostakovsky, 374
Shpajinsky, 314
Sklifasovsky, Volodia, 296
Slavinsky, 95
Smetana, 122
Smyth, Dame Ethel, 320
Snegiref, 32
Sokolof, Alexander, 69
Sokolof, N. A., 358
Solovief, N. F., 95, 282, 361–2
Solovieva, 49
Sophocles, 56–7
Spencer, Herbert, 394
Spinoza, 394, 443
Spontini, 77, 83
Stassof, Dimitri, 58, 105–6, 108, 132, 181, 206, 220, 351
Stassof, Vladimir, 9, 54, 56, 58, 60, 71, 77–82, 85–6, 89, 97–8, 105–6, 109–12, 115–6, 125, 127, 129, 131–2, 145, 148, 152–3, 156, 160, 164, 169–70, 172, 174–5, 178, 181, 184–5, 191–2, 195, 204–7, 209–17, 219–30, 232–7, 239–41, 243–4, 251, 273, 279, 283, 287, 312, 343, 351, 355, 367–8, 373, 380, 384, 389, 398, 400, 405, 415, 426, 428, 432, 434, 463–4
Steibelt, 14
Steinberg, 365, 417, 420–1
Stellovsky, 139
Stepanof, N. A., 40, 43
Stepanova, 47
Strauss, Johann, 25, 259, 457
Strauss, Richard, 142, 414, 417, 419, 448, 468, 492
Stravinsky, F. I., 376
Stravinsky, Gury, 416
Stravinsky, Igor, 121, 410, 416–7, 424, 435

T

Taneief, Alexander, 439
Taneief, Sergei, 140, 262, 307, 315–6, 329, 332, 358, 435, 439–49, 451, 456–7, 459–60, 463, 485–6, 488

INDEX

Taneief, Sergei—continued
  Chamber Music : 440, 443–4, 447
  John of Damascus : 443, 488
  Netherlandish Fantasia : 441
  On the Reading of a Psalm : 448
  Orestes : 443–6
  Overture in D minor : 440
  Overture on a Russian Theme : 442
  Pushkin Memorial Cantata : 441
  Symphony No. 1 in E minor : 440
  Symphony No. 2 (unfinished) : 441
  Symphony No. 3 : 443
  Symphony No. 4 in C minor (published as " No. 1 ") : 446
Tatishchef, 376
Tchaïkovskaya, A. I. (see Miliukova, Antonina)
Tchaïkovsky, Anatol, 249, 254, 269, 271, 275, 291, 293–7, 317–8, 330
Tchaïkovsky, Modest, 249 253–4, 269, 274, 284–5, 287, 295, 297, 306–7, 309, 312–3, 316, 318, 323, 326, 329, 331
Tchaïkovsky, P. I., 9, 44, 61–2, 76, 90, 94–5, 105, 113, 124–5, 130–1, 135–7, 152, 216–7, 225, 249–334, 364, 367–8, 376, 385, 397–8, 402, 405, 408, 427, 435–6, 439–45, 448, 457, 464–6, 491–2
  An die Freude : 260, 263, 266, 305
  Andante and Finale, Op. 79 : 329
  Boris Godunof : 261
  Chant sans paroles : 264
  Chorus of Insects (or Elves) : 273
  Concert Fantasia, Op. 56 : 311
  Coronation March : 309
  Dance of the Serving Maidens : 259, 261, 265–7, 270
  Eugene Onegin : 290–1, 293–4, 297–8, 301, 303, 310–1, 313–4, 322–4, 328, 333
  Fatum : 131, 268, 270–1
  Fifty Russian Folk-Songs : 272, 276
  Francesca da Rimini : 136, 284, 286–7, 308–9
  Hamlet : 321–2, 326
  Iolanta : 326–7, 329, 395

Tchaïkovsky—continued
  Italian Capriccio : 301–2
  Little Shoes (see Vakula the Smith)
  Liturgy of St. John : 298, 302
  Maid of Orleans : 299, 301, 304, 306
  Manfred : 136–7, 308–9, 313–7, 333
  Mazeppa : 307, 310, 317–8
  Mezza Notte : 254
  Military March : 330
  Moscow (cantata) : 309
  Mozartiana : 318–9
  Nutcracker : 326–9
  Opritchnik : 216, 273–8, 280–1
  Overture, 1812 : 249, 302, 307
  Overture in C minor : 259, 262–3
  Overture in F : 259–60, 262
  Overture on the Danish National Anthem : 264
  Oxana's Caprices (see Vakula the Smith)
  Piano Concerto No. 1 : 282–3, 299, 322, 334, 440
  Piano Concerto No. 2 : 301, 307
  Piano Concerto No. 3 : 328, 330
  Piano Pieces, Op. 72 : 330
  Piano Sonata : 298
  Queen of Spades : 323, 325, 329
  Rococo Variations : 287
  Romance, Op. 5 : 269
  Romeo and Juliet : 137, 272–4, 286, 308, 312, 360
  Scherzo à la russe : 260
  Serenade for Strings, Op. 48 : 302, 321
  Slavonic March : 287
  Sleeping Beauty : 322–3, 327, 402
  Snow Maiden : 279, 376
  Songs, Op. 6 : 273
  Songs, Op. 73 : 330
  Sorceress : 314, 316, 318–9, 323
  Souvenir de Hapsal : 264
  Storm : 258, 261
  String Quartet in B flat : 259–60
  String Quartet No. 1 : 275, 278, 286
  String Quartet No. 2 : 279, 283
  String Quartet No. 3 : 284
  String Sextet : 324, 329

Tchaïkovsky—continued
  Suite No. 1 : 298–9, 301, 320, 322
  Suite No. 2 : 309–11
  Suite No. 3 : 311, 314, 321
  Symphony No. 1 : 263–5, 267
  Symphony No. 2 : 277–9, 301
  Symphony No. 3 : 136, 283, 326
  Symphony No. 4 : 290, 294, 297, 330, 332–3
  Symphony No. 5 : 320–3, 333
  Symphony No. 6 (Pathétique) : 329–33
  Swan Lake : 283, 326
  Tempest : 279, 283, 299–300, 309
  Trio : 305–6
  Undine : 271–4, 277, 279, 298
  Vakula the Smith : 281–2, 286, 314, 318, 368, 397
  Violin Concerto : 298, 305, 307
  Voevoda (opera) : 259, 262, 264–70
  Voevoda (symphonic ballad) : 324, 327–8
Tchekhof, 378, 412
Tcherepnin, N., 154, 419
Tchernof, Constantine, 126, 134, 138–9, 142
Teliakovsky, 419–21
Teschner, 25, 26
Thalberg, 23
Theocritus, 81
Tichatschek, 18
Tilmant, 49
Timofeief, 107
Titof, 13
Tkatchenko, 303–4
Tolstoy, Alexei (Count), 234, 404
Tolstoy (Countess), 446–7
Tolstoy, Leo (Count), 62, 206, 245, 286, 393, 446
Tolstoy, Theophil, 21, 68, 89, 91, 94, 162, 207
Trubetskoy, S. N. (Prince), 468–9
Turgenef, 18, 52, 242, 300, 440
Tyndall, 363

U

Ulich, 339, 341
Ulybyshef, 48, 60, 83, 101, 103–4, 107, 109

V

Vasilko-Petrof, 59
Vasiltchikof (Prince), 45

INDEX

Vassilief, 157–8
Verdi, 23, 163
Vereshchagin, 227
Verstovsky, 13, 79
Viardot-Garcia, Pauline, 269
Viazemsky (Prince), 27, 54
Vielgorsky (Count), 21, 27, 30, 40, 46, 54, 105, 107, 141
Vieuxtemps, 81
Villebois, 40, 58, 272
Virchow, 242
Vladimir Alexandrovitch (Grand Duke), 402
Voiatchek, 210
Volkonsky, G. P. (Prince), 48
Volkonsky, S. M. (Prince), 408
Vorontsof, 66
Vorontsof-Dashkof (Count), 400
Vsevolojsky, 310, 318, 322–3, 402, 405–6, 408

W

Wagner, Johanna, 58, 60
Wagner, Richard, 57–8, 60, 83–5, 87–90, 93, 95, 117, 150, 152, 159, 258, 285, 309, 343, 388–90, 421, 433, 444, 448, 452, 460–1, 468, 473, 491, 497
Warlich, Hugo, 482
Weber, 59, 77, 152, 454
Weigl, 16
Weingartner, 143
Werth, Alexander, 446
Winckelmann, 79, 87
Wolf, Hugo, 78
Wood, Sir Henry, 492
Wordsworth, 245

Y

Yastrebtsef, 378, 395, 398–9, 403, 411, 416–7, 420, 422–3
Yusupof (Prince), 30

Z

Zabela, Nadejda, 406–7
Zamboni, 21
Zaremba, 207, 255–7, 263–4, 266, 352, 356
Zarlino, 60
Zeibich, 67
Zeleny, 347, 380
Zhukovsky, 20, 25, 26, 27–9, 31, 33, 40, 54, 68, 193, 271, 299, 318
Ziloti, 295, 415, 446, 456, 490–1
Zimin, 420
Zimmermann, 139, 478
Zinin, 157
Zotova, S. I., 349
Zveref, 455–6